Tales and Trails

New Jersey's Places, People, and Past

By

Henry F. Skirbst

Al Felzenberg,

Best Wishes,

Henry F. Skirbst

ISBN: 1-4107-8862-8 (e-book)
ISBN: 1-4107-8863-6 (Paperback)
ISBN: 1-4107-8864-4 (Dust Jacket)

Library of Congress Control Number: 2003095871

This book is printed on acid free paper.

Printed in the United States of America
Bloomington, IN

1stBooks - rev. 09/15/03

This book is a compilation of selected weekly articles
written by the author throughout the 1980's
which appeared in *The Star Gazette,*
a Hackettstown, NJ, newspaper.

To Ruth, my wife,
and our seven children:
Lynn, Ellen, Peter, Karen, John, Henry, and Frederick

Tales and Trails
New Jersey's Places, People, and Past

Table of Contents:

PREFACE

We live, today, in a society that has become very accustomed to fast-paced lifestyles of immediate gratification. As we live by the credo, "time is money," we find ourselves rushing around in search of the latter and realize that we desire more of the former. Our technology-based culture would have us believe that our reliance on machines has afforded us more time: time to relax, time to reflect, time to plan, time to interact (with humans), time to enjoy life. Nothing could be further from the truth!

Perhaps we have too much free time; and since nature abhors a vacuum, we have chosen to stuff every possible (unnecessary) activity into that finite resource so that we might feel fulfilled. There was a time, however, before today's modern conveniences, when life was simpler. Although more of our day may have been spent doing hard, physical labor, the little (free) time that remained, perchance, was more valuable to us than it is today.

In those days gone by, people could be found interacting with one another, remembering the past, sharing ideas, dreams, and plans for the future. So often, today, we lack the time to reflect on our identity as individuals or as a nation. In our rush to live life, we have lost sight of where we have been, where we are now, and where we are going; and more importantly, why?

So many children, today, are growing up with little sense of, much less a connection to, or appreciation for, the past: their own or their nation's. Without that foundation, it is difficult, if not impossible, to make intelligent decisions about tomorrow. Trees with shallow roots fall easily when strong winds blow. Taking time, today, to learn about and understand our history is not only important, it is essential to planning for a successful future!

As editor of this book, I have had the opportunity to read it – many times. In so doing, I have come to gain a greater appreciation for my own past, as an individual, as well as the history of our state and the nation as a whole. Every time I read, and re-read, an article, I also felt a greater sense of connection with the author – my father.

I have learned a great deal about him, as a person, through his words. I have learned about his passion for history, his love of the outdoors, his desire to preserve the past, and to teach others of its importance – in a way that makes it come alive for people today. I have come to appreciate the sacrifices he has made both big and small, in his fervent pursuit to serve his family, his community, his state, and his nation to insure a better future for all.

As a kid growing up in the 1980's, I must admit that I never really took the time to read many of his articles when they appeared in the paper each week. I was busy with my own interests. After all, like most teens, I was too self-absorbed to recognize my father's work as something worthwhile for me to take interest in. I am glad I no longer feel that way.

I am certain that you will be glad, too, when you take the time to read this book. You will gain a greater understanding of our past, and the lessons it has for our future. You will appreciate how the people of our state have contributed to this nation in such marvelous and unique ways. You will develop an awareness of the diversity that exists all around us. Most importantly, you will come to know my father for who he is.

As you read through each story, beginning with the Introduction, keep in mind that they were written during the 1980's. Occasionally, passing references are made to events of that decade. This in no way detracts from the content of the stories. You may also notice, at times, a slight bias in favor of the northwestern part of the state. This is simply due to the location of his audience as well as to the fact that he lives in Warren County.

I believe I can speak for each of my siblings when I say that I am truly grateful to our mother who inspired the compilation of this book. It has been many years in the making, but over the past year has jelled into the current form. What better tribute to a man who has devoted his life to public service, than to immortalize his words forever along the "Tales and Trails" of New Jersey.

HENRY M. SKIRBST, EDITOR

ABOUT THE AUTHOR

Henry Franklin Skirbst, born November 14, 1928, has devoted his life to public service. Growing up in Irvington, NJ, the son of a police officer, he learned early the importance of civic responsibility. His lifelong involvement, commitment, and leadership in education, church, and civic organizations, only add to the impact of his words written on the pages of "Tails and Trails."

A graduate of Irvington High School in 1946, Mr. Skirbst worked in industry for two years before entering Kean College. There, in 1952, he received his BA degree and later earned his Master of Education from Rutgers University. He was employed as a guidance counselor and as a teacher of History and Civics in the New Providence, and later Irvington Public School systems for many years. During this time, he was a founding member, and former President, of the Irvington Historical Society. Mr. Skirbst was also instrumental in the formation of the "Jerseymen" organization in Irvington, which was specifically intended to further the interest of "New Jersey History" among young people in the state. After retiring from teaching, he was afforded the time to research and write about the many interesting and profound happenings along the "Trails" of New Jersey. He shared these stories, throughout the 1980's, in a weekly column entitled "Tails and Trails of New Jersey," which he wrote for a local newspaper, "The Star Gazette." His passion for history and his love of the outdoors and open space were evident throughout his writings.

Active in church and fraternal organizations, Mr. Skirbst has been a church-school teacher, served as the secretary of the board of trustees, and since 1962 has been an ordained elder of the Presbyterian Church. He has been a member of the Franklin-Century Lodge, F&AM and was a leader in the American Boy Scouts in the 1950's. He, along with his wife, Ruth, have raised their own "troop" of seven children, over the past 46 years together, and are now enjoying time with their 10 grandchildren and two great-grandchildren.

After serving as a special agent with the US Army's Counter-Intelligence Corps in the 1950's, he first became involved in civic service with an appointment to the Irvington Planning Board. In the late 60's and early 70's, he was elected and served two terms on the Irvington Town Council. After moving to Harmony Township nearly a quarter century ago, he continued to be a civic leader. He served for 12 years on the township committee as a Committeeman. Four of those years, he served as Mayor. During that time, he encouraged the formation of the first Environmental Commission of the township. Before leaving politics, he was also able to help establish the Harmony Township Historic Preservation Commission.

Mr. Skirbst has devoted his life to public service. His desire to ignite the flames of curiosity in others to appreciate the significance and relevance of New Jersey's history and his passionate pleas of appropriate environmental stewardship have been driving forces of his. His lifelong accomplishments have done much to achieve these goals, perhaps more fully than he is aware.

ABOUT THE BOOK

Throughout the 1980's, Mr. Skirbst composed nearly 400 articles entitled the *Tales and Trails of New Jersey*. These articles appeared as a weekly column in a local newspaper, *The Star Gazette*. Dedicated readers from across the state (as well as from other states) faithfully followed his stories about the places, people, and past of the state. From week to week, his readers looked forward to the next tale along the trails of New Jersey.

In these stories, one thing was always clear, Mr. Skirbst was passionate in his writing. He was passionate about teaching others to understand and appreciate history and the vital role it plays in molding the pathway to the future. He was passionate about promoting responsible environmental stewardship and the need to preserve our remaining open spaces and conserve our state's natural resources. He was passionate about encouraging his readers to get out and experience the diversity of the state and visit the many historic sites and natural areas. He was passionate in his love for New Jersey.

Over twenty years later, selected articles from this series have come together to form the contents of this book. In celebration of the author's 75th birthday, his wife Ruth, and their children, have spent the last year (secretly) going through the many scrapbooks in which Mr. Skirbst kept copies of his typewritten stories over the years. After reading, and re-reading, every article, they were topically arranged into units and chapters to form the structure of this book. Selecting the most representative articles in each section, about 230 articles - out of almost 400 - were chosen. Each of these articles was then typed and saved as computer files, arranged, and edited, in order to be sent to the publisher.

This book serves as testimony to the author's passions. Many hours were spent by his family in compiling the articles for the book, but many more hours were spent by the author in researching and writing the stories themselves. In fact, an entire lifetime has been spent living along the trails of New Jersey, gathering information, going to visit various sites, and gaining a greater appreciation for the wonderful diversity of our state every day.

The contents of the book are arranged topically, not in the original order they appeared as a weekly column. It has been divided into 4 units and 18 chapters. The first unit explores the places of New Jersey. In it, the reader is taken on a tour of the various regions of New Jersey, through the state's 21 counties, and a visit to some interesting sites to see.

The second unit explores the people and their contributions to the state of New Jersey. Within this unit, the industrious nature of its citizenry is explored in chapters on agriculture, industry, and transportation. Various tales in a chapter on folklore and legends is followed by a chapter on famous people, with New Jersey Connections.

New Jersey's history is fully explored in the third unit. From the Lenape (Original People) to the first colonists, the beginnings of the state are explored. Two chapters on the American Revolution outline the significant role our state had in the formative years of our nation. The unit finishes up with a look at New Jersey's history during the Civil War era.

The fourth and final unit, entitled "Potpourri," includes a variety of subject matter. From a tour of the state through the seasons of the year to the various holiday celebrations, and their New Jersey connections, this unit finishes with a little bit of everything. In the last chapter, topics include population growth and diversity, the environment, recreation, medicine, and education.

"Tales and Trails," although focussing on the places, people, and past of New Jersey, is certainly relevant to the nation as a whole. Between historical events and famous people, "Tales and Trails" is a significant contribution to those that seek to learn more about our history and future.

HENRY M. SKIRBST

INTRODUCTION

Those who have taken the time to travel, hike, sightsee, or bike throughout the length and breadth of this compact little state called New Jersey cannot help but be impressed.

From its wooded, rocky hill country in the north, with its scattered small farms, through its residential, industrial, and hustling urban centers along its central piedmont, to its remote Pine Barrens, cranberry and blueberry bogs, and large flat farmlands in the south, to any one of its picturesque fishing villages along its extensive shoreline, there is a diversity that has its own charm.

You can view the spectacular natural physical features of the Delaware Water Gap region in the northwest. You can muse at the peculiar, perpendicular, rock formations of the Palisades in the northeast. You can visit what tourists of old once considered New Jersey's own Niagara, the 80-foot Great Falls of the Passaic. You can tour the vast, unspoiled wilderness known as the "Pine Barrens", which the government has set aside as a national reserve.

You can visit such different national wildlife preserves as the 8,000-acre Great Swamp in Morris County or the 36,000-acre Brigantine (now Forsythe) wetlands bird sanctuary along the shore. You can fish in its hundreds of streams, rivers and lakes or along its vast ocean front. Whatever you do, you will soon realize what a wonderfully diverse state we have.

Its people, too, are as diverse as its topography. It was first settled by its "Original People," the Lenapes, who lived for centuries in harmony with its natural features. Then came such Europeans as the Dutch, Swedes, and Finns. Later came the English, Irish and Scotch along with Germans, Swiss and French Huguenots, most of whom were farmers. Africans first came as slaves brought here by early Dutch and English sea captains. Each with their own religions and cultures, they lived side by side.

By the late 1800's and early 1900's, Italians, Poles, Hungarians, Russians, Lithuanians and many more were added to New Jersey's "melting pot." In more recent years, other groups such as Portuguese, Cubans, Puerto Ricans, Haitians, Asiatic Indians,

Chinese, Japanese, Vietnamese, Armenians, Iranians and many more have entered the mainstream of New Jersey's population. This state is truly a representation of what America purports to be - a "melting pot" of the world's people.

From its fairgrounds to its playgrounds, it also offers a wide variety of recreational opportunities to its people. In spite of its density of population, it still provides areas for hunting and fishing. Its many large, diverse shopping malls have got to be added to that recreational list as well, since they are no longer merely places to shop, but a diversion for millions of people both young and old.

From its Meadowlands Sports Arena to amusement parks such as "Great Adventure," to its many state, county and local parks, playfields, golf courses, playhouses and museums, there are a variety of activities in which its citizens may engage for leisure.

And much more is in various stages of development. A gigantic, world-class, hands-on Science Center, for example, is currently being planned by the state for the Liberty State Park area of Jersey City. An equally top-rate Aquarium, illustrating the aquatic life of both on-shore and offshore areas of the state, is being prepared for a waterfront park in Camden. And along it's Passaic riverfront, in the state's largest city, Newark, plans are under way for the development of a Cultural Arts Center with accompanying restaurants, etc. that compares to any in the country. So the best is yet to come!

Its history, too, runs the gamut of America's heritage. From colonization to wars, to industries and inventors, to poets and transportation, to native Americans and frontier living, New Jersey has it all.

National, state, county and local historic sites dot the state, covering the wide variety of eras in our state and nation's history. The first national historic park in the country was established here at Morristown and Jockey Hollow, illustrating the important role New Jersey played in the American Revolution. More than 100 battles were fought here and George Washington spent more time in this state than any place except his native Virginia. Numerous state historic sites such as Washington Crossing and the Monmouth Battlefield State Parks also depict that important era. Villages such as Clinton, Waterloo, Millbrook, Wheaton, Batsto, and Allaire illustrate life in by-gone times.

In folklore, too, New Jersey is rich and diverse. From the Jersey Devil to the Jersey Pirates (Capt. Kidd and Blackbeard); from Tom Quick - the Indian Slayer, to Oxford's "Jersey Samson," John Linn; from Molly Pitcher and Temp Wick, to the "Fighting Parson" and John Honeyman; the trails of New Jersey abound in legends as diverse as its rich heritage, natural features, and people. Yes, New Jersey has it all, and in such a small package, too!

HENRY F. SKIRBST, AUTHOR

UNIT 1: PLACES IN NEW JERSEY

This unit explores the varied physical and cultural geography of the state of New Jersey.

Chapter 1: Highlands
Chapter 2: Rivers
Chapter 3: The Jersey Shore
Chapter 4: Pinelands and Meadowlands
Chapter 5: Counties of New Jersey
Chapter 6: Sites to See Around the State

Henry F. Skirbst

CHAPTER 1: HIGHLANDS

Wooded Mountains

Like our seashore, our wooded mountains are a great New Jersey treasure. They both have attracted visitors from other places to our state. They both have been respites for weary travelers from crowded cities - vacationland for those seeking refuge from the hubbub of everyday life. They have given restoration and renewal for worn out minds and bodies. They served as places where people could go over the years for just plain fun. Some of our nation's first resorts were established in them. Both are well worth every effort it will take to preserve them for our posterity to enjoy.

Like our seashore region, our wooded mountain areas are suddenly in danger of becoming too overpopulated with year-round residents to serve their once restorative purpose. Their demise would be a sad day for future generations and a very sorry legacy by us to our children and grandchildren. For generations past, these two separate and different places in our tiny state were thinly populated most of the year. Both of them have had terrain and peculiar conditions of employment that have not been able to support large populations. It has been those factors, rather than a conscious effort by those who came before us that have kept them available for our generation to enjoy. But, if they are to remain here for tomorrow to delight in, it will only be because of a definite plan of preservation, for today's technology has created a threat to development that past generations did not face.

Each section had difficulties in settlement. The rugged, steep and rocky slopes of the wooded mountainous northwestern section made building good roads both difficult and expensive. It was not the best terrain for large housing developments or industry, and it only encouraged special kinds of agriculture. Both were originally settled by seekers of iron, and both seemed destined to serve the interests of that industry only to lose them when varying problems caused their

3

withdrawal. In the end, it was those difficulties that kept both areas preserved for today.

Our heavily wooded mountains with their pure lakes and streams and thin populations, however, encourage vacationers, fishermen, hunters, hikers, and those whom just enjoyed being in the great outdoors. Its many trees brought coolness to the landscape that refreshed the body as well as the soul. They also kept the rains from washing away too rapidly - helping to form a great natural aquifier, nature's own water reservoir. They sheltered an unknown number of the state's natural wildlife, so vital to the balance of nature. They breathed in polluted air and returned to it great quantities of the oxygen so essential for human existence.

There are some 200 kinds of native New Jersey trees. Though the red oak is the official state tree, New Jersey has a number of different kinds of oak as well as maples, beech, birch and willows. Knowing our trees as individuals makes wanting to keep them so much easier. Can you identify the sycamores, tulips, sassafras, and dogwoods? Do you recognize the walnut and poplar, the linden and pear, the locust, mulberry, cedar, spruce, fir, hemlock and pine? Many of our trees are more than 200 years old! They have a history all of their own - such as Belvidere's famed, "Shoe tree."

The state's highest wooded mountains are in the northwest, where they are known as the Kittatinny Range. High Point, which is 1803 feet above sea level, is the states' highest. From a vantage point in High Point State Park, you can get a beautiful vista of our state's natural heritage. Here, too, New Jersey is a participant in that intrastate natural paradise that begins in Maine and ends in Georgia - the Appalachian Trail.

Eternal vigilance is the price of keeping these priceless reserves. Lest you think that once they become state preserves they are safe forever, remember what is happening to Hamburg Mountain at this very moment! But for the almost single-handed vigilance of Hackettstown's Casey Kays, the same fate would have befallen the pristine Sunfish Pond in Worthington State Forest at the hands of a group of utilities.

Further to the east of the Kittatinnies are lower groups of mountains extending in the southeast to northwest direction. Many bear Indian names such as Pohatcong, Pochuck, Musconetcong,

Waywayanda, Ramapo, and the Watchungs. Others relate to folk tales, early settlers or conditions of terrain such as the Bowling Green, Kanouse, Ragged Ridge, Scotts, Schooley's, Jenny Jump, Bearfort, and the Sourlands. Within these mountains can also be found most of the state's vacation lakes.

Hopatcong, almost 7 miles long and 40 miles around, is the largest in the state. Greenwood, which we share with New York State, has a history all of its own. Spruce Run and Round Valley are man-made reservoirs. All have their own tales to tell along the trails of New Jersey.

Hiking the Appalachian Trail

As I write this week's column, my wife, Ruth, and I have just returned from the Delaware Water Gap. There we, and the Jack Shoemakers of Liberty Township, launched their son Dennis and our son Henry M. on one of the great adventures of their young lives. We saw them step off onto the beginning of New Jersey's portion of the Appalachian Trail with 55 lb. packs on their backs.

Heading north, the trail will take them past the beautiful Dunnfield Gorge. Through New Jersey's Worthington State Forest, they will ascend a difficult pathway to reach the spectacular Sunfish Pond. Lying in the unbroken quiet of a deep forest of tall trees, this 42-acre lake is described by the Audubon Society as being "cradled like a precious stone in an ice-scoured glacial basin atop the Kittatiny Mountains." It "personifies the unspoiled natural beauty of America," and is "one of the most scenic treasures of New Jersey."

In 1970, the Interior Department named it to the National Registry of Natural Landmarks. Yet, if it were not for the singular fighting spirit of Hackettstown's Casey Kays, this gem would have been destroyed by a group of utility companies.

Our young men are planning to hike north as far as their youthful legs will carry them by mid-July. They hope it will be at least to the Green Mountains of Vermont, or maybe even to the border of New Hampshire. They have been planning this trip for months - to live on their own in the solitude of nature. Man, after all, is part of nature. It is his natural habitat. Living within its realm, experiencing

5

its challenges helps him to get his priorities straight. To deny one this privilege is to rob him of his birthright. I pray that man's lust to subdue the wilderness for the financial gain it affords the few, will never be permitted to deny others the "space" they need in that simple and unperverted, sometimes raw, rustic and unrefined, unartificial, and often harsh expanse we call "nature."

That New Jersey still possesses some areas where nature holds supreme is the result of those with foresight who have gone this way before us. That our grandchildren might still be able to tread these ancient, unspoiled trails is our responsibility. The 2,070 - mile footpath through the wilderness known as the Appalachian Trail was the dream of a single forester named Benton Machaye. His untiring determination launched that dream via a published article back in 1921. That dream at long last became a reality when the final links were completed in 1937. The trail extended by then along the crest of the entire Appalachian Mountains of the eastern United States, through 14 states from Mount Katahdin, Maine to Mount Oglethorpe, Georgia.

Some 70 miles of the trail pass through a portion of northwestern New Jersey's precious little remaining wilderness environment. New Jersey became in 1982 the first of the 14 states, which contain parts of the trail, to locate its entire route on protected public land. This step was necessary here first because the pressure to develop had become so strong that its continued unbroken existence was threatened. In 1980, Congress designated the Appalachian Trail as a "National Scenic Trail," and provided funds for land purchases. The elimination of future threats of development along the entire length of the trail - the longest marked footpath in the world, was its goal.

New Jersey's portion of the trail north of Sunfish Pond in Warren County extends through the Delaware Water Gap National Park, past the Historic Village of Millbrook and atop the 1500-foot Mount Mohican. At that point, a side trip to the spectacular Buttermilk Falls near Flatbrookville is afforded. As the boys continue north they will experience the picturesque gorge called Tillman Ravine, a commanding view atop Rattlesnake Mountain and wooded ridges through Culver's Gap. As they come atop the 1653-foot

6

Sunrise Mountain, they will see a vista of farms and woodlands below them. Of course, they will be camping all along the way.

Still further to the north, they will enter High Point State Park. There at New Jersey's highest elevation they will view the tri-state vista of the Delaware Valley. The Kittatinny Mountains of New Jersey, Catskills of New York State, and the Poconos of Pennsylvania are all within view from this vantage point. This is thanks to the generous donation of land to the state by Col. Anthony Kuser, whose lodge still stands at High Point as a monument to his thoughtful foresight.

After traveling east out of the park past Mount Salem, the Appalachian Trail briefly enters New York State West Of Unionville. There, after crossing the Wallkill River, it will traverse the Shawangunk Mountains. Back in New Jersey, it continues through Wawayanda State Park. Above Upper Greenwood Lake, passing through the Bearfort Mountains of western Passaic County, it re-enters New York on its journey northward to its terminus in Maine.

Skylands

I keep returning to the beautiful forested mountains of northwestern New Jersey because they never cease to hold my interest. Though they attracted many tourists in the early years because of their rugged charm, they somehow did not continue to do so. Famous health spas had sprung up in the Schooley's Mountains east of Hackettstown. Large hotels lured tourists by train to view the sturdy beauty of the Kittatinny Range overlooking the Delaware Water Gap. But whereas the Catskills and Adirondacks of New York and the Poconos of Pennsylvania grew as meccas for the tourist trade, the Jersey Skylands over the years became more and more an exclusive private domain.

You were either one of the very select, fortunate few to own your own "cottage" on the banks of the many small lakes and streams dotting the Jersey uplands, or you belonged to that even more select group of wealthy folk who lived like barons-of-old in their large forested retreats. Much of the pristine Jersey countryside was like rural England, where a few "royal" families owned thousands of acres of their own exclusive woodlands. Such was the case of the affluent industrialist, C.C. Worthington.

With a 6,200-acre estate bordering on some four miles of the Delaware river in Warren County, Worthington, like an English Lord, hunted and fished on his own private domain. Now part of the Worthington State forest, his estate, once boasted several large private deer herds for his own exclusive use. Such, too, was the estate of Col. Anthony Kuser. His former 13,000-acre mountain retreat now encompasses High Point State Park in Sussex County. The former Kuser home, High Point Lodge will soon be undergoing a million-dollar renovation by the state to make it available for accommodations by hikers along the nearby Appalachian Trail.

Because of the state's long existence as the private "fief" of the opulent, we today are fortunate in having much more open space than we would have had otherwise. We can be thankful to this group of "Land Barons." Because of their love of Jersey's more picturesque primitive countryside, we have available today some of the state's most attractive scenic parks and forests. Their purchases are responsible for keeping them undeveloped over the years - at their expense. In more recent times, we have begun to see a return of some of those entrepreneurs of yore who once saw in the Jersey "Skylands," an ideal setting for drawing the tourist trade. The developers of the Great Gorge Ski Resort - and later, Action Park - in Sussex County are a prime example. One might expect to see in the future smaller tourist enterprises that fit into such a setting, such as "Dude Ranches," eventually sprouting up on their periphery.

I mentioned earlier some of the activities of the former Mayor of Philadelphia, William Allen, and his associate, Joseph Turner, who speculated in Jersey mines. In the 1740's, you recall, they developed the Union Iron Works in High Bridge. In the 1750's, we saw their involvement with the copper mines at Rocky Hill. And it was Allen and Turner who in 1763 originally built the Andover Iron Forge along the banks of the Musconetcong. This later became Waterloo Village.

A new shop of life came to the Andover Forge when the dying village was revived as a canal port with the completion of the Morris Canal in 1831. This 106-mile waterway, linking Phillipsburg on the Delaware with ports on the Hudson, did much, not only for North Jersey's iron industry, but for its farmers as well. The new life of

Andover Forge as a busy canal port also brought with it a new name - Waterloo Village. It was named after the site of the defeat of the arch-conqueror of that day. Napoleon's defeat in 1815 at Waterloo, in Belgium, inspired the villagers to this name change.

When Percy Leach and Louis Gualandi, two interior designers, found Waterloo, some 150 years later, it was returning to its natural state. The close of the Morris Canal brought about its demise. They saw its potential, purchased it, and began a long career of attempting its resuscitation - this time as an historic village. It was their individual drive, inspired by an imaginative dream of what could be, that brought about the rebirth of what promises eventually to be a major tourist attraction of Northwest Jersey.

This once important iron village, and later busy canal port has many tales to tell of Jersey's heritage. In its beautiful Allamuchy Mountain State Park setting, historic Waterloo Village, given the public support it so richly deserves, can prove to be the catalyst for other tourist attractions along the trails of this tri-county area of New Jersey.

Land 'O Lakes

With more than 3,000 lakes, reservoirs, and ponds nestled somewhere within our varied terrain, New Jersey could very easily lay claim to the title, "Minnesota," meaning in the Chippewa Indian tongue, "Land 'O Lakes." And, if modern engineers have their way, we will be returning still another gigantic lake to an area, which once boasted the state's largest glacial body of fresh water, Lake Passaic.

The continuously ravaging floods of the Passaic River Valley have been costing mid-20th century residents and taxpayers untold millions of dollars as a result of the area's increasing development since the 1920's.

In recreating the gigantic Lake Passaic as a flood control project, man, in a sense, is saying to nature, you win. A dam at the meeting place of both the Passaic and Pompton Rivers is now being proposed. It would permanently flood a portion of the man-filled wetlands, which once comprised Lake Passaic in ancient times. It

9

would return this region to the waters that seem to be saying time and again, "this is mine."

After 60 years of pompous idiocy, during which man thought he could outsmart nature by filling in this wetland - the remains of a once gigantic prehistoric glacial lake - he has finally decided to work with nature by coming up with a flood control plan that would save millions in dollars and immeasurable personal anguish.

He is starting to buy up the homes that were built there by a number of enterprising developers. Plans are to undo this work by tearing down these houses and building a multi-million dollar dam - returning the lands to the waters that have persistently laid claim to them over the years. The result would be the recreation of New Jersey's largest, freshwater lake, Lake Passaic. A recreation, water supply, and power producing paradise in harmony with nature's desires would then replace the annual agony that now accompanies man's insistence upon fighting natural forces.

To date, modern man's largest, strictly man-made lakes are the reservoirs created in Hunterdon's hills - known as Round Valley and Spruce Run. They not only provide backup water in times of drought - which are becoming increasingly frequent with new developments - but are sources of much-needed recreation as well. Recently, there has been testing to explore the possibility of creating a power-generating station at Spruce Run as well.

Man-made, natural, and glacial lakes, ponds, and reservoirs have created within New Jersey a recreational paradise - a mecca for tourists and permanent residents. They have also provided an abundant water supply for both man and industry over the centuries. The names of these bodies of water have served as living memorials to the once proud Native Americans who inhabited our forests and plains. Such names as Hopatcong and Musconetcong come immediately to mind, but there are many others. Some have remembered names of those that once lived near or worked at them - as with Erskine, Parvin, Swartswood, and Budd. Still others, like Sawmill or Millbrook, or Sunfish, refer to what one did or caught there. Some, like Crystal, Stony, Split Rock, White Meadow, or Horseshoe might refer to natural features. All tell some kind of tale about bygone days, ways, or people worth remembering.

New Jersey's natural lake-district is in its mountainous northern counties, such as Morris, Passaic, Sussex, and Warren. About 770 New Jersey lakes fall into this category. Sussex leads the way; Morris, Passaic, and Warren are next, though with considerable less. Sussex County's 33-acre Round Pond and 75-acre Rutherford Lake, at 1,359 feet and 1,309 feet, rank second and third highest in the state.

Man-made lakes and ponds are still another story, with a varied and often colorful history. Their sizes, uses, and tales could make an article in themselves. In this category, Warren leads the way with about 493 that are known.

Other New Jersey counties in order of the number of known man-created lakes and ponds found within them, are as follows: Essex, 396; Monmouth, 390; Morris, 346; Sussex, 227; Hunterdon, 200; Mercer, 173; Burlington, 149; Salem, 114; Gloucester, 104; Camden, 84; Cumberland, 73; Bergen, 69; Ocean and Passaic, 62; Somerset, 51; Middlesex, 43; Atlantic, 34; Cape May, 21; Union, 4; and Hudson, none.

New Jersey is truly a "Minnesota." There are, of course, more tales to relate about this magnificent array of natural, glacial, and man-made lakes, ponds, and reservoirs so abundantly to be found along the trails of New Jersey, but they will have to wait another time.

Palisades

During the period leading up to the Civil War in 1860, the region along the New Jersey side of the Hudson River known as the "Palisades" was both a national tourist attraction and a summer playground for nearby New Yorkers.

These unique cliffs stretch for some 15 miles along the state's northeastern border from above Hoboken to beyond Alpine, and then spill over into New York State to about Haverstraw.

They are another example of how one of our state's natural scenic splendors was almost lost, but was saved from the destruction of an uncaring group of New York developers by the enraged efforts of some determined New Jersey housewives. This is proof once again that citizens, when aroused, can "fight city hall."

The Palisades' first recorded recognition was by the Dutch in 1609. They were so captivated by them that the crew of Henry Hudson's "Half Moon" wrote of their reaction in the ship's log.

Offering a commanding view of the Hudson River, these awe-inspiring cliffs rise from 100 to 300 feet in height. Fantastic in their appearance, the rocky "palisades" with their peculiar perpendicular formations is considered one of the most picturesque cliff formations in the world.

Column-like in appearance, the "Palisades" came about millions of years ago when layers of hot lava intruded between layers of sandstone and shale. When it cooled in the cracks, the rock contracted into vertical columns. As the softer stone wore away and crumbled, these columns were exposed to view like tall fortifications - or palisades.

These rare cliff formations are not only one of the many "scenic wonders" of our tiny state, but are also the site of a number of historic events as well.

A Dutchman, Aert vanPutten, for example, started America's first brewery in this region in 1642. The area, except for the nearby Lenape, was solidly Dutch at that time.

Weehawken was also the scene in 1804 of that ill-fated duel between Vice President Aaron Burr Jr. and Alexander Hamilton. Hamilton was mortally wounded.

Col. John Stevens bought his lands there in 1794, where he raised his famous engineering family. "Stevens' Institute of Technology" was founded on his estate there in 1871. This, too, was where, at a place called the "Elysian Fields," the first organized baseball game of the world was played in 1846.

Its commanding view of the Hudson made the Jersey Palisades a strategic point during the American Revolution. Washington, who sought to keep control of the Hudson River, built two strongholds on its rocky heights. In an attempt to gain intelligence on British plans, the American spy, Nathan Hale, operated from there. His mission unfortunately failed when he was captured - and hung.

A great loss came to Gen. Washington when the British overwhelmed a force he left with Gen. Nathaniel Green at Fort Lee in late 1776. With some 4,000 men, Gen. Cornwallis skillfully scaled the treacherous cliffside under the guidance of a local Tory. Swarming up the Palisades, they were able to cut off the garrison of the fort. The Americans barely had time to escape, but with great loss of both men and supplies - a loss that almost dealt a deathblow to the budding revolutionary cause.

Among the prominent vacationers who frequented the area in pre Civil War, days were Washington Irving, Edgar Allan Poe, President Martin Van Buren, and William Cullen Bryant. The famed fur-trader and scion of one of New York's wealthiest families, John Jacob Astor, also built his "villa" along the "Palisades."

Then, in the late 1800's, a group of New York developers began eyeing its cliffs as a source of building material for their Manhattan structures. Seeing the Palisades thus threatened with virtual destruction by "quarriers" with little thought of their unique features, a group of outraged women finally marched on Trenton in 1896.

Feeling the sting of the anger of these women was more than New Jersey's politicians could bear. Finally, in 1900, they were successful in helping to create the "Palisades Interstate Park." Today some 30,000 acres of parkland and parkways have been set aside in both New Jersey and New York to protect these natural wonders.

From 1907 until World War I, this area was also the location of the nation's budding movie film industry. Pearl White was filmed on the Palisades' rugged bluffs in her famous, "The Perils of Pauline." Mary Pickford starred in "The Violin Maker of Crimona." Such early film stars as Rudolph Valentino, Lon Chaney, Charlie Chaplin, Fatty Arbuckle, Theda Bara, Lillian Gish, and Marie Dressler were also filmed along the trails of New Jersey's famous "Palisades."

Today you can visit and picnic in these parklands, and take a tour of the reconstructed gun batteries of the fort Lee Historic Park and Revolutionary War Museum. From the heights of the "Jersey Palisades", you can gain a panoramic view of the Hudson River and New York skyline, thanks to those determined women back in 1896.

CHAPTER 2: RIVERS

Major Rivers

I wonder how many people have ever stopped to think about the unique way our state is bounded by water. Only the short 48-mile northern boundary between New Jersey and New York, extending between the Delaware and the Hudson Rivers, is a land boundary. Our state is actually a peninsula, in a sense, surrounded on three sides by water.

We are unique in that no other state in the nation has water bounding it as extensively as does New Jersey. Our little state is bordered for some 432 miles by water - rivers, bays, or an ocean. We also have a considerable amount of water within our 8,000 square mile area. Almost 700 square miles of that space is devoted to various rivers and lakes. New Jersey has more than 100 fairly large rivers and steams, and numerous smaller, and more than 800 lakes and ponds of varying sizes.

All of New Jersey's land surface waters eventually flow into the Atlantic Ocean. Some go by way of the Hudson or Delaware rivers, but most of them have more direct outlets into the Atlantic. By far the greatest of our rivers is the Delaware - one of the major rivers of the eastern United States. Much of its northern stretch has been designated a part of the Wild and Scenic Rivers Network of the United States by the Department of the Interior. Its cut through the Appalachians at the Delaware Water Gap has been recognized as one of the scenic wonders of the East.

Rising in the Catskill Mountains of New York State, the Delaware flows in a generally southward direction, forming the boundary between New Jersey and Pennsylvania for the greater part of its length, and then between our state and the state of Delaware at its southern mouth. Many streams flow into this river, which is navigable for ocean-going ships as far north as Camden. Among the larger of its tributaries in our own northwest is the Flat Brook, which empties into the Delaware at the border of Sussex and Warren counties near Flatbrookville.

In Warren County alone, Paulins Kill reaches the Delaware at Columbia, while Beaver Brook and the Pequest River empty into its waters at Belvidere. The Pohatcong flows into it at Phillipsburg, and the Musconetcong River, which forms the county's boundary with Hunterdon County, ends its journey to the Delaware at Riegelsville.

On Jersey's northeastern border is the might Hudson River, which has been important in both state and national history and economics. Its border along New Jersey is highlighted by the unique rock cliffs known as the Palisades. Once an important tourist attraction, this prominent natural feature has been protected by the establishment of the Palisades Interstate Park. The Hudson's mouth also has one of the nation's best harbors. It serves both Jersey City and Hoboken on the Jersey side and New York City on its opposite shore.

The longest river entirely within the state's boundaries is the Raritan, which rises in Morris County. It, and its tributaries, drains about one-seventh of the entire state. It flows south and east, and eventually empties into the Raritan Bay east of New Brunswick at the Amboys. It flows through both forest and farmland, as well as through some of our most industrialized regions. One of its branches, the South Branch, actually flows only a few miles from the Delaware!

Another winding-river that flows through many diverse territories in its journey through the state is the Passaic. It also rises in Morris County. Along the journey of this river are two noteworthy descents. At Little Falls, it makes its first drop of some 40 feet through cascades and rapids. Then at Paterson it plunges a dramatic 77 feet through a rock-walled gorge at what was once one of the nation's leading tourist attractions - the Passaic Falls. From there, it flows south through a highly populated section of the state. It finally empties into Newark Bay, which has a fine harbor for large ships.

The Hackensack River has its source in New York State, flowing south into New Jersey about 5 miles west of the Hudson. It feeds into Tappan Lake, which straddles the two states and then the Oradell Reservoir before paralleling the Hudson, and finally emptying into Newark Bay. The valley through which this river flows is steeped in Jersey history, including an early Indian Village, examples of old

Dutch farmhouses and the site of the Massacre of Baylor's Dragoons during the American Revolution, just to mention a few. More about the numerous water bodies to be found along the trails of New Jersey, however, will have to wait another time.

Delaware River

Last week we mentioned the natural scenic beauty and historic value of the Hudson River Valley on New Jersey's northeastern border, which it shares with New York State through the 80,000-acre "Palisades Interstate Park System."

On New Jersey's northwestern border is still another of its natural scenic and historic wonders. One section of the Delaware River Valley is shared with Pennsylvania through the 70,000-acre "Delaware Water Gap National Recreation Area."

In addition to the national park, New Jersey also has a number of state parks along the Delaware, which help preserve the natural and historic wonders of this region.

The Delaware is one of the northeastern United States' larger rivers. Its unusual course, bordering between Pennsylvania and New Jersey for much of its length in what many describe as the profile of an Indian's bust, takes it some 410 miles from its headwaters in New York State to the end of its bay in Delaware. The river itself is about 296 miles from Hancock to the bay.

Its headwaters begin with two branches. The West Branch rises on the slopes of the Catskill Mountains in New York at an elevation of about 1,900 feet. It then flows southwestward to Deposit. From there, it flows to the southeast as it borders New York and Pennsylvania. Its East Branch rises on the slopes of the Catskills near Grand Gorge and then joins the main branch at Hancock. The Indians called this place "Sheehawken," or "the wedding of the waters." From there, it flows to Port Jervis where it begins its boundary between Pennsylvania and New Jersey above High Point State Park.

The Delaware River then flows south through that most spectacular of New Jersey's natural scenic wonders, the Delaware Water Gap. Known to the Lenapes as "the place where the water is gone," the gap is located in the rugged hill country of northwest

16

Warren County. It is a gorge some two miles in length where the river cuts through the Appalachian Mountains, known as Tammany on one side and Kittatinny on the other. The mountains rise to a height of about 1,600 feet on each side of the river.

The awe-inspiring scenic beauty of this natural wonder has attracted tourists and vacationers to this region for more than a century. President Teddy Roosevelt was one who frequented the region for hunting excursions.

Inns and public houses for the accommodation of travelers were known to have existed there as early as 1750. One such historic place, the VanCampen Inn, was used by many well-known personalities and is currently being preserved by the National Park Service. The first hotel for vacationers was the "Kittatinny House," built in 1829, and destroyed by fire in 1931. At one time, some 40 hotels dotted the region and vacationers played an important role in its economy.

During the French and Indian War, the New Jersey colonial governor directed the building of some 10 forts in this area for the protection of settlers against Indian attacks. At the time of the Revolution, George Washington on several occasions ordered armies into the area to settle Indian uprisings stirred up by the British. The Old Mine Road, built by Dutch mineral seekers as early as 1650, was still a well-known route between various points to the north and south of the colonies. Little has been done to remind our citizens of this rich heritage.

The bed of the Delaware is about 150 feet wide through the Gap, and is flanked by towering walls of quartzite rock. The Delaware Water Gap National Recreation Area aims to preserve the region's natural beauty. It flanks that portion of the Delaware, which was designated by Congress to be preserved forever as a "wild and scenic river."

The area was once an important center of Indian life, and the last home of the Lenapes who freely roamed the entire state. The fact that they were later concentrated along this river valley led to their designation by the colonists as the "Delaware" tribe. Millbrook Village, located in the Warren County section, is also being preserved and restored as an example of an early 1800's farming village.

From the Gap, the river flows south towards Easton, where it turns southeast to Trenton. Both Pennsylvania and New Jersey have dedicated "Washington Crossing State Parks" along the river's banks above Trenton to mark the spot from which Washington led his victorious armies to the Battles of Trenton and Princeton, considered by many to be the turning points of the Revolution.

The river, though navigable by ocean-going vessels only as far up as Camden, was once a travel route for Indians, fur traders and later a large lumber run. The southern end of the river was the site of early Swedish and Dutch settlements.

So the Delaware River Valley, by any measurement, has both scenic and historic significance both along the trails of New Jersey and in the saga of America.

Wickecheoke Creek

A few months ago, I wrote of a pleasant drive my wife and I took with my sister and her husband through Hunterdon County. During the course of our journey from Flemington to an old Inn in Stockton on the Delaware, we came through some picturesque country along the Wickecheoke Creek. On the Rosemont-Sergeantsville Road, I noted that we suddenly came upon the last remaining covered bridge in New Jersey. It is called the Green Sergeants Covered Bridge. It is to this bridge and this region that I would call your further attention today.

The bridge spans the Wickecheoke Creek. The creek gets its name from the tribe of Delaware Indians (Lenni Lenape) that once roamed the trails of this region. Between the early 1800's until the post Civil War Period, New Jersey had many such bridges. Covered bridges served also as shelters for travelers and farmers, during stormy weather. Travelers either on horseback or in open carriages, or farmers carrying hay back to their barns, might otherwise have been drenched with rain or pummeled with hail.

The original bridge across the Wickecheoke Creek at Sergeantsville is said to have been built around 1750. The present, single-lane, covered bridge, which is 81 feet long and 12 feet wide, was built of white oak in the period between 1860 and 1872. Because lovers often found their darkened interiors welcome shelters from the piercing eyes of onlookers, they sometimes earned the nickname of "Kissing Bridges."

The Wickecheoke Creek, with its little rock tributaries, is considered by many nature lovers to be one of the most attractive waterways in the state. Beginning at the Croton Plateau in Kingwood Township, northwest of Flemington, the rock-strewn Wickecheoke gently ambles its way to the Delaware passing between Sergeantsville and Rosemont. There it is spanned by the historic wooden bridge. Tumbling through picturesque rolling countryside and forested areas of hemlock and hardwoods, it reaches toward New Jersey's famous Delaware and Raritan Canal feed at Stockton, about 5 miles north of Lambertville. Stocked by the state, the Wickecheoke is a favorite spot for trout fishing.

Rural in character for three centuries, the landscape here has changed little over the years, and has been a popular region for a drive in the country for city folk. But the scenic and water quality values of the valley are now being threatened by the encroachment of both housing and industrial development. As a result, the New Jersey Conservation Foundation in cooperation with Delaware Township, the Covered Bridge Association and the Delaware River Mill Society have recently undertaken a project to protect the region along an eight-mile stretch of the creek. Through easements, purchases and donations from about 86 landowners along the stream, they hope to preserve a portion of this scenic and historic New Jersey countryside for the continued enjoyment of not only present, but future generations as well.

Though the region has been popular for hiking, cycling, fishing, and pleasure driving for many years, the stream itself can be reached by the public only at the Delaware and Raritan State Park and at Smith's Mill at Prallsville, just north of Stockton. Owned by the state, Smith's Mill is leased to the Delaware River Mill Society. The project, when completed, contemplates opening three more locations to the public. There will be a 40-acre area north of the Covered Bridge, in Wickecheoke Gorge. Another 12-acre section is planned north of that point at the largest waterfall of the creek. The third section will be at a floodplain about a mile north of Smith's Mill.

These three new points, plus the two already available, will make public access to highlights along the creek meaningful.

The groups are planning to tie three of these sites in with the Bel-Del bikeway and trail along the Delaware and Raritan Canal. All would then be part of a scenic trail program currently underway between Stockton and Bull's Island. The Delaware River Mill Society, which is a private group of concerned citizens, hopes to connect Lambertville to Frenchtown, eventually, with this scenic and historic trails system. The entire project is a unique effort by the people of one section of New Jersey to keep a small portion of their heritage intact. It is just another example of what interested citizens can make happen along the tails of New Jersey.

Passaic River

The Passaic River has its beginnings in the mountainous region of Morris County near Mendham about 600 feet above sea level. It is the longest and most winding river in the state. Its 90-mile pathway touches upon seven counties before finally emptying into Newark Bay. It flows in every direction imaginable. It passes through a wide and variable terrain. It moves swiftly through some regions. It is sluggish in others. It is prone to flooding badly in certain areas. It, or its tributaries, flows through the Morristown National Historic Park at Jockey Hollow and the Great Swamp National Wildlife Refuge in Morris, which abuts on Union and Somerset Counties as well.

The long, meandering, and once beautiful Passaic River is a good example of a New Jersey waterway that was early much used, and eventually over abused. It is a monument to man's never-ending pursuit of nature's resources to fulfill an insatiable appetite for individual profit. It has been an embarrassment to what man will do to his inheritance, if left unchecked.

The most dramatic change in the flow of the Passaic occurs at Little Falls. In this area, there is a drop in elevation of about 40 feet. The most impressionable is the 16-foot drop called Little Falls.

The most spectacular drop, however, occurs at the Great Falls in Paterson. There it drops 70 feet into a deep chasm some 60 feet in width, and then descends another 20 feet before leveling off. From there, it heads north to Hawthorne, then suddenly veers south. As it empties into Newark Bay, it unites with the Hackensack River. At Passaic, the Dundee Dam, completed across the river in 1859 for powering the Dundee Manufacturing Company, creates the man-made Dundee Lake. Once the site of a marvelous water recreation area, this lake has since been turned into a useless, stinking cesspool - a testament to the unscrupulous abuse that oft times results when uncontrolled avarice is left to run rampant.

The Passaic River, along with its many tributaries, is the drainage basin for some 950 square miles of northern New Jersey. It, and its main tributaries, the Pompton, Rockaway, and Saddle Rivers, encompasses 11 counties. The Rockaway, for example, starts in Sussex County. Because of the arrogant attitude man often has about his right to do whatever is profitable to him, this river system is plagued with problems. Careless, unchecked over-development along its riversides has led to serious and expensive flooding problems. Both human and industrial wastes that have been poured into it have made it one of the most polluted in the nation. As a result, this once beautiful Passaic River system became an environmental monstrosity. One would hope that people could learn from past mistakes. History, however, does not substantiate that hope.

The Passaic first provided the power man needed to move his machines back in colonial times. At the very beginning of the settlement of Newark in 1666, the need for a gristmill became apparent. A site along the Passaic was chosen to build its first mill. An agreement was finally reached with Richard Harrison to construct one in 1670. It was in operation by harvest time in 1671. The builders were paid chiefly in ground grain.

By the time a Geological Survey was taken in 1894, the Passaic, along with its branches, was home to a total of 79 mills. Among those included, there were 12 grist and flour mills, 15 sorts of woodworking, turning, and sawmills, 27 different kinds of textile mills, 3 paper mills, 11 assorted categories of ironworks mills, and a varied lot of 11 others put to a wide range of uses.

Between Mendham and Millington, where the Passaic is a fast-moving waterway, many good mill sites were found and used in great abundance. Some of these mill sites were still in operation as late as the end of the 1800's and early 1900's. Where the rivers did not move swiftly enough to provide power, such as between Millington and Chatham, man was not to be dissuaded. Dams were constructed there as early as 1727 to create the necessary power. Between Chatham and Little Falls, the flow of the river is so slow that it is more like a marshland. There, man had to turn to his many faster moving tributaries to build his mill sites.

But perhaps the most extensive and persistent abuse of this great river came in that 25-mile stretch from the Great Falls at Paterson to where it empties into the Newark Bay. There, a once-clear river, formerly an idyllic location for much water recreation along the trails of New Jersey, reaped the greatest effrontery from man's pollution.

Fishing, swimming and finally boating were all abandoned. One can now only hope that some day the Passaic River will once again run as clear and beautiful to the sea as it did in those days of yore. Perhaps we can yet leave our children a worthwhile inheritance.

CHAPTER 3: THE JERSEY SHORE

The Jersey Shore: Vacationland

To many people New Jersey is "the Shore." A vacationland 128- miles long, stretching from Sandy Hook to the tip of Cape May. Once past the Pine Barrens, it means an oceanfront cottage, and sandy beaches, with the Atlantic's thunderous surf breaking nearby. It is a place to go during July and August to beat the heat. It is where you find lots of sunshine, sunburn, and surfing - with cool sea breezes on those hot sultry days. It is water skiing, beach combing, and sunbathing in the lazy, hazy days of summer. It is cool nights, and the noisy, bustling excitement of the boardwalk.

The Lenni Lenape Indians were the first to flock to the Jersey shore. From the backcountry they came each summer to frolic on the beaches, bathe in the cool ocean waters, and to feast on the famous Jersey seafood. Mounds of clamshells were left as mementos of those happy days now gone. Indian trails from the north and west led south and east. "Big Sea Day," New Jersey's oldest festival is our heritage from those Indians of yore.

This Indian custom continued among the white settlers as "Beach Day" that for years was observed on the second Saturday in August. The "Day" began on Friday afternoon. Farmers from the backcountry hitched their wagons, after chores were done, and drove their families to "the shore." Picnicking along the way, they slept in their wagons overnight, arriving early on Saturday morning. Clouds of dust would start rolling in from all different directions. It was a time for meeting new friends and renewing old acquaintances.

After romping on the beach, picnicking, and bathing in the ocean throughout the day, they would then head for one of the local Inns. There, the remainder of the evening would be spent in dancing, drinking, and participating in various sporting events. Hitching their wagons again, most would head home late Saturday night, and arrive back home in time for Sunday morning chores and church.

Wealthy Philadelphians were known to stay at several boarding houses located in Cape May City as early as the 1760's. Day trips were rare when travel was difficult and expensive. For the New York crowd, Long Branch was known to keep boarders back as early as 1780. Both were among the earliest, and for many years, the most popular of Jersey's shore resorts.

With the coming of the railroads in the mid-1800's city-folk began to flock to the shore for weekly vacations. They stayed at the big boarding houses that began springing up in the various resort areas. It became the "in thing" for big names in the fields of entertainment or politics to spend July and August at the "summer places" on the "Jersey Shore." Southern aristocrats flooded the resorts of Cape May where casino gambling was prominent in the pre-Civil War period. Eight presidents set up summer residences over the years at Long Branch.

But the two events that have, perhaps, done most to make all points along the "Jersey Shore" accessible to the vast majority, have both occurred within the lifetime of those past 60. They were the introduction of the mass-produced automobile after World War I, especially in the 1920's and the opening of the Garden State Parkway in the early 1950's. Today there is not a place in the state that is not within two hours driving distance of New Jersey's most valuable natural resource - "The Shore."

The "Jersey Shore" is many things to many people. Some seek the busy boardwalks of places like Asbury Park, Seaside Heights, Point Pleasant, Atlantic City, and Wildwood. To others it is the serenity of places such as Spring Lake, Long Beach Island, Ocean Grove, Deal, or Cape May. To the deep-sea fishing enthusiasts, it's the offshore fishing from boats chartered anywhere from the Highlands south - including Brielle, Toms River, Barnegat, Forked River, and Sea Isle City. And there is the natural solitude of Brigantine and Stone Harbor, too.

But whatever it is they seek, almost every resident of New Jersey eventually joins the throngs of people, from inside and outside the state, who flood at some time during those lazy, hazy days of summer, down to the "Jersey Shore."

New Jersey's North Shore

As we have mentioned before, the "Jersey Shore" has been attracting people ever since the "Original People" (Lenni Lenape) arrived here in prehistoric days. And, since so many people "go to the shore" during the summer months, this would appear to be a good time to focus our attention on that region. If you are spending any amount of time at the "Jersey Shore" you will want to spend some of it exploring the number of interesting places there are to see in the area. Since we are talking about a span ranging almost 130 miles of oceanfront coastline from Sandy Hook to Cape May Point, let us start in the north first. Of course, what you will visit depends upon two things - your interests and the amount of time available.

Sandy Hook State Park at the Highlands is now part of the "Gateway National Recreation Area" and in addition to its fine beaches, it contains some other sites worthy of your attention. This is where the first European is reported to have been buried in New Jersey back in 1609, at what was called Coleman's Point. John Coleman was shot through the throat there with an arrow while exploring the area for the Dutch from Henry Hudson's ship the Half Moon.

It was there, too, that groups of merchants built and maintained the Sandy Hook Lighthouse back in 1764, to guide their ships around the treacherous sandbars. The British Commander-in-chief, Sir Henry Clinton, also escaped there with his army after the disaster at the Battle of Monmouth in 1778. Because of its key location for the defense of the Jersey City-New York-Newark Harbor areas, the US Army has some type of fortification there since 1807. Fort Hancock was built on the Hook in 1892. It served as a training center for US troops in World War I, as an anti-aircraft base in World War II, and a radar and missile base since the Korean War.

If your interests lie along botanical lines, you may want to see the almost 80 acres of wild holly trees nearby. It is supposed to be the best stand of wild holly forests in the nation. Or, if waterfowl turns you on, a wildfowl preserve there will offer you a spectacle you will not soon forget. Located along the Atlantic Flyway, you will not only see egrets and herons, but during the spring and fall migrations, you will see skies filled with duck and Canadian geese as well. And, since the New England whalers came there in colonial times, salt-water fishermen have continued to find this one of their favored spots.

This too, was the scene back in 1831 for the James Fennimore Cooper novel, "The Water Witch." Just before the bridge at Sandy Hook are the famous Navesink Twin Lights, which marked the entrance to New York Bay. Originally built back in 1746 with whale oil lights, its present twin towers were built in 1828. It threw a light that was visible at sea for 22 miles. The towers are open to visitors along with an interesting marine museum. An excellent view of the Bay area is visible there as well.

Further westward, off of the Garden State Parkway, at Holmdel, the state has erected a 9,000-seat amphitheater called, "The Garden State Arts Center." Here one may view a variety of classical, pop, and ethnic musical programs. For those with an equestrian bend, there is the Monmouth Park track featuring thoroughbred, flat, and turf racing at Oceanport. Further inland, at the Freehold raceway, harness racing, trotters, and pacers may be seen. New Jersey has become one of the nations leading horse-breeding states in recent years. Its tradition of horseracing and breeding, however, goes back to colonial times.

Also in the area is the Monmouth Battlefield State Park, where one may view this historic battle of the Revolution at the visitor's Center. A tour of the battle areas, and visit to the Old Tennent Church, Molly Pitcher's Spring and the Historic Craig House will give you a flavor of what time's were like in an area that has remained little changed since that period. You may also want to take in the gigantic 50-acre flea market in Englishtown, where some 700 vendors and antique dealers display their wares.

We will continue our tour of Jersey's Shore in the weeks to come. As we wend our way southward over some 130 miles of coastline, from the Hook to the Cape May Point, I hope you will gain new perspective on New Jersey. Its diversity just in this one section should give you a greater appreciation of the scope of living to be found within its confines.

Allaire's Village

As has been mentioned before, the "Jersey Shore" has been drawing visitors ever since its "Original People," the Lenape Indians, made their annual treks there centuries ago. Today, if you are spending any amount of time at the "Shore," you should explore some of its other interesting sites.

One place to take a day away from the beach, if you are in the Asbury Park to Point Pleasant area, is the Allaire State Park in Farmingdale. At the "Deserted Village of Allaire" you will witness a part of the shore region that was once the center of the now-long-gone New Jersey bog-iron industry.

Before the discoveries of magnetite made limonite, or bog-iron, too expensive to bother with, New Jersey's bog-iron industry was doing very well in its extensive offshore swamps.

The demand for iron for the manufacture of armaments, first at the time of the French and Indian War during the 1750's and early 60's, and later during the time of the American Revolution (1775-1783), gave New Jersey's bog iron industry the stimulus it needed to keep it profitable.

A chemical reaction in the swamp beds between the iron salts and decayed vegetable matter takes the iron to the surface where it oxidizes. The deposits then drop and gradually build up in the mud. While lying there they harden into rocky ore beds. These beds are formed under the roots of the grass found in the bogs. These beds are then "mined" producing the iron ore of the bog-iron industry.

The "War of 1812" with its new demands for iron armaments of various kinds, as well as peaceful iron products that could no longer be purchased overseas, created still another boom period that allowed the New Jersey shore's bog-iron industry to reach even greater heights.

In the scurry to make enormous quick profits, however, over-production depleted the limonite deposits faster than they could be replaced by nature. Though nature eventually replenishes bog-iron beds, the process takes about 30 years.

In the meantime, the Jersey furnaces were running 24 hours a day, seven days a week. They stopped only when winter weather froze the swamps or water wheels. In their greed to make immediate profits the industrialists, with no thoughts for the future, thus "killed the goose" that was laying their "golden eggs." How familiar that story has been over the years!

James Allaire, who built the cylinder in 1819 for the first steamboat to cross the Atlantic, the "SS Savannah," took over the rejuvenated Monmouth Furnace in 1822. Allaire was the leading steamboat-engine builder in the nation of that day. He produced the engines for many of Robert Fulton's steamboats. He bought out the Monmouth Furnace to be sure he would have the iron he needed for his prosperous steam boat-engine industry.

Allaire's original "company village," which was a typical 19th century way of doing business, was built to house some 500 workers and their families. In time, some 3,000 inhabitants and 70 buildings occupied Allaire's Village, which also included the first, free, public school of the area. He also built and financed an Episcopal Church, the beehive blast furnace, a four-story company store, a village bakery, the ironmaster's house, a blacksmith's forge, a grist and sawmill and a number of craft shops.

Allaire's Village was designed to be, and practically was self-sufficient. For a time he even went so far as to print his own money for exclusive use by his workers in his own private village! The dependence of an industrialist's workers upon the industry that housed them later became a sore point for reformers in America's burgeoning young industrial society.

By 1840, Allaire's Village was the largest iron producer in the nation. Then, about 1846, bog iron once again became exhausted. The village first went into decline, then shut down altogether with disastrous effects on its workers. Allaire became a ghost town. People left by the droves and grass grew in its streets.

The "Deserted Village of Allaire" remained in just that state for more than a century while the Pine Barrens grew up around it.

Finally, the State of New Jersey took it over and began its restoration as a tourist attraction.

Today, the "Historic Village of Allaire," located on some 3,000 acres of wooded state parklands, is a restored 19th century company village with tales to tell about life in a mid-1800's iron town along the trails of New Jersey.

There you will find picnic facilities, trout fishing, bridle paths, play-fields, a general store, and for railroad buffs, the narrow-gauge Pine Creek Railroad. Special events throughout the year make it a nice place to visit whether the beaches are open or not.

Ocean Grove

One of the state's most unique shore resorts is midway along the Atlantic coastline of Monmouth County. It wasn't until the coming of the New York and Long Branch Railroad in the late 1860's, the post Civil War period, that it was possible for average folk to afford a stay at such a North Jersey shore beachfront. Prior to that period, Long Branch, which had its beginnings as early as 1788, was the only North Shore resort of any substance, and it catered to the well to do. It competed in face, with Cape May as the place to go - for the elite.

In the summer of 1870, a novel organization, the Ocean Grove Camp Meeting Association, offered "a religious seaside resort" that would not subject vacationers to the intemperate behavior for which fashionable "watering places" had become so noted. People at the beginning pitched their tents along the beachfront at what was to become "God's square mile." Within a year, dozens of small cottages were being built. A second resort, named after the Methodist Bishop, Francis Asbury, soon rose up to its north. Then a third, named after James Bradley, one of the first lot owners at Ocean Grove, appeared to the south. By 1883, the railroad reported as many as 8,000 visitors in one day were coming to this formerly desolate stretch of beach.

A Methodist minister, the Rev. William Osborn of Farmingdale, is credited with dreaming up the idea of a family-style encampment along the Jersey Shore where one could find clean fun and Christian fellowship in sun and surf. It was to be a place of tranquility in a nation that had been recently torn asunder by a severe family trauma - the Civil War. The spiritual wounds incurred by that long, drawn out War Between the States, which had pitted brother against brother, and had divided many Protestant denominations into

29

northern and southern branches, are hard today to imagine. Ocean Grove was visualized as not only a place for bodily, but for spiritual refreshment. It was to be a religious gathering - a place for fun in an ideal setting, and for peaceful reflection.

To accomplish his dream resort, Osborn enlisted the aid in 1867 of the Rev. J. R. Andrews of Vineland. Together they searched the Jersey shoreline. Ocean air and water had long been considered a curative element for ailments of the body. Now it was to be enlisted as restorative, nourishment for the spirit. The ideal spot for their religious refuge was finally found in the summer of 1869. It was a 300-acre beachfront grove of trees, prickly plants, and low bushes. It was marvelously free of mosquitoes and protected by high sand ridges.

They soon had enlisted a group of 19 Methodists to be the founders of New Jersey's unique religious seashore camp. The first camp meeting was held on the evening of July 31, 1869 at a clearing near Long Pond in a candlelit tent. By December 22, the "Ocean Grove Camp Meeting Association of the Methodist Episcopal Church" had been formed. On March 3, 1870, they were granted a charter by the state of New Jersey, "providing...for the members and friends of the Methodist Episcopal Church, a proper, convenient and desirable permanent Camp Meeting ground and Christian seaside resort."

On July 14, 1877, the oldest building of worship in Ocean Grove, the James Memorial Tabernacle, was dedicated. It was named after Methodist Bishop Edmund James. In 1889 it was decided to build a smaller House of Worship, the Thornley Chapel arose, to be used for lesser gatherings. The Centennial Cottage, built in 1874, is now used as a museum of early life in Ocean Grove.

Amidst a growing seasonal settlement of tents and cottages, the association began building at the end of 1893 the gigantic wooden auditorium that was to become the centerpiece of their religious and cultural lives. It contained 262 windows and doors. Its central ceiling rose 55 feet. Its main tower was 131 feet high. Covering almost an acre, the dimensions of this now world-famous National Historic Landmark is 225 by 161 feet. Originally it seated 9,600 people. Today, abiding by state codes, it seats almost 7,000 on theater seats.

In 1907 the world's largest auditorium organ was installed at a cost of $27,000. It was dedicated on the evening of July 3, 1908.

New Jersey's unique religious resort, Ocean Grove, has been visited by Presidents Grant, Garfield, McKinley, Teddy Roosevelt, Taft, Wilson, Eisenhower, and Nixon. In addition many celebrities including world famous entertainers, evangelists, lecturers, musical groups and political leaders have appeared on its auditorium stage. Many tales can be told of the activities and people who have made their appearance at this unequalled spot along the trails of New Jersey.

Middle Shore Sites

As we continue our journey southward along the Jersey seashore, you might want to stop at the Forked River House, an eating place since colonial days. Capt. Joshua Huddy, whose heroic defense of the Toms River Saltworks cost him his life, made periodic stops at the Old Inn and Stage Stop that once occupied this spot. The present restaurant was build back in the 1820's for a sea captain. Also at Forked River is a state marina and 550-acre state game farm where tourists are allowed to view the 30,000 ring-necked pheasants that are raised in pens there. They are later released at various hunting grounds within the state.

Farther south is the once great port town of Tuckerton, which was founded about 1699. During the Revolution, it was an important port of entry and a hot bed for privateers. It was to this place, in October of 1778, that Sir Henry Clinton dispatched a British flotilla with some 500-armed men under the notorious Capt. Pat Ferguson. Their mission was to clean up this nest of rebels once and for all. This invasion led to the Battle of Chestnut Neck further up the Mullica River. There the fort was leveled, and many prize vessels were destroyed.

Brig. General Casimir Pulaski's daring horse brigade arrived at Tuckerton too late to save the fort. While one of his outposts was asleep at camp, 44 of his men were lost in an enemy bayonet massacre. When Col. Proctor arrived with his artillery from Batsto, Ferguson fled with his troops post haste. But first he sank his grounded flagship, the "Zebra" in Little Egg Harbor Inlet, in order to prevent its capture. The Pulaski Monument in Tuckerton commemorates the massacre. Tuckerton is also the site of a gigantic Indian Shell Mound, a reminder of the early Indian clambakes that once took place here.

The famed Renault Winery, founded by Louis Renault in the early 1870's is located at Egg Harbor City. German immigrants first settled this region in large numbers in the 1850's, and began the cultivation of grapes for home fermented wine. A small commercial winery opened in 1867 shortly before the large Renault Winery got underway. Public tours of the plant and museum are available, along with wine tasting. The first three weeks in September, when the grapes are being crushed, is the best time to visit, though the winery is open to visitors all year.

At the Bass River State Forest, the oldest in New Jersey, some 9,000 acres of pinelands offers family camping facilities. Campsites around Lake Absegami, with its fine beach and bathhouse, make it a great place to stop while touring the area. Nearby, the 20,000-acre Brigantine National wildlife Refuge offers both an auto route and hiking trails. Located along the migratory Atlantic Flyway, its population in the winter months reaches about 150,000 birds. Hiking and bird watching are its chief attractions. The refuge is also cut by the Inland Waterway.

While in this vicinity, you would also want to visit the restored Historic Towne of Smithville. The original Smithville Inn, founded in 1787, was a stage stop for a stagecoach line that ran between Leed's Point, on the edge of the wildlife Refuge, to Berlin, northeast of the Great Adventure Park in Jackson. The Inn was restored by the Noyes family in 1949, after a period of decline.

A number of old-time south Jersey buildings were brought there. The purpose of the restoration was to recreate an early "down Jersey village" atmosphere. Many shops for browsing have been clustered around the inn. At the Olde Village, for which there is an admission fee, a gristmill as well as various craft shops and other buildings typical of an old south Jersey village surround a millpond. A nearby farm makes the area a living museum of life in southern New Jersey in days gone by.

Surrounding the Mullica River, named after the Swedish Navigator, Erik Mullica, who explored the region for Sweden in the mid 1600's, is the 96,000-acre, state-owned Wharton Tract. Along this river, at the Forks, Erik Mullica later settled. He named the place Bad-stu, a Swedish name meaning "steam bath." We call it Batsto. This pine wilderness of some 150 square miles in the midst of the most densely populated state in the nation is a sight to behold. Some 60 miles of canoe routes are found within its borders. This will be the locale for our continuing journey along the "Jersey Shore," as we next explore another of south Jersey's famed bog-iron centers - Batsto.

Atlantic City

Like its mountains, New Jersey's seacoast has been both a source of livelihood and pleasure. Fortunately the state has been blessed with both of these natural features. Each has provided our state's people with a means of earning a living through the raw materials they have provided. But what is even more exciting is that both have been a source of livelihood as well because of the pleasure they have given. Recreation as a business is fast becoming New Jersey's economic giant. In both instances, nature has provided the basic raw material.

Although there are many resorts along New Jersey's 125 miles of Atlantic seacoast, it is to her "Queen of Resorts," her "City by the Sea," that I want to call your attention at this moment. Located in Atlantic County about 56 miles southeast of Philadelphia, the Atlantic City area is the most famous all-year-round sea resort in the United States. It draws tens of millions of visitors annually not only from throughout the United States, but from all over the world.

Situated on a narrow island, Atlantic City itself is separated from the mainland by the New Jersey Inland Waterway. The island was known to the Lenni Lenape Indians as Absegami, or "place of the swans." The first inhabitants called it Absecon when it was settled in about 1790. As early as the 1600's whalers were hunting off the coast of present-day Atlantic City and pirates, like Blackbeard, found its numerous bays and coves to be a most desirable haven.

33

The man who first envisioned this region as a resort area came there in 1820 from that other famed resort spa of his day - the Schooley Mountains of Morris County. Dr. Jonathan Pitney, who came to practice medicine, visualized the sea breezes of the shore and sunning on its wide, sandy beaches as an excellent source of good health. Only a handful of houses were on the island then. At first it was more of a sportsmen's than a bather's paradise. Bird life was plentiful and hunters stayed at Aunt Millie Leed's Boarding House. The bathers were more apt to stay at Uncle Ryan Adam's place.

By the mid-1840's, it had gained prominence as a summer resort. It took Pitney until 1852, however, to interest Gen. Enoch Doughty, Richard Osborne, and Samuel Richards to promote the area by bringing a railroad into their "Bathing Village." It was Osborne who coined its name, "Atlantic City," which was officially incorporated in 1854. In that same year, the United States Hotel opened and the Camden and Atlantic Railroad rolled into town.

It was Richard Osborne who in mapping the city named those streets running from the beach back to the marshes after the states of the Union. The streets paralleling the beach were named after the seven seas: Atlantic, Pacific, Arctic, Baltic, Adriatic, Mediterranean, and Caspian. These streets gained household fame through the introduction in 1930 of a genius of promotion - a game called Monopoly. As the little resort grew and prospered fine hotels originally were along the city's "Great White Way," Atlantic Avenue.

In 1870, Jacob Keim and Alex Boardman, tired of vacationers dragging sand into the plush hotels and railroad cars, promoted the building of a boardwalk on the sandy beach. And thus was born the famed, "Boardwalk in Atlantic City." In 1876, vast crowds watched the first of Atlantic City's Easter Parades. Today, the 60 foot wide and 5 miles long boardwalk takes more than 20 miles of new pine plank each year just to keep it in repair.

In 1882, the first of Atlantic City's famous piers was built. Before the turn of the century the idea of amusement piers over the ocean gave the Resort City a new first, and a new claim to fame. The following year, 1883, saw the introduction of salt-water taffy when a violent storm washed seawater over the boardwalk, splashing into a batch of David Bradley's stock of taffy candy. Picture post cards as a means of advertising were first introduced in Atlantic City in 1895.

They soon became a national fad. Many famed hotels of Atlantic City opened during the eras covered from the period of the Gay Nineties through that of the roaring twenties.

In 1920, the "Miss America Pageant" was born in order to extend the season well into September. The city's famed Convention Hall opened in 1929. It was just in time to witness the economic crash. Atlantic City, after the initial shock, weathered that storm with the introduction of the Big Band Era. Paul Whiteman launched his "The Rhythm Boys" with Bing Crosby as a member. Such big names as Jimmy Dorsey, Artie Shaw, Vaughn Monroe, and Glenn Miller performed in Atlantic City's Million-Dollar Pier Ballroom. Amos and Andy, Harry James and Frank Sinatra were among the famous names to follow.

In the summer of 1978, Atlantic City's latest claim to international prominence began with the opening of its first gambling casinos. The fabulous "Queen of the Seacoast" had done it again. It had captured the nation's imagination with still another first. Today, the first gambling resort on the eastern seacoast is in the midst of a casino boom era.

Visitors should not miss seeing other well-known attractions in the area. Famed seafood eateries such as Hackney's opened in 1912 to the delight of one of its favorite customers, Diamond Jim Brady. The more recent, Captain Starn's, opened in 1940, and with its fishing fleet was Atlantic City's answer to San Francisco's Fishermen's Wharf. Lucy, the Margate Elephant, a large 65-foot structure, was erected in 1881 by a promoter named Lafferty. Historic Gardner's Basin on the site of a once-busy fishing village was launched on the inlet in 1974. In recreating a 19th century seacoast village Atlantic City was hoping to compete with Mystic Seaport. Two square-riggers, "The Flying Cloud" and "Young America" recall the days of America's giant clipper ships. Illustrating New Jersey's nautical heritage, the Basin also contains exhibits of early sailing days. The newest novelty in seashore dining, the "Flying Cloud Café," adds an attractive dockside setting. The Historic Towne of Smithville with its 19th century South Jersey village is another attraction worth visiting 10 miles up Route 9. All of these places have helped make Atlantic City the "Queen of Seaside Resorts" and one of the most popular convention cities of the Atlantic coast.

"Lucy," the Margate Elephant

Ever since the Lenape Indians began their annual trek to the Jersey Shore, the place was recognized as a seasonal attraction for out-of-towners.

Following the American Revolution, certain Philadelphia entrepreneurs began to capitalize on this fact by opening boarding houses, first at Long Branch and in time all up and down the 127-mile coastline from Sandy Hook to Cape May.

Boarding houses were followed in their turn by hotels, summer cottages, boardwalks, public beaches, amusement parks, fishing piers, marinas and whatever also the mind could conceive that would make money out of the desires of people for a seasonal recreational get-away.

In the early 1800's, medical people began to view breathing in salt air and bathing in saltwater as a curative for all kinds of illnesses. Medical doctors began to prescribe a visit to the shore for their wealth patients. Average people did not have the luxury of a "vacation" in those days. In some cases, doctors even began to establish "health resorts" along the shore themselves.

One such individual was the young Dr. Jonathan Pitney, who searched out the area around Absecon Island in the 1820's. Eventually that place blossomed into the famed Atlantic City resort, once the now-older Dr. Pitney coaxed the railroads to come there in the early 1850's.

By the time the decade of the 1870's came to an end, the Jersey shore was a well-known and popular resort area for those New York City and Philadelphia families with enough substance to have "vacation" time.

Certain spots were also regularly frequented by the rich and the famous of that day from throughout the then-United States. But there were also many deserted beachfronts along the 127-mile New Jersey shoreline that remained untouched, and therefore practically worthless. It was to such an area south of the by-then-famous Atlantic City Resort to which the enterprising Philadelphia real estate broker, James V. Lafferty, turned his attention early in 1880.

Lafferty knew that to get people to buy something he first had to get their attention. To draw their attention to this deserted beachfront section south of the then-famed resort, he would need a really big "gimmick." What, he mused to himself, could be bigger than an elephant? And so in Lafferty's mind was first conceived, and then born, the famed "Lucy, the Margate Elephant," that would be a landmark for that area for the next century. It has since been named a State Historic site.

By the time Lafferty hauled in the lumber, 12,000 square feet of sheet metal, and all the other supplies needed to build this gigantic six-story "elephant," he had accumulated enough bulk for a 90-ton animal! Its four, over 20-feet high and 10-foot-in-diameter legs had to support a body that was 38 feet long with a circumference of 80 feet!

Its head alone stood out some 26 feet in length and 58 feet around. Added to this were a 26-foot tail, a 36-foot trunk, two 17-foot ears, and two 22-foot tusks.

On top of this elephant Lafferty had built the typical carrying seat with railing and canopy commonly found on the backs of elephants used in the East Indies, and called "howdahs." Only Lafferty's "howdah" was big enough to serve as an observation deck. The whole "gimmick" cost him an estimated $38,000 to build.

Inside of Lafferty's "elephant" were two spiral staircases in the rear legs leading to his real estate office and a restaurant. Up the sides from there were other stairs leading to the "howdah."

This served as an "observation deck" from which his prospective customers could get a tremendous view of both the Atlantic Ocean and the real estate he was there to sell them. He painted his elephant white and the "howdah" a number of bright colors.

It really was quite the sight to see. People did come from all over to see this "elephant," which somehow came to be called "Lucy." In time the development in South Atlantic City grew to such proportions that it became a separate community called "Margate City." It was named after an old, seaport summer resort in England.

By 1887, Lafferty had grown weary of this spot. His active mind visualized building other such elephants and selling other real estate all up and down the East Coast. He did build ones in Cape May and on Coney Island. Both are long gone.

"Lucy" also had her problems. Lafferty sold her to Sophie and John Gertzen, who over the years used her as part of their hotel and tavern. In 1903, she sank up to her knees in high water and had to be moved back 50 feet. In 1928, her "howdah" was blown off by high winds.

After John died, Sophie maintained "Lucy" as well as she could. At her death in 1963, "Lucy" was condemned. A "Save Lucy Committee" preserved her.

Today, the trails of New Jersey, thanks to that concerned citizen's committee, are still adorned with "Lucy, the Margate Elephant," a New Jersey landmark for more than a century now.

Cape May

When we think of a maritime heritage too often we think of New England rather than New Jersey. Yet the smell of fresh sea air permeates 125 miles of Jersey coastline. Seaport villages and wharves busy with fishermen are, and have been very much a part of New Jersey's heritage from the beginning. Vessels of all sorts moving into and away from its docks. Villages whose people are dependent upon the sea for their livelihood. A busy shipbuilding industry. Harbors that provide anchorage for the loading and unloading of cargoes. These are scenes of today and yesterday that provide the setting along the Jersey seaboard. From Sandy Hook to Cape May the Atlantic's waves roll and roar upon her shores.

A substantial body of legend and folklore related to the sea also has, as a result, become associated with New Jersey. Stories of bold sailors, notorious pirates, courageous privateers, and cunning smugglers abound in those areas of our state whose shores are washed by the Atlantic Ocean and the Delaware Bay.

For today, however, I want to concentrate on that particular section of our state that's almost totally surrounded by sea. It is an area that lies so far south it is below the Mason-Dixon Line. This peninsula, known both as "the Tidewater" and "the Cape" by the tourist trade, is another of New Jersey's unique regions that's worth your visit.

In 1621, a Dutch explorer, Capt. Cornelius Jacobsen Mey, entered Delaware Bay and gave to the peninsula the name, which today bears the English version - Cape May. Mey established Fr. Nassau further to the north in 1623, but it did not last. The Dutch tried again in 1632 to plant a colony in Cape May; however, trouble with the Kechemeches, a Lenni Lenape sub-tribe, prevented it from becoming permanent.

During this period of New Jersey's early settlement that great maritime nation of its day, Sweden decided to establish colonies there. In December of 1637, under one of its greatest Kings, Gustavus Adolphus, the Swedes sent out their first expedition. By March of 1638 under Peter Minuet, they entered Delaware Bay and began building settlements. But Sweden was unable to protect its American possessions for long because of setbacks in its European wars. After a series of engagements with the Swedes, another maritime people, the Dutch, overwhelmed them in the 1650's. When relations with Holland were poor, the greatest sea power of them all, England decided to strike the Dutch colonies in the New World. Cape May fell to the English after the British fleet's successful siege of New Netherland in September 1664.

The Dutch later won back Cape May in 1673, but early in the next year lost it to the English for the last time. When the English were firmly in possession of the Cape, New England and Long Island whalers eyed the land to carry on their trade. The whale-men first settled in Cape May on the Delaware Bay shore about 1685 and for a time the whaling industry prospered. They say there are more Mayflower descendants in Cape May today than in Plymouth, Massachusetts. And so, three great maritime nations, and a group of New England whalers have thus buried their roots in the Jersey Cape's nautical heritage.

In the late 1690's and early 1700's, pirates infested the Jersey coast from Sandy Hook to Cape May, and pirate vessels constantly prowled the waters of the Delaware Bay. In the period leading to the American Revolution, the Jersey coast became a hotbed of smugglers. On the lower Delaware Bay and up its Atlantic coast, smugglers abounded waiting to get rid of their illegal cargoes.

In 1778, a British ship, carrying a cargo of gold and other loot seized from plundered Spanish ships, sank off the coast of Cape May.

The contents, worth well over 30 million dollars, have yet to be found. The Dutch, English, and French were all guilty of bringing piracy to the Jersey shore, but the Dutch were first in 1653 to bury their booty there.

Cape May's real and lasting wealth was to come with her promotion of the benefits of bathing from her white sandy beaches. As early as the 1760's, physicians were praising the healthful benefits to be gained by Cape May bathers. In the early 1800's, visitors from Philadelphia were depended upon to bring summer wealth to the local citizens. Soon Baltimore and Washington added their guests to the growing list. By the pre-Civil War period, rich southerners were bringing in their entourages of servants to spend the entire summer gambling in the six gaming houses of the resorts. They brought in architects and competed with each other for the best "cottages" on the Cape. It soon had a reputation as the "watering place" for wealthy southern plantation owners.

Famous people, too, visited the Cape's resorts: President's Lincoln, Pierce, Buchanan, Grant, Arthur, and Benjamin Harrison to name only a few. Henry Ford raced one of his first automobiles on its wide beaches in 1903. Resorts like Ocean City, Sea Isle City, Cape May Point, Stone Harbor, Somer's Point and the Wildwoods began sprouting up. The charm and nostalgia of Cape May itself with its collection of Victorian buildings makes it an American resort classic. It has in fact the largest concentration of those architectural delights in the nation. So much so that in 1976 it was designated as a National Historic Landmark.

The clear silicate pebbles found on its beaches have become known as "Cape May Diamonds." Its sunken experimental concrete ship, "the Atlantis," Fisherman's Wharf, and the Cape May Lighthouse all have attracted visitors.

But perhaps its most famous folklore involves that of the archpirate of them all, the infamous Capt. Kidd. One story tells of his ship appearing off the Cape's coast and his approach with some of his crew bearing several treasure chests. They made their way to a remote spot on one of the offshore islands where they dug a deep pit. After burying the chests in the hole Kidd called for a volunteer to guard the chests until they could return. The unsuspecting seaman who volunteered found himself brutally walloped and shoved into the pit on top of the chests. While crying for mercy he was buried alive. It seems the pirates believed that a dead man's ghost was the best protection you could garner for a buried treasure chest. If anyone comes near the chest the ghost of the murdered sailor rises out of the pit and the potential finder flees in terror.

Lighthouses

New Jersey's nautical heritage makes it a natural for having historical lighthouses, such as "Old Barney" and "Old Sandy," among its well-known shoreline landmarks.

Lighthouses of one sort or another have been in existence for a long time. Built or set up as important landmarks to guide sailors at sea, they are known to have been in existence for more than 2,000 years. The ancient Egyptians, Romans, and Phoenicians all used them. They were few and far between in the American colonies, however, until the end of the 1700's.

The first lighthouse to be built in what is now the United States was the "Boston Light" built in 1716. New Jersey's "Old Story" was first lit on Sandy Hook in 1764. "Old Barney," by comparison, is just a youngster, having made its first appearance in 1858.

In 1789, the US Congress passed its first act concerning lighthouses when it created the Federal Lighthouse Service - now a part of the US Coast Guard.

The earliest known lighthouses were merely wood-fires burned in braziers. Coal fires were also in early use. Animal or vegetable oils burned in lamps specifically designed for lighthouses came to be the chief source of illumination at the end of the 1700's. Batteries of candles had also previously served this purpose. About the middle of the 1800's, mineral oil burned on wicks was introduced. By the end of that century, burners of vaporized mineral oil on mantles were in use and were another improvement.

The biggest improvement, of course, came with the introduction of the electric incandescent lamps. Once oil lamps and candles replaced wood and coal fires, various types of optical devices and reflectors were also introduced. In 1820, the introduction of the

Fresnel lens of ground and polished glass was a great advancement in lighthouse illumination.

The Sandy Hook Lighthouse at the Highlands in Monmouth County, New Jersey, is the oldest original light still operating in the United States. Built as a guide for ships heading in and out through the narrow, winding channel into Lower New York Bay around Sandy Hook, "Old Sandy" has been a welcome sight for mariners for some 225 years now. Prior to its construction, which was first suggested in 1761, many ships and their valuable cargoes were lost there on shifting sandbars and dangerous shoals.

This 103-foot octagonal structure's beacon was originally lighted with 48 oil fires located within glass lanterns. The lighthouse-keeper, whose quarters were at its base nine stories below, had to climb the stairs to light it every day before sunset, and again to put it out once the sun came back up.

During the American Revolution, "Old Sandy" served the British navy royally and was thus the object of constant attacks by patriots.

Since 1790, it was operated by the US Lighthouse Service, which in 1939 became a part of the US Coast Guard. Its beacon, which is visible for some 20 miles, is now, of course, a modern lamp.

"Old Barney," which was designed by Gen. George Meade, the commander of the Union Army at Gettysburg, when he was a young lieutenant in 1858 replaced the first lighthouse that was built there in 1814.

"Old Barney" stands 150 feet high with another 17-foot light-holder on top of that. Its light, which is composed of 1,024 separate prisms set into bull's-eye lenses, could be seen some 30 miles out at sea. This lighthouse was first put into operation on Jan. 1, 1859. Darkened during the air-raid scares of WWII, it today has been replaced by a lightship anchored offshore and is no longer operational.

The light-keeper for "Old Barney" had to climb up 217 steps to reach the lard-oil lamp that once warned mariners from its location south of the inlet where Barnegat joins the Atlantic Ocean.

In 1866, some 200 tons of stone had to be dumped onto the stretch of washed-away sand between the inlet and the lighthouse to keep it from toppling. This process had to be repeated each year with greater amounts as the forces of nature took their continuing toll. Finally, in 1920 the US Lighthouse Service decided to replace "Old Barney" with a lightship anchored at sea.

Once again, concerned citizens came to the rescue. With their own money and work, a jetty was built to save the old lighthouse landmark from destruction. Though the lightship did finally replace "Old Barney" in 1927, the old lighthouse still continued to illumine the sea from along the trails of New Jersey until WWII darkened it forever. But it, like "Old Sandy," still stands today as a reminder of New Jersey's nautical heritage.

While America's Atlantic coastline was once the most poorly lighted in the world, it is today one the world's best lighted. An array of modern light-aids, from the old lighthouses to gas and electric lighted buoys, radio-beams and lightships, assist the US Coast Guard in this formidable task.

CHAPTER 4: PINELANDS AND MEADOWLANDS

Pine Barrens

Though small in area, New Jersey is large in natural phenomena. An interesting illustration is the "Jersey Pine Barrens." Just one of the natural wonders of our great state, these Barrens make up the largest area of unspoiled wilderness in the entire eastern coast of the United States.

A vast region of desolate sand trails, mysterious marshes and wild pine stands, as well as extensive cranberry bogs and luscious blueberry plantations, the Pine Barrens cover some 2,000 square miles of Jersey's terrain. This area accounts for our state ranking number one in the nation in the production of blueberries, and third in cranberry production. The forest wilderness of the region is equal to that of many of our large western national parks. The Barrens are also the largest source of pure water in the entire United States.

The many rivers and streams of the Pine Barrens have an orange-colored hue from the large cedar forests and the scattered bogs of iron ore that still lie within this vast domain. Stretching across seven counties of southern Jersey, you can travel through their amazing desolation for miles without coming upon any signs of civilization. The remarkable wild beauty of this place is even more outstanding because of its location within the boundaries of the most densely populated state in the United States.

The Barrens are a naturalist's paradise. Hundreds of varieties of wild flowers, rare species of orchids and lilies, the insect-eating pitcher plants, dense pine, oak and cedar forests, the unique dwarf pine that stretches for miles, fur-bearing animals, birds, and reptiles all inhabit this primitive, wild region in the most urbanized state in the nation.

The centuries-old isolation of the Pine Barrens and its few scattered inhabitants, known as the "Pineys," was not broken until the twentieth century. It came about as a proliferation of modern roads began to make the Barrens more accessible to outsiders and "the

44

Pineys" more within reach of modern civilization. Old-timers have (with frustrating displeasure) observed the gradual nibbling away of their private pristine paradise.

But others, too, have more recently watched with concern the infringement of modern man upon this vast wilderness. So much distress was exhibited by naturalists, outdoorsmen, fishermen and others disturbed at the frightening speed with which man suddenly encroached upon this unique region that the national and state governments have moved in. As a result, "the Pinelands National Reserve" was created. The reserve at its outer fringes encompasses a million acres of New Jersey's Pine Barrens. This south Jersey area, which includes about one-fourth of the state, is to be permanently protected by the cooperative efforts of both state and national governments. It will hopefully remain as a haven for all who seek its peaceful sanctuary.

Hiking, canoeing, fishing, wildlife study, timber production, berry farming, picnicking, camping, and swimming all are important parts of this extraordinary wilderness. Some of the finest wilderness canoeing in the East is available there. The Mullica and Wading rivers are among the favorites. At least five state forests - Bass River, Belleplain, Lebanon, Penn and Wharton are found within the bounds of the Barrens.

Picturesque names such as Mt. Misery, Double Trouble, Apple Pie Hill, Hog Wallow, and Ong's Hat add local color to the intrigue of the area. Folklore abounds in this region dating back to the 17th century. Lumbering succeeded where farming failed for the early settlers. Loggers once shipped quantities of cedar and pine to a thriving shipbuilding industry along the coast. Local artisans made their living on the manufacture of valuable cedar shingles. With the discovery of bog iron, furnaces and forges also once prospered there. These early industries turned out munitions vital to both the Revolution and the War of 1812. When a better grade of iron in the West brought an end to the iron enterprises, attempts were made for a time to produce products of paper and glass.

In time, all industry collapsed and crumbling ghost towns added a new dimension to the eerie nature of the landscape. History buffs have been delighted by several of the ghost towns that have been restored by the state as authentic examples of early Pine Barrens iron villages. Batsto, lying inland from the vicinity of Atlantic City, and Allaire, just a short distance inland from the Asbury Park region, are two notable restored settlements. They have become prominent tourist attractions and are well worth a visit.

Stories of pirates and robbers, of smugglers, Tories, privateers, and iron kings have all abounded in this region. The one legend for which the Barrens have been most notorious, however, is the legend of a creature whose antics have terrorized the countryside. Since colonial times, this ogre has haunted the Pine Barrens. Other areas of New Jersey, including Warren County and eastern Pennsylvania, have also been subjected to the nocturnal visitation of this hideous monster. What is its name? They call it the "Jersey Devil." But we will have to tell you about this eerie creature next time.

Pine Barren History

South Jersey is the location of the Pine Barrens, a vast area so ecologically sensitive and unique that the United States government has declared that the almost 1.1-million acre wilderness be set aside as the "Pinelands National Reserve." It is the largest such area on the eastern seaboard. This is a region in which development is to be controlled for the most part, and prohibited entirely in certain very sensitive enclaves.

Parts of these Pinelands sustained a prosperous iron industry, whose chief ingredient was the bog iron once found in great abundance in its swamps. Also in abundance were its trees, which were turned into charcoal for firing not only iron furnaces, but also those of another early Pine Barrens industry - glass making. The silica found in its sand once nourished these flourishing glass-works. The specific kinds of clay found in its soil also nourished both pottery and brick-making industries. Its boundless forests of pine, cedar and scrub oak fed shipbuilding, papermaking, cedar shingles cutting and decoy carving industries in its heyday as well. Keep in mind, however, that they were chiefly family enterprises and never of the magnitude as would be found in today's giant manufacturing centers.

A number of families in the Pinelands realized the great American dream of achieving great wealth through hard work and the free enterprise system. The William Richard's family was one of those that so prospered. From its original 19 children and 40 grandchildren, countless glassworks, ironworks, paper mills and railroad enterprises, all of which engaged more than a number of generations, became part of this family's financial domain. Played out in a region stretching from the Atlantic Ocean to the Delaware Valley, its might and influence lasted over a period of time encompassing both the American Revolution and the Civil War.

William Richards of Batsto had two wives, 19 children, and 40 grandchildren. Over the generations that followed, they were involved in just about every industry ever found in the Pinelands, and eventually became the biggest landowners in the eastern United States. Born in Pennsylvania in 1738, William died in Mount Holly in 1832. He outlived 10 of his 19 children. His first wife, Mary Patrick, bore his first 11 children. His second wife, Margaretta Wood, 34 years younger than he, bore his remaining eight, the last only eight years before his death at 85.

Young Richards was apprenticed to an ironworks in 1754 in Pennsylvania where he grew up. There he met John Patrick, who taught him the trade and later became his father-in-law. While living with the Patricks, William met, wooed and married Mary, six years younger the he, when she 19. Four years and two children later (1768), he moved to New Jersey to find work at a place called Batsto, where a new iron furnace had just opened in the Pinelands on the Mullica River. Fortunately, he left his family back in Pennsylvania because the Batsto Furnace closed down temporarily and he soon had to return.

A Philadelphia friend, Col. John Cox, bought Batsto in 1770 and in 1773 hired Richards as his new manager. This time he moved his wife and by then five children with him. In 1775, however, they all moved back to Pennsylvania where Richards joined the Provincial Army as the American Revolution burst into flame. By 1781, he was once again manager at Batsto while his family, then numbering eight children, remained 80 miles and a two-day trip away in Pennsylvania. It seemed that the manager at the time, his nephew, Joseph Ball was too much involved in a very prosperous sport of the day, privateering along the Jersey coast - or piracy as the British called it. He was using

Batsto on the Mullica as his headquarters. Needless to say the iron business was being ignored.

When Richards returned to Batsto, it once again prospered and a new forge was built on the nearby Nescochague Creek. An additional 8,000 acres of woodlands had to be purchased to provide it with enough fuel. By the time it was in full swing producing more guns for the American Army, however, the British had surrendered at Yorktown and the need dropped sharply. Batsto again went up for sale. With no interest being shown for three years, Richards was in a position to purchase it with two others. They took title on July 1, 1784.

Four fire-backs for George Washington's fireplaces at Mount Vernon were sold that year. Two Batsto fire-backs are still there today. This turned out to be the beginning of the Richards family's financial dominions in the Pinelands.

Batsto still remains along the trails of New Jersey, but now as part of a state historic village nestled in the 100,000-acre Wharton State Forest - a monument in a sense to the American dream and the industrious Richards family who achieved it.

Joseph Wharton

In the decade after the Civil War period, Joseph Wharton of Philadelphia began purchasing large chunks of land I what was known as the "Jersey Pine Barrens." His purpose at the time was to build reservoirs throughout the region to harness a large enough potable water supply to meet the growing needs of that Pennsylvania metropolis. Even at that time ghost towns and ruins of once prosperous mills and furnaces were to be found scattered throughout the area.

In the midst of this ambitious project, the state passed laws prohibiting the removal of water to other states. Wharton, by then fascinated with the area for its own sake, changed gears, and decided to remain and use his gigantic land holdings for various agricultural pursuits. Today it is part of the 100,000-acre Wharton State Forest, a unique wilderness hopefully preserved for posterity.

Before Wharton got there, the Pine Barrens had been inhabited by a series of diverse groups. The Lenape Indians, of course, were the first to occupy the region, leaving it pretty much as they found it when they were driven further west in the early to mid 1700's. In fact, by a treaty signed in Easton, PA, in1758, this nation's first Indian Reservation was established in the Pine Barrens.

Today the town of Indian Mills is the only reminder that the proud Lenape nation was once rounded up from throughout New Jersey and relegated to this small region. This was where the Indians had to stay, if they wanted to remain at all on the east banks of the Delaware. Most chose eventually to move west. Some sooner, some later. By 1800, most were gone.

The lumber people were the next wave to move in. The alarming number of saw mills that were erected there created such a scare that early conservationist sentiments were aroused at a time when exploitation of natural resources was accepted and commonplace practice in America. Even those who generally supported the "natural right to man" to consume for profit as much of "God's gifts" as he was able to avail himself of, recoiled at the unconscionable lack of restraint shown in hacking down the area" forests.

With the discovery of the large amount of a low-grade form of iron that lay dormant in the bogs along its many streambeds, another group of entrepreneurs began swarming over the Pine Barrens. First discovered along the Shrewsbury in Monmouth County back in 1675, the bog iron industry actually began in New Jersey there at Tinton Falls Iron Works. Not until wars created greater demands for large quantities of iron products in the colonies did iron men begin harvesting the bog iron ore deposits found along the Mullica and Wading rivers.

The tremendous demands, for example, that were created by both the needs of the armies of the American Revolution, and the cut-off of English iron during that period, gave the bog-iron industry added life. Available waterpower, and the abundant nearby forests for fueling its furnaces and forges, were added ingredients to foster this once flourishing bog-iron enterprise. The nearby availability of seashore shells to be ground into flux was another plus.

Competition from cheaper methods and better grade ores, diminishing resources, and the coming of the railroads all had their toll as one Pine Barrens ironworks after another eventually folded. As the iron industry collapsed, it was replaced for a time by paper mills, cotton mills, and glassworks. By the time the Civil had faded, so did most of the Pine Barren's industry. Decaying ghost towns, roads fading into oblivion, the return of the forests all make it hard to believe that any industry ever thrived in those "Pine Barren" of South Jersey. But it did.

Joseph Wharton was there with the needed cash when Batsto foreclosed in 1876. Wharton bought up acre after acre until his land holdings reached 125,000 acres of Pine Barrens. When his plans for turning the region into a gigantic source of fresh water for Philadelphia went sour, he raised sugar beets, cultivated cranberries and even herded beef cattle. He died in 1909 at the age of 83 – a contented man.

The state of New Jersey almost immediately became interested in obtaining his land holdings in the Pines as its own vast reserve watershed. The issue was finally put up to the voters in a statewide referendum held Nov. 2, 1915. It was defeated principally by South Jersey voters whose chief concern was that its purchase would mean a loss of ratables.

Some 39 years later in 1954 the state bought the tract for three times the original price. Today, Wharton offers the largest uninterrupted source of release from the tensions of modern life to be found anywhere along the trails of New Jersey. It also contains the Historic Village of Batsto, a memento to a once thriving industry. The National Park Service is considering constructing an interpretive visitor's center where people would be able to learn more about the flora, fauna, and folklore of the Jersey Pinelands.

Batsto Village

Probably no site in the Jersey Pinelands more epitomizes the story of that vast region and the various enterprises that once occupied it than that of the village of Batsto on the Mullica River.

The gigantic 100,000-acre Wharton State Forest, within which that historic village is situated, was acquired by the State of New Jersey in 1954.

Originally offered for $1 million in 1912 as a valuable water aquifer, it was rejected by the voters at a referendum held in 1915 because development promoters waged a propaganda campaign arguing that it would be lost forever to the tax rolls. When it finally was acquired years later the price, of course, had risen considerably. It was still, however, a valuable acquisition for the state and its people.

The "West Jersey Proprietors," led by John Munrow, were the first to begin assembling these vast stretches of pine, oak, and cedar forestlands as early as 1758. But it was Charles Read of Burlington, along with four associates, who were first to build the Batsto Furnace there in 1766. It was one of four pineland ironworks they built. All of them made use of the area's valuable resources: the bog iron, then found so abundantly in the area, from which they extracted the iron ore; the vast woodlands which were turned into charcoal to fuel the furnaces; and the many streams which were dammed for power.

Within two years, Read, a distinguished lawyer who went on to become an Assemblyman and New Jersey Supreme Court Justice, sold his interest in the furnace to his partners, Reuben Haines of Philadelphia, John Wilson and John Cooper of Burlington, and Walter Franklin of New York. They, in turn sold a controlling interest two years after that to Col. John Cox of Philadelphia.

Col. Cox, who was a patriot, became an assistant Quartermaster General in Washington's Continental Army. Because cannon and cannon balls for the Revolutionary Army were cast at the Batsto Furnace, the men working there were exempted from military service.

In 1778, as an indication of the importance the British attached to the area, a British fleet, with accompanying foot soldiers, attacked Chestnut Neck. This was an important shipping harbor of that day about 15 miles east of Batsto at the mouth of the Mullica River. The British force, after hitting Chestnut Neck, attempted to move on to destroy a second harbor at Forks, as well as destroy the Batsto Ironworks. Quick action by Gen. Pulaski's Cavalry Legion, however, repulsed the attack and they retreated.

That same year the furnace was sold to Thomas Mayberry who, within six months, sold it again to Joseph Ball. Ball had been manager at Batsto under Col. Cox. He built a forge and slitting mill there on the Nescochague Creek around 1783.

Joseph Ball's uncle, William Richards, acquired the Batsto Ironworks in 1784. In 1809, he retired to Mount Holly and left his son, Jesse, to run the works. Batsto again furnished munitions for the nation during the War of 1812.

When William died in 1823, his grandson, Thomas Richards, bought the place at an auction. His son, Jesse, who had stayed on as a manager, bought a half-interest in the works in 1829 and rebuilt the furnace. Water pipes for eastern cities were made there as well as firebacks. Other notable projects included the iron fence that once surrounded Independence Square in Philadelphia and the cylinder for John Fitch's fourth steamboat.

By the 1840's, bog iron was on the decline and Batsto's last furnace fires went out in 1848. But to diversify, a glass factory had been built at Batsto in 1846 that made use of another valuable resource of the region - sand. When Jesse died in 1854, his son, Thomas Richards, not only carried on the glassmaking industry at Batsto, but had included a large lumbering operation as well. Flat glass for windows and glass for gas lamps were made at Batsto. A brickyard was also added.

By 1867, the glassmaking enterprise also failed. Then, in 1874 another crippling blow came when more than half of the once-thriving village went up in flames. An era had obviously ended.

Joseph Wharton, a Philadelphia financier, acquired the property at a master's sale in 1878. He continued with the lumbering business and experimented with cultivating cranberries and raising livestock. He also greatly expanded his land holdings and enlarged the former ironmaster's mansion, adding the tower.

His acquisition of lands in the pines was aimed towards acquiring an aquifer of such size that it could supply the City of Philadelphia with a water reserve. He died in 1909 without achieving his goal. A law forbidding the export of water from the state had been passed by the state legislature.

Today, the restored Batsto Village, in the 100,000-acre Wharton State Forest, serves as a reminder of the important part this vast Pinelands along the trails of New Jersey once played in the industrial development of the United States - a use its current appearance could hardly have conveyed - if it weren't for the preservation of historic Batsto Village.

Meadowlands

We find another of New Jersey's unique natural areas in the "Jersey Meadows," which are found in the northeastern section of the state. Encompassing Bergen, Hudson, Passaic, and Essex Counties, this vast open region of marshes, meadows, and woodlands lies within the most highly urbanized portion of New Jersey. For several generations, this area has been looked upon as an immense Wasteland. This was not always so, and once again is changing.

The result of a retreating glacier that formed the giant, Lake Hackensack, the Meadowlands eventually came about after years of a natural draining away of the water. Today, the lower Passaic River, the Hackensack River, Berry's Creek, Sawmill Creek, the Lower Saddle River, and the swamplands surrounding them are all that remain of this once great lake.

The Hackingsackie Indians, a sub-tribe of the Lenni Lenape, ruled these lands under their wise sachem, Oratam, when the Dutch first established a fur-trading post there in the early 1600's. Panthers, wolves, and large numbers of fur-bearing animals were in great abundance at that time. Various crustaceans, fish, and birds provided both Indians and the early Dutch with a plentiful food supply. Mussels, clams, shrimp, and crabs were sought after not only by local Indians, but by tribes who made the trek there from other areas.

Early attempts of settlers to produce farmlands by damming the tidal waters met with failure. Eventually, aside from trapping, highways, and railroads merely crossed over the land, leaving it a vast open space in the midst of the most densely populated region of the nation.

Though developments came to selected areas within the Meadows as large groups of German and Irish immigrants were sold building lots in the 1840's and 50's, the region remained basically untouched. Unfortunately, in time, it became a dumping ground – first only by individuals. Ultimately, though, some 50,000 tons of garbage from six counties were dumped there each week. This one unique region became an eyesore, devastated, and despoiled by man's ruinous treatment.

As a new attitude about our environment gradually evolved, demands to rehabilitate this remarkable land began to arise. Large portions of the Meadowlands were restored to former greatness. Land was set aside for open spaces, marsh preservation for the use of wildlife, and for various forms of recreation. All kinds of wildlife returned and fishermen, hunters, and crabbers were again able to catch their legal goals.

A 2,000-acre DeKorte State Park has been developed with areas for sports, camping, biking, skiing, and picnicking. The Sawmill Creek Wildlife Management Area protects the marshlands and has once again created a migratory stop for birds in the Atlantic Flyway, and spawning and nesting ground for fish, waterfowl, and crabs. Walkways, horseback riding trails, canoeing, and wildlife observation centers are also found there.

Probably the most notable development in this region was the Meadowlands Sports and Entertainment Center, that rose from the surrounding swamplands. Various teams, the Giants in football, the Cosmos in soccer, the Jersey Nets in basketball and the Jersey Devils in Ice Hockey, call it home. This vast entertainment center also hosts thoroughbred racing, concerts, the circus, and other special events. The hockey team, the Jersey Devils, was named after that famous Jersey legend to which I shall now turn.

Though associated today with the Meadowlands Sports Center, the Jersey Devil originally, as I mentioned before, arose in the Pine Barrens of south Jersey. There this mysterious creature regularly terrorized the local citizenry. It seems that in colonial days a woman named Mrs. Leeds was in labor with her 13th child. On a particularly dark night, a violent storm was brewing in those eerie Barrens, while a group of old women were attending to her needs. She cried out something to the effect that this unlucky child could go to the devil. Mother Leeds then delivered what at first seemed to be a fine baby boy.

Then suddenly to everyone's horror, the child began to take on the likeness of some devilish creature! Its head bore the features of a horse, its arms those of a bat's wings. Its legs were a mixture of a large bird with the hooves of a goat. A dragon-like tail and the horns of a devil appeared. The old women were frozen with terror. With a shrieking bawl, the creature took off out of the room. It was said that it blared out something about belonging to the devil, and this forever after it became known as the Jersey Devil.

This frightening creature has since been seen, after that first appearance in 1735, in various places within the state. It has been sited in the Delaware Valley and in eastern Pennsylvania. Over a period of some 250 years, the exploits of this devilish mixture of folklore and history have been documented by both local folk and famous personages alike. But more about this infamous being will have to wait for another time.

Great Swamp

Every year around this time our attention is drawn to another of New Jersey's unique wilderness areas.

On the edge of one of the most densely populated state's high population centers lies the 7,000-plus-acre Great Swamp National Wildlife Refuge.

It is a monument to how people who love their natural surroundings can, if they unite their efforts, fight back against even overwhelming odds and still come out on top in this great democracy of ours.

In southeastern Morris County, edging upon Somerset and Union counties, south and east of the Morristown National Historic Park, there still lies this wilderness paradise. This is thanks to the untiring efforts of a group of determined citizens in the 1960's who would not give in to the power, money, and political clout of the mighty New York Port Authority.

Some of the most powerful men in this state had determined to fill in "this useless piece of real estate" and turn it into the fourth jetport in the metropolitan area. In their infinite wisdom, they had decided that they alone knew how best to correct nature's "wasteland" and turn it into a financial masterpiece.

Like the nearby Watchung Mountains, this Great Swamp once afforded protection to the hopelessly out-numbered, and ill-prepared little revolutionary army of Gen. George Washington against the mightiest power of their day.

The parallel between the patriots' seemingly hopeless fight to gain their independence from the mighty British Crown and these local citizens' fight to keep their beloved wilderness from the grasp of the powerful financial interests of the Port Authority did not go unnoticed. That in both instances "the people" won their impossible dreams against seemingly insurmountable odds reinforces one's faith in the power of the people.

The area has both natural and historic significance. Arrowheads and primitive tools found there give evidence of the presence once of the Lenape Indians, who made their seasonal camps in this pristine wilderness.

They hunted, fished, and found there the necessary materials of stone, bone, wood, and clay to make their simple tools, weapons, and utensils. The skins of animals, feathers of birds, and various plant-life provided the resources for their ceremonial, medicinal and other life-support needs. They lived there peacefully, abundantly, and in harmony with their environment.

On several occasions, seeking safe sanctuary from threatening British troops, encampments of soldiers of the American Revolution were held along the Loantaka Brook within the confines of "the Great Swamp." The patriots of that now-long-ago time had nicknamed, "Fevertown," because of the frequent illnesses the region had inflicted upon them. But it provided them temporary safety from the menacing British troops. It was a godsend.

More than 200 species of birds and waterfowl find solace there, along with some 30 different mammals more than 600 different kinds of plants, 24 species of freshwater fish, 18 amphibians, and 21 reptiles. Among its mammal inhabitants are herds of white-tailed deer, beaver, otter, raccoon, muskrat, mink, fox and rabbits.

It is not merely a swamp, either. Open fields and hardwood forests, as well as freshwater marshlands and bogs, make up its terrain. It is alive with the sounds, smells, and hues of nature.

Once it was part of the ancient, Lake Passaic. The lake was left behind when a great glacier melted some 15,000 years ago and retreated. As the glacier drew back northwestward across the Passaic Valley, it left in the depression it created the great, Lake Passaic. This glacial lake was created as was the one further to the east called Lake Hackensack, by the terminal moraine. Both eventually evolved into their present state. Lake Hackensack became today's "Jersey Meadowlands."

Ever since the coming of the Europeans into New Jersey, attempts were constantly made to alter this area. It was by no means a new encounter, therefore, when the Port Authority's attempts were made in the 1960's.

Forests were cut and canals were dug there throughout colonial times in an effort by man to drain the region for use in farming. Forests were also cut for tools and building materials and to fuel the industries that were regularly being attempted. Indian paths were also widened into logging roads. But no matter how man had tried throughout the centuries to alter it, nature always seemed to win out in the end.

In this most recent plan, however, harnessing the power of man's mighty earthmovers to create a gigantic 10,000-acre jetport seemed to have finally sounded the death knell. Nature had surely met its match! The tranquility of the "Great Swamp" would no longer be a refuge for man nor beast.

Then, other men became nature's allies. The thousands who had come to cherish this wilderness paradise banded in the fight to save it.

As a result, the "Great Swamp National Wildlife Refuge and Wilderness Area" still stands along the trails of New Jersey – a sanctuary of nature for the enjoyment of both man and the wildlife that continue to inhabit it – and New Jersey is the better for it.

CHAPTER 5: COUNTIES OF NEW JERSEY

Atlantic County

The first Europeans to come to what New Jersey today calls Atlantic County were English whalers who had been fishing previously off of the coast of New England. Whale blubber had once been in considerable demand throughout the world as a source of the fats used for oil lamps. For centuries immemorial, these lamps were the principal means of lighting for our homes. During the early colonial period, before candles came into common use, the sale of whale oil brought a healthy income to Jersey's whale-boatmen.

But these whalers were not settlers, for the most part. The first really permanent settlers were Swedes who came under the direction of Eric Palsson Mullica in the 1690's, long after Sweden had given up her American claims. The river, which today serves as the boundary line between Atlantic and Burlington Counties, was named in his honor, as was the Town of Mullica Hill in Gloucester County. By the mid 1700's a considerable number of Swedes were working as lumbermen in this heavily forested region.

Today this area lies within an expanse almost as wild and wooded as in Mullica's time, thanks to the persistent preservation efforts of the State of New Jersey. Much of the Mullica River flows through the more than 100,000-acre Wharton State Forest. Slightly north of the Mullica's mouth it passes between the Swan Bay and Port Republic Fish and Wildlife Management Areas. At its mouth lies the Bass River State Forest to the north and the Brigantine National Wildlife Refuge on its southern banks. Considering the tremendous pressures for development in this area with the advent of gambling casinos in Atlantic City, its serene beauty will hopefully be preserved for untold future generations to enjoy. We should be eternally grateful for those who had the foresight to set aside these vast tracts in the midst of the most densely populated state of the nation.

As to the iron hills of the northwest, so too the iron bogs of the southeast, many people came to New Jersey to make their fortunes, or spend their energies, in the promotion of Jersey's early iron industry. Charles Read of Philadelphia was one of those early ironmasters whose efforts on the banks of the Mullica in the mid 1700's led him to great wealth. There at Sweetwater he lived like a baron in medieval splendor. His iron, too, was to be of great importance to America's War for Independence. Just a short distance to the north is Batsto, another old iron village across the border in Burlington County, which the state has preserved as an historic site and popular tourist attraction.

Like Ocean's bays and inlets, Atlantic's, too, served as hideaways for numerous privateers who preyed upon British shipping during the American Revolution. It was here, then, at the Battle of Chestnut Neck, that the British command decided in October of 1778 to put an end to these sea-raiders. They would send a small army into the heart of this nest of terrorists and burn them out of existence. The village was indeed torched and the American defenders routed, sent fleeing north, up the Mullica River.

An opportunity for a double kill presented itself. The Triumphant British forces would now not only blot out one of the persistent nests of rebel stingers which had been constantly molesting British shipping, but they would also pursue them to a valuable source of supplies being used by their insurgent armies – the iron works along the Mullica! Having only about one-eighth the number who were in the ranks of the well-trained British Regulars, the Americans had to plan their strategy well.

Scattered throughout the dense forests surrounding the Mullica, the Americans waited – Indian style, outnumbered eight to one! When the highly organized red-coats, beating their drums and thus signaling their every move, came marching forward through the woods, the locals were ready. The volunteers "cut loose" with a volley of musket fire that sent the British reeling. The well-trained Europeans were soon fleeing for cover. Another round of this type of "heat" would surely rout the lobster backs. After a short skirmish of this "guerilla-type warfare," the far-more-numerous British soldiers found their ranks demoralized in wild retreat. It was an embarrassment to the world's greatest military power of that day. They never again ventured into that part of the Jersey Pines. Other tales – of pirates and pine robbers, such as Jersey's own "Robin

Hood," Joe Milliner, still wait to be told to those who would travel along these trails of New Jersey.

Bergen County

New Jersey's Bergen County, sometimes referred to as New York City's bedroom, is a prime example of a rural area suddenly gone urban. It also contains some of the state's most affluent communities, Alpine, the most opulent of the state, and Saddle River, home of former President and Mrs. Richard Nixon, are excellent examples. The more populated areas of the original Bergen County were removed with the creation of Passaic County in 1837 and Hudson in 1840. What was left was the land that made up the present Bergen County, whose character for the next 100 years would be strictly agricultural.

The opening of the George Washington Bridge in 1932 set the state for Bergen's metamorphosis from farmlands to suburban sprawl. The cables for that famed structure were made by a New Jersey firm, John A. Roebling & Sons of Trenton. Since the 1980 census, Bergen has been competing with Essex for the honor of being the most populated county in the state.

A French Huguenot seeking religious freedom established the first settlement in 1677 in what is now Bergen. The place is called New Milford. By 1700, farmers were tilling the soil in the region of the Ramapo Mountains in present-day western Bergen. The little village of Oakland (then called Yaughpaugh) was established there. In 1709 Hackensack, a port of call on the river of the same name, became the county seat.

Known in the tourist trade as part of New Jersey's "Gateway Region," it was so considered by the British, who had established New York City as their headquarters after they lost Boston to the patriots in the early days of the American Revolution. Driving Washington and his small army from Manhattan in the fall of 1776, the British pursued him into New Jersey by way of Bergen's Fort Lee. The Visitor's Center at the Fort Lee Historic Park vividly tells the story of their dramatic entrance into the state, and Washington's subsequent flight to the banks of the Delaware, via New Brunswick.

Another historic site to visit in Bergen is the state's Von Steuben House. It was used as a headquarters during the Revolution by both British and American officers. Located north of Hackensack in New Bridge, this characteristic Dutch homestead was owned during the revolt by a notorious Loyalist, Isaac Zabriskie. It was built in 1739 by John Zabriskie, who operated a big gristmill there for local farmers. The house was taken from him by the state and given to Gen. Von Steuben in appreciation for his contribution to American independence. Today, its museum contains, among other artifacts, relics from New Jersey's long-time operating Wampum Factory, once located in Bergen's Park Ridge.

This Wampum Factory was started by John Campbell back in 1775. There, he and his sons manufactured "wampum" out of Jersey seashells. It was used in trading with Indians throughout the American colonies. Fur traders began coming from near and far to New Jersey's Wampum Factory. The famed Astor Fur-Trading Company, which operated in the Oregon country, obtained their wampum there in the 1800's. Fur traders from throughout the American West got their wampum from this New Jersey factory until 1889, when it was finally forced to close for lack of business. That is the year the last free American Indian was driven onto a reservation. Congress then declared that date to be the end of the "American Frontier."

From 1907, in the days following World War I, Bergen's Fort Lee was known as the motion-picture capital of the world. The rugged Palisades became the backdrop for many of those early "flicks." Pearl White and Mary Pickford were among the heroines of filmdom in those pioneer days. Other early movie stars who performed in Jersey's film capital were Fatty Arbuckle, Theda Bara, Lon Chaney, Charlie Chaplin, Marie Dressler, Lillian Gish, and Rudy Valentino. Today, Bergen's plush community of Alpine is the hideaway locale for many a millionaire of America's entertainment industry. The unique Palisades are preserved for posterity by the Interstate Park, which straddles both New York and New Jersey.

Bergen's Teterboro Airport was home base for that well-known radio and television talk-show star of the 1940's and 50's, Arthur Godfrey. It still harbors celebrities of the 1980's, including the John Gambling Show's traffic helicopter. It is also home for an important Museum of American Aviation.

From colonial relics to modern aircraft, the trails of Bergen tell many tales of interesting New Jersey heritage.

Burlington County

At one time, Burlington County was far larger than it is today, though it still reaches from the Delaware River to the Atlantic Ocean. When it was first created in 1676, it stretched from the west all along the banks of the Delaware, taking in the verdant forests of present-day Warren, Morris, and Hunterdon Counties to the north, the fields of Mercer and Hunterdon further to the south, and its own Pine Barrens. It then moved eastward to include both Atlantic and Ocean Counties in the far south. Bits and pieces were whittled from its boundaries between 1713 and 1891 until it has taken its present form. With a land area of 819 square miles, it still remains New Jersey's largest county - and one of its more sparsely settled.

In 1677, five years before founding Philadelphia, the Quakers first settled at Burlington, after having purchased West Jersey from Berkeley and Carteret in 1675. Their settlement was originally called New Beverly. Shortly afterwards, William Penn received title from one of the purchasers and began selling portions of his claims to persecuted "Friends" from Great Britain. While visiting Holland and several German states along the Rhine Valley during this same period, Penn influenced many who were being harassed for their religious beliefs to consider coming to his lands in the New World. On a second visit in 1688, his ardent assurances of religious toleration ignited a mass emigration of Germans into Pennsylvania and West Jersey that extended well into the early 18th century.

In 1861, West Jersey had been made a separate Province, and Burlington City was named as its capital. The next year Bordentown (then called Farnsworth's Landing) was founded. Mount Holly (first named Bridgetown) was also settled during this period. Mount Holly became the county seat after the Revolution - in 1796.

An indication of the wide diversity of this large county's interests might be shown by a number of its early famous Americans. Both the novelist who wrote of Indians and frontier life, James Fenimore Cooper, and the naval hero of "Don't Give Up the Ship" fame, James Lawrence, came from Burlington. Also Francis Hopkinson, a signer of the Declaration of Independence, who also designed the Great Seal of the United States, and William, the Tory son of Benjamin Franklin and the last royal governor of New Jersey, were once residents of Burlington County. So, too, was Tom Paine, who wrote those inciting papers during the Revolution, the "Crises" and "Common Sense."

In Burlington, also, in 1758, at a place now called Indian Mills, the nation's first Indian Reservation was established. Delaware (Lenni Lenape) Indians from present day Warren and Sussex Counties were sent there as part of the treaty settling the terrible Indian Wars along the northwestern Jersey frontier. The famed Indian missionary, John Brainerd, who once preached among the Indians of Warren and Sussex, taught school for a time among the Reservation Indians.

There, too, the first iron plow was invented by a Burlington County farmer, Charles Newbold, in 1796. Farming has always played an important role in the county's history. In 1816, Joseph Bonaparte, brother of Napoleon, and the former King of Spain came there to live in exile following his brother's defeat.

Although industry, agriculture, and shipping all have had their important roles in Burlington, it is probably most noted for its extensive Pine Barrens. That may also account for the fact that, though it contains 11 per cent of New Jersey's land area, it has less that 4 per cent of the state's population. Most of those people are located along the Delaware Valley where they are within easy commuting distance of cities such as Philadelphia, Camden, and Trenton.

About two-thirds of Burlington County are covered with the great Pine Barrens. In 1766, Charles Read began the iron works there on the banks of the Mullica River that is now preserved by the state as the Historic Village of Batsto, in the midst of the 100,000-acre Wharton Tract. At one time, more than a dozen such works operated in the county. Both bog iron and lumber for charcoal were then found in great abundance.

It was such an important source of iron products during the American Revolution that numerous attempts were made by the British to capture these resources. So important was it considered to the war effort that a special detachment of troops was established there, and its ironworkers were exempt from military service elsewhere. But more about this fascinating region will have to await other times along the trails of New Jersey.

Camden County

We hear much about Raleigh's mysterious Lost Colony of Roanoke in Virginia. Every history test from the founding of our nation related that tale to untold generations of school children. Yet how many have ever heard of Captain Cornelius Mey's Lost Colony of Nassau in Camden County? It has only been in recent years that we have come out from under the shadows of Philadelphia and New York, and begun to let the world know that we, too, have an exciting and interesting heritage of our own to tell. Even more so than many others!

In 1623, the Dutch explorer, Captain Cornelius May, sailed up the Delaware river and, at a point where Big Timber Creek empties into it, disembarked. There, on the shores of New Jersey, in what is now Camden County near present-day Gloucester point, he established the first Dutch colony along the banks of the Delaware. Before he sailed away, he and his crew helped those Dutch colonists who were left behind to build a fort - for their protection against the Indians or anyone else. They named it Fort Nassau after the ruling house of Orange-Nassau back in the Netherlands.

Just as at the Lost Colony of Roanoke in Virginia, the Lost Colony of Nassau in New Jersey was left with ample provisions to keep them going until they could plant their crops and be on their own. And, like Roanoke, they were promised that new shiploads of supplies and settlers would soon be forthcoming. As at Roanoke, some years went by. Finally, in 1631, another Dutch ship sailed up the Delaware laden with supplies for the settlement at the mouth of Big Timber Creek. And, just as mysteriously as Raleigh's Lost Colony in Virginia, Mey's Dutch colony at Nassau was nowhere to be found. Nothing remained. Its disappearance was as much of a puzzle to the Dutch as was that of those at Roanoke to the English. No trace of the settlers or of what happened to them has ever been uncovered.

It was up to the English and Irish Quakers, then, to establish the first permanent settlements in what is present-day Camden County in the 1680's. William Cooper first settled the region at the site of the present city of Camden in 1681. He called it "Pyne Point," from the extensive growth of pine trees visible from the riverbank. But after taking over the ferry service started in 1688 between there and the city of Philadelphia, just across the river, by William Royden, the little settlement that grew up there came to be known as "Cooper's Ferry." And Cooper's Ferry it was still called at the time of the American Revolution when George Washington frequently used the ferry service there to cross and re-cross the Delaware between Philadelphia and New Jersey.

One of William's descendants, however, Jacob Cooper, is responsible for its present name. There, in 1773, he established a real estate development on some 40 acres of land. He named his "Towne" Camden, after Charles Pratt, the Earl of Camden. Camden, as a champion of constitutional liberty in the British parliament and an opposer of the taxation program being imposed upon the American colonies, was a popular figure in America at that time. Not until 1828, however, did the name finally stick, when community leaders officially adopted it as a more suitable name for their town.

It took the coming of the Camden and Amboy Railroad in 1834, then the longest in the nation, to finally bring industry and spur the town's growth. Ten years later, in 1844, Camden was newly created from Gloucester County for the state legislature. The city of Camden was named as county seat in 1848. Both the county and the city from which it was named continued to grow. Farmers' fields were rapidly becoming city streets. Today, both the city and the county are part of what has become known as New Jersey's City Belt. It stretches diagonally across the state's neck. It is part of "the corridor" connecting New York and Philadelphia. The width of this corridor has been gradually widening in recent years to include areas once considered to be strictly rural.

In 1858, Richard Esterbrook established his pen factory in Camden. In 1869, Joseph Campbell began packing vegetables. In 1901, Eldridge Johnson opened his Victor Talking Machine Company. The New York Shipbuilding Company began production in earnest about the same time. Atco, Clementon, and Waterford became centers of glass production. Gloucester saw the opening of a gigantic textile mill. And, for a time, the J. L. Mason Company made its famous Mason jars at Winslow. Camden County became a land of housing developments and industry, of slums and of culture, of noise and traffic. Of course, there is more to be told of Camden - its backcountry and its heritage - but that can wait for other days along the trails of New Jersey.

Cape May County

You may have noticed that we have been moving rather rapidly down the New Jersey coastline since the onset of those hazy, lazy days of summer - as befits any true Jersey traveler. Well, we have finally reached the Cape where, along with fishing and farming, taking care of tourists is one of its main means of earning a livelihood. Though it has never reached the year-round status of an Atlantic City-type resort, Cape May has been in the tourist business longer than any other Jersey shore region - save possibly Long Branch. Today, its extensive collection of Victorian homes is touted as a tourist attraction.

It was visited earliest by the Dutch back around 1620, but its first permanent residents were definitely of English background. Dutch fishermen came and went in those early years, but New Englanders and Long Islanders, in search of new fishing grounds, built the first permanent towns and gave the Cape its distinctly New England flavor. It was named, however, after the familiar Dutch sea Captain who first touted its pleasant characteristics to Europeans - Cornelius Jacobsen Mey.

Cape May County was originally constituted by the colonial Assembly in the year 1692 - one of the oldest in the state. You would think, as a result, that it would have been one of those well-established and populated counties by the turn of the century. It was not. Its population over three decades later was still under 700. One of the major factors was its isolation. Extensive marshlands several miles inland from the Atlantic coastline, deep cedar forests along its western and northern borders, and the accompanying lack of roads in or out, were all contributing elements. As were, perhaps, the exceptionally large numbers of notorious pirates infesting its waters in those early years. European piracy was running rampant in America in the late 17th and early 18th centuries.

Strategically located for either guarding or hampering shipping up the Delaware River on its way to such important ports as Philadelphia, Cape May's seafarers soon found themselves embroiled in the American Revolution. Their role obviously was sea-oriented. Depending upon which side held Philadelphia, they did what they could in either aiding or foiling attempts to reach that port. Smuggling of illegal goods into the Cape's ports was rampant, as was attacking British shipping off of its extensive coastline. Though no land battles took place there, its dense forests did shelter much contraband heading for rebel forces in the vicinity of Philadelphia, and numbers of spies sending messages concerning British movements in either direction.

Cold Spring and Cape May Point were already in the tourist business at the turn of the 18th century. Not only Philadelphians came there to vacation, but southern city dwellers from Baltimore and Washington were also attracted to its seashore hotels before the War of 1812. By the time of the Civil War, plantation owners had practically annexed the area to the Southland. The fact that it was below the Mason - Dixon Line might well have influenced their thinking! The war, however, soon ended southern domination of Jersey's Cape.

With the coming of the railroad in 1863, Cape May's population soared to more than 7,000. Its summer population, however, was almost 10 times that number. A few years before the railroad came, Cape May town had played host to Presidents Franklin Pierce, and later, James Buchanan. Lincoln was there, too, but that was before he became president. After the War Between the States, the newly elected President Ulysses S. Grant was a visitor at Cape May, as was President Chester A. Arthur. President Benjamin Harrison even had his own "cottage" built there for him in 1890.

Many popular seaside resorts have come into being on the Jersey Cape between Ocean City in the north (which was started as a Methodist summer resort in 1880) and the much older Cape May Point in the far south. These Cape resorts range from the hectic to the sedate, and cover the gamut of what you might seek in the way of rest or recreation. The most notable are such places as Sea Isle City, Avalon, Stone Harbor, and the three Wildwoods. The Wildwoods have become the mecca for thousands of French Canadians in recent years as the result of an intensive tourist campaign. But more tales of the Cape will have to come along future trails of New Jersey.

Cumberland County

Along with Cape May, New Jersey's Tidewater Country includes Cumberland County. Here, as the oyster fleets come in at Bivalve where the Maurice River empties into the Delaware Bay, you get a distinctly "down south" feeling that sets the place apart from the rest of the state.

First settled by the Swedes in the 1630's, about the only trace of that Swedish influence that remains in Cumberland is the name of one of its main rivers, the Maurice. It was named after the Swedish ship, "The Maurice," which brought those first settlers to what is now Dorchester and Leesburg.

It was the English Quakers under John Fenwick who really set the tone for the county's settlement in the 1680's. There, on the Cohansey, they established the village of Greenwich in 1682 (the same year Penn set up Philadelphia) and Bridgeton in 1686. Once part of Salem (which was an anglicized version of the Hebrew "shalom," meaning peace), Cumberland was sliced off of that county in 1748. Its county seat was established at Bridgeton that same year.

Greenwich, which sits inland a ways on the Cohansey, soon became its largest town, however, and its leading port. Because it was a part of the brisk colonial trade route between Philadelphia and Boston, Greenwich was one of New Jersey's earliest communities to become actively embroiled in the American War for Independence. Two years before the Continental Congress issued its Declaration of Independence at Philadelphia, and one year before the first shot was fired on the village green at Lexington, Greenwich committed an act of defiance against the British Crown which was to mark it forever as a den of rebels.

In 1774, a Captain J. Allen brought his brig, "The Greyhound," into the port of Greenwich with a shipload of the hated tea. The captain feared landing that cargo at the rebel hornet's nest, Philadelphia. So he figured he would unload it on the docks at the peaceful Greenwich port, store it, and in due time ship it overland to markets in and around Philadelphia, unmolested. He was in for the surprise of his life!

Angry Greenwich area residents under the leadership of the Howell brothers, Richard and Lewis, held a secret meeting at Shiloh to plan their course of action. There, they decided to organize into three bands of "Indians," led by the "Fighting Parson" Phil Fithian, his cousin Joel, and Andrew Hunter. Swooping down on the sleeping village of Greenwich in the middle of the night, they first uncovered the tea stored at the home of Dan Bowen, a Tory. Hauling it off to a nearby field, they set off the largest bonfire ever seen in the memory of the oldest villager. But at the time, it was considered an act of treason, and the perpetrators - when their names were uncovered - were brought to trial.

Bridgeton, which has since grown larger than Greenwich, had its own Liberty Bell peal the news of the Declaration of Independence in July of 1776 from its place in the tower of the County Courthouse. There, it may still be viewed, but now it sits in the main corridor of the Courthouse. Across the street is Potter's Tavern, where patriots once gathered to stir up insurrection and print the "Plain Dealer," a news-sheet that was designed to incite thoughts of independence among the local Jersey populace.

Though distinctly rural in nature and an outdoorsman's paradise, being home to a half-dozen, State Fish and Wildlife Management Areas, Cumberland is also noted for its glassmaking industry. Glassmaking had its origins in Cumberland as early as 1799 when James Lee set up his glassworks at Port Elizabeth, upland on the Maurice River. Millville, further upriver, was next in 1806. Bridgeton, on the Cohansey, got its start in 1830, and Vineland after the Civil War. But in the industrial boom that bloomed in the North following the War Between the States, the glassmaking triangle formed by those three latter Jersey communities gained a national reputation.

Its location on a bed of fine silica sand deposits, estimated to be some 300 feet in depth, was the chief contributing factor toward making this Cumberland County region -along with that of nearby

Salem - one of the nation's six major producers of glass products. Today, the Historic Glassmaking Village of Wheaton in Millville has become a leading tourist attraction. But more tales of Cumberland's varied heritage will have to wait for other days as we continue to travel along the trails of New Jersey.

Essex County

It's hard to believe that in 1800, the population of Sussex County, which then included Warren, was greater than that of Essex, which at that time also included present day Union. But time and circumstances do change. Sussex turned to agriculture while Essex turned to industry. Today, Essex, even with Union gone since 1857, is the most populated of all 21 New Jersey counties. In 1800, much of it was rural outside of the city of Newark. Even Newark at the time of the American Revolution only housed a thousand people.

English Puritans from Connecticut, led by Robert Treat, were the first to settle the area we now call Essex. They founded NewWork in 1666 as a theocracy. Only members of the Congregationalist Church were allowed to vote or hold office. Trinity Episcopal Church, the second church to be established, did not come into existence until 1733 and then only because the Ogden family had been ostracized for farming on Sunday! The Congregationalists, in the meantime, had become Newark's First Presbyterian Church whose leaders ruled that community until well after the Revolution.

Though Dutch farmers had moved into the areas of what is now West Essex by the late 1600's from their settlements in Bergen, it was not until the middle 1700's that farmers from the Newark settlements began moving up and over the Orange Mountain. Their early communities were soon named after their prominent farm families. Dodd's Town later became East Orange. Camp's Town was eventually called Irvington. Crane's Town was renamed Montclair. Freeman's Town became a part of West Orange.

Though privately built turnpikes began turning the population tide in the early 1800's by providing better transportation, industry didn't get its real impetus until the opening of the Morris Canal in 1832. Its completion brought into Newark cheap coal from

Pennsylvania via Phillipsburg. The Morris and Essex railroad soon followed. Along with shipping on its prosperous waterfront, Newark soon became the transportation hub that made industry hum. By the 1840's, transportation and industry brought thousands of Irish and German immigrants. The latter soon made Newark a famous brewery center.

Although it first looked as though the Civil War would shatter Newark's strong, industry-centered economy because of the loss of its important southern markets, this proved otherwise. The fact was that contracts for shoes and uniforms for the northern army, as well as harnesses and saddles for its cavalry, soon had Newark's industry buzzing. Its iron foundries also received large military contracts. So prosperous had the war made its industry that by 1870, Italian and Polish as well as German and Irish immigrants were pouring into a city of more than 100,000 people. All of Essex had only 40,000 more. By 1900, Essex's population had risen to 360,000, mostly in Newark.

A number of noted American inventors played vital roles in Essex County's early industrial edge. First was Seth Boyden, a transplanted New Englander who, by the time of his death in Maplewood in 1870, had contributed much to Newark's early leather and iron industries. Another was Thomas Edison, a transplanted mid-westerner who, by the time of his death in West Orange in 1933, had more inventions to his credit than any other man who ever lived. A National Historic Park now incorporates his early "think tank" in West Orange. John Hyatt, who worked with celluloid, and Edward Weston, the electrical genius, are two others who also contributed much to Essex's industrial prominence.

By the 1890's, the alarming population growth that industry and commerce had brought to Essex led to the establishment of the nation's first county park system. Foresighted men began setting aside several thousands of acres of natural beauty for the enjoyment of both present and future inhabitants. Such large tracts as the 3,000 acres encompassed by the South Mountain and Eagle Rock reservations, as well as the extensive Branch Brook and Wequahic parks, soon gave city dwellers the needed natural respite that all humans crave.

In the meantime, in the late 1800's and early 1900's thousands of city folk enjoyed picnics and outdoor sports in the many private centers which began springing up to fill that need. Such places as

Vailsburg's "Electric Park," Cable Lake of the Oranges, and Becker's Grove in Irvington, which featured German songfests (it was later called Olympic Park), became popular. Unfortunately, private facilities eventually give way to developers as well.

Essex is just one of the half-dozen counties in what is loosely termed New Jersey's "City Belt." Although it is a sad commentary on what unbridled development can do to the livability of a region, it at least had men of foresight who had the wisdom to set up a county park system in this most populous of counties along the trails of new Jersey.

Gloucester County

As we come up the Delaware River off of the Delaware Bay, Gloucester is the first of New Jersey's counties to be totally within the Delaware Valley. Though once a part of Burlington, Gloucester broke away early, in 1686 to be exact, and became one of New Jersey's oldest. At first, it included both present day Atlantic and Camden Counties, but these were separated by the state legislature in 1837 and 1844 respectively.

Originally, like most of southwestern New Jersey, it was settled by the Swedes, the Finns, and some Danes, and officially became a part of New Sweden from 1638 to 1655. From 1655 to 1664, it was incorporated into New Netherlands when the Dutch took over all of the Delaware Valley. For the next 100 years, however, it was to become a part of the British Empire. This is until the American colonies broke away in their War for Independence. During that period the English Quaker influence became dominant.

Of all the New Jersey counties that were once a part of New Sweden, however, Gloucester, except for its name, remained under the Swedish cultural dominance for the longest period of time. English Quakers, soon after the takeover by Great Britain, did give the county its English name, and did enter their influence around Woodbury, which became the county seat. But the Swedish language and its culture held sway over the rest of the county until well into the 18th century.

Communities such as Repaupo, Mullica Hill, and Rackon (now Swedesboro), with their surrounding countryside, remained centers of the Swedish population. The Swedish Lutheran Church in Swedesboro (now Episcopal) stubbornly kept its service, and all of its records in the Swedish language for almost 100 years after the beginning of British rule in New Jersey.

The early Swedes, contrary to popular belief, fought gallantly in their struggle to keep their Swedish culture in America intact. This, in spite of the fact that they seemed to care little what country claimed sovereignty over their lands. Their churches and schools as well as their homes attempted valiantly to preserve both the language and ways of living they had brought with them from the old country. They even continued for well over 100 years to import their ministers from Sweden! The last clergyman sent to American by the King of Sweden was the Rev. Nicholas Collin, whose pastorate ended in 1786. The famous Swedish naturalist, Peter Kalm, was once a pastor there, and lived for a time in Swedesboro.

Old Swedes Church on Kings Highway and Church Street in Swedesboro, though now Episcopal, is almost unchanged from that built under the tenure of Collin. Its old pews and hand-blown windowpanes remain intact. In its historic cemetery you will find the names of old Swedish settlers on weather-beaten tombstones, among those of soldiers of the American Revolution. South of Swedesboro is also an old Moravian Church built by the followers of John Hus. These same people founded Bethlehem, PA and Hope in Warren County. Pastor Schmidt, who was preaching there during the Battle of Red Bank, which was occurring about 20 miles away, reported in his diary of hearing the noise of cannons on that historic October day in 1777.

About a mile south of Gibbstown, on the Repaupo Road, attached to a two-story frame house, is to be found what is believed to be the oldest log cabin in the United States. Built about 1640 by one of the early settlers of New Sweden, Anthony Neilson, it is a forerunner of the log cabins that were soon to dot the American frontier from Kentucky westward.

Neilson is recorded in the county courthouse at Woodbury as being the earliest taxpayer in Gloucester County. Historians and architects, who have been studying his log cabin in recent years, now tell us that these log cabins were the type from which the frontier cabins, that have since become the symbol of America's western pioneers, were copied. They were built first in America by the early Swedish settlers in New Jersey, and later by the Pennsylvania Germans. And with which every aspirant to the American presidency tried to associate himself for many campaigns.

Of course there is much more of our American heritage to be found in Gloucester County. Included among these is one of the major battles of the American Revolution, which was fought on New Jersey soil - the Battle of Red Bank. But those tales will have to wait for another day along the trails of New Jersey.

Hudson County

In our whirlwind tour of New Jersey's 21 counties, we have now devoted at least one article to all but two. Those two have one dominant trait in common - they are in the most urbanized section of the state. We will look now at New Jersey's most citified county - Hudson.

With roughly 15,000 people per square mile, crowded into a county of 45 square miles, Hudson now holds the not-too-proud distinction of being the most densely populated county of New Jersey. By comparison, the entire state as a whole recently realized an average density of 1,000 people per square mile - the highest in the nation. Warren County in 1985 attained the figure of about 250 people per square mile, from 171 just 10 years ago.

Hudson is a prime example of the result of unbridled development. It is almost impossible today to believe that Hudson - now an overcrowded industrial and transportation hub, once was called the "Garden Spot of the East." Hoboken's once beautiful "Elysian Fields," for example, was the site of the nation's first major league baseball game on June 19, 1846, between the Knickerbocker Giants and the New York Metropolitans.

Aside from once being the play land of the wealthy New Yorkers, Hudson also had achieved prominence for its beautiful large estates. In the 1850's, Gen. Philip Kearny, just to mention one, bought his charming country estate, "Belgrove." In 1855, he had "Kearny's

Castle" built on it. Just before his death in 1862 at Chantilly, during the Civil War, he commented on his desire to enjoy, once again, the beauty of his beloved "Belgrove." His funeral was held there shortly after. In 1867, that section of Harrison became the independent community of Kearny - in his honor.

Hoboken was best known for its numerous beer gardens and picnic groves along the Hudson riverbanks. Summer weekends saw thousands of New Yorkers strolling its pleasant countryside, or engaging in one of the many games played on its sports fields, Bayonne was dubbed, "The Newport of New York." Large, wealthy estates overlooked the Bay as New York's aristocracy competed with each other for the finest country "cottages."

The Mansion House and LaTourette's Hotel accommodated the well-known vacationers who enjoyed Hudson's country air and riverside view. Among the frequent distinguished visitors to this once popular Hudson County "play-land" were such luminaries of the nation as the John Jacob Astors, William Cullen Bryant, Washington Irving, Edgar Allan Poe, and Martin Van Buren. The Asters were, in fact, among those who eventually built their own "villa" there on that Jersey riverfront. Most also indulged in the "sport of kings," at the Beacon Racecourse in Jersey City.

In the mid 1800's, large numbers of German and Irish immigrants came to Hudson's shores. The Germans tended to gravitate to Hoboken and North Hudson while the Irish settled in Jersey City. Large numbers of Scotch immigrants came to Harrison and Kearny in the next several decades, and Union City saw an influx of Swiss mechanics. By the early 1900's, Italian immigrants came in increasing numbers. All were put to work in the many new industries that were beginning to saturate the area following the Civil War period.

Less than 100 years had seen a phenomenal change in the character and population of this New Jersey riverfront county. From only 9,500 people in 1840, Hudson's population had multiplied about 17 times in 35 years. By 1875, it had reached 165,000. From these 1840 figures, it had increased about 41 times within 60 years. By 1900, as a result, 390.000 inhabitants were along its shores. Today that figure has about doubled again.

With the coming of industry and transportation, large numbers of people followed. A stark change gradually unfolded. Wealthy New York families began closing their large estates when the oil industry started arriving in 1875. Within a short time, its numerous fishermen, bathing beaches, and prominent vacation hotels were gone. Though its German beer gardens were still popular up until WWI, prejudices put a "damper" on that sort of activity. Most of its "play-lands" had left by the 1900's.

With the coming of the 20th century, dozens of railroad and shipping lines, as well as industries and oil refineries had completely changed the character of this New Jersey waterfront. During his reelection campaign of 1912, President Taft referred to Hudson as a "hive of industry." Severed from Bergen in 1840, Hudson has had an interesting heritage, most of which will have to await later columns along the trails of New Jersey.

Hunterdon County

Once one of the state's largest counties, Hunterdon, when it was first formed in 1714, started at the Assunpink Creek in what is now Mercer County, and extended north all the way to New York State, including most of present day Morris and all of Sussex County.

It also spread west to the Delaware River and took in today's Warren County. Morris County, which first encompassed Sussex and Warren, broke off in 1738. Trenton was still in Hunterdon during the American Revolution. Mercer was not lopped-off until 1838 by a line drawn through the Sourland Mountains.

Though the county's first settlers were English Quakers from Burlington County, the Dutch soon followed in the early 1700's traveling up the Raritan River from their settlements in Somerset. By the 1750's, so many Germans had come to the county from nearby Pennsylvania that a whole region around Tewksbury became know as German Valley. In fact, until the anti-German hysteria of World War I forced a name-change Oldwick was called New Germantown.

The Irish soon followed. One young Irishman, Sam Fleming, built himself an impressive home, called Fleming's Castle, in 1756, and gave the town of Flemington its name. Another, Robert Taylor began buying into the Union Iron Works in 1758, and eventually it became know as Taylor's Forge. A century later it was renamed High Bridge. A Swiss-Frenchman, Paul Henry Mallet-Prevost, bought almost 1,000 acres along the Delaware from Fleming's son-in-law, Thomas Lowery, and it became known as Frenchtown. Hunterdon, as you can see, like most of New Jersey, was a mixture of people from many national backgrounds early in its history.

Presently, Hunterdon extends north along the Delaware, until it reaches the Musconetcong, which separates it from Warren, and south just below Lambertville. Except for the Lamington River, which forms a boundary with part of Morris in the northeast, there are no natural boundaries separating Hunterdon from Morris, Somerset, and Mercer Counties to its north and east. Hunterdon's hills have remained an impressive attraction to visitors throughout the centuries, and many country inns soon sprouted along its roads for their convenience. Its picturesque countryside still draws people for a relaxing drive into a land that has remained essentially a retreat from the present.

My brother-in-law, Robert Conway, whose mother once owned a 100-acre farm outside of Flemington, and is therefore familiar with the back-roads of that region, took myself, my wife, Ruth, and my sister, Betty, for a drive through that picturesque country. After a brief visit to the hustle and bustle of the busy, but still small-town atmosphere of Flemington, we took the back roads to see the old farmstead, which still remains pretty much as it was. The narrow roads were bordered that June day with an endless procession of wild roses. We passed across bubbling brooks and soon came upon an old country store somewhere between Sergeantville and Rosemont. Then, suddenly, before our eyes, spanning the Wichecheoke Creek as though out of an old Currier and Ives calendar, stood the only wooden covered bride still standing in the state of New Jersey! Shades of the past.

Continuing on to Route 519, and then to 29 along the Delaware, we stopped at the rambling old Stockton Inn. Built in 1832 by Asher Johnson, when the Delaware and Raritan Canal was under construction, we had a pleasant outdoor lunch in an atmosphere among trees and running water that reminded me again what so many people in our great state are missing. The road from Stockton to

77

Lambertville, Route 29, runs near the feeder to the Delaware and Raritan Canal that was completed in 1834. The D & R is celebrating its 150th anniversary this year. Among the celebration activities will be an ongoing exhibit at the Trenton State Museum.

Arriving at Lambertville, which from 1732 to 1812 was called Coreyell's Ferry, we remembered that before John Lambert built the first bridge here to cross the Delaware, you had to take the Coreyll's Ferry to get to Pennsylvania. And that is just what Washington's Army did on several occasions back in the 1700's. We passed the Lambertville House on Bridge Street, which opened as a hotel when Lambert built his bridge back in 1812, and changed the name of the town.

We also saw the Marshall House, where the young man, James Marshall lived before he headed west in 1832 to make his fortune in the lumbering business in the Sacramento Valley of California. Instead, this son of New Jersey discovered gold in 1848 on the land of John Sutter. Thus started the wildest Gold Rush of 1849 the world had ever seen. Just another tale that began here on the trails of New Jersey.

Mercer County

Although Mercer County did not come into existence until 1838 that is not to say that it had not any history prior to that date. It was, in fact, originally settled back in 1680 when Mahlon Stacy established his mill at the Falls of the Delaware. William Penn's Quakers were already settling its banks along about that same time. And soon thereafter, English Puritans from Long Island started communities at Hopewell and Lawrenceville (originally known as Maidenhead).

It was the joining point, however, for a number of New Jersey's earlier counties. Since 1713, for example, those who lived to the north of Assunpink Creek had been a part of Hunterdon County. To the south of that point, they were still residents of Burlington County. Of those living in the Princeton area, the village itself was the dividing line between Middlesex (founded in 1682) and Somerset (established in 1688). So it was from those four counties that Mercer finally emerged by an act of the state Legislature back in 1838.

Its chief city, Trenton, got its name from Colonial William Trent, who bought a farm and built his home there in the period between 1714 and 1719. His house still stands on Warren Street as an historic site. New Jersey's first Royal Governor, Lewis Morris, once lived there also, as did Col. John Cox, his wife, and six lovely daughters. Cox had previously owned the now historic Batsto Iron Furnace further to the south in Burlington County.

Several of New Jersey's governors made their homes at the Trent House, as well, back in the mid 1800's. Trent, who was instrumental in having Trenton named as the county seat of Hunterdon, went on to become New Jersey's first Chief Justice. Unfortunately, Flemington replaced Trenton as Hunterdon's county seat in 1785 when Trenton was seriously being considered as the new national capital.

So sure were New Englanders, who strongly favored the Trenton site, that Trenton would be selected, that a commission established by the United States Congress, which met at Trenton in 1784, set to work marking out the site of the government's capital buildings. The South, however, lobbied so unceasingly for a southern location, that with strong backing from Washington, it finally won out with the selection of the now-well-known location on the Potomac - instead of on the Delaware.

In the meantime, Trenton was stripped of its governmental importance for a period of some five years after losing the county seat. Finally in 1790, the state Legislature decided to soothe the little village's pride by naming it the state capital. It would take the Delaware and Raritan Canal and the Camden and Amboy Railroad, which came in the 1830's, to change Trenton from a sleepy little village to a bustling metropolis, however. Both brought with them industry and people.

Mercer County's other focal point, Princeton, gained importance when the College of New Jersey (now Princeton University) moved there from Newark in 1754. The little village pledged money and land if the college would honor them with its presence. It was probably the best investment they ever made. The college accepted their offer. The educational center and its surrounding communities have since become a lodestone for cultural, educational, and scientific note-worthies from throughout the world.

Besides becoming home for such a distinguished scholar as Albert Einstein, Princeton has attracted a number of outstanding institutions to its borders. The Forrestal Research Center, The Institute for Advanced Study, The Rockefeller Institute for Medical Research, the Westminster Choir College, and more recently a gigantic computer center all have added new luster to both Princeton and the county.

Princeton was also the home of two of the nation's presidents. Thomas Woodrow Wilson who once was a professor and president of the college as well as the state's governor, and Grover Cleveland who, though born in Caldwell, went on to become governor of New York before ascending to the presidency. Cleveland died at his home in Princeton in 1908.

Much of the state's Revolutionary War heritage centered in what is now Mercer County. It was along the banks of the Delaware at Titusville, at what is now Washington Crossing State Park, that George Washington made his fateful moves across the Delaware in 1776 and early 1777. He then went on to win the two important battles at Trenton and Princeton, which subsequently became turning points of the war. But more of Mercer's heritage will have to await other days along the trails of New Jersey.

Middlesex County

One of New Jersey's original English counties, Middlesex, once included a large chunk of Somerset as well. It also had close links with Warren and Hunterdon Counties because of its key location. Though given its present designation as Middlesex in 1682, its present county seat, New Brunswick, was not so designated until 1778. Before that time, two communities that had been established in the late 1600's, Woodbridge and Piscataway served alternately as its county seat. During that time, another thriving town, Perth Amboy, had in 1686 been designated as the provincial capital of the new English province of East Jersey.

Both Woodbridge and Piscataway were settled by the English soon after the takeover of New Jersey from the Dutch in 1664. While Woodbridge's early settlers were from Connecticut via Long Island, Piscataway was settled by Englishmen who came the long distance south from the Piscataqua River in Maine. Those who traveled the greatest distance, however, came in 1685 when the Earl of Perth allowed a group of persecuted Scotsmen to sail for Ambo Point in New Jersey. First called, "New Perth," Perth Amboy soon became its official name.

New Brunswick was also settled in the late 1600's by a group of English settlers from Long Island led by John Inian. At first, the place was called Prigmore's Swamp. Not a very attractive name, it was later designated as Inian's Ferry, after John established a ferry service there across the Raritan River. Not until 1724 was the name New Brunswick adopted. The name was borrowed from the German Royal House of Braunschweig, which was anglicized to Brunswick when, through marriage, it became part of the British royal family.

Because of its location, Middlesex has always been a key transportation link between New York and points west. Even the early Dutch followed the banks of its Raritan River west to settle first Somerset, then Hunterdon, and eventually Warren counties. Indian paths became roads linking Perth Amboy southwest to the capital of the West Jersey province, Burlington, along the Delaware. Later roads took early travelers in the same direction for stops at Princeton and Trenton.

During the American Revolution, this key route location was much trafficked by both the British and American troops, and the pillaging of its countryside became commonplace. New Brunswick, in fact, alternated as British or American headquarters throughout the war. More than likely, it was British controlled in the early years, and later American. Perth Amboy, which faced British permanent headquarters in Staten Island, was almost permanently a British outpost. It was from New Brunswick that Washington made his decision to move on Yorktown, VA, and thus end the war at that fateful battle. Both American and French troops were thus rushed across New Jersey at that time.

Over the New Jersey Turnpike in the first third of the 1800's - from Easton via Phillipsburg, to ships awaiting them at New

Brunswick's wharves - rolled enormous, sometimes six-horse-drawn wagons loaded with fruit and grain shipped from farms in Warren, Hunterdon, and Somerset Counties. The waterfront was abuzz with activity as the horse-drawn wagons stayed overnight to be unloaded for shipment to the markets of New York. South River (then called Washington) became another port of embarkation for the west Jersey farmer's goods. Steamships and stagecoaches aided both people and goods between New York and Pennsylvania via Middlesex communities.

By the late 1830's, the horse-drawn stagecoaches and wagons, however, were being replaced by the cheaper Delaware and Raritan Canal barges, and the Camden and Amboy and New Jersey railroad cars. Jamesburg grew in importance because of its location on the rail line. New Brunswick soon became an industrial as well as a commercial center.

Perth Amboy and Sayreville also became industrial centers when the Lehigh Valley Railroad was built in the 1870's from Easton via Phillipsburg, to Perth Amboy. The Lehigh Valley railroad brought with it huge shipments of Pennsylvania coal. Easton's coal shipments soon powered newly created industries that changed the face of east Middlesex communities by the late 1890's and early 1900's.

With industry humming and population soaring, the inventive genius of the age, Thomas Alva Edison, moved his "invention factory" in 1876 to Middlesex's Menlo Park - to be near the new era's action. Many new inventions were born in Middlesex as it roared into the 20th century. But more of Middlesex's colorful history will have to await other days along the trails of New Jersey.

Monmouth County

One of New Jersey's four oldest counties is along the "Jersey Shore." When it first came into existence, however, it was called by an entirely different name than that which it now bears. As soon as the British took over the territory from the Dutch in 1664, a group of Englishmen from Long Island immediately began settlements at the Atlantic Highlands. Middletown and Shrewsbury were the names given to their new communities. By 1675, the "County of Navesink" was established - named after the local Indians from whom they bought their lands.

However, a gentleman named Lewis Morris, whose family name appears in connection with other New Jersey places, became one of the most influential citizens of the area. Morris became ironmaster of the first iron works in the state - at the Falls of the Shrewsbury River. He was originally from Monmouthshire in Wales, Great Britain. The litmus test of his importance in the area came when he suggested that the county be named Monmouth - after his old homestead. In 1682, Monmouth it became.

Stretching westward to Burlington and Mercer, which before 1838 was part of southern Hunterdon, Monmouth is more than a "shore county." Its iron industry was once at Shrewsbury and later at Allaire. The latter is now the site of a fabulous tourist attraction at Allaire State Park. Farming is still centered near Freehold, whose orchards witnessed the blistering Battle of Monmouth in June of 1778. The state has commemorated this famous scene with the newly opened Monmouth Battlefield State Park. Its horse breeding predates the Revolution. However, its seashore resorts, which attracted Philadelphia's elite since the late 1700's are probably its most noted feature.

I mentioned before that Long Branch was the state's earliest and, in some respects, nationally famous resort. It once served as the summer residence of five of the nation's presidents and many other notables as well. Like most resorts of its day, it catered to the nation's well to do.

Ocean Grove first became famous in the years following the Civil War. It was established as a religious, seaside resort by the Methodist Church. Its clientele and atmosphere were quite "different" from anything the nation had yet seen. One of its early residents, James Bradley, soon established another nearby, where "average" people could enjoy a few weeks at hotels or boarding houses along the beach. It was named after the Methodist Bishop, Francis Asbury, and called Asbury Park. More exclusive resorts in Monmouth were established at Spring Lake, Elberon, Monmouth Beach, and Rumson. Popular beaches below Asbury today include Belmar and Manasquan. Probably the most popular to its north is the new Sandy Hook National Park.

Along with its shore resorts, Monmouth has always been noted for its horse-breeding farms. Though many new horse ranches have sprung up throughout New Jersey in recent years, Monmouth farmers have been breeding fine racehorses since colonial times. Some, however, have taken to this more lucrative type of farming lately because running other kinds of farms in New Jersey has become too expensive for the returns received. Monmouth Park at Oceanport and the Freehold Raceway provide the outlet for either thoroughbred racehorses or standard-bred trotters. Non-racing horses are also raised for people who enjoy riding for pleasure on many bridle paths throughout the state.

Because it faces upon both the Raritan Bay and the Atlantic Ocean, it stands to reason that the sea has always played a prominent role in Monmouth's lifestyle. Such navigable rivers as the Manasquan, the Navesink, the Shark, and the Shrewsbury once brought much shipping to her shores. Though commercial trading ships no longer tread her waters, deep sea fishing vessels, particularly at such places as the Atlantic Highlands, are very popular. Beacons from its lighthouses at Sandy Hook and Navesink Highlands were guiding ships at sea since before the Revolution. Both are now tourist attractions as historic sites.

Many folk tales arose relating to Monmouth's many-faceted life-style. Stories of its Pine Bandits were prominent in the period before and after the Revolution. Tales of the legendary "Molly Pitcher," who became a heroine at the Battle of Monmouth, have been told throughout the nation. Monmouth's special hero, Captain Joshua Huddy, who was captured by the British at the Battle of Toms River, has niched his special place in history. It came about as a result of his notorious hanging on the gallows at Navesink. Pirates, bootleggers, and sea wrecks are all part of Monmouth's past, but tales such as these will have to await other times along the trails of New Jersey.

Morris County

Morris County was first settled by Dutch migrants from Bergen as early as 1695. It wasn't until 1738, however, that Morris, which at the time included both present day Sussex and Warren

Counties as well, broke away from the then gigantic Hunterdon County to gain its own identity. Not much later, Sussex, which also included today's Warren County, was severed from Morris. That move, in 1753, finally left the present county's borders, as we know them today. Morristown was named as the county seat in 1740. It set aside its famous Town Green in 1771.

Aside from the Dutch, Morris was the recipient of an influx of Germans who first moved into its Schooley's Mountain, between the Musconetcong and South Branch of the Raritan, in 1707. They came from the west, where they had first been invited by William Penn. Both of these early colonists were chiefly farmers, though the Dutch were ever on the alert for mineral ores.

Whippanong, (now Whippany) was the first settlement in Morris to be established by the English. That was in 1710. They had been transplanted New Englanders more recently from Essex County, seeking iron. This they found in mines shown them by the Lenapes at Succasunna (meaning "black-stone").

Not long after their arrival, a forge was going at what was soon called Morristown. Forges began popping up all along the Whippanong and Rockaway rivers. Iron forges opened in Dover in 1722 and Rockaway in 1730.

Other scattered early settlements soon were found at Pompton, Chester, German Valley, and Mendham. Iron was already the center of the county's economy when in 1772, John Jacob Faesch, fresh from running the Ringwood mines in what is now Passaic County, arrived. He soon had a gigantic operation centered near his newly acquired iron mine at Mount Hope.

By the time of the American War for Independence, Morris was ripe for its role as the "Arsenal of the Revolution." In addition to cannons, cannonballs, and grapeshot, it provided many supplies to the Continental Army throughout the war.

George Washington, finding the area not only exceedingly defensible, but well worth defending, set up his military headquarters at Morristown.

While he stayed at the wealthy ironmaster, Jacob Ford's place, his troops encamped in nearby woods. In 1833, the first National Historic Park in the country was established there to commemorate this vital colonial heritage.

Morris soon became home to many of the colony's wealthy and influential people. Large estates sprang up. When the Morristown-Phillipsburg Turnpike opened in the early 1800's, along with another toll pike from Elizabethtown earlier in that same period, the health-giving spring waters found in Schooley's Mountain turned that area into the young nation's leading "health resort." Wealthy families from other nearby states soon began eyeing the beautifully wooded Morris hills.

The Morris & Essex Railroad made it possible for men of great wealth to commute to New York City, while raising their families on huge estates in the healthy Morris environment.

By the end of the 1800's, such famous national writers and artists as Bret Harte, Rudyard Kipling, and Thomas Nast were calling Morristown their home.

The surrounding area became a virtual nesting ground for millionaires. Though its iron-based economy was eventually lost to the new mines in the Midwest, the whole county still sits atop an estimated iron-ore reserve of some 600 million tons, which someday may have to be sought after once again.

Aside from harboring America's first National Historic Park at Morristown and Jockey Hollow, Morris County is home to several other unique federal preserves.

Back in 1880 the government purchased several thousand acres east of Green Pond Mountain to establish its Picatinny Arsenal. There, experiments would be carried on with various explosives for its war needs.

Today, a gigantic national weapons research center encompasses its over 6,000 acre preserve.

Back in the 1960's residents surrounding the Great Swamp were aroused by plans to build a giant regional airport there. An area housewife led a movement that eventually resulted in the preservation of the some 8,000-acre "Great Swamp National Wildlife Refuge" instead.

Fortunately for Morris, now in the grips of an unprecedented growth spurt, it already has one of the best county-open-space-preserve systems in the state. Many of its extensive county park acres were donated by landowners who wanted to see their beloved open-space heritage preserved for posterity.

"Fosterfields," a 132-acre farm, was donated to the park system in 1973. It is being restored to depict farming methods of the 19th century in a "living historical farm." Another bit of American's rich farming heritage is thus being preserved along the trails of New Jersey - by people with foresight.

Ocean County

Monmouth County, one of the state's four oldest counties, once extended along the Atlantic coastline as far south as Little Egg Harbor. But that all changed in 1850 when the state Legislature made that 50-mile strip of land from Point Pleasant south, into a separate county. Though its land extended inland to Burlington, its thoughts were definitely turned outward to the ocean, and so Ocean County it was named.

Its history is somewhat varied. The Dutch explorer, Cornelius Mey, gave two of its most notable seamarks their names as early as 1614. One body of water, which separates a major portion of its main coastline from the Atlantic Ocean, runs all the way from the Metedeconk River in the north, below Bay Head, to Mill Creek in the south, below Manahawkin. He called it "Barende gat," or "Inlet of Breakers." It has been anglicized today to read Barnegat Bay. Midway along this stretch, the historic Barnegat Lighthouse still guards the inlet between Island Beach and Barnegat Lighthouse State Parks.

South of the Barnegat National Wildlife Refuge extending to the Great Bay State Fish and Wildlife Management Area is the second largest Ocean County water body named by the Dutch explorer, Capt. Mey. Like Barnegat Bay, it, too, separates the mainland from the Atlantic Ocean with a long, narrow strip island of famous beach resorts. Mey named that sheltered, body of water, "Eyre Haven." In case you do not recognize what that was translated into by English settlers – it's Egg Harbor.

A few years after the English takeover of New Jersey in 1664, an Englishman named Capt. William Tom explored the region. That was sometime in the early 1670's. He sailed into one of its larger inlets and named the river that still bears his name - as well as the town that was to become Ocean's county seat - Toms River.

Toms River later turned out to be the site of an historic battle in the American Revolution. Armies of the period depended upon vast amounts of salt, for making gunpowder and preserving food. Congress, therefore, set up such establishments for its manufacture. It was at Toms River that the British Army in 1778 attempted to take over one of Washington's vital saltworks. Capt. Joshua Huddy, leader of its defenders, became another of Jersey's heroes of the Revolution as a result of this battle. The county has in recent years set aside Huddy Park to commemorate this event.

Farther south, along Little Egg Harbor, another Ocean County community grew in seafaring importance. A German immigrant named Henry Falkinburg was the first to settle the area around Tuckerton in 1698. He was soon followed by two English Quakers, Edward, and Mordecai Andrews. It was Edward Andrews who, as far as we know, in 1704 built the first gristmill along the coastline. Other gristmills, as well as sawmills, inland, were soon to follow.

Both Toms River and Tuckerton became important seaports in the period before the American Revolution. When other ports were closed as a result of the British blockades during the War for Independence, the importance of those two Jersey seaports was compounded considerably. Because of the fierce independence of their seafaring citizenry, they also became hotbeds of insurrection.

Barnegat Bay and Little Egg Harbor served as convenient hideaways for a considerable number of privateers who constantly molested British shipping in that part of the Atlantic during the war. Numerous private fortunes were accumulated in the conduct of these "patriotic" activities. The British government was not unaware of the deeds being perpetrated from these Ocean County seaports and a number of attempts were made at various times to flush them out. After the Revolution, during the presidency of George Washington, Tuckerton was named as an official port of entry - an action deemed very important to its booming shipping interests.

By the second decade of the 1800's, Ocean County communities, such as Barnegat, Forked River, Toms River, Tuckerton, and Waretown had established booming shipbuilding industries. In a day when nearby lumber was considerable more plentiful, and shipping by water of far more importance than it is today, sea trade and the construction of the vessels that plied the waters, with all of their related trades, made a powerful economic impact on the area.

Tuckerton became the center for large, ocean-going vessels being built in Ocean County communities. The other towns mentioned meanwhile were concentrating on the construction of smaller coastal craft - including both oyster and whaleboats. A two-masted, square-rigged brig built by Tuckerton's famed shipbuilders, the Shrouds, became one of the nation's most popular sailing ships of that day. But more tales of Ocean's interesting past will have to await other times.

Passaic County

Dutch settlers began moving into the lands we now call Passaic County as early as 1678 about 12 years after the British take-over of the New Netherlands. In 1682, the region called Acquackanonk was purchased from the Lenni Lenape Indians by a group of Dutch families. It included most of the area that makes up the present day cities of Passaic, Clifton, and Paterson. Until 1873, the City of Passaic was called Acquackanonk. By 1697, Dutch landholders had purchased all the region around Pompton Lakes, and by 1730 either Dutch or German settlers owned all of the highlands that are included in present day Passaic County. The Bearfort Kanouse and Ramapo Mountains lie within this rugged hill country.

Before 1740, Dutchmen were still tramping the countryside looking for copper ore within these hills, such as they had found a century before in what is now Warren County - far to the west. Instead of copper, however, they discovered rich veins of iron. The smelting of iron began in 1741 northwest of the Ramapos at a place purchased by the wealthy Ogden family of Newark. They called it the Ringwood Iron Company. Soon affluent English interests in London bought it out, along with about 50,000-acres of virgin woodlands in the surrounding region.

The Englishmen hired a German iron-master, Peter Hasenclever, in 1765 to manage their mines. They authorized him to import about 500 German ironworkers to run them. Soon furnaces were established in Charlottesburg, New Foundland, and Pompton. The nearby, forested hills became a German enclave, and Hasenclever, who lived like a feudal lord was dubbed the "Iron Baron." He moved on to manage other mines in the region while first John Faesch and then Robert Erskine succeeded him at the Ringwood mines. Today, this is all part of the Ringwood State Park.

Erskine was running the Ringwood Company during the American Revolution, and became fast friends with the American Commander, George Washington. In fact he became Washington's personal mapmaker. Washington later stayed at Ringwood, while Erskine was there. He also stayed elsewhere in what is now Passaic County during the course of the American Revolution. His armies were encamped at such places as Pompton, Totowa, and Wayne in 1780 and 1781. Washington was at the home of a wealthy Dutchman, Theunis Dey, at what is now the historic Dey mansion in Preakness. It is an historic site worth seeing. During one of his visits he was hiding from an assassination attempt.

It was while Washington was visiting in Passaic in 1778 that he and his young aide, Alexander Hamilton, observed the potential for industry offered by the Little and Great Falls of the Passaic River. When Hamilton became Washington's Secretary of the Treasury in the new government, set up by the Constitution of 1787, he remembered those falls in his "Report on Manufactures," sent to the U.S, Congress in 1791.

This report led eventually to the founding of the "Society for the Establishing of Useful Manufacturers:" (SUM) in November of 1791. In 1792, the city of Paterson, the first planned industrial city of the new nation, was born as a result. It was named after the then Governor of New Jersey, William Paterson, in appreciation for his signing of the society's charter. The same engineer, Pierre L'Enfant, who later planned the nation's capital, was hired to design the new city. His plans, however, were too elaborate for the society's limited pocketbook and were dropped.

The story of Paterson's industrial growth, first from its many cotton mills, and then to the varied interest of the Colt family, including Sam Colt's famed gun, is long and colorful. It includes the manufacture of the nation's first locomotives and submarines. It became famous as an iron as well as silk center. For a time it manufactured airplanes, including the engine for Charles Lindbergh's "Spirit of St. Louis." Today an Historic District at the Great Falls of the Passaic commemorates the nation's first planned industrial city. The year 1991 will mark the 200th anniversary of the establishment of SUM.

In the midst of all of this growth, in the year 1837, the people of the region then still a part of Bergen County petitioned the state legislature to set up two new counties - Pompton and Paterson. The County of Paterson would include the more urbanized region surrounding the Passaic River to the east. Southern interest would have no part of two new northern counties. In fact, approval hinged on the establishment of Atlantic in the south. Thus was born, Passaic, really two distinct counties in one, along the trails of New Jersey.

Salem County

The most northern of the Jersey Tidewater region, and the most southern of its Delaware Valley counties, is Salem. Its western border is about half on the Delaware River and half on the Bay. Like the other southernmost counties, it was first settled by the Swedes and Finns. For the short period of Swedish rule from the 1630's to the 1650's, it, along with the present state of Delaware, was called "New Sweden."

Elsinboro Point near the present community of Elsinboro is the site of the former Fort Elfborg. It was built by Johann Printz, then Governor of New Sweden, who was the Swedish equivalent of the colorful Dutch governor of New Netherlands, Peter Stuyvesant. Like Stuyvesant, Printz was an autocratic, though capable ruler. Not much liked, but much needed in that wilderness bastion. The outpost was nicknamed Fort Myggenborg, which means Fort Mosquito, because it was plagued with those famous Jersey bugs. In fact, it has been claimed that it was the Jersey mosquito, not the Dutch that ended Swedish rule in America.

Since many of the colonizers among the Swedish territories were Finns, and since some say Finnish explorers even preceded the Swedes, it's not surprising that a small protrusion of Jersey land in

91

that area is called, "Finn's Point." It lies near the mouth of the Delaware between New Castle, on the Delaware side, and Salem in New Jersey. In the 1830's, the United States government saw fit to set up a battery of guns there to control shipping coming up the Delaware. It was part of the paranoia concerning sea invasions that had plagued America since the successful raids of our shores by the British, during the war of 1812. Today, it is the site of a National Cemetery commemorating the thousands of Confederate soldiers who died at the infamous Pea Patch Island Prison - opposite Finn's Point.

During the Civil War, Fort Delaware was established on Pea Patch Island, and it was fortified to prevent a Southern invasion of New Jersey and Pennsylvania by the way of the Delaware. Such an invasion was considered to be very imminent. Though south Jersey, much of which was below the Mason-Dixon Line (from about Atlantic City south) had definite pro-south leanings. Salem's Quaker heritage made that region both anti-war and anti-slavery.

The naval battle that was anticipated never materialized, but thousands of southern soldiers did make it to Fort Delaware - as prisoners of war. And a despicable prison it was, too. It is a chapter of our history of which we are not proud. The prisoners were so horribly treated that they welcomed death. And die they did, at the rate of at least 20 a day. Some 2,500 of them eventually made their way to the mainland where they were buried. In 1875, it was dedicated as a national cemetery, and a monument was raised to their memory.

Nearby Elsinboro Point also played a prominent, but humane role in the Civil War period. It served as one of the "stations" for the famous "Underground Railroad." Here, hundreds of runaway slaves, who were transported from points south crossed the Delaware River and began their northward journey to Canada - and freedom. Again the anti-slavery Quakers of the region aided and abetted what had become an illegal act according to the runaway slave laws enacted by the national government.

The lands surrounding the Finns' Point National Cemetery were later set aside as the 1500-acre Killcohook National Wildlife Refuge. It serves today mostly as a sanctuary for waterfowl. To its south is another former federal outpost on the Delaware. It's called Fort Mott, after the Commander of the New Jersey Volunteers during the Civil War, Gen. Geershom Mott. It was built in 1896 during the pre-Spanish-American War days when invasion by sea was still very much on the minds of America's military leaders. A garrison of soldiers remained there until 1922. Today, it is a part of the Fort Mott State Park - where its moat, tunnels and gun emplacements serve as reminders of those days not so long ago when America itself was still considered a fortress protected by the sea from foreign invasions. It offers a fine view of the Delaware, and ships that sail its lower waters.

There is much more to be told of Salem's heritage. Stories of its settlement by the Quakers abound. Its role during the American Revolution is full of drama - including the infamous massacre at Hancock's Bridge. Its early role in shipbuilding, glassmaking, and farming all make interesting stories. But more tales of Salem will have to wait for other times along the trails of New Jersey.

Somerset County

Only two of New Jersey's 21 counties do not border at some point on one of the outside boundaries of the state. One of them, Somerset, was created in 1688 when it was separated from Middlesex. It took until 1713, however, before it finally established its own county seat. This it did at what is now Franklin Park (it was then called Six Mill Run.) When its courthouse burned down, however, in 1738, the county government was moved to Millstone.

That was not to be Somerset's permanent county seat either, however. In 1779, during the American Revolution, that courthouse, in turn, was consumed by flames during a British raid. Under direct orders from the notorious cavalryman, Colonel John Simcoe, leader of the Queen's Rangers, it was torched. Somerset's third county seat was then established at Raritan (now Somerville) in 1782. There it has remained.

Somerset has also been required in the course of time to give up both some of its territory as well as its prestige. For awhile, the county housed two of the state's oldest and most prestigious colleges - Princeton and Rutgers. In 1838, the legislature, in creating Mercer County, took away any claims Somerset had to Princeton when it relocated all of that university town within the borders of the new county. Somerset, before that date, shared part of Princeton with

Hunterdon. In 1850, it took away that section of Franklin Township where Rutgers was located and returned it to Middlesex. Thus, within the short span of a dozen years, Somerset lost both of its famous colleges.

But its colleges were not its only claim to fame. It was in Somerset's Basking Ridge that the perplexing Gen. Charles Lee, once a British officer who joined the American cause, was mysteriously captured by his once comrade in arms. Lee was then returned to the American lines only to later commit what Washington charged was a traitorous act at the Battle of Monmouth. The enigma surrounding this strange officer has never been cleared.

It was there, too, in Somerset's Griggstown, that the family of John Honeyman was scorned and jeered and all but driven from town because, under orders from Washington, he assumed the "cover" of a notorious staunch Tory. Honeyman, you may recall, was all of that time the personal spy of the American Commander-in-chief behind British lines. When Washington exonerated Honeyman after the war, the former top-notch spy was so stigmatized by then that he had to pack up his family and live out the remainder of his life in Hunterdon's Lamington.

It was through Somerset's Millstone Valley, too, that Washington marched his war-weary command after its startling victories at first in Trenton and then Princeton. He escaped the wrath of the reorganized British regulars by hiding that winter in the protective Watchung Hills surrounding Morristown. It was at a summit in what is now Washington Rock State Park in Somerset that he was enabled to observe British troop movements as far away as Newark Bay that following spring. And, while encamped nearby at Middlebrook on June 14, 1777, he flew the first American flag after its adoption by Congress. By order of the Congress, it is never lowered at the park created there. It is one of the few places authorized to fly the flag, day and night.

While headquartered at Somerville's "Wallace House," now a state historic site, in the mild winter of 1778-79, Washington and Martha enjoyed their most pleasurable stay of the war. Parties included one at Gen. Nathaniel Green's headquarters at Finderne and Gen. Henry Knox's headquarters at Pluckemin. It was also Somerset's Berrien Mansion at Rocky Hill; called Rockingham (now a state historic site), that Washington wrote his farewell address to his troops at the war's end.

But Somerset is probably most noted for its abundance of wealthy estates. The affluent in the British colony began buying up Dutch farmlands from the former settlers early on. Probably the most prominent estate, however, was that of James Buchanan Duke (after whom Duke University in North Carolina was named).

Making his millions in the tobacco industry, Duke settled in Somerset in the early 1890's. There he began to assemble more than 2,000-acres. At the cost of some $15 million, by importing thousands of tons of dirt and an entire forest, he transformed its flat plains into wooded hills. Hundreds of thousands of rhododendrons and myriads of other woodland shrubs and flowers were added over time to his private forested hills. The fabulous "Duke Gardens" resulted when his daughter, Doris, became the world-famous rich girl after she inherited his estate in 1933. There is more to tell of Somerset's "rich" heritage, but it will have to wait for other days along the trails of New Jersey.

Sussex County

"Minnesota" is the Chippewa Indian term for "Land of the Lakes." It well could be the name used to describe parts of New Jersey's northernmost county, Sussex. Along with nearby Morris and Passaic Counties, the hills of Sussex contribute a large share of the lakes and ponds that make up the state's Lakeland region. Though it shares Lake Hopatcong, the state's biggest lake, with Morris county, it has many other large lakes contained solely within its borders, including Cranberry, Culver, Highland, Mohawk, Owassa, Swartswood, and Wawayanda. In addition, there are many smaller lakes and ponds in Sussex such as Pochung, Girard, Beaver, Grinnell, Morris, Lenape, Lackawanna, Fairview, Paulinskill, and Kemah, to name just a few.

These blue lakes, when coupled with its verdant woodlands, mountain vistas, sparkling streams and tumbling waterfalls, make Sussex and its nearby environs a land of scenic beauty and sylvan relaxation. It has attracted visitors from nearby metropolitan areas for centuries. In more recent years, ski resorts have been added to make Sussex a year-round vacationland.

Since its rocky hills have been difficult for farming, it is no accident that the state chose this area to reserve large tracts of land for public recreational purposes as early as World War I. In order that all its citizens might enjoy this scenic wonderland for posterity, the state began a program of land acquisition for which we now can be thankful.

Stokes State Forest, which comprises some 12,000-acres along the slopes of the Kittatinny Mountains, is an early example of the wise preservation of recreational lands by the state. Thanks to the generosity of Col. and Mrs. Anthony Kuser of Bernardsville, the nearby 11,000-acre High Point tract became an additional state park in 1923. It includes the state's highest elevation, 1803 feet above sea level. Add to these, the vast Sussex portion of the 77,000-acre Delaware Water Gap Recreation Area along both sides of the Delaware River, purchased in the late 60's and early 70's, and you have an attractive area of scenic beauty for the public's enjoyment that beats any other in the state. The famed Appalachian Trail, now totally on state-owned land in Sussex, is another area set aside for the hikers among us to relish forever.

Dutchmen were among the first Europeans to come to Sussex County from their settlements around Esopus, along the Hudson. English, Irish, and Scotch immigrants came overland from the eastern part of the state, and Germans came up from the Philadelphia region, all in the early 1700's. There were barely 600 people in Sussex in 1753 when it broke away from Morris County and set up its own county seat at Newton.

By 1820, with some 33,000 people, Sussex was the most populated county in the state. Essex, now the most populated and then including present-day Union as well, was second. Since most of the people of Sussex were centered near Oxford, that area of the county soon demanded its own county seat. In 1824, Warren was cut off from southern Sussex. What remained of Sussex was rugged, isolated country. Its population, therefore, never competed with Essex again.

For a time the building of the Morris Canal in the 1830's brought increased activity to the Sussex iron mines, and it appeared that Sussex might regain its population status. Forges and furnaces at

Andover, Franklin, Stanhope, and Waterloo prospered. Then came the discovery of zinc in the Sussex hills by Dr. Samuel Fowler. Later, the Scranton family built a huge iron furnace at Franklin (in 1872). Around 1891, Thomas Edison poured $2.5 million into the Ogden iron mines. By the turn of the century, however, only zinc remained a profitable industry in Sussex.

The coming of the railroads to the large cattle ranches of the mid-west in the late 1850's and early 1860's virtually killed the beef industry in Sussex. But the farmers of the area soon found that the trains could be used by them to bring fresh milk quickly to nearby cities. So dairy farming came to Sussex in the 1860's in a big way and, until recently, remained its chief means of livelihood.

Today the trails of Sussex, like so many rural areas of New Jersey, are under great pressure by developers. Route 80 has made the county within quick commuter distance of the eastern metropolitan areas. Unless steps are taken soon to balance these demands for development, with the preservation needs of the natural environment, Sussex's bucolic rural charm, too, will become, unbelievable as it may now seem, just another quaint tale about a by-gone era that once was so pleasant along the trails of New Jersey.

Union County

When Union County was cut from Essex in 1857, it settled a dispute of long standing between the cities of Elizabeth and Newark. Ever since Newark was founded by a group of Connecticut Puritans under Robert Treat in 1666, each of these two cities contended that they should be the county seat. When elections were finally held to decide the dispute, the vote, instead of dousing the flames, only added more fuel to the fires of enmity that were burning between them.

The hostility from Elizabeth's point of view was based upon age - she was the senior city. Newark's advantage was population. The outcome of elections, unfortunately for Elizabeth, was based upon the number of votes received and thus Newark had the decided advantage. Elizabeth, nevertheless, charged fraud and so the antagonisms continued until the state legislature finally gave

Elizabeth its coveted reward, with the Establishment of Union County on March 18, 1857.

The Ogden family had been the leading settlers of Elizabeth almost two centuries before. John Ogden and his five grown sons, along with John Baker, John Bayley, Daniel Denton, and Luke Watson, were the principal early property owners. Part of this same Ogden family was later to play a pioneer role in the development of Sussex County. It was Robert Ogden who in 1778 brought his family to Sparta, and later became prominent in the iron industry of that region. The name lives on in Sussex in the community of Ogdensburg.

The original boundaries of Elizabeth Town, as it was initially called were approximately the same as those of present-day Union County. Founded in 1664, it was the first English settlement in New Jersey, which had been, as you know, a Dutch province before that date. Gov. George Carteret designated the settlement as the new English colony's first capital in 1668. It was there then that Jersey's first General Assembly met. Thus the stage was set for Elizabeth's belief that it, and not Newark, was the county's most prominent city.

Farming, leather making and the whaling industry were the major occupations of those who first settled within the boundaries of present-day Union County. As early as 1667, farmers from Connecticut came to its rich lands to ply their trade. And so they called their new homelands Connecticut Farms (since changed to Union). Scotchmen, who had originally settled at Perth Amboy, were moving into the farmlands south of the Watchung Mountains as early as the 1680's. So they called their settlements, Scotch Plains.

The farmlands lying to the west of Elizabeth Town were being tilled around the period of the early 1700's. Because of their location, they were dubbed the West Fields. When settlers began moving into the wooded top-lands of the Watchungs at the turn of the 18th century, the name Summit was given to their region as befitted its location. About the same time farmers moving into the fields along the Reawake River found them studded with numerous springs and so named their settlements, the Spring Fields. All became battlefields in the contest that was soon to rage between the mother country and the fiercely independent farmers whose families had been tilling that soil for several generations by the time of the Revolution.

Princeton University (then called the College of New Jersey) was founded in Elizabeth Town in 1746. Its first president, the Rev. Jonathan Dickinson, was pastor of the Presbyterian Church there. He was also a very reputable doctor, teacher, and farmer of the area at the time. When Princeton decided to move its college to Newark (for a short time before settling in its present location) the fires of ferment between these two cities were fanned further.

Elizabeth Town's once proud position of eminence in this state was due not alone to the fact that it housed Jersey's capital - with its governor and colonial Assembly and all the perquisites that went . with the center of government. Nor was it because it housed the colony's most prestigious college, with the aura that such a center of learning spewed forth. Another very important factor for Elizabeth was the considerable number of outstanding families that resided within its borders. They later played important roles throughout the state.

As the first of signs of Revolution began to spring up in the colonies, Elizabeth Town, an area we now call Union County, found itself embroiled in the conflict with fierce partisans taking positions on both sides. But these tales will have to wait for other days to be told along the trails of New Jersey.

Warren County

Though the state legislature first broke Warren County from Sussex on Nov. 29, 1824, that date could hardly be considered the beginning of the historical existence of Warren. Even its name reflects events of an earlier date. It goes back to the period of the American Revolution. Gen. Joseph Warren was a hero in that war at the Battle of Bunker Hill in 1775. He actually had nothing to do with this area, but rather was chosen as an echo of the esteem with which his deeds were held by the people of the young nation, including those in the hills of Warren. The people of Warren were, after all, very much involved in that historic event, even though they were still a part of Sussex County.

In reflecting upon the history of Warren County, we must realize that it was once an integral part of a much larger region, especially northwestern New Jersey's frontier. When counties were first established by the English in West Jersey, Warren was found within the gigantic Burlington County. In 1738, it was removed from Hunterdon and made a part of the newly created Morris County at the behest of the iron interests of that area. As the population of the more western area of Morris grew, it too demanded its own county seat. In the shadow of the French and Indian War, the colonial legislature decided to remove it from Morris in order to create the new county of Sussex, with its own county seat at New Town. The history of Warren and Sussex continued to be one until 1824 when the state legislature, with pressure from Sussex's southern communities, particularly centered near Oxford, created the separate county called Warren.

The history of Warren cannot be divorced from that region of which it was for so long a vital part. Its heritage is a part of its larger birthplace. Its earliest European settlers also came not only before its identity as a separate county, but even before the English takeover of New Jersey, and the establishment of any counties at all in the colony. The Dutch, rather than the English, were its first non-native inhabitants.

The area we now know of as Warren County was not only not born with the English takeover of New Jersey in 1664, but also not with the coming of the Dutch to its soil in the earlier 1600's. It was, after all, inhabited for perhaps thousands of years before the coming of the first Europeans. Though Americans have a habit of referring to the history of any given region in the "New World" as beginning some time after its European discovery and settlement, we both flatter ourselves and insult those earlier inhabitants whom we have come to know as the American Indians.

Warren County's "Original People," the Lenapes are very much a part of its history. We are, in more recent years, just beginning to give them their "due," and recognizing their existence as a part of the heritage of the region. The Indian's concept of the land, their concern for preserving nature's gifts for future generation's use, their attitude towards their environment, and their role in it as a sharing member rather than as a conqueror, all are part of that heritage which we are now first beginning to appreciate.

"Nature" itself also had a vital role in the evolving history of Warren County. Those who lived here over those many centuries were as much influenced by what they found here as part of the county's natural features, as by what they brought here as part of their own makeup's. This was perhaps much more true in the past than it is today, but even now our natural features cannot help but influence our growing personalities.

The "Original People" of Warren County were that branch of the Lenape known as the Minsi, People of the Stone County. Who can deny this vital feature of the county - the result of the once mighty "Terminal Moraine," dumped here by the Wisconsin Ice Age?" Its result lives with us still. Much of the early history of Warren has evolved out of what nature has set down before it. We owe the history of its early industry and the way its people earned a living to the geography they found here. So the geography of Warren County is also a vital part of its heritage. In the material to follow we will examine all of these aspects of the unfolding drama of the history of Warren County.

CHAPTER 6: SITES TO SEE IN THE STATE

Many Sites to See

Diversity is New Jersey's middle name. From High Point to Cape May more is packed into this little state than any other place of comparable size in the nation. That includes people, motor vehicles, and highways, as well as historic and geographical points of interest.

From tip to tip it is less than 170 miles as the crow flies. It is less than 40 miles wide from the Delaware River to the Atlantic Ocean at its narrow neck and no more than another 20 miles anywhere else. It is surrounded by water on three sides while sharing a small land border to its north with New York State.

Within its 7,500 square land miles are to be found the nation's greatest concentration of people per square mile (more than 1,000) and the world's greatest concentration of traffic and transportation facilities.

Yet also within this small area can be found some 127 miles of a seashore playground hugging its coastal plain and a variety of lakes, woodlands and streams scattered from south to north across coastal plains, piedmont and mountains. Yet New Jersey is about six times smaller in size than its two neighbors, Pennsylvania and New York.

While holding so many people (some 7,500,000) in such a concentrated space, New Jersey has still managed to possess considerable woodlands and a viable agricultural acreage (though both are being threatened by overwhelming development pressures).

At the same time, it is the only state in which no community lies outside of a metropolitan area. Along its northwestern border it shares the 70,000-acre Delaware Water Gap National Recreation Area with neighboring Pennsylvania. There, Millbrook Village is being restored to depict life in a 19th century northwestern New Jersey farming village.

At the northern tip of its 127-mile seacoast, Sandy Hook Park is the New Jersey section of the Gateway National Recreation Area, which it shares with New York. At its northeastern border lie the natural wonders of the Palisades Interstate Park, which it also shares with New York State.

More than 100 battles were fought within its borders during the American Revolution, and a number of historic parks have been set aside to commemorate some of them. At the site of Washington's Military Headquarters at Morristown and its adjoining army encampment at nearby Jockey Hollow is one of the nation's first National Historic Parks.

Monmouth Battlefield State Park has preserved much of the area around the battle where Molly Pitcher became a national folk heroine. Washington's Crossing State Park in New Jersey is across the river from a similar one in Pennsylvania, reminding us of the Battles of Trenton and Princeton, which proved to be turning points of the Revolution.

The Trenton Barracks depicts events not only of that war but of the part New Jersey played in the French and Indian War when a number of such barracks were built in the state to house British troops sent to protect the colonies.

The Edison National Historic Site in West Orange, the Great Falls Historic District in Paterson, and Speedwell Village in Morristown are all sites of some of America's great inventions and growing industry.

Wheaton Village in Millville displays more than 7,000 glass objects and demonstrates 19th century glassmaking in what was once an important glassmaking region. The Historic Village of Batsto, sitting in the midst of the 100,000-acre Wharton State Forest in the Pine Barrens, not only commemorates New Jersey's once-thriving glassmaking industry, but also its bog-iron industry, as well as does the Deserted Village of Allaire in Monmouth County.

Shippen Manor at Oxford in Warren County is being restored as a reminder of the once prosperous iron industry in northwest New Jersey. The Franklin Mineral Museum displays minerals from Sussex County's once-thriving zinc mines. Waterloo Village illustrates not only an old iron center, but also a village reborn with the coming of the Morris Canal.

For those more oriented to the great outdoors, a number of state parks and forests provide camping, boating, fishing, hiking, picnicking and swimming facilities. New Jersey has more than 100 rivers and streams and some 800 lakes and ponds. There is also the modern fish-breeding station and environmental center at the Pequest State Trout Hatchery at Oxford.

In Morris County we can find the 7,000-acre Great Swamp National Wildlife Refuge with observation trails and environmental center. The gigantic 36,000-acre Brigantine National Wildlife Refuge (recently renamed after the late Rep. Edwin Forsythe) with its bird sanctuary is located along the seashore in the Atlantic City area.

For the flying enthusiasts in New Jersey the Aviation Museum at Teterboro Airport is dedicated to the history of flight. A military museum can be found at the Picatinny Arsenal near Dover. The Meadowlands has an attractive sports center.

There are many additional historic sites depicting varying eras, people, and events in our state and national history, too numerous to mention in any one article; but I do hope this brief overview does give some idea of what lies before you, if you travel along the many diverse trails of New Jersey.

Historic Sites

Having devoted half of my life to teaching, writing, and lecturing about history, I think it is excusable that I take great delight in the groundswell of public interest that has been developing over the past two decades in places of historic interest in our state. I trace the beginnings of this current movement to preparations for the celebrations of our state's Tercentenary in 1964, followed by that of our nation's Bicentennial in 1976. Both have given new impetus to the value of preserving the state's diverse heritage.

This is not to say that the state does not need to devote even greater emphasis on seeking out, preserving, and promoting its authentic examples of life in times gone by.

There is much to do and one hopes that a union of private historic preservation groups, business interest, and governmental agencies can together supply the force needed to prevent the loss of any more of our historical gems which, from a strictly economic view, can be important tourist attractions as well.

We might here note that the preservation movement in this nation as well as in this state got its start not from government, but from private groups. Nationally, George Washington's Mount Vernon and the Williamsburg Restorations come to mind. Statewide, probably the most significant was Washington's Headquarters in Morristown, now a part of the nation's historic parks system. The Old Barracks in Trenton and Waterloo Village in Stanhope are other prime examples. The Monmouth County Historical Association has been in the forefront of preserving and restoring historic houses and sites, and the Monmouth Battlefield State Park, which grew out of their efforts, is destined to become an important tourist attraction.

Some 11 county and more than 20 local historical societies are now housed in houses of historic interest. Historical associations have preserved the Proprietary House in Perth Amboy and the Old Barracks and Trent House in Trenton, as well as the Walt Whitman House in Camden, Kingsland Manor in Nutley, the Crane House in Montclair, the Drake House in Plainfield, the Dey Mansion in Wayne, and the Nail House in Bridgeton to name a few. The Watson House in Trenton and the Schuyler-Hamilton House in Morristown are among those maintained by the DAR.

Historic villages are adding to the state's attraction as a place to see life as it once was. The state administers the Deserted Village of Allaire, west of Asbury Park, and Batsto, northwest of Atlantic City. Other examples are Speedwell Village in Morristown and Waterloo Village near the Delaware Water Gap. The Middlesex County Park Commission maintains Ye Olde Towne on the Raritan River near Piscataway.

Historic mills around the Great Falls of the Passaic are being preserved by the city of Paterson and the Great Falls Historic Corporation with the help of state and federal funds. This area reminds us of our role in the nation's Industrial Revolution. Private citizens are developing a Victorian Village at Cape May Courthouse. The Cumberland county Historical Society has been doing much to preserve and restore Old Greenwich, where New Jersey's tea party took place. Warren County has recently taken over the Oxford Furnace and its ironmaster's mansion, the Shippen House. Hopefully, a major tourist attraction can be created there centered near North Jersey's once important iron industry.

The Culver Brook Restoration foundation has been struggling to restore a complex at Branchville in Sussex County, as has the Clinton Museum Association at Hunterdon County's Red Mill in Clinton, where a village is slowly taking shape. A unique shopping center has developed at Flemington out of Liberty Village and Turntable Junction. Atlantic County offers the very successful Historic Olde Towne of Smithville 10 miles north of Atlantic City. Wheaton Village at Millville in Cumberland County centers near an operating old-time glass factory, along with a Glass Museum and a group of antique craft shops.

The list goes on and on as New Jersey has finally come into its own as a state with much to offer in the way of buildings and places that typify periods in our nation's past worth preserving and seeing. History happened here in every aspect of our nation's life, and the state's new Office of Historic Preservation and Division of Travel and Tourism are at last mobilizing the efforts necessary to take advantage of their significance for educational, economic, and recreational values. It is a good time to be alive along the trails of New Jersey, and writing about its past.

Historic Sites Act

Until half a century ago there was no national program for preserving our nation's historic buildings or sites. Whatever was preserved was the result of some private individuals or group's interests in this or that place as the spirit moved them. Some important places were thus lost forever. Some of less than national importance, but of keen local interest, might therefore have been preserved through the efforts of inspired local leadership.

Historic preservation in the United States was at best haphazard. The nation was too young to be interested in the past. All eyes were keenly focused on the present and future. New Jersey was very much a part of that scene.

Then came one of the worst national catastrophes this young nation had ever encountered. The stock market crash of 1929 brought a sudden and dramatic end to one of the nation's greatest periods of prosperity following World War I - the roaring 20's. As so often happens in moments of national, family, or individual crises, one becomes introspective. The tendency is to look back at more pleasant or more memorable times. One seeks moments of triumph upon which to hang for stability and purpose, for meaning to it all - and for hope in the future.

So it was during the administration of President Herbert Hoover, at the onset of the Great Depression, the National Park Service, seeing the need to reemphasize the roots from whence we came, established a new division. National historic parks were thus born.

Before leaving office in March of 1933, President Hoover established the Morristown National Historic Park in New Jersey, which thus became the nation's first. It was to become the centerpiece, the model around which was to be built a new system of national historic parks. As the administration of President Franklin Roosevelt took office, measures were undertaken to ward off the effects of the Great Depression. New Jersey's new national park at Morristown was thus able to take immediate advantage of a flow of federal funds and public workers.

Fortunately, in the years following the Civil War, some people felt that the Nation's Revolutionary War sites were worth preserving. Along those lines of thought, a highly effective private organization, the Washington Association of New Jersey, was founded. As a result, the Ford mansion (Washington's military headquarters during much of the Revolution) had been maintained by a private group since the 1870's.

Not much thought had been given, however, to preserving the surrounding woodlands where his troops had encamped during some four separate winters. They were, after all, in great abundance and had always been there. Under those circumstances, it was deemed foolish to take steps to preserve them. Then came the building boom of the 1920's.

Thanks to strong local efforts of Morris County's citizens in the period from 1929 to 1932, parts of Washington's troops' military campgrounds, including the significant Jockey Hollow section, were saved from being felled by tremendous pressure for commercial development. As a result, when public works money and workers became available at the end of 1933 and the beginning of 1934, Morristown's new national historic park site was ready.

National research teams were sent to Morristown where evolving plans for preservation eventually included not only the restoration of the Ford mansion; scholarly researchers decided that the Wick farmhouse and the Guerin house in the Jockey Hollow area were also worth preservation. They further included plans for the restoration of a Revolutionary War camp hospital and officers' huts in the project.

In 1935, Congress passed the Historic Sites Act, greatly expanding the federal government's role in historic preservation. It declared that it was now "national policy to preserve for public use historic sites, buildings and objects of national significance for the inspiration and benefit of the people of the United States." In 1938, a library museum was dedicated at the New Jersey site, and the Morristown restoration project was declared complete in 1940.

Of course, much more has been done to enhance the effectiveness of this National Historic Park in New Jersey in the ensuing years. Included in this ongoing development have been such things as the evolution of the Tempe Wick site into a typical 18th century farm. Also, an interpretive visitor's center has been built at the Jockey Hollow site. More recently, dramatic presentations have added more realism. Since the inception in 1933 of the national historic park, the federal government, with strong citizen involvement, has wrought along the trails of New Jersey fundamental changes in the nation's historic preservation movement.

Sites in Sussex

Ever on the alert for places to go and things to see in New Jersey, my wife Ruth, and I decided the other day to journey north into the beautiful Sussex hills to a place we had heard about that lies between Newton and Franklin. It is pretty countryside anytime of the year. It is invigorating and gives one the feeling of being on top of the earth looking down at it, but away from its problems. Regardless of whether our journey's destination would give us pleasure or disappointment, we were determined the trip there and back would be pleasurable.

In order to further enhance the day's outing, therefore, we decided to go and come back via different routes. We chose as our pathway north one that was to take us past the Rockport State Game Farm and Hayford State Fish Hatcheries. As we continued northward, our journey also skirted along the Allamuchy Mountain State Park. Pretty farm-sites and a picturesque countryside were our constant companions as we crossed the Warren county line and entered Sussex near Cranberry Lake. We continued on through Andover and the pleasant Lake Mohawk resort area, turning northwest above Sparta onto Route 15. Our destination was nearing. Pleasant feelings about our beautiful state were already rewarding us.

We had heard that a little village in Sussex County wanted to bring in more taxes and more employment for its people, but that it didn't want to sacrifice its bucolic atmosphere. The idea was to capitalize on what it already had - using it to accomplish this other purpose.

The promoters of the project suggested that a retention of their country charm could be attained through the creation of a special kind of shopping center at the edge of their existing cluster of antique and craft shops. It would not be the usual commercial development - which destroys the pleasant, relaxed country look. Instead, it would recreate the warm friendly atmosphere of the old-time individual shops, each with their own proprietors.

If you haven't guessed it as yet, our destination was "Ye Olde Lafayette Village" - a spanking new country-colonial complex of stores and shops that gives you the feeling of visiting an old country village instead of an impersonal mall.

If you've been to see "Olde Mystic Village" in Mystic, CT, or the "Peddler's Village" in Lahaska, PA, (outside New Hope), you'll know what to expect.

The people of Lafayette, in Sussex County, wanted a shopping center that would enhance, rather than destroy, the character and history of their community. We believe that this new, "old village," will do just that. Its success and expansion, of course, will depend upon its promoters' belief that people are looking for this old-time atmosphere. And that they will be willing to travel miles to get it. As a result, the trails of New Jersey now have their own "Peddler's Village" - in the hills of Sussex.

Some 60 or more country and colonial shopping outlets are eventually contemplated, along with restaurants with the same motif. Also coming will be a motel and banquet center to accommodate visitors from all over the state and hopefully nearby states. It is located "out in the country," which is what makes it attractive, and makes its developer partners in keeping it that way. It will cater to tourists coming to see such comparatively nearby outdoor attractions as the Delaware Water Gap National Park and the Vernon Valley Action Park and Ski Resort.

Because it will add about $6 million to the little villages' tax base, take care of its own 24-hour security, waste disposal and refuse collection, while providing hundreds of new jobs for local residents, and at the same time retain and enhance the area's rural atmosphere, most people in the area are delighted with their new "tourist" attraction. As for Ruth and I, we are glad we went. We think you would be, too.

Coming home, we headed southwest to Newton, passed by the Whittingham State Wildlife Management Area, and re-crossed back into Warren's rolling farmlands above Johnsonburg. We passed the beautiful Jenny Jump State Forest lands, and eventually reached one of the state's reviving agricultural ventures - a vineyard and winery. It was Warren County's new, "Four Sisters Winery" in White Township. We capped our day's adventure by stopping for a tour of its operation, which is available to the public on weekends.

For a small state, my wife and I have never ceased to wonder at the variety to be found in its remarkable heritage, the diversity of its terrain and croplands, and of the many interesting places there are to visit - along the trails of New Jersey.

Space Farm Zoo and Museum

Back in 1876, great-grandfather Space was attending a one-room schoolhouse in Beemersville, Sussex County, New Jersey. Nothing unusual about that. So were most other Jersey youngsters of that day. It was not even very odd that when the consolidated schools began appearing with the coming of the 20th century, some local folk bought the one-room schoolhouses and adopted them to their own use. So, when the Space family bought the school to which several generations had gone, that did not come across as anything particularly fantastic either.

So why, then, have Ralph Space and the Space family farm become synonymous with Beemersville? And why do people travel from all over the state and nearby states to visit this place? It is not just the old schoolhouse that still stands as a reminder of a simpler day. It is not even the old general store and blacksmith shop, which hearken us back to a by-gone era. Ralph Space, one-time trapper and automobile repairman, has, over his lifetime, managed to preserve a tremendous chunk of early Americana. Talk about the squirrel instinct and you have got some idea of what Ralph Space has accomplished on his Space Farm Zoo and Museum.

You ride up Route 519 through lonely farm country and begin to conjure up in your mind what you will expect to find way out there: perhaps a wired-in tract with half-a-dozen moth-eaten animals roaming inside. You know, the kind you have come across on the roadsides. Maybe a few old showcases in his barn with a pathetic collection of Indian arrowheads.

Unless you are one of those sophisticated cosmopolitans who are impressed by nothing, you will definitely be surprised by what this individual has done. For in the midst of this 425-acre Space family farm, out in the rolling Sussex Countryside, there is both an unexpectedly large zoo, and an unbelievably extensive one-man museum of America's rural heritage.

After leaving your car in the graveled parking area, you cross the quiet country road and enter a very large, white, impressive-looking building. This houses the gift shop and restaurant downstairs amidst stuffed animals, rifle collections, early jukeboxes, and other collector's items of a by-gone era. Upstairs is a surprisingly extensive museum of weaponry, dolls, Indian artifacts, glassware, etc. which leaves you wondering. How, you ask yourself, could one man, or even family, have accomplished all of this?

Outside of this building, there are 45 acres of roaming wildlife. They are kept in large, fenced-in open areas that would put any big-city zoo to shame. Though North American animals

111

predominate, there are enough good representations of tigers, lions, and monkeys present to give added interest to those who just want to see animals. The various species of bear, deer, elk, American bison, wolves, sheep, goats, and fowl joined with a herd of Texas Longhorn cattle gives the place a distinctively American flavor. One expects to see a group of cowboys riding off into the horizon.

The Space farm, now in the possession of the third generation of the Space family, is an operative farm providing the hay and grain necessary for feeding the animals. It also contains an extensive mink ranch, which brings in adequate income totally divorced from the zoo and museum. Originally not intended as an income-producing enterprise, the zoo and museum are now being advertised as a definite tourist attraction with the hope of being self-supporting in their own right.

The Space Museum has the most extensive collection of old cars, carriages, coaches, wagons, sleighs, tools, farm implements, kitchen utensils, and other bits of old-Americana you could hope to see anywhere. All of these items are housed in a museum complex of eight buildings. They are located between the main entrance building and the zoo and, in your emphasis on the zoo, might be missed. But whatever you do, do not skip them!

If you have not visited this extra-ordinary, one-man dream operation in the heart of northwestern New Jersey's farmlands you owe it to yourself and family to do so. It is just another of those interesting sites to see as you travel along the trails of New Jersey. And it adds further proof to what you have grown more and more to believe that though small in size, New Jersey is large in things to do and see.

Millbrook Village

As I have mentioned before, many a village sprang up in New Jersey's northwestern frontier country following the arrival of a gristmill. Warren County's Millbrook Village was just such a place. Soon after a sufficient number of farmers moved into a region, there was always an urgent need for a miller to settle in at a nearby swift-moving stream to grind their grain. Grinding their own grain was one task both the farmer and his wife were soon anxious to abandon. Home grinding was both such a time-consuming and arduous chore that most farmers would take on two days of rough travel over difficult Indian paths to the nearest miller to avoid subjecting their wives to doing it.

Of course the first task a pioneer farmer had to undertake in arriving at a new site was the erection of a crude shelter. Those trees best suited to the building of a cabin were first to be cut in clearing a site for farming. Most of the land was heavily forested. Clearing it was a backbreaking job that was undertaken in small sections at a time. After the cabin, trees would be cut for crude shelters for the farm animals. Other farm building, such as the more elaborate barns, would have to wait - often for the arrival of a sawmill. Many of these outlying gristmills were eventually joined by a sawmill. Thus did the nucleus of a village begin to take shape.

In the meantime, those early farmers put into piles those smaller trees and brush that were cleared and were not suited for fencing. They would be burned during the winter months. The huge piles of wood ashes that resulted were not wasted. Water was run through the ashes and lye was evaporated from it in large iron pots. This was then boiled with leftover animal fats from cooking, and made into crude soap. Surplus potash derived from the wood-burning process could also be sold. It was in great demand. The arrival of a merchant operating a general store provided the place where a farmer could sell it. Usually it was bartered.

With the arrival of a sawmill, the original cabin often became the kitchen of a more elaborate farmhouse. How elaborate depended upon the prosperity of the farmer. He often built on to the original cabin with cut wood from the mill. The larger storage barns and stables and other farm buildings were also erected with wood that could be more precisely and easily cut to order at the sawmill.

Warren County's historic Millbrook Village is a typical example of the many little hamlets that began to grow in the once wild New Jersey countryside to fulfill the needs of its early isolated farmers and their families. It was in 1832 that Abram Garris built his gristmill over a brook that flowed through the region near the Old Mine road in what is now the very northern tip of Warren County. In time, a flourishing little village sprang up around the Garris gristmill

113

as other entrepreneurs moved nearby to service the local farmers. In the period following the Civil War, Millbrook had grown to a population of 75 people with 19 major buildings. The George Trauger family was among the most prosperous at that time.

The blacksmith was another early craftsman to appear in any village, and Millbrook was no exception. In addition to making many of the iron tools needed by the farmer and his family, he repaired them, sharpened blades and made horseshoes. The general store was also vital to any community's life. It provided everything from hardware to dry goods to medicines. Its merchant-owner often bartered his goods with the local farmers for their produce. He usually served as the village postmaster as well. A shoemaker was another early craftsman to arrive in the village. Coopers, cabinetmakers, wheelwrights and weavers all began appearing in Millbrook by the late 1800's.

Millbrook continued to thrive throughout the remainder of the 19th century. A school, a church, and a local cemetery all became part of its flourishing cultural and religious life. Then, as the 20th century arrived it brought with it, better transportation to bigger places. Millbrook, like so many others, lost its purpose in being. It began to decline. In time, its people left for places with greater opportunities. It became a ghost town. Today, historic Millbrook Village is being recreated as an example of what those typical, rural, mill-centered villages of northwestern New Jersey were like back in their heyday in the late 1800's.

Through three summer months Millbrook comes back to life along the trails of New Jersey. Volunteers dressed in period costumes perform traditional crafts much as they might have in a crossroads mill-village of 100 years ago. They are also helping the National Park Service to reconstruct the village's old gristmill, as well as other old buildings. To help celebrate the rebirth, "Millbrook Days" are held the first weekend in October. Show your support of this intriguing venture in Warren County. Be there!

Waterloo Village

Living in or near small, friendly villages nestled in a rural setting, couched in a society chiefly centered around agriculture; that was the way of life most Americans followed until the ever-increasing influence of the industrial revolution forced a bland urban existence upon them. As they increasingly abandoned their farms for life in the cities, problems beset them with which many were not prepared to cope. As the years rolled on, this compact, unfriendly, city life began to take its toll. In recent times we have been fondly seeking to recapture that way of life that most Americans once embraced. The movement "out into the country" is just one response. A "nostalgia for the past" that has spawned the creation of a number of historic villages is still another. There is an attempt afoot to recapture that less hectic, much simpler period in America's past.

My wife, Ruth, our eldest son, Peter, his wife, Kathy, and our grandson Erik, along with another son, Henry, visited such a site this summer at nearby Waterloo Village in Allamuchy Mountain State Park. I mentioned in a previous article a visit to Sturbridge Village in Massachusetts, and expressed the hope that such an historic site could someday come into existence in New Jersey. I believe that the nucleus of one such place exists here at Waterloo. I would urge those of you who want to encourage such a development to happen here, to show your support by both visiting Waterloo Village and encouraging others to do likewise.

Like all of life, the village is always changing. My wife and I were delighted to find a number of additions to Waterloo that had not been there the last time we visited. It has become much more a "living" museum. Two mills are now in operation - a working saw mill and a gristmill. Though we only witnessed the gristmill, we were assured that the sawmill was operative, as well. Other activities have also been added, and some exciting new ones are being planned. The key is public support.

Because the area was once a meeting place for various members of the Minsee tribe of the Lenape nation, a site has been selected there for the development of a "live" project never before attempted in New Jersey's state parks. An authentic, full-sized eastern woodlands Indian village of the Lenape nation is being undertaken by John Kraft, son of the well-known expert on New Jersey Indians, and Seton Hall University Professor, Herbert C. Kraft. He hopes that the Indian village will be in operation by next year. If he can break through the state's building code bureaucracy, it will.

In the meantime, a movie, excellently done dioramas and displays, plus a very fine oral presentation by John Kraft, himself an experienced anthropologist, is taking place at the village's Carriage Barn and Visitor Orientation Center. This program and display itself is well worth the visit to Waterloo, and is a must for the many Indian-life enthusiasts residing in New Jersey. Books and other materials on the subject are also on sale there.

Waterloo was once the site of the Andover Forge, established by the firm of Allen and Turner of Philadelphia in 1760. In fact, it had its beginnings as a community as a result of the iron industry. The first sawmills and gristmills in the village were built by the ironworks - as well as the forge. Though the site of the original forge still remains, a restored one has yet to be undertaken. There is a blacksmith shop in operation, and the old Ironmaster's House is open as well.

The original settlement was named Andover Forge in honor of Joseph Turner's birthplace back in England. Waterloo came into existence as a name for the village when the ironworks, after a period of decline, was revived following the War of 1812. The dictator who had been running rampant over the Europe of that day was Napoleon. In 1815 he was defeated at the Battle of Waterloo. The new ironworks was named The Waterloo Foundry in honor of that defeat. Since it was the main business of the village, the name came to be associated with it. Even after iron's decline, the name stuck.

Because the Morris Canal gave new life to the floundering community when it was built in 1831, the Canal Society of New Jersey has established a Canal Museum at Waterloo Village as well. It is located in the former home of Harrison Smith, a canal boatman. Excellent views of segments of this once important canal are to be seen in the village, and restorations of a lock and an inclined plane are in the making. Dioramas of the operation of the canal are on view in the museum.

The Sussex and Morris and Essex railroads intersected at Waterloo Station starting in 1854. When they chose to bypass the village in 1901, they brought about its demise. A complete history of transportation along the trails of NJ could be accomplished by including the role of the railroad era at Waterloo as well. Maybe the railroad buffs out there will work on it!

Clinton Museum Village

While visiting Historic Millbrook Village several weeks ago with my wife, Ruth, I was reminded once again of just how many villages came into existence as a result of their mill sites. Some still hold on to names reflecting those early beginnings. But more, like Hackettstown, have dropped that original designation and taken on another name - usually that of a prominent citizen of some later time.

The majority of those original mill sites are long-since gone. The purpose that brought them into being has been lost to antiquity. Millbrook was one of those villages that lost its mills and was about to lose its very existence when the National Park Service and a group of volunteers, "the Millbrook Village Society," came to its rescue. Through their efforts, Millbrook Village is having a rebirth. It is being both recreated and expanded to serve a new purpose. This and future generations will be able to understand first-hand what rural life was like during the period of the 1800's along the frontier region of northwestern New Jersey.

These industrious volunteers who make up "the Millbrook Village Society" are seeking both financial and volunteer assistance so that they may also rebuild the two original working mills that gave this village its birth - a gristmill and a sawmill. It is a big undertaking and they welcome all the help they can get.

Another place that was born as a result of its original mills, and reborn as a result of some determined citizens, is the Clinton Historic Museum Village in Hunterdon County. There were two mills where the South Branch of the Raritan converges with Spruce Run. They served the needs of the local farmers. The little community that eventually sprung up around them came to be known as Hunt's Mills, after Daniel Hunt who in 1782 made them the center of local activity.

117

"The Old Red Mill" is the hub of today's Clinton Historical Museum Village. It stands on 10 ½-acres at the edge of an amphitheater of limestone cliffs. The Museum Village, in addition to two old lime kilns and a stone-crusher from its lime-quarrying days, contains such other features as a general store, with barbershop and post office, a little one-room school house, a typical log cabin home with an herb garden, and such other buildings as might have been found in a small mill-centered village of the 18th and 19th century.

The mill at Clinton Museum Village was originally built around 1763 by a miller named David McKinney. It ground flaxseeds to make linseed oil. The crushed seeds were then formed into cakes and sold as feed for farm animals. Today it houses four stories of exhibits as well as an operational mill. The exhibits portray various farm family activities and crafts covering some 200 years of northwestern New Jersey heritage. The mill can be seen in operation on the top floor. It is open to the public from April to November.

Mahlon Kirdbride bought the mill around 1770 and sold it six months later to Mahlon Taylor. Taylor turned it into a gristmill. Daniel Hunt's arrival in 1728 brought with it the operation of two mills and the gradual development of a thriving little village around them. It came to be called Hunt's Mills. His son, Ralph, took over in 1809. The family continued operating them as a flaxmill and a gristmill until 1828.

About that time, two partners, Taylor and Bray, bought them. They, in time, were influential in renaming the village, Clinton, after Gov. DeWitt Clinton of New York who had become a national hero of that day for his role in developing a popular route to the west, the Erie Canal. They were operated as pumice and graphite mills by Taylor and Bray. The nearby limestone quarry and kilns were run by the Mulligan family. Between 1834 and 1903, first John Snyder and later Philip Gulick owned the Old Red Mill. Once again, it was used as a gristmill to grind the grain of the local farmers. Between 1903 and 1920, the Tomson family ground talc and graphite at the mill. After that, it gradually fell into disuse.

In 1960, a group of five men bought if for its historic value. They worked unceasingly to restore it. In 1963, the Old Red Mill at Clinton was re-opened as a non-profit museum of 18th and 19th century life around a mill. Today, the Historic Clinton Museum

Village, the Clinton House Inn, the Hunterdon Art Center (which opened at the second mill), and Clinton's burgeoning shopping area are developing into another of those delightfully pleasant tourist attractions now popping up along the trails of New Jersey in a nostalgic attempt to recapture some of the state's charming bygone eras. Both the Millbrook and Clinton Historic Villages deserve your support.

Liberty State Park

One cannot write a column on New Jersey, at a time when the whole nation has been celebrating the 100th birthday of Lady Liberty in Liberty Harbor, and focusing its attention on a mighty national symbol just 1,750 feet from the state's shoreline, without pausing to reflect upon the New Jersey connection. A ferry service to Liberty Island operates out of the 700-acre Liberty State Park just off the NJ Turnpike in Jersey City. It would be worth your time, after the dust settles, to take a trip out to see the refurbished Statue of Liberty - especially if you have never been there.

Aside from the fact that Lady Liberty sits in New Jersey's front yard (or should I say harbor), and that it can best be reached from a ferry ride that leaves Liberty State Park in New Jersey every hour, it was also first dedicated on Oct. 28, 1886, by the only President of the United States who was born in New Jersey - Stephen Grover Cleveland. And, when President Cleveland came up from Washington, DC on Oct. 27, 1886, to participate in the dedication ceremonies, the presidential party, which included members of his cabinet, arrived by train at the Jersey City railroad station. After the program, they also returned to Jersey City for their rail trip back to Washington.

As you stand on the New Jersey shore, you cannot help but be impressed by this enormous symbol of our national purpose, which stands more that 305 feet tall from the bottom of its base to the tip of its torch. The new torch itself is now a gold-plated flame lighted by 200 candlepower lamps. The base has been turned into a museum - emphasizing our immigrant heritage. As you view the statue from the harbor, it is the New Jersey shoreline that serves as its backdrop - a

119

fact that was not lost upon the developers of the state's most used of all its recreation facilities, Liberty State Park.

As those millions of immigrants arrived in this country each year after 1892, it was through the portals of still another national shrine even closer to the Jersey shoreline, the Immigration Center at Ellis Island. This historic gateway is also being refurbished for its 100th birthday in 1992. Those who passed the required tests there were then boarded on ferries that took them to the Central RR of New Jersey's Terminal Building in Jersey City (now a part of the Liberty State Park). At that currently restored building there were some 20 tracks of departing trains awaiting them, which embarked the eager immigrants to various points throughout America - and a new life. The CRRNJ Terminal was built in 1889. It is now officially listed as a State and National Historic Site. The whole area is thus steeped in memory-provoking history of a great and inspiring era in America's past.

President Cleveland's New Jersey birthplace at 207 Bloomfield Avenue in Caldwell is also an historic shrine that could be visited on weekends while taking in the Statue of Liberty and related sites. Cleveland was born there on March 18, 1837, while it served as the Manse for the Caldwell Presbyterian Church. His father, the Rev. Richard S. Cleveland, was pastor there from 1832, when the Manse was first built, until 1841, when he accepted a call to a church in Fayeteville, NJ.

The town of Caldwell itself was named after still another historic New Jersey figure, the Rev. James Caldwell. Though Caldwell was born in Virginia in 1734, he was New Jersey's "Fighting Parson" during the American Revolution. He gained national folk-hero status for his famous cry, "Give 'em Watts boys," uttered at the Battle of Springfield in June of 1780 when the call went up and down the line that the citizen-soldiers were running out of wadding for their muskets.

The "Fighting Parson," then pastor of the Elizabethtown Presbyterian Church, hearing of the urgent need, entered the Springfield Presbyterian Church, now the site of the nation's smallest national park, and grabbed handfuls of the Isaac Watts hymnals lying there. Caldwell then rode up and down the lines of embattled farmers, passing the hymnals out to the minutemen, from which they took the paper for the much-needed wadding.

The historic Caldwell House in Union, (the Connecticut Farms) can also be visited. It was while sitting at the window of that house that Caldwell's wife, Hannah, was mortally shot by a passing British trooper during the Battle of Connecticut Farms. Local farmers were so enraged by this act that they fought evermore fiercely. Caldwell himself was shot on Nov. 24, 1781, and is buried at the graveyard of the historic First Presbyterian Church of Elizabeth. These are just a few more of the many tales to be found along the trails of New Jersey.

The Deserted Village of the Watchungs

When we hear of "ghost towns" chances are that we conjure up thoughts of the old west. Most people relate that term to mining towns in the Rocky Mountains whose mother lodes gave out. A picture comes to mind of tumbleweed gently rolling down the main street past false-front taverns, a general store, and a hotel. Seldom, if ever, do we think of it in relation to New Jersey. Unfortunately, very little of New Jersey's romantic past has been exploited. Our image is too much that of an industrial present.

New Jersey, however, does have a great many "ghost towns" whose stories are linked to its dramatic days of yore. Most of them, but not all, are in the Pinelands of South Jersey, and are connected to its once thriving bog-iron industry. Two of those, which were taken over by the state and restored as historic sites, I have already written about. The Deserted Village of Allaire and Batsto Village. Another restored "ghost town", this one in the midst of Allamuchy Mountain State Park, that I have mentioned before is the old canal town of Waterloo. Its demise came with the folding of the Morris Canal. Waterloo's past, it was once called Andover Forge, also had its link to the early iron industry.

But the "ghost town" that I will talk about today is a little-known and not much developed one in New Jersey's crowded northeast. Nestled in the Watchung Mountains of Union County, this "Deserted Village" is part of the Union County Park System. It is located in the midst of the heavily wooded Watchung Reservation. Unlike the south Jersey "ghost towns," whose rise and fall centered on one industry, the "Deserted Village of the Watchungs" had a varied past.

From prehistoric times until the early 1700's, it was an Indian village. It was the winter quarters of a tribe of the Lenni Lenapes, who spent the warmer months fishing along the Raritan Bay. The Lenni Lenape also gave the "wach unks" their name. It means "high hills." Sold through their chief, Warinaco, to the Elizabethtown Associates, 424 acres were purchased from them by Peter Wilcox in 1736. He built a house, saw mill, gristmill, a dam and a millrace. With settlers from Great Britain he obtained the manpower to operate a copper mine. The area became known as Peter's Hill. During the American Revolution, between 1775 and 1783, a powder mill was added. This continued to operate through the War of 1812.

It was not until 1845 that an actual village, known as Feltsville, came into existence. In that year, David Felt bought 760-acres to develop his bookbinding and papermaking village. To the three mills and dam he added his Manor House and barn, 13 double cottages and two, boarding houses for his workers, a school, a church, store, blacksmith shop, warehouse, and a dye-house.

Known as "King David," Felt ruled his 300 to 400 villagers like a feudal lord. It was a company town so typical of that era in our history. Built to be as nearly self-contained as possible, his workers were subjected to his rules not only in the conduct of their work, but in their private lives as well. When southern slave-owners argued that northern factory workers were practically held in bondage, too, they were not far off. The uprooting Civil War period, however, dealt a fatal blow to "King David's" feudal manor and the village entered a period of decline.

Between 1864 and 1882, another entrepreneur, Dr. Samuel Townsend, "The Sarsaparilla King," bought and ran the village. He tried unsuccessfully to manufacture sarsaparilla there. But being unable to adapt the mills to that endeavor, he shifted his operation to the making of cigars. He even grew his own tobacco, brought in black field hands from the South and Cuban cigar makers. The village could no longer be held together after the war, however, and it went into decline between 1880 and 1882. By 1882, it finally succumbed and became a "ghost town."

The last attempt at its survival was made by Warren Ackerman. He bought the tract and operated it as a successful resort village in an era when city folk who could afford it were flooding to "the country" for a respite. Known as Glenside, it was a prosperous vacation spot for several decades prior to World War I. With changes in our lifestyle brought about by the Great War, it too folded. By 1919, it once again became a "ghost town." Finally purchased by the County Park Commission in 1930, it is now operated as a part of its Education Center. Visitors to the trails of the Watchung Reservation can, with a little imagination, recapture several chapters of New Jersey's heritage by a tour of this "Deserted Village" now hidden away in its tranquil woods.

Great Adventure

New Jersey is one of the six states in the United States that was chosen to be a part of the nationally famous "Six Flags Amusement Parks" family. Texas, Georgia, California, Florida, and Missouri are the other five. The fact that this large, successful company chose New Jersey as one of its sites tells us something special about our state.

It had to meet the corporation's three criteria: 1) being in the heart of a major population center; 2) being a popular tourist attraction region in its own right; and 3) being able to provide a large, open-space area suitable for a major regional theme park with adequate parking and traffic-flow facilities.

New Jersey, the most densely populated state in the entire United States and lying between two of the nation's largest cities, New York and Philadelphia, certainly met the first criteria. With some 130 miles of the nation's finest saltwater beaches from Sandy Hook to Cape May drawing visitors from throughout the United States and foreign countries, New Jersey was well on its way toward meeting the second criteria.

In addition to its world-renowned beaches, however, it also has hundreds of beautiful lakes nestled in wooded mountain resorts.

There are the increasingly popular ski areas for winter sports enthusiasts, the famous Meadowlands Sports Complex and the "Queen of Resorts," Atlantic City, fast becoming the casino capital of the world.

Add to these the internationally known Pine Barrens, some one-third of the nation's historic sites related to the American Revolution, natural sites such as the Delaware Water Gap National Park, and the Great Falls of the Passaic, and you begin to realize that New Jersey certainly does meet the second criteria. In fact, tourism is New Jersey's foremost industry today! It now employs more than 175,000 people, and generates more than $7.5 billion annually in income.

Surprisingly enough, the nation's most densely populated state also met the third criteria. There are still many millions of acres of open-space in New Jersey. Mid-way between the state's northernmost tip at High Point, and its most southerly end at Cape May point, is the northern edge of its Pine Barrens. Surrounded by thousands of acres of open-space, yet reasonably accessible to the population centers of New York, New Jersey and Pennsylvania, is Jackson Township and there in Jackson is New Jersey's "Six Flags Great Adventure."

Its location having been scientifically arrived at, some 1,700-acres of developed entertainment now lie in the midst of thousands of acres of undeveloped pinelands. This makes it uniquely suitable to the third criteria.

With more than 100 amusement rides ranging from the 3200 feet of "Rolling Thunder" to the northeast's only man-made river, the "Roaring Rapids," the park provides a variety of daring to pleasant experiences. Its zoo, a 450-acre drive-through safari, has more than 2,000 wild and exotic animals. It is the largest outside of Africa. Its aquatic shows, both on the Great Lake of the park, with nationally famous water ski experts, and in the Aqua Stadium where dolphins perform, are well worth the visit alone. And, even if you are not particularly a nature lover, you will enjoy the beauty of the park's thousands of flowers set in the midst of its beautiful, professionally landscaped woodland gardens.

The Six Flags Parks Corporation started in 1961 with the opening of its first regional park, the "Six Flags Over Texas" in Dallas. Its park in Atlanta, "Six Flags Over Georgia" was next to be opened in 1967. The third regional park to be established was in St. Louis, MO where in 1971, "Six Flags Over Mid-America" was opened. New Jersey's "Six Flags Great Adventure" was added in 1977. It finally became a coast to coast institution when "Six Flags Magic Mountain" was added in Los Angeles in 1979.

Long touted by man for its unique location, and always admired by its long-time residents for its many attractive settings, New Jersey has finally come of age as a tourist mecca by being scientifically spit-out of the "Six Flags" computers as an ideal location for its northeastern park. With over 3 million visitors a season, New Jersey's Great Adventure has become one of the nation's largest parks of its kind, and growing more popular each year. If you live in New Jersey, you owe it to yourself to visit this major Park at least once. But, if it is to be a one-time visit, be sure you plan your time well in order to get it all in.

Burlington

About halfway between Trenton and Philadelphia along the banks of the Delaware River lies another historic New Jersey town worth visiting. Burlington can be reached from Route 130 after leaving Bordentown. A walk in the area along Broad Street, High Street and the Delaware River will bring you into contact with an interesting collection of Jersey's diverse heritage. At the foot of High Street, for example, is Burlington Island, where Swedes set up an outpost in 1624 to carry on trade with the Indians.

Burlington itself was founded in 1677 by a group of Quakers, who, under William Penn, had received permission to settle in the newly partitioned west Jersey Province. Burlington became West Jersey's capital in 1681. The little, redbrick Lord's Office still stands on Broad Street near High. Along with the Lords of East Jersey Office in Perth Amboy, it is one of the two oldest corporate offices still operating in the nation. It contains the Concessions and Agreement of 1677, guaranteeing such basic rights as that of the secret ballot, religious toleration, and trial by jury. The General Council still meets there once a year to dispose of any new unclaimed lands west of the province line.

On High Street near Broad is the Old Friends Meeting House. This one, built in 1784, replaced the original meeting house built by the founding Quakers, which had been in use for 100 years by that time. Among the graves in the cemetery in the rear is that of an Indian Chief, Ockanikon, symbolic of the good relations that existed between those early Quaker settles and the local members of the Delaware (Lenni Lenape) tribe. Three houses in the area, the Gov. Bloomfield House, the Thomas Revell House and the Boudinot House, could tell tales of the American Revolution and of participants in it. All are privately owned.

A state Historic Site, also on High Street in Burlington, illustrates several other events in American history. It is the James Lawrence House, which was built around 1742. James Lawrence, American Naval Hero, was born there in 1781 and remained until joining the Navy at 17. It was James Lawrence's famous cry, "Don't give up the ship," which became the motto of the US Navy. Lawrence gave that command while lying mortally wounded aboard his ship, "Chesapeake," after bloody hand-to-hand combat with the crew of the British ship, "Shannon," during the War of 1812. In a previous war with Tripoli in the early 1800's, Lawrence had heroically boarded the captured American ship, "Philadelphia," under enemy fire and burned it - both to tie up the harbor and to keep the Tripolitans from using it. Five American naval vessels have since been named after this famous Jerseyman.

A few doors from the Lawrence House is the James Fennimore Cooper birthplace, which was built around 1780. Cooper was born there in 1789. The Burlington county Historical Society has since turned it into a museum. Among the documents on display is part of Cooper's manuscript for his novel, "The Spy." Another famous Jerseyman, John Honeyman, is believed to have been the hero of this book about America's intelligence network during the Revolution.

Another of Cooper's novels, "The Water Witch," brought international attention to New Jersey's Atlantic Highlands. This Jersey port area was the setting for the hero of the mysterious shop in this story. "Skimmer of the Sea," as he was called, operated his vessel "The Water Witch," from out of the coves in this area of Sandy Hook Bay. Cooper whose father went on to found Cooperstown, NY, where he grew up, died there in 1851. But his death came only after he wrote many, many more stories depicting various aspects of American life in the early 1800's, and getting involved in all sorts of international disputes. The poor coverage he received from the American press during the intervening years eventually led Cooper to sue for damages. Among his better known books today are probably the five · Leatherstocking novels, "The Pioneers," "The Last of the Mohicans," "The Prairie," "The Pathfinder," and the "The Deerslayer." Many books were also written about such diverse topics as the Sea, Democracy, and the American way of life.

There are other places of historic interest in Burlington, including the house in which Gen. U.S. Grant's family was living while he was commander of the Union armies during the Civil War. But they are far too numerous to mention here. From those I have brought to your attention, however, you can get a flavor of the diversity of tales related to America's heritage here on the trails of New Jersey.

Batsto Village

Inland from New Jersey's south shore, and lying in the midst of more than a million acres of National Pinelands Reserve, is the nearly 100,000-acre Wharton State Forest. Flowing through this forest of pines and cedar is the Mullica River. It was named after Erik Mullica, a 17th century Swedish explorer of the region. The Mullica flows into Great Bay just north of the Brigantine National Wildlife Refuge. Along the Mullica, on the southwestern edge of the Wharton Tract, just beyond Pleasant Mills, is another of New Jersey's restored bog-iron communities - a living monument to New Jersey's role in that once-important industry.

Back in colonial days, and during the American Revolution and the War of 1812, Batsto Village was a thriving iron-making settlement of some 1,000 people. The Batsto Furnace was built in 1766 by Charles Read. Read, presiding at the foreclosure auction of the site, which then housed a sawmill, noted that the area contained the necessary elements for a successful iron-making industry. Aside from large deposits of bog-iron, there were endless forests for the making of charcoal, and power from the swift-moving Batsto Creek. Nearby in Pleasant Mills was the labor force he would need to operate his iron-making enterprise. A furnace was soon built along Batsto Creek. A few years later, a forge was built at nearby Nescochague Creek. Permits to dam these waterways had to be obtained first from the Assembly. Read obviously had political influence.

Within two years of the erection of the Batsto Iron Works, Read sold out to four partners. They continued the operation until 1770 when Col. John Cox, an ardent Philadelphia patriot, along with a partner, Charles Thompson, bought them out. Thompson sold his share to Cox in 1773. Cox expanded the Iron Works to include the manufacture of a large variety of iron products. With the onset of the American Revolution, he turned the Iron Works into an important supplier for Washington's Continental Army. So important was Batsto's contribution, in fact, that his ironworkers were exempt from military service. Cox also played a role at Batsto in running the British blockade. His privateers were responsible for smuggling goods up the Mullica River, and then transporting them overland to the American Army. In 1778, he was made assistant Quartermaster General by the Congress. Near the end of that year, he sold Batsto for a handsome profit. A British attempt to capture the village was repulsed, though they destroyed nearby Chestnut Creek.

A fighting Quaker named Joseph Ball, who had managed the Ironworks under Cox, gained control of Batsto in 1779. Then a William Richards bought Ball out in 1784, and turned Batsto into a feudal estate, which he ruled like the Lord of the Manor. The Richards family remained in control for the remainder of the village's life. Jesse Richards Sr. was the prime mover during most of those years. Changing times and diminishing bog-iron saw the production of iron diminish. But by using imported iron, Jesse retained iron as Batsto's main source of prosperity. Other industries, however, such as sawmills, brick making, cranberry, culture, shipbuilding, were added by the enterprising Jesse to help insure the villages' continuity.

In 1846, while the iron industry was still in operation, Jesse Richards decided that a new venture was needed. And so he build the Batsto Glass Works. Unfortunately, fire destroyed the first Glass House in 1848, and the second in 1851. And fires continued to plague this venture over the next 28 years of its operation. The death of Jesse

Richards Sr. in 1854, however, marked the real turning point in the Batsto enterprises. None of his sons possessed his skill or drive. Continuing fires, along with a series of strikes beginning in 1867, plus the growing disinterest of the remaining Richards's family, brought on the eventual demise of Batsto Village.

A tremendous fire swept through the Village in 1874 providing the final blow. By 1876, Joseph Wharton purchased the property for only $14,000. It remained in this family until the state took it over in 1954 when it had become a ghost town.

Today, a stroll through the restored Village of Batsto, starting at the Visitor's Center, makes an interesting journey into the past, and a day's outing away from the beaches in and around Atlantic City. The Ironmaster's Mansion, a blacksmith's shop, a gristmill, company store, sawmill, the sites of the iron and glass furnaces, and the restored workers' cottages are among the sites to see. On the edge of this unbelievably vast wilderness stands this unique living monument to a page out of New Jersey and the nation's industrial heritage.

Atlantic City: "Queen of Resorts"

Unlike people, it is sometimes far more difficult to pinpoint the birth date of a city. Such was the case for New Jersey's "Queen of Resorts." Even with the existence of records, there is disagreement as to which date should be regarded as its birth date.

We can, of course, rule out that unknown period when the Lenape Indians used to set up their temporary villages on Absegami Island (or Absecon as later white settlers called it) because no permanent settlement of any kind arose there. The same is true of the time when swarms of pirates were attracted there as a temporary haven.

But what of those late dates? Which was its actual birth date?

We know, for example, that Jeremiah Leeds came to settle on Absecon Island back in 1783. Should that be established as the year of its birth? In fact, the Leeds family had become a well-established institution in that area by the time a young graduate of Columbia College Medical School arrived in 1820.

Dr. Jonathan Pitney, who is often called the "Father of Atlantic City," was embued with the possibilities of the island as a health resort. He spent the next 49 years promoting it as a place where people could come to absorb the salt air and salt water and recover from their illnesses or, if healthy, maintain it, by drinking in its heady atmosphere. Perhaps the date of his arrival should be considered its birth date.

Throughout the ensuing years, Dr. Pitney involved himself in the commercial and political life of the area in his attempts to "sell" its attributes. In 1837, he was behind a move to have Atlantic County separated from Gloucester, and became its first freeholder director. From 1845 to 1851, he enlisted the support of Gen. Enoch Doughty in a campaign to have a railroad built to their island paradise from Philadelphia, 56 miles to the northwest. They finally gained a charter in 1852. Is that its birthday?

Some say the birth date was in January 1853, when a railroad engineer named Richard B. Osborne presented his plans for the city on a gigantic map entitled, "Atlantic City." This was, after all, the first time that its name appeared in public. The railroad's backers loved it.

It was Osborne, too, who gave the streets running from the beach to the marshes the names of the states, and those paralleling the ocean the names of the seven seas - Atlantic, Pacific, Arctic, Baltic, Adriatic, Mediterranean, and Caspian.

Maybe he should be called the "Father of Atlantic City."

When the first train of the Camden and Atlantic Railroad finally pulled out of Philadelphia on July 1, 1854, headed for "Atlantic City," it was a fact; the name had stuck!

A new Absecon Lighthouse soon was warning ships off of its coast. That lighthouse continued to light its waters until 1932. Yet, since Atlantic City was also incorporated in 1854, there are those who consider that year as its birth date.

Well, whatever date is chosen as the birth date of New Jersey's "Queen of Atlantic Resorts," there are other dates that are also important landmarks in its continuing saga of growth and development. When Pitney died in August of 1869, he did have the pleasure of knowing that his "health spa" had achieved popular favor.

But much more was still to come! Because people were constantly dragging sand from the beaches onto the fine rugs in the plush new hotels that were rising along the city's "Great White Way," Atlantic Avenue, Alex Boardman, a railroader, got the idea of building a boardwalk along its beachfront. There, people could shed the sand before returning to their hotel.

Thus was born in 1879 the famed, "Boardwalk in Atlantic City." Today, it stands above the sand, 60-feet wide, and 5 miles long. That first boardwalk was only 8-feet wide and was built directly on the sand.

In 1876, promoters conceived of the idea of a gimmick to bring in the tourists before the summer season. And so was introduced the city's famed "Easter Parade." In 1882 the Steel Pier came into being to attract more tourists. "Salt Water Taffy" came along in 1883 - the result of an accidental wave of seawater over a taffy stand during a violent storm. At the height of the era of the "Gay Nineties," picture postcards were introduced to the nation at Atlantic City as an advertising gimmick. It soon became a national fad.

At the beginning of the "Roaring Twenties" the "Miss America Pageant" was born to extend the season into September. In 1929 the then world's largest convention center was opened. Big-name bands appeared regularly.

For a time following World War II, bad times fell upon the city until 1976, when the voters approved legalized gambling. Since the first casino opened its doors in May, 1978, the trails of New Jersey have seen a rebirth of that place where Dr. Pitney envisioned his "health spa" now so long ago.

Wheaton Village

As we continue southward along New Jersey's famous shoreline, we find ourselves at her southernmost tip - Cape May. It was named after the Dutch navigator, Cornelius Jacobsen Mey, who explored the region in the early 1600's. It was first settled, however, mostly by New England whalers and fishermen in the early 1700's. By early 1800, it had already gained renown as a seashore resort of national prominence, particularly favored by the southern plantation owners. Today, it is most famous for its Victorian architecture, and as a summer mecca for large numbers of French-Canadians. Since I have already devoted a previous column to the history of Cape May itself, we spend this one visiting some of its interesting nearby sites.

After leaving Ocean City, there are a series of well-known resort communities along the cape's Atlantic shoreline - Sea Isle City, Avalon, Stone Harbor and the Wildwoods, as well as Cape May and Cape May Point. Sandy beaches, saltwater fishing, boating and strolling the boardwalks are among the typical shore activities they all share. The Wildwoods also offer extensive amusement rides. Cape May, in addition to its Victorian architecture, has its "diamonds" and its lighthouse. There are dozens of private campgrounds on the cape; while nearby Belleplain State Park in Woodbine offers camping facilities, too. An abundance of private, boat marinas are found throughout the region. Six miles west of Wildwood on fishing Creek Road are the famed "Hedge Gardens." There you will see enough sculptured hedges to suit your fancy. There are 175 varieties of hedges in this unique place. At Cold Spring is a recreated Historical South Jersey Village.

As you begin to make your way north along the resorts on the bay side, you are in Jersey's "Tidewater Country." Both Bridgeton on the Cohansey and Millville on the Maurice are up-water towns. The Swedes were first to settle this region in the 1630's. In fact, the Maurice River is supposed to have been named after a Swedish ship, "The Prince Maurice." In Bivalve, at the mouth of the Maurice River, you can see some of Jersey's large oyster fleets tied up. There, too, you can learn about still another of the states varied specialties - the oyster industry. Visits to the oyster shucking houses, the shellfish Research Center and the Oyster Museum are all available to those who are interested.

Journeying inland paralleling the Maurice River, you will arrive in Millville. Four miles to the east is Holly Farms, USA, containing the largest holly orchard in the entire nation! A holly museum and gift shop makes this an attractive tourist stop. But a visitor's must at Millville is the recreated glass town, known as Wheaton Village. Tiny Jersey's big diversity is revealed again here in its early glassmaking industry. Millville, once called Shingle Landing, was begun in 1750. However, it first experienced its real growth with the coming of the glassmakers. An Irishman named James Lee is credited with bringing glassmaking to this area in 1799, with the founding of the Eagle Glass Works. He opened his Millville Glass Works in 1806. Soon the area became the center of New Jersey's glassmaking industry. Sandpits at Mauricetown further south on the Maurice River supplied the necessary raw material.

The T.C. Wheaton & Co. Glass Factory was opened in Millville in the 1880's. It manufactured glassware for druggists, chemists, and perfumers. Wheaton Village, a recreated glass town of the late 1800's, is run by a non-profit foundation to remind us of what that important industry was to the lives of south Jersey's people. An extensive Museum of American Glass presents a "panorama of American glassmaking." At the 1888 glass factory, skilled artisans take you through the steps of transforming hot, molten glass into pitchers, bottles, vases, and other items.

In another area of the village, The Prince Maurice Pottery Co. demonstrates its wares. Other craftsmen practice their trades in the shops of the village Crafts Arcade. Special events such as antique shows, etc. are put on at the village throughout the year as announced. Exhibits on the history of New Jersey farm life are on view at the agriculture center. There are a variety of specialty shops, a turn-of-the-century drug store and a general store. I hope that this journey along the Jersey shore gives you a new perspective on our state, and a greater appreciation of that many-faceted region we call New Jersey.

Henry F. Skirbst

UNIT 2: PEOPLE OF NEW JERSEY

This unit explores the role people and their various endeavors have contributed to the cultural heritage of the state of New Jersey.

Chapter 7: Agriculture
Chapter 8: Industry
Chapter 9: Transportation
Chapter 10: Folklore and Legends
Chapter 11: Famous People

Henry F. Skirbst

CHAPTER 7: AGRICULTURE

The Garden State

In designing the Great Seal of the State of New Jersey back in the late 1700s, the Goddess of the Harvest was chosen, along with that of Liberty, to be prominently portrayed. To further the point being made, the center shield of the seal contains three plows and a horse's head. But just in case one still had not got the idea, the state's nickname was contrived to get the message across. We are, as you know, called the "Garden State." It should be amply clear, then, that the idea these early citizens were trying to convey was that New Jersey was a state deeply committed to farming!

Of course when the state's seal was designed, more than 200 years ago, New Jersey's population was, in fact, primarily made up of farmers. Over the years, and right up to the present, agriculture has been a very important part of the state's economy. Farming is not only one of New Jersey's oldest, but it remains one of its most important industries. Even when the first Europeans arrived in the 1600's, they found that New Jersey's soil had already been under cultivation for generations by its native Indians, the Lenni Lenape, or Delaware as the English called them.

In the valley along New Jersey's many rivers and streams the Indians were growing such native crops as corn, beans, pumpkins, and squash. And in its many wooded and swampy areas they were harvesting its many wild berries. It is no coincidence that these native foods became a part of so traditional an American holiday as Thanksgiving. Friendly Indians, in fact, taught New Jersey's first settlers how to grow these Native American crops.

Our early colonists were soon clearing many wooded acres of the state and planting seeds imported from their native European lands as well. In fact during the American Revolution New Jersey had been nicknamed the "Breadbasket of the Colonies." Its farms suffered heavily from marauding bands of soldiers raiding its abundant supplies of beef, pork and poultry, as well as its ample fruits and grains. Its fine horses, too, were taken often by raiding parties. In fact, one of our popular folk tales, the story of Tempe Wick, is centered on just such an attempt by soldiers to steal her favorite riding horse.

Over the years, the small general farms of New Jersey gave way to the more specialized ones in order to meet the insatiable needs of the growing numbers of nearby city-dwellers. Depending upon terrain as well as interest and economics, some took to dairy farming, particularly in Warren, Sussex, and Hunterdon counties, while others began to specialize in poultry raising, or the harvesting of fruits. Various vegetable crops, particularly in Burlington, Cumberland, and Salem counties became the chief agricultural pursuit. More than two-fifths of Jersey's land today is still in farming, though the shovels of developers have recently made harsh inroads. Small in comparison to the nations' Midwest, New Jersey's farm yield per acre, nevertheless is among the highest in the nation!

At this time of the year, with the celebrations uppermost in our minds of two traditionally family holidays, Thanksgiving and Christmas, we think of a Jersey crop that has become synonymous with the season - cranberries. Berry production of all kinds - blueberries, raspberries, blackberries, strawberries, and gooseberries, as well as cranberries, are widely grown in New Jersey. But it is in the production of cranberries, a traditional American holiday fare, that New Jersey ranks third in the entire nation! Only Massachusetts and Wisconsin exceed the state in their annual production.

Though Indians picked Jersey's wild cranberries before the colonists arrived, the cultivation of cranberries as we know them today began in the 1830's. The bog lands in the Jersey Pine Barrens of Atlantic, Burlington, and Ocean Counties are the primary locations for the harvesting of this important crop in the state today. The type of large cranberry in use in the United States is grown only in North America, and is therefore a truly American fruit. First cultivated by Captain Henry Hall in Massachusetts in the 1820's and by Benjamin Thomas of Pemberton in 1830, it was sold only fresh for years.

Since harvest time for the Jersey cranberry is late September and October, it was ideally suited for use during the Thanksgiving and Christmas holidays. Thus it was that this uniquely American fruit became an integral part of our traditional holiday celebration. And thus it was, too, that the trails of New Jersey became important to families throughout America in the keeping of that tradition.

Agricultural Heritage

As we continue the pursuit of the state's agricultural heritage, we need to be reminded that the Native American Indian was the original New Jersey farmer. The first New Jersey Indians, to our knowledge, were members of the Algonquin nation, and called themselves the Lenni Lenapes, or "original people." The English called them the "Delawares," presumably because they seemed to be using that river and its fertile valley as their home base. They called their lands, "Scheyichbi," or "lands between the waters." This was an obvious reference to the fact that it lay between the Hudson River and the Atlantic Ocean to the east, and the Delaware River and Bay to the west. It has always been blessed with more than adequate water for its agricultural needs.

The first European farmers to settle the lands called it at varying times, New Sweden, New Netherlands, Nova Caesaria, and finally New Jersey. They were a mixed lot, unlike those in New England and Virginia. Sweden, the Netherlands, England, and Scotland contributed the first farmers from Europe. The Dutch farmers first came in the 1630's and moved westward from their Hudson River settlements. The Swedes settled the area of southwestern New Jersey along the Delaware Bay and River, and moved north and east. The English and Scotch started settlements in the Newark and Raritan Bay regions and gradually moved west and south. Each brought with them their own knowledge and skills of farming which they had gained in their native lands.

William Penn invited large numbers of Germans, most notably Rhinelanders, to settle his holdings in eastern Pennsylvania and western New Jersey. They started coming in the late 1600's and gradually moved eastward from Philadelphia. They were particularly noted for their skills in agriculture. New Jersey thus benefited early from a blend of farming customs that enriched all of its agricultural practices. This diversity in backgrounds soon drove the state's farming recognition to the high status for which it achieved its nickname, "the Garden State." Even today, 300 years later, agriculture ranks (with tourism and the petrochemical industry) among the top three income producers in the state.

Promotion of the state to possible immigrants from Europe soon centered on its agricultural potential as the "Garden of the World." This reference appeared in literature distributed in Scotland as early as 1684. Along with the introduction by the Indians of the growing of corn, unknown in Europe, shipments of seeds from Europe soon resulted in the planting of extensive fields of barley, buckwheat, oats, rye, and wheat. The growing of grain early in the 17th century eventually led to the state's being dubbed as "the nation's breadbasket" during the American Revolution. Barley and hops were grown by Dutch and Swedish settlers for the production of beer as early as 1630.

New Jersey's strength in agriculture throughout its history has been the result of its diversity and its adaptability to changing trends. Early records indicate that the growing of fresh fruit as apples, peaches, plums, and grapes have always been an important aspect of the state's farming capability. Cider early became a prominent beverage in colonial America and apple orchards soon were conspicuous throughout the state.

Grape culture, which is witnessing a rebirth in New Jersey of great promise, has had its ups and downs, notably because the fruit of the native, or labrusca grape, was tart and not particularly suited to wine production. The introduction of new varieties today is changing that picture. Commercial cranberry and blueberry production since the mid 1800's has elevated the state to one of the three producers in the nation. The whole country is familiar with the famous "Jersey peaches."

But farming in New Jersey is not only centered in the production of food and beverages. The growing of trees for timber and fuel has always been important, but more recently trees along with shrubs of various types has become a highly valuable agricultural pursuit in the state. Both the "Christmas tree" and the ornamental trees and shrubs industry have been skyrocketing in the state. The rise of suburban living has played a prominent role in these farming pursuits.

Horse breeding for various uses is of growing importance today, but has also been prominent since colonial days. It is no accident the horse is the state animal and features prominently in the state seal. In colonial days, flax was a highly visible crop. It, along with sheep raising, was important sources of textiles. Linen fiber and oil were exported as early as 1630. Much more still awaits to be told about farming's importance along the trails of New Jersey - past, present and future. Its preservation should be of high priority.

Silk

We know that New Jersey's farmers have experimented with a wide variety of products over the years. I wonder, though, how many are aware of the silk-culture craze that hit this state in the mid 1830's? Warren County farmers, in fact, were the first to succumb to the fad in the spring of 1835.

The mulberry tree is native to the mild climates of Asia, Europe, and America. It can be propagated by seeds, cuttings, and grafting. It thrives in almost any soil. It does well on rocky hillsides or in gravely soils. It can be cultivated, like any other fruit, in orchards. Though its fruit may be used for desserts or wine, its true economic value lies with that particular variety whose foliage provides food for the silkworm. It was to this tree that the Warren County farmers turned in a get-rich-quick furor that led to the temporary desertion of their wheat fields.

The silk industry was flourishing in China as early as 1523 BC. It remained their well-kept secret until about 552 AD, when two monks who had been traveling in China brought some silkworm eggs secretly back with them to Constantinople. Its culture eventually spread up the Balkan Peninsula.

For centuries, Greece became the center of the European silk industry. In time, it spread to Spain, Portugal, and Italy. Eventually, it became an important industry of the French. When the French Huguenots, many of whom were silk workers, were driven from France in 1685, they took the industry with them to England. By 1718, English silks replaced French silks in the markets of Europe. By the 19th century, the manufacture of silk was flourishing in Germany, Belgium and the Netherlands, as well as the United States.

Silk culture had an early start in the American colonies. King James I arranged to have silk worms sent to Jamestown, Virginia as early as 1613, eight years before the Pilgrims landed at Plymouth Rock. The Virginia House of Burgesses required by law that at least 10 mulberry trees be planted for every 100 acres under cultivation. Not until a group of French Huguenots settled in South Carolina in the late 17th century, however, did any real interest in the silk industry take hold in America. By the 18th century, it had spread to Louisiana and Georgia. Following the American Revolution, a number of states offered their farmers bounties for planting mulberry trees for the production of silk.

A national interest in silk production was aroused in 1826 when the House Committee on Agriculture called for a manual on the growth of silk-producing mulberry trees. A publication in 1828 aroused enough interest to get several states to pass laws encouraging their growth. New Jersey was among them. A state silk convention was held. By February 21, 1838, the legislature passed a resolution authorizing a state bounty of 15 cents per pound for cocoons of silk produced in the state of New Jersey. John Van Dyke of Princeton was the first to qualify. He took his cocoons to Trenton that June amid a great celebration.

In the meantime, the first mulberry orchards in New Jersey had begun springing up in Warren County. There, by the spring of 1836, aroused by news that New England farmers were cashing in on all the riches to be had by silk production, a charter had been secured by silkworm zealots for a silk company. The madness was being spread by newspaper accounts of this farmer or that whose production of silk was making him rich. Visions of becoming overnight millionaires were dancing in many a Warren County farm family's head.

The "Hunterdon County Democrat" protested the state bounty offered in 1838. It complained that "the wheat growers (were being) taxed to support the silk-stocking aristocrats." The madness continued to rage throughout the state, however. Silk companies were established in such places as Allentown, Belvidere, Burlington, Elizabeth, Freehold, Newark, Princeton, Trenton, and Woodbury. By

1838, when the bounty was offered by the state, more than 300,000 mulberry trees had been planted in Burlington County alone. A Princeton farmer got $4,000 for trees he sold at 27 cents per tree. Speculators were running rampant with little knowledge of the business.

Then came the cold spring of 1839. Thousands of trees died. The price had dropped to ¾ cents per tree. By the spring of 1840, most discouraged farmers had returned to the planting of wheat, or some other crop. Although the growing of silk-producing mulberry trees ended, the trails of New Jersey had not been deserted by domestic silk manufacturers. In fact, at the Centennial Exposition held in Philadelphia in 1876, American-made silk competed well, and Paterson, New Jersey had become the leading silk-producing city in the United States. A position it held well into the 20th century.

Viniculture

Partially because of the rediscovery of New Jersey's excellent soil and climate for wine making, and because it meets the current demand for a high return on its diminishing availability, a profitable agricultural industry is having a rebirth in the Garden State. It is the redevelopment of "viniculture," the growing of grapes for wine making. Plantations of grapevines, called vineyards, are not new to this state. In fact, historically, New Jersey vineyards were being cultivated before the California and upstate New York grape farms. Though for a long time now the state has taken a back seat in the cultivation of the grape commercially, a new day is dawning for this phase of New Jersey's agriculture.

John Wild, encouraged by the large settlement of wine drinking Germans in the Egg Harbor area of Atlantic County, introduced the cultivation of grapes to that region in the 1850's. Many small, local wineries grew up around it. In 1867, H.T. Dewey and Sons opened the first large commercial winery there. But it was the Frenchman, Louis Renault, who put Egg Harbor's wine-making region on the map with the establishment of the Renault Winery there in the 1860's. Eventually his company went on to become America's largest distributor of champagne.

Still another use for the cultivated grape was arising about the same time in neighboring Cumberland County. There, a Methodist minister, Dr. Thomas Welch, used the newly introduced pasteurizing techniques of Louis Pasteur of France to develop an unfermented wine. The nation's first nonalcoholic "grape juice" had its start in the vineyards of Vineland. Welch's grape juice became a popular American drink. The nation's "teetotalers" now had a refreshing grape drink that did not violate their objections to alcoholic beverages. Since it was not affected by the ban on alcoholic beverages resulting from the passage of the Prohibition Amendment in 1919, its production could continue during that era as well.

The Renault Winery was also enabled to continue its operations during the Prohibition Era (from 1919 to 1933). Instead of bottling wines for taverns and liquor stores, however, the government allowed it to continue with the production of a special 22-percent alcohol-content wine product. This "Renault Wine Tonic" was to be sold instead in the nation's drug stores!

Founded almost 125 years ago, the Renault Winery is listed today on the state Register of Historic Places. It is the oldest winery and vineyard in continuous operation in the nation. Though Renault originally planted his grapes in California, he soon learned that the Native American Labrusca grape, which was disease resistant, flourished best in New Jersey. He was attracted to the Egg Harbor area of the state because he knew of the small wineries that the early German vintners had already established there. Egg Harbor soon gained an international reputation as the "Wine City."

The Renault Winery has since opened a museum that houses the historic wine-making equipment used originally more than 100 years ago by Louis Renault. It also contains a large collection of masterpiece wine glasses, many originally made for European royalty. A chateau style Hospitality House and an art gallery have been added as well. The Renault Winery has added to its viniculture to become a unique tourist attraction as well. Visitors to this historic site can view its cavernous wine cellar and beautiful flower garden. It continues to grow 110 acres of grapes in its vineyards, and puts on a number of festival days during the fall months.

A new wine law enacted by the state legislature in 1981 had much to do with the encouragement of the state's expanding wine industry. Its designed purpose was to boost two of the state's leading industries - tourism and agriculture. The number of wineries in the state has doubled since its enactment, and the New Jersey's Wine Growers Association predicts that the state will once again return to the forefront in the production of fine wines with a national reputation.

Jersey grown grapes have the unique quality of not having to be fortified with acids in its wines, as do the California grown varieties. There are today some 25 vineyards growing these New Jersey grapes. Some 14 wineries can now be found along the trails of New Jersey. That does not match what it contained in its heyday, but it is a step in that direction nevertheless.

Hunterdon and Warren Counties have more recently proven to be excellent locations for viniculture in the state, and their family-run wineries are bottling the full range red, white, sweet, and dry domestic wines with a "Jersey label." History, it appears, is about to repeat itself in the "Garden State."

Livestock

When we think of cattle drives, we are most apt to conjure up visions of cowboys on horseback, moving gigantic herds of long horns over the Great Plains of our western states into such cow towns as Abilene or Dodge City. I bet there are very few people today, however, who are aware of just how the pioneer farmers of New Jersey, whose chief marketable produce was livestock, got their product to market. In the early days, in fact, they drove them over land on a crisscross of Indian trails often at great distances. In many cases these were reminiscent of the picturesque drives of the Old West with which we are all so familiar.

Among the earliest recorded market towns for cattle drives in New Jersey were those at Burlington in West Jersey, which opened in 1681, and at Perth Amboy in East Jersey, which opened in 1686. While already existing Indian trails were the first roads of commerce for West Jersey's pioneer farmers, they were, after all, only footpaths. For quicker, easier movement of herds of livestock and later the large wagons that served as carriers, these Indian pathways had to eventually be widened and leveled.

The first organized set of rules regarding road construction in New Jersey that eventually led to a network of early roadways was by act of the Assembly in 1716. This act established the required width of roadway right-of-ways and to some extent the course they should take with the least inconvenience to abutting landowners. Early roads were built by the labor of local residents, who were, for the most part, reluctant workers to say the least. As commerce increased, private road construction increased. Often those who would profit most by their construction paid road builders out of their own pockets to do the job for them; naturally along certain areas providing for their personal convenience. Turnpikes were also constructed by private companies to whom you paid a toll for the convenience of their use. The government was not, for the most part, initially in the road building business.

The early Burlington and Perth Amboy cattle markets were in time added to as settlement in New Jersey's northwestern counties demanded more, and in some cases closer, marketplaces. Trenton, then still a part of Hunterdon County, opened its market in 1746. By 1749, New Brunswick became an important outlet, and in 1768, Newark opened its farmer's market. In terms of travel time, however, New Brunswick became the preferred outlet of many cattle drives from northwestern New Jersey's pioneer farms. In the early days, the Phillipsburg to Trenton Road intersected at Pittstown with the road to New Brunswick.

To keep up with the competition for the farmer's produce, Trenton started its annual three-day agricultural fair in April and Newark in October during the mid 1700's. Its initial purpose was in attracting farmers to their market places. The profitable buying and selling of all manner of livestock, as well as other agricultural produce, in a festive atmosphere became a much looked-forward-to event in the pioneer farmers' lives. They provided not only a market for their produce, but a much-needed social outlet for the otherwise lonely farmers and their families. In today's close-knit, overcrowded, fast moving society, it is almost impossible to imagine how isolated and lonely farm life was like at one time in New Jersey.

In spite of these annual fairs, New Brunswick's comparable ease of access, plus the fact that it also carried on a brisk trade with a wide area all along the Atlantic seaboard, including sloops going daily into the port of New York, continued to make that town the favored terminus for West Jersey's pioneer farmers. Because of transportation difficulties, especially in the winter, however, it cannot be overlooked that Easton was growing into an important center of trade for nearby farmers seeking a local outlet.

Those who complain of roads today cannot begin to imagine the poor condition of roads throughout New Jersey in the 18th century, even in the more developed regions. What they were like in the hinterlands was even more unbelievable. The roads were not only badly constructed, but were so poorly marked and so lacking in adequate bridges over the many swift moving streams that crisscrossed the rugged woodlands, that they were often rendered useless. Heavy rains or snows made them impassable.

As a result of road conditions, the horse remained the primary means of transportation throughout northwestern New Jersey. Horseback riding was a necessary and universal skill. As roads improved during the 19th century, the transportation of both goods and people moved from pack and riding horses, to carts and sleds, and eventually to wagons and coaches. Though this was a picturesque era along the trails of New Jersey, it is doubtful that any today could endure its inconveniences.

Horse Breeding

Whether it was the dashing horse troops of American or British forces during the Revolution, the arrival of the cavalry at the nick of time during an Indian attack, or the romantic era of the cowboy on the trail, the horse has played an important role throughout America's history. There always seems to have been a love affair between Americans and the horse. Since about 1899, in fact, there have been more horses in the United States than in any other country in the world.

That the National Horse Show moved from Madison Square Garden this year to be held at the Meadowlands Sports and

Entertainment Center in New Jersey should come as no surprise. This very prestigious gathering, after leaving a long trail of history at the Garden behind it, decided that its best interests would be served by bringing the nation's finest horses for exhibition to a state which has a history of horse-breeding that goes back to its colonial days. They brought this horse show, after all, to a state which recognizes the horse as its "state animal." They brought it to a state that is so enamored with that animal that it has featured it at the head of its "Great State Seal" since 1777.

Horse breeding, which has taken on an even greater role in New Jersey's agricultural economy in recent years, has a long history in this state. Monmouth County probably has the earliest reputation for breeding horses, dating back to before the 1700's. It is still the leading county.

Figures released by the State Department of Agriculture in 1987 show New Jersey's current horse industry with assets above $4.1 billion. It is contained on some 120,000 acres that are allotted to horse related operations. While by far the largest number of horses in New Jersey are still stabled in Monmouth County, the next six counties include: Burlington, with more than 7,000; Hunterdon, with about 6,500; Morris and Sussex with about 4,500 each; and Salem and Somerset, with close to 4,000 each. The rest are found scattered throughout the state in its remaining 14 counties. Hudson, with 100 horses, accounts for the smallest.

The horse industry in New Jersey employs more than 10,500 people. Its operations spend about $631 million at about 7,100 locations. Acreage in New Jersey devoted to horse breeding has increased by some 44,000 within the last six years. The number of horses in New Jersey has doubled since 1971. It is the fastest growing segment of the state's agricultural economy.

In addition, there are miles of trails within New Jersey which are designated as bridle paths. The numerous horseback riding academies, saddle clubs and livery stables found within the state also attest to the popularity of the equestrian sport. In fact, one of our nearby colleges, Centenary in Hackettstown, has equestrian studies in its curriculum for the more serious student of horsemanship.

Another indication of the important role that New Jersey plays in the field of horse husbandry is the fact that the training center for the U.S. Olympic Equestrian Team is at Hamilton Farms in Gladstone. Many national horse competitions, such as the Gladstone Driving Event where the national pairs championship is contested, is also held in New Jersey. This competition is the biggest event of its kind in the nation. This is only one example of a number of such events that are held within New Jersey.

It might surprise many to know that New Jersey has also been on the National Rodeo Circuit for over half a century. At a place called Cowtown (near Woodstown) in southwestern New Jersey's Salem County, real, western-style rodeos have been held regularly in season every weekend since the 1930's. In recent years, more and more annual farmers' fairs have been featuring horse shows and rodeos as part of their regular programs, recognizing the increasing importance of the horse in New Jersey's agricultural economy.

Back before the turn of the 18th century the "Middletown Cup" was being held near Red Bank, in Monmouth County. The first "derby" ever run in America was sponsored by the Passaic Jockey Club in 1861. Back in 1840, the little mare, "Fashion," bred in Colt's Neck, was nationally famous. One of the most notable horses of all time, "Man 'O War," was bred and trained in Monmouth County.

A popular folk tale is about a young New Jersey girl from Jockey Hollow who hid her favorite horse in her bedroom to keep it from being sequestered by a foraging party of soldiers. The girl, of course, was Tempe Wick, daughter of Henry Wick, whose farmhouse served as headquarters for Gen. Arthur St. Clair during Washington's encampment at Morristown.

The trails of New Jersey have certainly been a favored locale for the horse throughout its history, and all indications seem to point to an even greater role for its favorite animal in the future.

Mills to Villages

One of my readers, whose name and address I must apologize has been lost in the unkempt shuffle of papers on my desk, asked me to write more about those early mills once so prominent in this area. As I had mentioned previously, one of the earliest industrialists who came to any frontier region was the miller. Northwest New Jersey was true to form with one exception. In and around the many iron forges that began popping up in north Jersey's "iron hills," the miller followed the iron master. Otherwise, he followed the pioneer farmer into the remotest countryside. His arrival, of course, depended upon the existence of a fast moving stream to generate the needed power for his wheels. For the most part, the miller thus became the first industrialist of an area.

To insure a more reliable source of water power during those seasons when water was low, or when there was an unseasonable drought, crude dams were constructed by the early millers. Those dams would also bring increased power by raising the water level, and thus providing a "fall." Dams usually were built of stones hauled in from the rock-strewn woodlands, or of a combination of heavy timber, earth, and gravel.

As pioneer farmers moved into any region in large enough numbers to warrant it, millers moved in nearby shortly afterwards. These colorful mills with their waterwheels on the outside churning their machinery on the inside soon became a prominent part of the northwest New Jersey landscape. Many a fond memory is generated in the minds of old timers still living in the region who recall their grandfather's mills. Such was the case of the reader referred to, who remembered his grandfather's mill, first in Hainesburg and later in Hackettstown.

Gristmills for grinding the farmer's grains and sawmills for meeting his needs for cut wood for homes and farm buildings were not only first to arrive, but the most prominent. Many communities were founded surrounding one or two mills. They were, in fact, its central reason for existence. Such was the case at Beatty's Mills, later Beattystown. Sometimes just its existence gave the community its name, as in the case of Milford or Millbrook. Mills were often subject to destruction by fire, which was one explanation of their moving from place to place. This sometimes gave rise to another name for a village, such as Burnt Mill.

If there was not a nearby mill, farmers would have to travel many miles to avoid the arduous task of home grinding on the part of their wives. One can see, then, why the arrival of a miller nearby was an event of great importance in their lives, and reason enough to name a town after him. Because of the wooden materials of which these first mills were constructed, their utter uselessness after abandonment, and often their destruction by fire or vandals, precious few of these many early mills remain. This colorful era in our heritage is thus being lost to us. So, when a mill is still standing in an area, every effort ought to be made to preserve it, lest still another part of our unique heritage be lost forever.

As the population in northwest New Jersey increased, the demand for mills heightened. Evidence indicates the existence of gristmills as early as the 1750's in this region. Asbury, Anderson, Beattystown, Bloomsbury, Changewater, Finesville, Hackettstown, and Waterloo all have documented evidence of the existence of these early regional mills. Many smaller, scattered mills, called "tub mills," serving a much smaller capacity, also existed. Most of the early, larger mills served local farmers' immediate needs. They would come in once or twice a week for the grinding of their buckwheat, corn, oats, rye, or wheat for personal use. Later mills purchased grain for the marketing of flour in nearby towns. Usually this originated by the fact that farmers paid for the grinding in "kind." This was then ground to be sold. As the market increased, millers bought additional grain to be ground and sold.

Sawmills were also an important early industry. This was especially true near iron forges. Often grist and sawmills shared one building. Before saw mills, lumber had to be laboriously squared with a broadaxes and sawed by two men operating a pit saw. This was far too slow to meet the demands of a growing population.

The need for clothing brought in the "fulling mill." These vigorously beat "homespun" with paddles and then compressed it in water, avoiding another onerous task for the over-worked farmer's wife. She still had to spin and weave it, then sew it into clothing after the "fullling."

Other mills arising along the trails of New Jersey were for crushing flaxseed into linseed oil, tanning leather, crushing apples for cider, grain for stills, and limestone for lime. Mills were indeed an important part of the lives of those who once tread these pathways.

151

The Old Red Mill

Many an old Jersey village sprung up around a mill site. These mills were built along our numerous waterways. One of those waterways originating at Budd Lake in Morris County, and meandering first to the east through the Schooley's Mountain past Bartley, and then south past Long Valley and Middle Valley before entering Hunterdon County, is New Jersey's longest. Continuing south past Califon, it finally breaks through the mountains at High Bridge, and topples over a 75-foot dam before reaching Clinton, the site of today's tale. It then winds generally east again through Hamden, Flemington Junction, and Three Bridges before entering Somerset.

Flowing past Neshanic, its general wandering direction is then north to South Branch and Raritan. There it starts its twisting journey in a northeasterly direction in the vicinity of Somerville, Finderne, and Bound Brook. Its pathway then wanders eastward through Middlesex County past New Brunswick and Sayerville until it reaches the end of its long passage. Between Perth and South Amboy, it empties into the Raritan Bay. The Raritan River, thus regularly traverses more than 100 miles in its wandering, winding waterway from start to finish.

Some claim its name comes from the Lenni Lenape Indians who referred to it as Laletan, meaning "forked river." That tribe of the Delaware (Lenni Lenape) known as the Naraticongs planted its villages all along its shores from Budd Lake to Raritan Bay, canoeing its waterways long before the white man came to these shores. The Dutch wrote of it as early as 1650, claiming that the land was inhabited by a tribe known as the Raritangs. Early European settlement throughout its pathway was by Dutch colonists. They were first to harness its waters to drive the wheels that ran their many mills. These mills were used to grind the grain produced on their prosperous farms. Following the Dutch were the Germans, who also farmed these lands before the Irish, Scotch, and English arrived.

At Clinton there are two old gristmills where the South Branch of the Raritan converges with Spruce Run. One of these, "The Old

Red Mill," is the center of today's Clinton Historical Museum Village, now situated on 10 ½ acres at the edge of an amphitheater of limestone cliffs. The Museum Village, in addition to two old lime kilns and a stone crusher from its lime quarrying days, contains a General Store, with barbershop and post office, a Blacksmith Shop, a little Red Schoolhouse, a Log Cabin with Herb Garden and a Gift Shop. All are open from April through October.

The Hunterdon Art Center is housed in the second mill across from the 200-foot wide dam. The mill at the Museum Village was originally built by a miller named David McKinney around 1763. Now called the "Old Red Mill," it once ground flax seeds to make linseed oil. The crushed seeds were then formed into cakes to feed the farm animals. Today, it houses four stories of exhibits tastefully arranged to portray rooms or shops illustrating various farm family activities or crafts spanning some 200 years of northwestern Jersey history. The top floor shows the mill operation.

Around 1770, Mahlon Kirkbride bought the mill, and in 1776 sold it to Mahlon Taylor, who used it to grind grain. In 1782, Daniel Hunt bought both mills. He did so well that a thriving little community developed around his mills which became known as Hunt's Mills. In 1809, Daniel's son, Ralph, took over. Both mills continued to operate as flax and grist mills in the Hunt family until 1828. In that year, Archibald Taylor, in partnership with a man named Bray, bought them out. The Hunts not only lost their mills to Taylor in this transaction, but he was also influential in renaming their village. DeWitt Clinton, Governor of New York, had become somewhat of a national hero for his part in the building of the Erie Canal. Hunt's Mills was renamed Clinton in his honor.

Taylor operated the mills as graphite and pumice mills. The nearby limestone quarry and kilns were sold to the Mulligan family. John Snyder and then Philip Gulick owned the Old Red Mill between 1834 and 1903, being the last to use it as a gristmill. From 1903 to 1920, it was used by the Tomson family to grind talc and graphite. Gradually falling into disuse, it was purchased in 1960 by a group determined to save it known as the "Red Mill Five."

These men restored the mill, replaced the water wheel, and gradually opened it as a nonprofit museum in 1963. Today, the Museum Village, the historic Inn, The Clinton House, the Art Center and Clinton's burgeoning shopping area, which is emerging as another "New Hope," make Clinton another delightful tourist attraction worth visiting along the trails of New Jersey.

Types of Mills

New Jersey was once the site of a myriad of different mills. Each had a story to tell of the life and times of the people surrounding it. The might of our waters was, in those times, the main source of power for moving our machines. New Jersey was fortunate enough to have many waterways that could provide that power. It was the sawmill that turned out the lumber needed to build our homes, barns, and other structures. It was the gristmill that provided the needed flour by grinding our farmer's grains. Mills ground limestone for our fields. They fulled wool for our cloth. They mashed apples for our cider.

Locating near swift-moving streams brought visions of power-producing waterwheels to early settlers' heads. Lands so located were, therefore, of greater value, and often became the sites of our first villages. Many New Jersey villages had "mill" somewhere in their name.

Though other sources of power had arrived by that date, waterwheels were still turning mills in some sections of New Jersey as late as the early 1900's. Even when the flow of rivers was too slow to move the wheels, dams at various locations were constructed to provide the power necessary to move them. As a result of this activity, though old mill buildings were long-time gone, their dams, and ponds remained behind to remind us of the once-thriving mills that were so important to the lives of the early settlers.

We often think of the picturesque sawmill and gristmill of an earlier day as the only mills in existence. Though they were the earliest types in use, a survey in 1894 gives us some insight into both the number and variety of water-driven mills that once were in operation in the state even as we approached the 20th century.

Just a small stream, Peckman's Brook, which emptied into the Passaic at Little Falls, serves as a good example. Within its relatively short distance, there were several bronze powder mills, a bolt and nuts mill, a carpet mill, a cotton mill, a dyeing mill, a felt mill, a gristmill, a hub mill, two sawmills, a wool scouring mill, and a wool mill. As so often happens in our small state, man tends to overdo a good thing when there is a profit to be made. Needless to say, this small waterway eventually became overburdened.

Some early mills served a dual purpose. The one now at Allaire State Park is an example of one of those early New Jersey mills. It had been run by the Crane family for more than a century. When its last owner, Herbert Crane, passed away in the late 1960's, the state dismantled it and had it reassembled at the Historic Village of Allaire. Originally constructed on Pine Brook by Cornelius Hetfield before the time of the American Revolution, it was first used as a sawmill. The Crane family bought the mill after Hetfield, who was a Tory, had his property confiscated because of his loyalty to the Crown. From the mid to late 1800's, it served both as a saw and gristmill. The water power would be diverted from the saw and made to turn two large millstones instead. The stones, of course, would grind various kinds of grain into flour. There are a number of these type mills in operation at various historic villages in New Jersey today.

Mills sometimes created problems among the local citizenry. Capt. James Gray, for example, built an iron foundry and casting mill as well as a saw and gristmill on his property along the Passaic River near Little Falls in the early 1770's. The large dam he built to provide the necessary power caused the water to overflow the banks upstream in certain seasons. It would flood nearby farms. The farmers involved sought relief at these times. Gray refused to alter his operation. In anger, they demolished his dam. During the Revolution, Gray became a captain in the British Army. As such, he led a number of revenge raids on the farms of those who had destroyed his dam. In turn his lands were confiscated, because of his loyalty to the Crown, and sold in 1784 at a public auction.

The classic example of how the influx of mills changed an area's whole-way-of-life involved what happened to Paterson. The year was 1791. That quiet little village of 10 homes, two small stores, a church, and the Godwin Hotel was made up, at the time, chiefly of descendants of its first Dutch settlers. The biggest activity in their lives were the tourists who came to view the Great Falls of the

Passaic, and stay at their hotel. Most of those living in the area were farmers. Then came "The Society for Establishing Useful Manufacturers." It had recently received a charter from then governor, William Paterson. It began advertising for mills to come use the power of the Great Falls. The tale of the change that was to come along that section of the trails of New Jersey, is a story in itself, and will have to wait another time.

CHAPTER 8: INDUSTRY

Types of Mills

New Jersey was once the site of a myriad of different mills. Each had a story to tell of the life and times of the people surrounding it. The might of our waters was, in those times, the main source of power for moving our machines. New Jersey was fortunate enough to have many waterways that could provide that power. It was the sawmill that turned out the lumber needed to build our homes, barns, and other structures. It was the gristmill that provided the needed flour by grinding our farmer's grains. Mills ground limestone for our fields. They fulled wool for our cloth. They mashed apples for our cider.

Locating near swift-moving streams brought visions of power-producing waterwheels to early settlers' heads. Lands so located were, therefore, of greater value, and often became the sites of our first villages. Many New Jersey villages had "mill" somewhere in their name.

Though other sources of power had arrived by that date, waterwheels were still turning mills in some sections of New Jersey as late as the early 1900's. Even when the flow of rivers was too slow to move the wheels, dams at various locations were constructed to provide the power necessary to move them. As a result of this activity, though old mill buildings were long-time gone, the mills' dams and ponds remained behind to remind us of the once-thriving mills that were so important to the lives of the early settlers.

We often think of the picturesque sawmill and gristmill of an earlier day as the only mills in existence. Though they were the earliest types in use, a survey in 1894 gives us some insight into both the number and variety of water-driven mills that once were in operation in the state even as we approached the 20th century.

Just a small stream, Peckman's Brook, which emptied into the Passaic at Little Falls, serves as a good example. Within its relatively short distance there were several bronze powder mills, a bolt and nuts mill, a carpet mill, a cotton mill, a dyeing mill, a felt mill, a gristmill, a hub mill, two sawmills, a wool scouring mill, and a wool mill. As so often happens in our small state, man tends to overdo a good thing when there is a profit to be made. Needless to say, this small waterway eventually became overburdened.

Some early mills served a dual purpose. The one now at Allaire State Park is an example of one of those early New Jersey mills. It had been run by the Crane family for more than a century. When its last owner, Herbert Crane, passed away in the late 1960's, the state dismantled it and had it reassembled at the Historic Village of Allaire. Originally constructed on Pine Brook by Cornelius Hetfield before the time of the American Revolution, it was first used as a sawmill. The Crane family bought the mill after Hetfield, who was a Tory, had his property confiscated because of his loyalty to the Crown. From the mid to late 1800's, it served both as a saw and gristmill. The water power would be diverted from the saw and made to turn two large millstones instead. The stones, of course, would grind various kinds of grain into flour. There are a number of these type mills in operation at various historic villages in New Jersey today.

Mills sometimes created problems among the local citizenry. Capt. James Gray, for example, built an iron foundry and casting mill as well as a saw and gristmill on his property along the Passaic River near Little Falls in the early 1770's. The large dam he built to provide the necessary power caused the water to overflow the banks upstream in certain seasons. It would flood nearby farms. The farmers involved sought relief at these times. Gray refused to alter his operation. In anger, they demolished his dam. During the Revolution, Gray became a captain in the British Army. As such, he led a number of revenge raids on the farms of those who had destroyed his dam. In turn his lands were confiscated, because of his loyalty to the Crown, and sold in 1784 at a public auction.

The classic example of how the influx of mills changed an area's whole way of life involved what happened to Paterson. The year was 1791. That quiet little village of 10 homes, two small stores, a church, and the Godwin Hotel was made up, at the time, chiefly of descendants of its first Dutch settlers. The biggest activity in their lives were the tourists who came to view the Great Falls of the

Passaic, and stay at their hotel. Most of those living in the area were farmers. Then came "The Society for Establishing Useful Manufacturers." It had recently received a charter from then governor, William Paterson. It began advertising for mills to come use the power of the Great Falls. The tale of the change that was to come along that section of the trails of New Jersey, is a story in itself, and will have to wait another time.

Early Industry

Like its excellent location near the nation's greatest harbor, the diversity of its surface features is another reason New Jersey has attracted so many people over the years. Its population has nearly doubled since the 1940's, indicating that its drawing power seems to increase with the passage of time. Back in 1800, there were only about 200,000 people in the state. By 1880, it had reached a population of one million. Almost two million were in the state by 1900. A population of three million was attained by 1920, four million by the 1940's, and by 1980 the state's population was almost eight million.

Whether for work or for play, there are assorted activities lending themselves to the state's varied terrain. Catering to the millions who want to play in New Jersey is big business in itself. In fact, it is the second largest industry in the state. Such major tourist attractions as the casinos in Atlantic City, the Sportsplex in the Meadowlands, and the ski resorts in the Skylands are only the tip of the iceberg.

Countless other places lend themselves to drawing people and, with them, services. Among these lodestones are hundreds of lakes, innumerable historic sites, endless miles of seashore, rivers and streams, parks, campgrounds, woodlands, and beautiful scenery. Horseback riding ranches and horse racing tracks not only attract people and services, but they also have made horse breeding an important agricultural pursuit in New Jersey.

Because of its abundant waterways, New Jersey also provides the scene for a deep-sea fishing industry off its extensive coastline and the valuable shellfish industry, particularly around the Delaware

Bay area. Its bounteous supply of sandy soil makes the state one of the major producers in the nation of sand and gravel. Jersey sands are not only used in the road building and construction industries, but certain kinds have attracted glassmakers to this state since colonial times. Old Wheaton Village in Millville has an interesting museum illustrating the state's early involvement in glassmaking. Other Jersey sands have found uses in welding, filters, metal polishes, scouring soaps, paints, and even face powders!

Limestone from Jersey and large deposits of green sand marl, which contains potash, have been valuable as fertilizers. The Museum Village in Clinton has some of the old limestone kilns used in the region. Jersey's thick clay beds also made the state among the top producers in the nation. These clay beds have been responsible since colonial times for attracting skilled potters to our borders. Brick making, the manufacture of tiles, and certain plumbing fixtures have also used Jersey clay.

When the Dutch first came to our shores, nine-tenths of the state was forested. Early colonists used it for fuel and home building. It was converted to charcoal for the ravenous appetite of the iron industry. Furniture making, shipbuilding, and papermaking all became important. As late as World War II, several million board feet of Jersey lumber went into the production of ships in Jersey shipyards. Today, Jersey's forests are probably more important as places to hunt, camp, and hike, or as a means for preventing floods and erosion and storing underground water, though they still do provide a means of livelihood for some.

Rich deposits of hard iron ore in its forested hill country, as well as bog iron in its swampy Pine Barrens, once made the iron industry important in the state. For almost two centuries, large numbers of immigrants came to Jersey to work the mines, furnaces, and forges. Ringwood State Park, the Deserted Village of Allaire, Batsto, and Waterloo Village are among historic sites that at least partially commemorate the days when "iron was king" in New Jersey. The Oxford Furnace in Warren, the Taylor Furnaces (High Bridge) in Hunterdon, and the Ringwood Mines in Passaic were the last, of the once-thriving iron centers in the state, to close down. Though they ceased operations in the first half of the 20th century, it was from the 1850's to the 1880's that iron making in Jersey was at its zenith.

One of the oldest and most important industries attracted to New Jersey has been agriculture. Even before the state's first Europeans arrived, the Delaware Indians were growing beans, corn, pumpkins, and squash. From seeds and livestock brought from Europe, the state became the nation's "breadbasket" by the time of the American Revolution. Jersey's agriculture is as varied as its terrain. The hill country lends itself more to dairying and fruit culture. Flatlands are better suited to vegetable crops. But of whatever type, farming is still alive and well in the Garden State and will not be going the way of the iron industry along the trails of New Jersey.

Early Prospecting

The search for valuable minerals was as much a part of New Jersey's history as it was anywhere else in early America.

The Dutch prospectors, in search of the gold that was supposed to be everywhere in America, first came upon the copper mines in Pahaquarry. Those mines led to the building of the nation's first interstate highway, the Old Mine road, from Pahaquarry on the Delaware to Esopus on the Hudson.

They also led to the early settlement of the remote, heavily forested hill country of northwestern New Jersey by the pioneer farmers who followed.

Though copper and zinc were found in sufficient quantity to be mined in New Jersey, for the most part the mining that struck a valuable chord in the state was iron.

It was the New Jersey iron mines and forges which served as the arsenal of both the first War for Independence (the American Revolution) and the second one (the War of 1812). Both the bog iron of its Pine Barrens and the iron mines of its northern hill country served the young nation in providing much of the needed munitions and supplies for the Revolution.

The first European settlers to our northern hill country found it to be densely forested and already inhabited (though sparsely) by small tribes of the Lenape. The immense forests soon began serving as fuel for its iron furnaces and forges. Their gluttony for wood,

161

unfortunately, so denuded the virgin forests that for a time the iron industry was brought to its knees for lack of fuel.

Not until the Morris Canal was dug in the 1830's was a cheap source of fuel (coal) hauled in from Pennsylvania; this revived the iron industry and enabled it to become "king" once again.

It was the Lenape who first showed New Jersey's early settlers where to find iron ore. They called it "suckle sunnal," or black stone. It was first mined around 1700 in Morris County's Schooley's Mountains.

In 1710, Hanover, on the Whippanong (now Whippany) River, had one of the earliest of the iron forges that soon were dotting New Jersey's "iron hills," West Hanover (later Morristown) had a forge shortly thereafter. Dover followed in 1722 and Rockaway in 1732.

Waterpower from the Rockaway River later helped keep the power-hungry forges going.

While Morris County became the first center of New Jersey's prosperous iron industry, it did not retain this title. Its great abundance was soon discovered to be elsewhere in New Jersey's northern rock-strewn hills.

By 1740, the famed Ringwood mines and furnaces of northwestern Passaic County were equally important. About that same time, the furnace at Oxford in Sussex (now Warren) County came into existence. In the late 1700's, Andover Forge in the Sparta Mountains of Sussex was opened. In fact, New Jersey's northwest hill country had become the center of America's blossoming iron industry.

The ironworks prospered and with them, their ironmasters. Soon, wealthy ironmasters were building mansions in northern New Jersey's "iron hills."

The Oxford Furnace in Warren County was one of those early iron operations, which played a key role in our state and national history. Innovations later introduced at Oxford were adopted by the young nation's growing steel industry. Early Oxford entrepreneurs, such as the Scranton brothers, moved on to establish gigantic steel centers, to the west in Pennsylvania and Ohio.

John Axford first settled in the area in 1726 and gave it its name. But it was Jonathan Robeson, coming from Philadelphia, who built the furnace in the early 1740's. Robeson built his ironworks on land that was owned by Joseph Shippen, also of Philadelphia. In

1745, Robeson sold a part interest in the furnace to Dr. William Shippen, Joseph's younger brother. With the money he received, he built another forge at Changewater on the Musconetcong River.

In 1754, the Shippens built a large stone manor house at the Oxford Furnace. Shippen Manor soon became the focal point for many social events by Philadelphia's high society. At the time of the American Revolution, the Shippens had become the sole owners of the Oxford Furnace. A number of famous personages are purported to have visited there during that period as well as at later dates in its long history.

Some two tons of iron a day were being produced at the Oxford Furnace. Its forge had been an important producer of cannon and cannon balls for his majesty's army. The British were, therefore, well aware of its value to the patriots. Twice, abortive attempts were made to seize its products as they were shipped down river to Philadelphia on Durham boats, or overland to Morristown during the Revolution.

The Oxford Furnace played a vital role along the tails of New Jersey for some 200 years. It put the area "on the map" in those days while "iron was king" in the hills of northern New Jersey.

Mineral Mining

Though New Jersey's prominence as a mining state has become largely a part of its history, Sussex County, at one point in the 1830's, had gained noteworthy national attention and even international recognition.

Thanks to the experiments of Dr. Samuel Fowler, attention focused on the unique mineral deposits of northwestern New Jersey. Fowler had an established career as a distinguished physician throughout northwestern New Jersey when, in 1810, he decided to move from his home in Hamburg to a place a few miles further south. There he would discover ore deposits in the limestone formations that were to bring Sussex County, and the community he founded, enduring fame among geologists, mineralogists, and just plain "rock hounds" from throughout the world.

Fowler was the son-in-law of Robert Ogden, who, you may remember, had purchased property in what was then western Morris County in the 1740's, and gotten into the iron industry.

Ogdensburg took its name from him, and was a leading iron center by the time Sam Fowler began building the homes, shops, and mills at the place, which he named Franklin. That area had long since broken away from Morris and become Sussex County.

While Fowler was at his new village, he enlisted the aid of a friend from New York City, Dr. Archibald Bruce, to examine the chemical nature of the rock materials he had been examining there. It was Bruce who discovered what he believed to be zincite in the rock formations.

Within a short time thereafter, the international scientific community had heard of, and become interested in, this new mineral find in the hills of northwest New Jersey's Sussex County of which Warren was then still a part.

Pierre Berthier, the French mineralogist who had discovered Bauxite, examined this new find in Franklin in 1819. He soon realized that he had a substance that contained ores of both zinc and manganese. In view of the location of the find it was he who gave the now famous zinc ore its name. He called in "franklinite."

Though Dr. Fowler did not get to see the production of the metal zinc from his holdings in Franklin before his death in 1844, he did succeed in developing a bluish-white zinc oxide powder. This became an important non-corrosive base used in the production of paints. In fact, the first white, house paint made in the US using a zinc-oxide base was made in Franklin.

Primitive man had been smelting copper for a long time when he discovered that it varied with location. These variations had, it was later found, been the result of accidental additions. These additions were, in fact, producing alloys. An alloy of copper and tin, for example, produced bronze. An alloy of copper and zinc produces brass.

Zinc ores were thus unwittingly used in the making of brass products by ancient man, long before its recognition as a free metal in its own right. In 1838, the United States government, by order of Congress, used zincite from Franklin, to produce the metal zinc, which was "of an admirable pure quality," in the manufacture of this nation's first standard set of brass weights and measures.

In 1848 the zinc ores at "Mine Hill" in Franklin were to be extracted by the newly organized Sussex Zinc and Copper Manufacturing Co. It failed. In 1849, the NJ Exploring and Mining Co was founded for the same purpose. With a smelting plant in Newark, it succeeded, however, only in marketing zinc-oxide powder from the Franklin mine ores.

Finally, in 1896, the NJ Zinc Co. began the production of the metal zinc from ores mined at Franklin. Zinc production from that company set a record for the American zinc industry, and New Jersey was front and center. These mines were in full production until 1954. New Jersey's zinc mines contributed mightily during this period to America's industrial economy and its war efforts, which were highly dependent upon zinc. Until the late-1940's, New Jersey was second in the nation in the production of zinc. The Franklin mine was reopened in 1961, but never regained its once great status. It closed, probably for the last time, just about one-year ago.

Nevertheless, the zinc mining region in the Franklin area has brought enduring fame to the trails of New Jersey. Amateur and professional "rock hounds," from all over the world, are aware of Sussex County as a treasure trove of rare minerals. Some 212 species and varieties of minerals have been discovered there. It possesses one of the most productive mineral deposits of rare and unusual minerals to be found anywhere in the world.

Thanks to the curiosity of Dr. Samuel Fowler, the Franklin area has gained fame as one of the most interesting and sought after mineral finds on earth!

Copper Mining

America was for generations the "pot of gold" at the end of the rainbow for many Europeans. The idea that great wealth with little labor could be found there attracted many a colonizer. But are you aware that New Jersey was once one of those places in the colonies considered to be a leading source of precious metals? In the colonial period, the state was turning up enough rumors about the sought after minerals to whet the appetites of a considerable number of prospectors and investors.

Of course, they were hoping that their efforts would be crowned with the discovery of rich veins of gold or silver, visions of which dancing in their heads continued to lure many of our earlier colonizers. But if other metals, such as iron or copper, were uncovered, there were still those who were willing to take second best. Iron, in time, proved to be New Jersey's most enduring metal of value, but for a while it looked as though copper would put up a mighty fight for that honor.

Most have heard, by now, of the Pahaquarry copper mines in what is now Warren County that were opened by the Dutch probably in the 1650's. The Dutch, like the others, had been on the alert for precious metals since the founding of their American colonies before the 1630's. Was not that, after all, what America was all about? When stories began recurring about valuable metals that could be found in the area we call northwestern New Jersey today, the Dutch Commissioners in Amsterdam instructed the directors in their colony to look into these reports (with hopes, of course, that they would uncover the long-sought-after gold and silver veins everyone knew were there somewhere.)

The discovery of potentially valuable rich veins of copper ore in Pahaquarry led to the construction of the first inter-colonial highway in the colonies, the "Old Mine Road" from Pahaquarry in New Jersey to the Hudson River port of Kingston in New York. Since there were no shipping ports on the Delaware in those days, (Philadelphia had not yet been founded), the road was originally built to haul copper ore overland to ports on the Hudson.

When the English took over the Dutch colonies in 1664, the search for these precious metals as a quick source of wealth was by no means halted. But, like the Dutch, the English also settled for copper, and later iron, when gold and silver eluded them. In 1714, English Governor Robert Hunter, after whom Hunterdon County was named, proposed the minting of copper coins with the copper being taken from the Schuyler Mine in Bergen County. By the 1720's, there was sufficient copper being mined to precipitate a minor trade war over the Jersey copper trade. Continued squabbling went on for the next two decades among the Holland merchants, the English Copper

Company, and proprietors of the Jersey Mine, over who was to receive the copper exports.

In the late 1730's, Richard and John Stevens inherited the "Rockey Hill" Copper Mine in Franklin Township in Somerset County. It was about 8 miles north of Princeton, 3 miles north of Rockey Hill and 1 mile south of Griggstown, just east of the Millstone River. They went into the copper mining business in earnest, instituting significant technological advances by the 1740's to interest investors. In 1753, William Allen, mayor of Philadelphia and a mining speculator, along with Joseph Turner and other associates, invested considerable sums of money in the "Rockey Hill" Mine. Unlike the Schuyler Mine, most of its ore was shipped directly to England via the ports of New York or Philadelphia.

By 1755, Robert Hunter Morris, son of Lewis Morris, governor of New Jersey, and himself Deputy Governor of Pennsylvania, began investing in "Rockey Hill." As the mine prospered, he increased his investments. Unlike the Schuyler operation, "Rockey Hill" had been using unskilled labor - indentured servants, slaves, and part-time farmers. In 1756, it was decided to import skilled Europeans. Furthermore, a large house was built on a 160-acre "Mine Farme" to house an overseer and bunkhouses for laborers.

The high cost of shipping raw ore to England for smelting led the owners to investigate the possibility of constructing their own furnace. Parliament, however, had passed laws forbidding manufacturing in the colonies. The political position of the Morris family made it inappropriate to violate that law, even though many iron mines were doing just that. The high cost of shipping plus other unfortunate incidents at the mine eventually led to the owner's decision to "put the mine to sleep," thus ending another tale along the trails of New Jersey.

Industry in Warren County

The kinds of industry that developed in the upper Delaware Valley region of Sussex and Warren counties primarily were related to the farming, mining, and lumbering activities that were carried on nearby. As I have mentioned earlier, the first Dutch immigrants from Kingston came into the area along the Old Mine Road for the purpose of bringing out copper, which was discovered around Pahaquarry in the mid 1600's. But others soon came to farm, hunt furs, and to cut timber as well as to mine copper and later iron.

Members of the Depui family have left records indicating that the planting of extensive apple orchards took place in the region as early as the 1730's and that there was exporting of large quantities of apple cider to Kingston at that time. So cider mills were one of the earliest of industries in the region. The handmade presses of that day accommodated about 75 bushels of apples at one time, producing some 200 gallons of cider for each squeezing. By the mid-1700's, cider making had become a large and important industry.

We know, too, that wheat was so extensively grown in, and exported from, the Delaware Valley country, that by the 1760's the valley became known as "the breadbasket." So it is not surprising that a number of gristmills arose along its swift-moving streams. Records point to one operated by the father of the legendary Tom Quick in Milford during the 1730's. One was also being run by the Depui family at the same time in Flatbrookeville. With more people, the number and size of the mills grew, and the millers became important to the economy of the region.

The presence of the Delaware River and the large number of streams entering it made water transportation, as well as water power, important contributing factors to the region's early industry. Sawmills were in operation at least as early as the 1730's. At first, the timber was cut to prepare the land for crops. Starting with the mid 1700's and continuing into the mid 1800's, lumbering for export was a major activity. Tall trees from the region were sent to Easton, Trenton, and Philadelphia for their shipbuilding industries via rafts along the Delaware. Lumber for railroad ties became increasingly important from the 1830's on, and the need for building purposes increased with the ever-growing population.

Rafting of lumber down the Delaware was still going on in 1910, according to the J. Blanchard Michael family records. Rafts about 100 yards long and 40 feet wide would leave Port Jervis in the morning and arrive at Pahaquarry in time for lunch. They would be seen zooming through Foul Rift, near Belvidere, at about a mile a minute. These rafts could transport other goods, but were considered by most to be too dangerous for carrying people.

By the end of the 1700's, the wool industry had become important to the economy of this region. Lower Smithfield Township boasted a wool mill as early as 1780. The Depui family records indicate the presence of large numbers of sheep in the area as early as 1744. By 1820, with the growth in population, there were three mills in operation that produced a linsey-woolsey, a combination of linen and wool. Linen was produced from the large quantities of flax being grown. By 1830, fulling was added, a special process in the manufacture of wool that cleanses and thickens the cloth to produce a better quality product.

The manufacture of cloth had reached a peak in the Delaware Valley by the mid 1800's. And this may explain why there were so many clothing makers advertised in Belvidere, in the 1850 issue of the "Warren Journal." The Depui and Stroud family ledgers indicated that many types of wool materials were being produced in the area by then. In the 1870's, farmers of the region were shearing 73,000 pounds of wool per year, while by 1880, it had risen to almost 90,000 pounds. Many workers were being employed in the wool mills operating throughout the region during that period.

But by the 1890's, growing sheep and producing cloth had become of little import to the region. This industry, too, joined those others of the past that had come and gone along the trails of the Delaware Valley in New Jersey. But more tales of other early industries will have to wait for other times, since time and space have once again run their course.

Andover Forge

Whether we speak of the hills and mountains of North Jersey or the Pine Barrens of South Jersey, at some period in their history, "iron was king." Bog iron still exists in the Barrens, but it is no longer profitable to "mine." I've heard that some 600 million tons of iron still resides in North Jersey's iron hills, but shafts to recover it must now go too deep. New sources are cheaper to obtain.

At one time several hundred mines, furnaces, and forges dotted the North Jersey Mountains. Ironmasters made fortunes, and built great manor houses. Iron was the chief material needed for the farm tools, the kitchen utensils, and the wheels of industry and transportation of early America. It was essential to the very existence of a civilized life in the colonial era. It provided the nails for our homes, shoes for our horses, axles for our wagons, and the munitions and tools for war. Jersey's ironworks were vital to the very continuance of the American Revolution. Whole villages in Jersey were born, prospered, and died based upon iron. Ironworkers were considered so important that they were relieved of the necessity of serving in the army. Iron was important to America's survival, and New Jersey had it.

There were certain essentials to keep the iron industry in operation. Primary, of course, was the source of the mineral itself. Next came the necessity of having a large nearby forest resource to keep the furnace burning. Limestone also had to be available for the forges. To keep them going, waterpower was needed. Since these requirements could only be obtained in isolated areas, the workers to man the industry had to be brought in from elsewhere. Thus, we saw the creation in New Jersey of whole new villages based solely upon the production of iron.

When the iron industry collapsed, so often did the little villages that surrounded them. Unless they could import another industry to give their existence purpose - they became "ghost towns." New Jersey had many such ghost towns following the demise of their iron industry. Two notable examples of such towns in South Jersey, which were restored as historic sites, are Allaire - near Asbury Park, and Batsto - near Atlantic City.

One such place in North Jersey was Andover Forge, later known as Waterloo Village. This little iron village came into existence when William Allen and Joseph Turner of Philadelphia bought the land from the Penn family. There on the Musconetcong River, in 1763, they built their iron forge. Thousands of acres of heavily forested land and the rushing waters of the Musconetcong in the heart of North Jersey's iron mountains provided the ideal setting. The production of iron was Andover Forge's purpose for existence.

It became an important producer of material for the American Army during the American Revolution. Its cannon balls were especially sought because of their fine quality. First it had to be seized by the patriots from its owners, who were outspoken Tories. American soldiers, wounded in nearby skirmishes, were also said to have been hospitalized there. The original village was built around the Furnace and Forge. The ironmaster's house, a store, a gristmill, and living quarters for its workers were nearby.

A general economic decline in the nation followed the end of the American Revolution. This recession, plus a shortage of wood for fuel in the area, created hard times for the people of Andover Forge in the post-Revolutionary period. The iron furnace made a gluttonous demand on its once seemingly endless forests. The land was finally purchased in 1799 by John Smith. He saved the village from collapse by opening a flax mill. Smith himself also established a large farm.

The defeat of the arch devil of his day, Napoleon, by the British at the Battle of Waterloo in 1815 was received with joy all over the world. Napoleon had been viewed by many as another Atilla, bent upon world conquest. His defeat was a cause of much relief in many quarters of the young nation. In honor of this English victory, Smith renamed his village, Waterloo, around 1820.

Waterloo was nearly asleep again when construction of the Morris Canal in 1831 brought it a new lease on life. Prosperity returned by 1834, as the little village became a busy canal port. Life in Waterloo seemed destined for a new permanence as the villagers built a church, and the gristmill took on greater importance. The Morris Canal was the greatest engineering feat of its day. Its presence at Waterloo now connected that little village to new outlets for its milled flour. Local farmers as well as villagers prospered. Waterloo became a bristling commercial center along the canal route.

With the coming of the railroad, traffic on the canal declined. Waterloo could hold on no longer. Its reason for existence gone, it joined the ranks of the New Jersey ghost towns. Percival Leach and Louis Gualandi purchased the overgrown site and formed the Waterloo Foundation in the late 1960's. Their dream was to recreate the village as a living museum portraying the social and economic life of that period in New Jersey between 1750 and 1850. Waterloo Village, once again, had a purpose. This time its purpose was to reveal its past. Having lived through both iron and the canal eras, it is unquestionably among the most important historic sites in New Jersey.

Waterloo Village in Byram Township is administered by a private, non-profit Foundation, though it sits in the midst of the 10,000 acre Allamuchy Mountain State Park. Named to both the New Jersey and the National Registers of Historic Places, it is located off of Route 206 and 80 near Stanhope in Sussex County. Reawakened after a century of sleep, Waterloo's resurgence into a New Jersey Williamsburg can only be realized with public support for its purpose in existence. A visit there would be well worth your time.

Long Ponds Ironworks

Another reminder of the days when "Iron was King" in New Jersey's northern highlands is being threatened with extinction. Attention was focused on the historic Long Pong Ironworks near West Milford as plans for the Minksville Reservoir came to light. When the Hackensack Water Company, in conjunction with the North Jersey District Water Supply Commission, announced its plans to build the reservoir by 1985, the "Friends of the Long Pond Ironworks" came into existence.

On land owned by the state, the Monksville Reservoir is also being proposed as part of a state recreational area similar to that at Spruce Run and Round Valley. What the "Friends of the Long Pong Ironworks" are hoping is that this historic Ironworks can also be incorporated into the recreational plans as a state historic iron village. Many of the old village's original buildings are still standing. In addition to the ruins of three furnaces, a forge and a waterpower system, there is an Old Inn, a church, a country store, and several homes.

Founded by a German immigrant, Peter Hasenclever, in 1766, the Long Pond Ironworks, like so many others in North Jersey's Iron Hills, played an important role in providing weapons needed by the colonists during the American Revolution. One of the ironmasters at that time was Robert Erskine, who later became George Washington's geographer and surveyor-general. Long Pond was what the Lenni

172

Lenape Indians called the body of water we now know of as Greenwood Lake. The Long Pond Ironworks gained tremendous waterpower by the damming of that lake.

Hasenclever brought over about 500 German immigrants to work the mines and ironworks not only at Long Pond, but at the charcoal driven furnaces at Ringwood and Charlottesburg as well, where he later served as ironmaster. Johann Jacob Faesch replaced him at Long Pond, and later founded another ironworks at Morris County's Mount Hope. It is believed that sections of the "Great Chain," used by the Americans to block travel by the British on the Hudson River, were forged at the Long Pond Ironworks.

Martin Ryerson, who later founded what is now called the Ryerson Steel Co. of Chicago, also served as one of the Long Pond's ironmasters. Other famous Ironmasters at Long Pond were the industrialist-inventor, Peter Cooper, and his son-in-law, Abraham Hewitt. It was during their period that iron from Long Pond provided gun barrels used at the time of the Civil War, and the iron plates for the North's ironclad ship, "The Monitor," manufactured by Cooper-Hewitt & Co.

Although many of the original buildings of the old iron village are still intact, three of them, the Wanaque Valley Inn and the Patterson House, both built around 1767, and the Writenour House, built in the early 1800's, are threatened to be underwater unless moved. The Long Pond Ironworks Historic Sites Committee, the Friends of the Ironworks and the Northern Highlands Historical Society have all joined forces to explore ways to find the help and funds needed to keep New Jersey from losing another of its links to its unique heritage. The Long Pond Ironworks is just one more historical window that is threatened to be closed on a view of New Jersey's role in those epics of American history - the Revolutionary and Civil Wars.

The last fires of Long Pond's Furnaces were finally blown out around 1882, ending another era in New Jersey's long, and the illustrious heritage. The days when "Iron was King" in New Jersey's northern hills was ending. It was Pennsylvania's anthracite coal which finally caused the downfall of Jersey's ironworks. After New Jersey's once dense forests, the source of its charcoal, became depleted, railroads and the Morris Canal, at first, imported the needed coal to the Jersey ironworks. But in time, it proved to be far more economical to operate the blast furnaces near the sites of Pennsylvania's coal mines.

The loss to the state's economy was probably considered by many late generations to be gain in its environment as the gigantic steel mills which replaced the old ironworks spewed forth their daily tons of noxious gases. Today, some of the economic loss the state suffered when its ironworks industry died could be recouped, at least in part, by a much cleaner industry - the tourist trade, which its restored old iron villages could attract back to the trails of New Jersey a century later.

Ringwood Mines

I spoke last week of the threatened extinction of the Long Pond Ironworks above West Milford, nestled on the edge of the Bearfort Mountains, near the border of Sussex in eastern Passaic County. It seems appropriate at this time that I call your attention to its sister ironworks at Ringwood. Ringwood lies nearby to the east of Long Pond, between the Bearfort and Ramapo Ranges. This was the eastern edge of Jersey's iron hills, which extended from western Passaic, through Morris, northern Hunterdon, Sussex, and Warren Counties.

Unlike Long Pond, Ringwood has been preserved and developed into a popular state park. By the 1730's, Dutch and German families had migrated into these rugged, wooded highlands in sufficient numbers so that a mountain range of that area, the Kanouse Mountain, bears one of their family names. It was the Ogden family of Newark, however, who formed the "Ringwood Company" and began smelting iron there in 1741, at a forge built earlier by Cornelius Board.

When English financial interest heard of the rich iron deposits in the North Jersey highlands, they hired a German iron expert, Peter Hasenclever, to come to the colony in the 1760's. He was to buy up suitable lands to develop an iron industry there for them. By 1764, he had purchased some 50,000 acres of the heavily forested North Jersey hill country, including Ringwood and Long Pond. By 1765, he had some 535 German immigrants there building roads, ironworks, and the prosperous little village of Ringwood. A year later, the Long Pond Ironworks was underway at the southern end of what is now Greenwood Lake.

"Baron" Peter Hasenclever rode about those wild-forested hills in a coach-and-four like a feudal lord. While the German colonists he brought over lived humbly in the nearby forest, Hasenclever lived in luxury in the Big House where a brass band entertained him every evening. His sponsors in England were so delighted with the profits he brought them, that it is said he was enabled to dine from a dinner setting of gold plates! Tales of the "German Baron" became a unique part of Jersey's iron hills.

In 1769, Hasenclever was succeeded at Ringwood by John Faesch, who in turn was succeeded in 1771 by a Scotch engineer, Robert Erskine. It was to Erskine, that Washington's Quartermaster, General Henry Knox, gave high praise. Knox obtained shells from Ringwood for the American army under Erskine's reign, which he extolled as "nearly perfect." Erskine, it later turned out, was Washington's secret mapmaker during the war. Washington also stayed at Ringwood with Erskine, after the aborted mutiny of the "Jersey Brigade" at Pompton, in January of 1781, forced him to reluctantly call for the execution of two of its leaders, as examples.

Many of North Jersey's ironmasters were familiar faces, at more than one of the ironworks, in Jersey's iron hills. One of those who served at Ringwood after 1807 was Martin Ryerson, a descendant of an early Dutch family of the area. Ryerson was at Ringwood when the ironworks furnished shop for the War of 1812. The Ryerson parlors are a part of the display at the ironmaster's house, Ringwood Manor, where the Ryerson family lived until 1853.

Peter Cooper bought the Ringwood Manor and 22,000 acres of surrounding land in 1853, and brought the Ringwood iron mines to their greatest heights. This he was enabled to do with the combined fortunes of his son-in-law, Abram Hewitt. The wealthy Hewitt married Cooper's daughter, Amelia, in 1855. Cooper, who was born so poor that he had to make his own shoes, never forgot his humble origins. He established Cooper Union in New York in 1859, where penniless boys could gain an excellent technical education. Peter Cooper died in 1883 at the age of 92.

By the 1880's, the Ringwood mines had reached their peak - with about 900,000 tons annually begin taken from some 20 mines by the Cooper-Hewitt combine. From then on, it was downhill. Though still being mined in the early days of the "Great Depression" during the 1930's, it was an infrequent operation. Eventually the descendants of the Cooper and Hewitt families gave the rambling chateau called "Ringwood Manor," with its 78 rooms, a symbol of a day that had long passed, to the State of New Jersey. Today it is an historic site in the midst of a State Park - with a lot of tales to tell about "barons" who once roamed the trails of North Jersey's highlands in the days when "Iron was King."

Oxford Furnace

Oxford Furnace in Warren County deserves far more attention for its role in both the state and the nation's industrial heritage than it receives. It seems odd that an ironworks that pre-dates the nation's birth, that played a role in supplying material in just about every war from its inception until World War II, and that made a significant contribution to the technology that made possible our modern steel industry, should stand practically unnoticed today. The very fact of its existence in the midst of rural Warren, should, by itself, make its origins of interest to those with even a modicum of curiosity. This monument to our industrial heritage deserves to be elevated to its proper status among the state's historic sites.

As the longest operating ironworks in our nation's history, spanning three centuries from its inception in the early 1740's to its demise about 1940, it qualifies for noteworthy recognition. Its significant role in the provision of iron products for the armies of the Revolution should stir the emotions of at least the American Revolution buffs. The fact that it was the innovator in 1834 for the utilization in the United States of the then newly discovered hot-air blast furnace, which revolutionized the steel industry of our nation, should certainly put the icing on its cake. It was this technology, after all, which plunged the United States into its role as the mightiest manufacturing nation the world had ever seen. And to think, the breakthrough occurred in Oxford, New Jersey! Add to this the interesting history surrounding its iron-master's mansion, "The Shippen Manor," and you have the makings of a unique tourist attraction.

When Jonathan Robeson emigrated there in 1741-42 from England, via Philadelphia, I am sure that he had no idea what a prominent role his ironworks was to play in the history of our nation. Built on fellow Philadelphia Joseph Shippen's land, the ironworks came into the complete control of the Shippen brothers, Joseph and William, by the time of the American Revolution. When they built "The Shippen Manor" in 1754, Robeson, who did not approve, sold out more of his interest. By 1762, he had pulled out of the Oxford Furnace operation, and was operating a large iron forge of his own at Changewater on the nearby Musconetcong River.

But apparently the Robeson family either did not get out of the Oxford ironworks entirely, or got back into it at a later date. Because in the Thursday, June 13 issue of an old 1850 newspaper, "The Warren Journal," the name reappears in connection with the proposed sale of the Oxford Furnace. A former Warren County resident, William H. Young, now living in Florida, who reads this column, was gracious enough to lend me this paper. And much to my delight, an ad appeared in it, placed by a William P. Robeson, dated April 18, 1850, and entitled, "FOR SALE, Oxford Furnace, With Mines, Farms and Woodland."

In this ad Robeson offers, "the celebrated Furnace, situated in Warren County, New Jersey, two and a half miles from the Morris Canal, and five miles from Belvidere, the county town." He goes on to say, "The Iron made at this Furnace is proved to be equal to any in the world." Robeson further notes in his ad that, "The Ore obtained within a quarter of a mile of the Furnace is of the richest quality and appears to be abundant." "A new vein of Ore of the best quality," he says, "has been found and opened within the last month. The exclusive right of mining extends over about 8,000 acres of land."

Robeson goes on to point out, "The FURNACE TRACT...contains... 5,850-acres, situated principally in the townships of Oxford, Hope, Washington, and Mansfield, all within six miles of the Furnace, that includes five farms, which he goes on to describe, and also a number of acres of woodlands in various stages."

In this ad back in 1850, Robeson further states that, "improvements at the Furnace are a large stone mansion, stone mill, stone store house, and a number of dwellings for work-hands, with sufficient stabling for mules, etc., etc." The price he places on all this is "the low sum of $100,000 or a little over $16.00 per acre payable in three annual payments with interest." To me an ad such as this, appearing as it does in the actual newspaper of its day puts flesh on the bones and blood in the veins of what otherwise is merely an historical character. It makes this account of the Oxford Furnace more than just another tale of what went on along the trails of New Jersey so long ago.

Union and Taylor Iron Works

One of America's longest operating ironworks, Union Forge at High Bridge, provided Hunterdon County with its earliest industry. Dating back to the early 1700's, this industry was almost lost to Hunterdon in the early years following the American Revolution because its furnaces had gobbled up the nearby forests faster than they could reproduce themselves. This was done in an overly eager attempt to provide the much-needed military supplies made of iron for America's war effort. No consideration was given to the effect this overuse would have upon the future needs of the area. This often happens in time of war. Modern wars, with their gigantic involvement of people, places, and products, are even guiltier than those of the past are.

You may perhaps wonder why a bountiful supply of nearby forests was so vital to the early production of iron. Very simply put, in order to reduce iron ore deposits to the metallic substance that may be turned into useful products, it was necessary to smelt it.

Smelting is the process of separating the metallic iron from the ore, by putting it under tremendous heat in a furnace. This operation needed the three nearby essentials of iron ore, fuel, and flux (usually lime) in order to make it profitable. The iron ore and lime was found in great amounts in Jersey's northern hills. Wood from its abundant nearby forests was converted into the much-needed charcoal for fueling the iron furnaces.

These iron furnaces produced the simple pig iron or iron bars from which varying products were to be made. Charcoal was the fuel, which also provided the heat to work the pig iron into a variety of useful forms. This was done under the hammer in the forge. Since coal was not yet available, lavish amounts of charcoal made from nearby forests was the essential fuel needed in any iron production; thus the necessity of an extensive nearby forest.

Taylor's Forge (now High Bridge) owed its rebirth to the coming of the DL&W Railroads in the mid 1800's. Now anthracite coal could be brought in cheaply enough to provide fuel for its ever-hungry furnaces. Within a few years after the coming of the railroads, the Hunterdon Hills were back to their former heydays. Iron products for railway use became a leading manufacturer. Iron mining at High Bridge (a name given to Taylor's Forge by the railroads), Cokesbury, Asbury, Jugtown, and Glen Gardner was operating in full swing.

Robert Taylor's son, Archibald had succeeded him as head of the Union Iron Works upon his death in 1821, and he in turn was succeeded by his son, Lewis, following his death in 1860.

After undergoing several name changes, the Union Iron Works became the Taylor Iron Works in 1868. By then production at the north Jersey ironworks had more than doubled.

As in previous wars, the Union Iron Works had been providing much needed iron products for America's Civil War efforts. By the late 1870's, after Lewis' son William Taylor had taken charge of the Taylor Iron Works, the newly patented process of manufacturing manganese steel was added to improve the company's railway products. By 1892, it had changed its name to the Taylor Iron and Steel Co. in keeping with this innovation. A new industry was, in fact, added to Jersey's contribution to America's growing industrial might. During the Spanish-American War, the Taylor Iron and Steel Co. was called upon to manufacture cast steel shells for the American war effort. This production continued a tradition carried on since casting cannon balls for Washington's army so long ago.

Adding to its continuing contributions to America's leading historic events, this northwest Jersey industry at High Bridge made steel power shovels that made possible the digging of the Panama Canal.

179

Knox Taylor, William's son, had succeeded him in 1910. He was to be the last of five generations of Taylors to direct this company. In 1912, he absorbed the Wm. Wharton Co. into the Taylor-Wharton Iron and Steel Co. In time, it became one of the foremost manufacturers of naval guns in the nation, for use in World War I. Throughout these years, it continued to manufacture railway equipment. World War II saw it again deeply involved in war productions. By 1960, exhausted iron ore brought an end to the iron saga in northwestern Jersey's Iron Hills. Iron was no longer king along those Jersey trails where it had reigned for more than 200 years.

Belvidere's Promising Beginnings

Belvidere, the county seat of rural Warren County, had an inception that seemed to point to a far different destiny. The circumstances surrounding its settlement appeared to indicate that this little community was destined to become the heart of New Jersey's industrial region. Perhaps even its first Paterson! There were sources of power where the Pequest emptied into the Delaware, and at Foul Rift where the Delaware took a sudden plunge downward some 16 feet on its journey south, that gave early entrepreneurs reason to believe this area offered potential to move the wheels of some mighty industries.

Further factors, such as the nearby abundance of certain raw materials, seemed to affirm these possibilities. Copper mines had, after all, been discovered in the mid 1600's by Dutch further to the north at Pahaquarry. And then there was the unearthing in the early 1700's of rich veins of iron in the town's surrounding hills. You may also add to these the accessible hoard of dense forests, which were suitable for the production of untold quantities of the much-needed fuel, charcoal. It took about 350 bushels of charcoal, by the way, for every ton of iron produced. And the Oxford Furnace was putting out some 15 tons per week of pig iron. Forges could soon turn this pig iron into highly demanded iron products for farms, homes, and other industries.

In addition there was the easy availability of cheap water transportation to the then largest city in the colonies, Philadelphia.

This could be accomplished via the large flat-bottomed Durham boats as well as rafts that were easily launched down the Delaware from there. The Old Mine Road could be reached for transporting goods northeast to ports on the upper Hudson. Later, new overland routes would be developed for wagons through the mountain passes to Morristown and other points, east.

With many of these facts in mind, Robert Paterson, in about 1750, purchased a tract of land from William Penn's extensive holdings where the Pequest emptied into the Delaware. There he established a settlement he called Greenwich-on-the-Delaware. It was named after George Green, who was the first to settle the region back in 1738.

Nineteen years later, Major Robert Hoops, who also had visions of industry dancing in his head, bought Paterson out. The year was 1769. It was he who actually set about harnessing the power of the Pequest to set up several mills - a gristmill to grind the grain produced by local farmers, and a sawmill to provide building lumber from the endless forests of the region. He, too, shipped his products down the Delaware to Philadelphia. Hoops renamed the place Mercer, but continuously referred to it as "belvidere," from the Italian work for "a beautiful view." Eventually that name was officially adopted.

Hoops also established a slaughterhouse at this place. There, local farmers could ship their livestock for processing prior to their sale in the marketplaces of Philadelphia. Belvidere, by the time of the American Revolution, had become quite the center for trade for both nearby farmers and local industry. Washington's Army was being supplied with both Oxford iron products and Hoops' grain and meats at Philadelphia, via Belvidere. During the horrendous 1779-80 winter encampment, both grain and meat from Belvidere were being sent overland by wagons, through treacherous mountain passes, to Washington's half-starved troops in the Morristown area.

In the years following the American Revolution, the nation was plunged into a severe post-war economic depression. In the early 1790's, Hoops was among those who suffered financial losses. He was forced to sell out. The famous financier of the Revolution, Robert Morris of Philadelphia, bought out Hoops' interest in Belvidere and gave the lands to his daughter, Mary, and her husband, Charles Croxall. A provision was made in their deed, however, which restricted the land to the Croxalls, or their heirs, forever. Since this placed severe restrictions on what could develop in Belvidere, it is believed that it was a contributing factor in Belvidere's inability to grow industry.

It finally took an act of the state Legislature, at the end of the second decade of the 19th century, to undo this obstacle. Valuable time, however, had been lost. Other industrial centers began to develop in the meantime on the Pennsylvania side of the Delaware. But more on rural Warren County's industrial beginnings will have to await other times and other tales along the trails of New Jersey.

Industry and Hackettstown

The Delaware, the Paulins Kill, the Pequest, the Pohatcong, and the Musconetcong rivers were once considered sources of potential industrial power in Warren County. A huge industrial complex was envisioned there, as America entered the Industrial Revolution. Located on the Musconetcong River, and originally known as Musconetcong, Hackettstown was another Warren County community that had the potential for developing into the hub of a huge industrial center. When the first settlers came there in the mid 1700's, they built several mills which utilized the power from their river. The little settlement came to be called Helm's Mills; until a prominent landowner named Samuel Hackett indulged his ego and convinced the town-folk to rename it after him.

But it was not only saw mills and gristmills that developed in Hackett's Town. The blacksmiths that settled in the area using iron from nearby furnaces, and the woodworkers, whose skills were fed by the heavily forested areas surrounding the town, soon found a valuable outlet in Jacob Day's Wagon & Carriage Manufactory, which opened in the period near the close of the War of 1812. Its carriage industry was doing quite well, in fact, when on March 3, 1853, Hackettstown was finally incorporated.

So well did business boom, catering to the carriage trade that visited regularly at the fashionable Schooley's Mountain Springs health resorts nearby, that by the 1880's, Hackettstown had almost a dozen carriage factories in operation. However, I am sure it was not these factories that encouraged the Newark Methodist Conference to choose this bustling community in 1867 as the site in which to build its Collegiate Institute as part of its centennial celebration in America. That has since evolved into Centenary College. Between the social events that were encouraged by the patrons of the health resorts and the students of the institute, Hackettstown was developing into quite the cultural center.

Industry was indeed flourishing in the mid 1800's when the Hackettstown Mills placed an advertisement in the Warren Journal on Feb. 27, 1850. The ad gave "notice to the farmers of Warren, Sussex, and Morris that they can find ground plaster in any quantity, at all times from the 1st of April next, through the season of using Plaster, at his Mills, and which he will exchange for either Cash or Grain to suit the customer, and at as low a rate as possible."

The Morris Canal had come to Hackettstown in the mid 1830's, and by the mid-19th century the Morris & Essex Railroad, forerunner of the DL&W, had made its debut. In time, the town did manufacture such things as sawmill machinery, circular saws, wire and cables, leather and hosiery. But the great industrial city, heralded to develop along the Musconetcong River of Warren County, somehow eluded its predicted destiny. Hackettstown, like Belvidere, at the juncture of the Pequest and the Delaware, and Phillipsburg, across from where the Lehigh enters the Delaware, remained comparatively small towns in the midst of a basically rural county.

Throughout it all, agriculture has persisted and grown in Warren County, despite the inroads of early industry. Perhaps we will never really know why people did not come in great numbers to Warren County. In fact, in the 1870's, when other farming regions of the state were losing out to an influx of people and industry, Warren County's Great Meadows were being reclaimed from the swamps by an extensive drainage program, and thousands of acres were added to its agricultural production. And, as the coming of the railroads were making the production of cheap, western beef too competitive for the state's large cattle-herds, Warren's cattlemen shifted to milk cows, and by the 1880's and 1890's, had expanded its agricultural production into an even larger dairy industry.

In 1912, the state established an immense fish hatchery in Hackettstown, and the county was launched into a new era - a sportsmen's paradise. In keeping with its image, a larger and more modern hatchery was launched in 1983 on the Pequest. In the 1970's, the national government opened the Delaware Water Gap National Park north of the already extensive Worthington State Forest. Perhaps this is where the county's destiny really lies. Much will depend, of course, upon how ready Warren is this time for a new industrial revolution that's sweeping New Jersey, the tourist industry! Already the state's number two moneymaking industry, tourism has arrived as the industry of today and tomorrow along the trails of New Jersey.

Industrial Roots of Phillipsburg

For two centuries, one way, or another, it was New Jersey's "Gateway to the West." Though not incorporated as a township until 1851 and as a town until 10 years later, Phillipsburg, Warren County's largest community has roots that go back much further in time.

Its settlement along the Delaware as a Lenni Lenape Indian Village, called Chintewink, goes back to antiquity. It traces its history as a frontier settlement, however, as far back as about 1735. For many years, it was the last outpost of civilization before entering the uncharted West. It retained its frontier outpost characteristics throughout most of the 18th century. Having been a trading center with the Indians of the Delaware Valley, Phillipsburg is said by some to have been named after one of the famous sachems of the Delawares (Lenni Lenapes), Chief Phillip.

Formerly an Indian Village, a frontier Trading Post, the terminus for several stage lines linking points West to Morristown and New Brunswick, and the western port town for the famous Morris Canal, which provided a water route to Newark and Jersey City, Phillipsburg already had a colorful career by the early 1830's. But it was the coming of the railroads in the mid-1800's, that really put Phillipsburg on the map as New Jersey's "Gateway to the West."

By 1852, Phillipsburg not only saw the coming of the Jersey Central RR, but two major industries, the J.R Templin Iron and Brass Foundry and the Trenton Iron Company as well. With the arrival of the Belvidere and Delaware RR, and also the Lehigh Valley, by 1855,

Phillipsburg was well on its way to becoming the transportation hub of northwestern New Jersey. Being in the center of deposits of iron ore, limestone, cement rock, sand and gravel, having excellent transportation facilities, and easy access to sources of power, made Phillipsburg look like a sure bet, in those pre and post Civil War days, for becoming northwest Jersey's industrial hub.

Located just about 60 miles due west of Newark, and about 40 miles northwest of Trenton, Phillipsburg seemed to have everything going for it. By 1865, the Morris and Essex Railroad arrived in town. As I mentioned in a previous article, attempts were even made in 1860 to establish a regular steamship line between Phillipsburg and Port Jervis, NY, via Belvidere, which ended in a tragedy. The iron industry was well established by the post-Civil War period. The Warren Iron Foundry and the Andover Iron Company were expanding their facilities in Phillipsburg after the war. Rolling Mills, Boiler Works, and a Stove Manufacturer were prospering there by the time Ulysses S. Grant assumed the presidency in the 1870's. Phillipsburg had indeed become a railroad and industrial center of that day. And, for a time its silk mills contributed to Hunterdon County's short-lived silk craze.

But you could hardly mention Phillipsburg's railroad-induced prosperity without remembering the most famous and illustrious citizen of Warren County, the nationally renowned Railroad Baron, John Insley Blair. Born near Belvidere in 1802, Blair eventually settled in what was then known as Gravel Hill. With the Scranton Brothers, with whom he was associated at the Oxford Furnace for a time, he built what came to known as the Delaware, Lackawanna & Western RR. Eventually, he went on to become the sole owner of more miles of railroad property than any other man in the entire world! Blair amassed a fortune of more than 70 million dollars at a time when that amount was probably more like a billion would be today. Blair was so wealthy that during the Civil War he loaned the U.S. Government more than a million dollars.

In 1839, Gravel Hill changed its name to Blairstown. John Blair, despite his great wealth, maintained his home there for some 80 years. While there he built and endowed the Presbyterian Academy, which came to be known as Blair Academy. He also built Blair Hall at Princeton University, rebuilt Grinnel College in Iowa, and gave

185

generously to Lafayette College. During his lifetime he built more than 100 churches throughout the American West, and also founded many towns and villages along his numerous railroad lines throughout the country. But his roots were buried deepest along the trails of Warren County, New Jersey, where he died at his home in Blairstown in 1899 at the age of 97. Though Phillipsburg's rail hub did not ensure its continued growth into a great industrial city, the move there in 1904 by the Ingersal-Rand Co. from Easton, did help to maintain an industrial base in the economy of this comparatively small Warren County community.

"Cradle of American Industry"

As I have mentioned before, though we are one of a handful of the nation's smallest states in area, New Jersey is at the top on many specifics - one of them being industry. The City of Paterson, for example, was recognized as the "Cradle of American Industry" when President Gerald Ford set aside the 119-acre "Great Falls of the Passaic National Historic District" to help preserve an important segment of the nation's industrial heritage.

Likewise, our role in the nation's industrial research has been nationally recognized with the creation of the "Edison National Historic Site" in West Orange. This place preserves the original laboratories of the man who is credited with the creation of more inventions (he held 1,093 US patents) than any other individual in United States history. Both places should be visited, and revisited, by all who want to know more about their state's and their nation's heritage. And remember, too, that your visit to all of these historic sites is a vote to both continue and increase financial support for these kinds of endeavors. For, like anything else in our free-enterprise society, the money goes where the demand calls for it.

Though Virginia has its Williamsburg and Massachusetts its Sturbridge, the little state of New Jersey has entire villages devoted to either specific crafts, or the entire gamut of Early-American trades. There are periodic craft fairs throughout the state as well, and craft museums that emphasize those basic crafts of our early days. Live demonstrations of these crafts may be seen at various times and places in order to give you an idea of how the people of past generations provided themselves with the basic essentials of life. These old craftsmen - the forerunners of today's mass-production industries - took great pride in their work. There has been a revival of interest in recent years in these activities of an earlier time. And, also a longing to recapture that pride in workmanship and sense of accomplishment which those early crafts encouraged. A visit to some of these Jersey sites can help you to regain that spirit - and also start you on some interesting life-long hobbies.

However, you will have to watch your newspapers for the most up-to-date information about when and where local and regional historical societies, or other groups, are sponsoring these varied craft fairs and demonstrations. Again, their continuance depends upon public support. A prime example of a once promising enterprise that fell by the wayside for lack of public support was "Liberty Village" in Flemington.

This fledgling craft village had high hopes when it opened, of providing the public with both first-hand knowledge about, and the fine products of many of the state's early crafts. Tradesmen in the areas of spinning and weaving, blacksmithing, tinsmithing, candle-making, glassblowing, woodworking, printing, gunsmithing, clock-making, pottery making, chair rushing, and others tried desperately to maintain a living there. It was a unique attempt to bring back in one village traditional American crafts to today's society. It failed and eventually folded, for lack of public support of its enriching endeavor. It failed in a short time, in much the same way that all of the old American Craftsmen folded at some point in the past. They could no longer compete with the public demand for mass-produced goods. Its failure was an interesting parallel to what took place in American society over a much longer period of time in the past as the Industrial Revolution overwhelmed us.

One unique place to visit in the state is run by an individual with a burning desire to recapture the best of this early craft age. Along with a host of volunteers he has opened his "Museum of Early Trades and Crafts" in an old church building on Main Street and Green Village road in Madison. There, Edgar Land has displays and reconstructed shops of the early trades. They are changed regularly so that revisits are encouraged. In order to develop a better understanding of the work of an early America and its people, he intermittently sets up displays and demonstrations, covering about 50 early crafts and trades. He is still collecting and researching another equally large number for future use.

I have already mentioned the villages of Allaire, Batsto, Millbrook, Waterloo, and Wheaton in previous articles. All are scattered throughout every part of the state. All deserve your continuing support. They encompass either specific crafts or trades, or include combinations of them. Since time and space have once again enclosed us, we will continue our tales of those early crafts and trades along the trails of New Jersey at a later date.

Paterson: The Nation's First, Planned Industrial City

In a description of north Jersey's natural features, written back in 1778, the Passaic was called "a very crooked river" that rose in "a large swamp in Morris County" and emptied into Newark Bay. The river was said to "abound with fish of various kinds." A great falls in this river, at the "new manufacturing town of Paterson," was said to be "one of the greatest natural curiosities in the state. And, there was spanning the Passaic, as part of the Post Road from New York to Philadelphia, a bridge of 500 feet long."

In the early days of our nation, New Jersey's spectacular Passaic River Falls ranked as one of America's natural wonders. Travelers came, from near and far, to see this scene of roaring water plunging over a rocky shelf. It dropped some 77 feet through a 280-foot-wide gorge. Probably the earliest written accounts of this natural phenomenon were by Dutch travelers, back in the period of 1679-80. They described the Jersey Falls as a sight that put them in awe of "the power and wonder of God."

Under the guidance of the first Secretary of the Treasury, Alexander Hamilton, back in 1778, the falls area became the nation's first planned industrial city. It used the power of some one billion gallons a day of water that plunged over the rocky ledge of the river at this place. The governor of New Jersey at the time was William Paterson. The "Society of Useful Manufacturers," for whom he arranged the receipt of a charter, graciously named their new manufacturing city after him.

Over the years Paterson, "The Cradle of America's Industry," became a bustling, prosperous community. By the end of the 19th century, it was at its apex. At one time, in the 1800's, it was the home for Samuel Colt's famous 45 Revolver, credited with the "taming of the West." It was also once the nation's locomotive capital, which pulled the trains which settled the West. All the sails of America's Navy were once made in this New Jersey City. Foundries, forges, and mills sprang up along its riverbanks. Paterson paper mills once produced paper for the nation's leading publishers. One of the earliest submarines was produced here.

By the 1880's, Paterson had become the nation's "Silk City," gaining international fame for its products. New immigrants poured into its borders by the thousands. By 1900, it had become the 15th largest city in the United States. In 1912, a new hydroelectric power plant introduced the age of electricity, generating some 21 million kilowatts of electricity annually from its powerful falls. It was here, too, that Lindbergh's "Spirit of St. Louis" received its engine for its famous flight across the Atlantic in 1927. By the mid-1900's, however, it seemed that the bustling activity of two World Wars had thoroughly exhausted this once proud city. It was in the throes of death.

Then, as part of plans to celebrate the nation's Bicentennial, former Mayor Pat Kraemer and his wife saw a possible golden fleece for the city - in tourism. They spearheaded a drive for the development of a Great Falls Historic District surrounding Paterson's Passaic Falls. A new life was injected into the dying city - centered on its natural wonder, coupled with its historic significance. Today, after much heartbreaking and heart-building effort, 119 acres of the area around the Great Falls and its early industry are being refurbished with trees, walkways, ornamental lighting, and newly paved street.

The Great Falls Park, with picnic benches for visitors, is in a setting of restored buildings, each figuring some way in America's Industrial Development. It lies along the banks of a river over which hurtles its famous roaring falls. The refurbished former hydroelectric plant now provides electricity for the district. Channels, once constructed in the 1800's to harness waterpower for its industry, are being restored and landscaped.

Boutiques, restaurants, studios of artists and craftsmen, and high-class merchandise outlets are adding to the lure of visitors, who are beginning to be attracted to this scene once again. Only this time, the allurement is for both natural and historic.

The Great Falls of the Passaic, with its park and historic district, is another example of how imaginative individuals of this great State of New Jersey have given us new tales to tell, by capitalizing on the old - along the trails of New Jersey. And tourism is the name of the tool that is accomplishing this goal.

Edison: Invention and Research

We would be remiss in talking about New Jersey, if we ignored the obvious. We are, after all, a leading research and manufacturing state. What has made us wealthy, unfortunately, has also made us ugly.

But it need not be so. Through better planning and architecture, our modern industrial and research plants are attempting to blend more comparatively into the surrounding countryside. Beautiful industrial parks make living together with farms and homes far easier that did those ugly industrial factories that haunted our immediate past. Hopefully, a new age of research and industry is slowly dawning in New Jersey: an age that will bring with it a greater pride in our industrial heritage.

We must recognize that today our basic needs are generally met with mass-produced goods manufactured by unseen persons, or even non-persons, often in places far from where they are consumed. This was not so just a few centuries ago - even less in some areas. A relatively short period of time, in the history of mankind, has seen tremendous changes in the way we meet the necessities of life. Even what we today consider as necessary would have been challenged just a short time ago.

Because what we eat, what we wear, and what we house ourselves in are, for the most, part mass-produced, few people today have had experience in even handling the raw materials from which they are made, much less the process of actually producing them. Observing the manufacturing process itself in today's gigantic factories could be mind-boggling. To witness the complicated machinery at work makes one wonder how the human intellect ever conceived of such wondrous devices.

Yet, New Jersey has been in the forefront from the very beginning of the Industrial Revolution. Perhaps no state has seen the evolution of manufacturing, from the simple craft stage to today's modern industrial giants, developing before its very eyes so clearly, and in so short a period of time, as has New Jersey. In witnessing "the Great Falls of the Passaic" during the American Revolution (with his commanding officer, Gen. George Washington), Alexander Hamilton dreamt that the power of these falls would some day run the machinery that would make this small Republic into a great manufacturing nation. This dream gave birth here in New Jersey in "the Society of Useful Manufactures" (S.U.M.) following the war. The City of Paterson evolved. It was named after the New Jersey governor of that day. In a short time, New Jersey, with its excellent transportation facilities by rail and by sea, its easy access to raw materials, and its large labor force of skilled craftsmen, was a center of the new manufacturing age.

In 1976, President Gerald R. Ford, acknowledging that New Jersey's City of Paterson was "the Cradle of American Industry," established a unique national district in the region. Setting aside 119-acrea at the Great Falls of the Passaic to preserve the nation's industrial heritage, he declared it a National Historic Landmark District. Today, you can visit the Great Falls District, and enjoy still another aspect of this great state's heritage, its industry, being recognized for what it is, a great contribution to the miracle of modern America.

New Jersey's role in the development of invention and research - the mother of industrial might - is given national recognition in still another place in our state. The Thomas A. Edison National Historic Site in West Orange memorializes the remarkable achievements of America's most prolific inventor. The original buildings housing his laboratories for investigating, discovering, and developing those new inventions for bettering the lives of millions both here and throughout the world, have been preserved. Lying in the midst of the old factory buildings of the Edison industries, it will someday be in stark contrast to the modern buildings of today's industry, and then will perhaps be more appreciated. Along with it, is his beautiful country estate, in nearby Glenmont. Edison called his family residence, with its large library and beautiful wooded setting, his "thought bench."

Edison's laboratory was the forerunner of the gigantic corporate research centers that are now sprouting up throughout the Jersey countryside. In the same manner, other historic sites in our state preserve the "Craft Stage" that preceded the modern factories that now represent the industrial age in New Jersey. But a visit to some of those places, that will help us view Jersey's evolution into modern American, will have to await another time and other tales along the trails of New Jersey.

Glassmaking

Glassmaking. Were you aware that New Jersey was once one of this nation's major producers of glass, and Warren County was one of the few areas outside of South Jersey to be a part of that industry?

The fires of New Jersey's glassworks have been burning in its South Jersey glass mills since 1738.

So well known was the state for its glass production that the noted American poet, Carl Sandburg, once immortalized it in these words appearing in one of his poems written in 1904: "Down in Southern New Jersey, they make glass. By day and by night the fires burn on in Millville and bid the sand let in the light."

Though glassmaking in the American colonies did not begin in New Jersey, none of the others came close in either its importance or persistence.

Glassblowing was introduced in Jamestown, VA, as early as 1608. Salem, MA had a glassworks in 1639. Both New York City and Philadelphia had begun glassmaking prior to the 1700's. But it was in New Jersey that the first permanent and persistent glass manufacturing industry in the colonies was undertaken.

Warren County (then part of Sussex) got in the act during the period of the War of 1812.

To a German immigrant, Caspar Wistar belongs the distinction of establishing in New Jersey the first glassmaking industry in the American colonies to last more than a decade. Wistar, who was born in the German "Electorate" of Heidelberg in 1695, came to Philadelphia in 1717.

Realizing the need for a native glass industry in America, the by-then-prosperous Wistar launched his glass furnace across the Delaware River in Salem County, New Jersey, in 1738. He brought skilled craftsmen to New Jersey from both the Netherlands and the various German "States" to operate his glassworks. His craftsmen both plied their trade and taught the art of glassmaking to Wistar and his son, Richard.

The combination of an abundance of excellent glassmaking sand, endless woodlands, and navigable streams for transportation made Wistar's self-supporting glassmaking community, situated on Alloway's Creek in Salem County, an immediate, and a long-lasting success. He called it Wistarberg. New Jersey's then-deep woodlands provided plenty of fuel for the tremendous heat needed in the glass furnaces. The necessary potash came from the wood-ash residue resulting from the burning. The superior sand of the area guaranteed the necessary silica.

In the process of making glass, the intense heat of the furnace melts the "batch." Alkalies, such as potash, cause the ingredients to fuse into a molten, metal-like substance. Traces of varying metals provide the range of colors. While in its molten state, glass is manipulated into shapes, drawn into varying lengths and blown into a variety of sizes and shapes.

One of Wistar's apprentices, Jacob Stanger, went on to found New Jersey's second glassworks at Glassboro in Gloucester County around 1780. The Stanger family also became involved in the founding of many other glassworks during the 19th century. Around 1799, a James Lee founded the Eagle Glassworks at Port Elizabeth near the mouth of the Maurice River in Cumberland County. A few years later, in 1806, he was part of the group that built the original glassworks in Millville.

Throughout the 1800's, the glass industry prospered in South Jersey. Some were built at the sites of old ironworks. Such was the case at Batsto, where Jesse Richards built the "Batsto Glassworks" in 1846.

Though Salem, Gloucester, and Cumberland counties became the main centers of New Jersey's glass-making industry, other areas did get involved as well. Some 28 glassworks were in operation throughout South Jersey by the 1840's.

Two places outside of that area, however, also had important glassworks. One was in Hudson County where the Jersey Glass Co., founded in 1824, was to be found at Paulus Hook (Jersey City). The second was the Columbia Glass Works in what is now Warren County. Founded along the Delaware River during the War of 1812, this Warren County glassworks, which was probably located there to avoid British attacks, lasted well into the mid 1800's.

The T.C. Wheaton & Co. Glass Factory opened in Millville in the 1880's. By then, Bridgeton, Glassboro, and Millville had become known nationwide as the "Glass Triangle."

In 1971, the "Wheaton Historic Village" was established there, commemorating the once-prosperous glassmaking industry found along the trails of New Jersey. Today, it is run by a non-profit foundation to remind us of what that once-important industry was for the lives of South Jersey's people.

An extensive Museum of American Glass there presents a "panorama of American glassmaking" for visiting tourists. At the glass furnace, skilled artisans take you through the steps of transforming hot, molten glass into pitchers, bottles, vases, and other items of glass. It is worth a visit for a better understanding of New Jersey's heritage.

Industry at the Shore

We generally lose sight of the Jersey Shore's year round means of livelihood when we think of it only as a place to go in the summer. Those who were permanent residents were always few - until the opening of the Garden State Parkway in the early 1950's made the region so accessible. But in the past, those who did live there, for the most part, had been dependent upon the sea for a living. This was true of the early whalers who came there from New England in the 1700's. It was self-evident to those who watched its fishing boats busily moving in and out of its many harbors. The former shipbuilders and merchantmen, too, who once plied such prosperous port towns as Tuckerton, and the salt-makers of Toms River, all depended upon the sea. So, too, did those who catered to the tourist trade. Or, those craftsmen who provided the tools and equipment for other artisans of the sea. And those less-legitimately employed in piracy. Or the salvagers, who watched for the shipwrecks that often washed their bounty ashore. All had their eyes ever turned outward upon the sea.

But there have also been a few other interesting industries on the fringe of the shore area as well, which played important roles in the economic life and folklore of the region. One of these was the hunting of waterfowl. Game birds were in great demand in the marketplaces of New York and Philadelphia in the latter part of the 1800's. These birds were found in great abundance along Jersey's shore regions, and thus provided some of the year round residents with an excellent means of livelihood.

Not only did some natives engage in the shooting of waterfowl for the marketplace, but a whole industry of decoy carving grew up along the Jersey Shore as well. Artisans working in the craft, either carved them by hand at home, or were employed in one of the small factories that sprang up in the area. The purpose of the decoy, of course, was to entice live waterfowl to come to the spot where they were floating, which would then put them within firing range of the waiting hunters.

Another means of income connected with the marketing of these birds was the building of the small, shallow boats that were used by the hunters to hide in the marshlands. These Jersey Shore boat-builders eventually invented their own special boat in the late 1800's, known as the "sneakbox." It was developed especially to carry a hunter, his dog, and a supply of decoys into the shallow salt marshes. There they would remain out of sight of the unsuspecting waterfowl until they were within range.

Still another occupation among early shore dwellers was the making of cedar shingles. These were in great demand in the 18th and 19th centuries for roofing. Extensive cedar swamps inland from the shoreline made it a profitable business for the artisans of the time who

195

became quite expert at cutting them by hand. Still another means of earning a living, also related to the nearby woods, was the manufacture of charcoal. In great demand by the bog iron forges that dotted the area, charcoal was made from the ever-present scrub pines. It was a booming business until the post Civil War period when the bog iron industry collapsed. The bog iron forges were so important to both this region and to our nation in the 1700's and up until after the Civil War, that it will require special attention in separate articles.

The glassmakers, too, carried on their trade in this region for many years - using the excellent sand of the shore area. And, that too is worth some extra time to explore in greater depth. The growing of blueberries and cranberries became so extensive in the shore area that New Jersey is now one of the leading growers of these berries in the nation. So, while the roll and roar of the ever-present Atlantic breakers had indelibly marked the hearts and souls of most who resided from the Hook to the Cape, there have always been those fiercely independent creatures who invariable found other means to earn their living from that unique region we call - the "Jersey Shore." We will talk more about some of them in the weeks to come.

General Stores

Back in 1805, Samuel Temple wrote about the "General Store" of his day. It contained, he said, "salt pork and powder, shot and flints, cheese, sugar, rum and peppermints." Also to be found, he went on, were "tobacco, raisins, flour and spice, flax, wool, cotton and sometimes rice." There, too, you would see "Old Holland gin and gingerbread, brandy and wine, and all sorts of thread." Or you could get "biscuits and butter, eggs and fishes, molasses, beer, and earthen dishes."

Also to be had were "spades, shovels, whetstones, scythes and rakes, as good as any person makes." There you could find "shirts, frocks, shoes, mittens and hose, also many other kinds of clothes." Then, too, there would be "shears, scissors, awls and bonnet paper, old violin and catgut scrapper."

They would have "tubs, buckets, pails and pudding pans, Bandana handkerchiefs and fans." You could find "perfume most grateful to the nose, when mixed with snuff or dropped on clothes."

In the 18th century, isolated frontier New Jersey farmers often depended more upon peddlers on horseback to supply them with the goods they couldn't produce on their farm or in the home. His arrival was greeted with great excitement by the entire family. Not only did he bring breath-taking gadgets to work, and pungent items to smell, stimulating books to read, but news of the outside world as well. The latter was without cost, and probably as much desired by the lonely, news-hungry families. Their remoteness is hard for us to fathom today.

As transportation facilities gradually improved, the general store began to make its appearance throughout the New Jersey countryside. Most likely, it would be located near the gristmill and sawmill. The outlying farm families were already in the habit of making regular treks to them. If there were no mills, a crossroad or rail line could be inviting. Any place that might already attract people was fine.

By the 1860's, with the coming of the railroads, the general store was a fixture familiar to any New Jersey community worth its salt.

Farmers came in to barter with both the produce of their farms and products made by their wives. For these, they hoped to exchange manufactured goods or some other item they couldn't provide themselves.

The weekly Saturday night trip to "town," after all chores were done, soon was eagerly awaited by all in the family. It was more than an opportunity to refill one's larder; it was a much-relished chance to meet with other people.

There are many who still have nostalgic memories of the profusion of smells that greeted the nostrils of those who entered the doors of the old general store. The blending of odors was a co-mingling of pickle barrels and butter tubs, of cheese wheels and sauerkraut. The delightful fragrance of home-ground coffee seemed to intermix with the aroma of perfumes and spices and stacks of dry goods. The pungent scent of tobacco smoke of all flavors combined with that of the hardware goods. All seemed to fuse into that separate

197

and distinct scent that was peculiarly characteristic of the general store they frequented.

The general store typically found, along New Jersey's 19th and early 20th century byways, was a frame building with a front porch and a hitching post for horses.

Upstairs there would often be a meeting room - for it was more than just a place to buy and leave. The town's local "characters" would likely be found sitting on benches out front. A bulletin board would keep folks informed of local goings on. A US Post Office was more often included than not.

In the winter or on cold evenings, a nice, hot, pot-bellied stove with a nearby cracker barrel was at hand. There, chairs full of old-timers sat around solving the world's problems. It was a meeting place, newspaper, mail carrier, supermarket, and social hall all wrapped in one.

But changes began taking place in American society in the post-WWI era. New Jersey was in the forefront of those changes. Part of it had to do with the fact that soldiers were taken from the farms and sent to exotic places. Part of it was the result of the revolution in transportation brought about by Henry Ford's mass production of cars for the average man.

At any rate, "chain stores" started moving into many New Jersey communities and stores "specializing" in the sale of one product became popular. The old general store was being replaced.

By the 1930's, chain stores, along with retail "collectives," had weakened the hold of the independent grocer.

As gigantic self-service supermarkets with immense parking lots moved in, the auto-minded public was ready for them in droves. With the 20th century coming to a close, general stores have all but disappeared from the trails of New Jersey. They have faded into a sort of nostalgic folkway of a bygone era. For some, like an old friend, they are very much missed.

CHAPTER 9: TRANSPORTATION

Transportation in New Jersey

If you could travel in a straight line from Port Jervis, which is in New York State just across the border from New Jersey's northernmost point, to the tip of Cape May, the state's most southern reach, you would have measured only 166 miles. Of course there is no route that travels from north to south in such a direct line, but it does give you an idea of how small New Jersey is.

Other comparisons also help put the state in perspective. It would take, for instance, some 33 New Jerseys to make just one Texas. Furthermore, you could put two of Texas into one Alaska, and still have room for about eight more New Jerseys. Or, to put it another way, only Connecticut, Hawaii, Delaware, and Rhode Island are smaller than New Jersey. To travel a straight line from east to west, starting at Raritan Bay and ending at Trenton on the Delaware, which is the state's narrowest neck, you would cover some 32 miles. That is about the distance by road from Washington to Morristown.

Within the borders of this tiny state, however, we have almost 8 million people. That is only a few million less than the gigantic state of Texas! So you can see why we have more people per square mile than any other state in the union. Why do so many people insist upon crowding into our little state? One reason is our location. We are, after all, the "Gateway to America," and have been since the colonial period. The English recognized this when they took us from the Dutch. We face one of the finest and busiest harbors in the world. Jersey, in other words, is in a very accessible position for taking advantage of a very rich worldwide trade.

Beyond this busy harbor area lies a narrow strip of lowland stretching to the southwest. That land makes an excellent corridor for carting goods and people both south and west into the American heartland. It also is a perfect site for warehouses and oil storage tanks to hold those goods until they are ready for shipping, or for factories and chemical plants to convert those goods into more lucrative products. This key location has affected Jersey's growth, economy, and politics throughout its history.

Even the Indians saw the value of the state as a corridor to the west. Two major trails, the Minisink and the Assunpink, traversed the state from shoreline to frontier. The Dutch also carried on a rich trade through the state, much to the dismay of the British. Shortly after the English takeover they, too, established stagecoach routes across New Jersey linking their major cities, New York, Boston, and Philadelphia, to points south and west. The Morris Pike, the Old York Road, Laurie's Road, and the Kings Highway became major links to points west and south.

During the Canal Era, starting in the 1820's two major canals were constructed across the state. The Delaware and Raritan used the lowland corridor between Trenton and the Raritan Bay. The Morris used a far more challenging route through the mountains, in order to accommodate the rich iron forges scattered through Jersey's northern hill country. Both also served the farmers on their peripheries. Everyone benefited from the state's key location.

When America entered the railroad era in the mid 1800's, New Jersey was again the route of choice for major railways linking the harbor area with the western interior and the southlands. Its prime location at the nation's "front door," once again, was the key factor. New Jersey, with 11 major railroads operating some 2,000 miles of rail lines, led the nation in rail density and had the busiest stretch of railroad in the world! Is it any wonder then, that the state's most noted millionaire, John I. Blair, was a railroad magnate?

The state's leading railway line, in so far as miles covered, was the Central Railroad of New Jersey. Some others which played key roles in linking the harbor areas with points west and south were the Erie and Lackawanna, the Lehigh and Hudson River, the Lehigh Valley, the Pennsylvania, the Reading, and of course, for a time the Camden and Amboy and the Belvidere and Delaware Railroads.

Excellent 20th century roads became cheaper and more convenient means of transportation, and eventually led to the decline of the railroads, after a century of dominance. Across state roads, this time trucks replaced wagons and their colorful teamsters, returned as the major transporters of goods within the state by the mid 1900's. New Jersey's prime location, so vital throughout history in carrying trade and commerce to points west and south from the world's busiest port, continued to serve that role well. The New Jersey Turnpike, Routes 46 and later 80, 22, 287, 78, 9 and 1 have all been key links in this chain. Everybody wants to be where the action is, and the trails of New Jersey have been witnessing that action since the beginning of our nation.

The New Jersey "Corridor"

More than half of New Jersey's total area of some 8,000 square miles is mountainous or sandy, leaving one to wonder why the state's land has become among the most valuable in the nation. When it was one of the 13 original colonies, it was often regarded only as a "corridor" between New York and Philadelphia.

That narrow strip between the mountainous north and the sandy south connecting these two great cities was the only area of the state that saw any significant growth for centuries. It was no accident that five major battles and 100 smaller skirmishes and encounters took place on Jersey soil.

Because of its position, the state became "the Crossroad of the Revolution." And because it was a vital crossroad, its countryside also became the "Crucible of the Revolution." Is it any wonder, then, that George Washington had to spend so much of his time in New Jersey during the eight years of that conflict?

This same unique position as a "connector" route also put the state in the limelight during four successive stages in the history of transportation. The early turnpike routes, which carried both stages lines and large cartage wagons, the Canal Period, the Railroad Era, and the epoch of our modern superhighways have all seen New Jersey taking an important role as a "link" between here and there.

Though this "link" role has brought economic advantage, it has also had its bad aspects. Hurried people tend to drop their trash in places they are just passing through. Harried people are apt to be impatient with the valuable time this "passageway" is consuming. They think of where they have been and where they are going, and regard this "land in between" as nothing more than an inconvenience. Travelers, back in the colonial period, wrote of their many

201

"complaints" about their long, tiring trip across New Jersey. New Jersey became something to be tolerated.

For those who ventured beyond this "corridor," though, many surprises awaited. A very diverse and beautiful countryside greeted them. Over the years some stayed – mostly to farm. Others, however, came to enjoy vacations – either at its many lakes, nestled among forested mountains, or at its sandy beaches along miles of seashore.

Eventually, New Jersey gained a reputation as a vacationland. At first, only wealthy New Yorkers or Philadelphians came to build "cottages" on thousands of acres of wooded lands. These served as "retreats" away from the hustle and bustle of the city. Cape May became the play-land of wealthy southern plantation owners. With the coming of the railroads, great hotels, boarding houses, and "spas" sprung up in the mountains and the seashore. Fresh air and water were eagerly sought after as "cures." The Schooley's Mountains, Delaware Water Gap, Palisades, and the salt air of places such as Long Branch were popular health resorts for well-to-do city folk. Presidents, politicians of national renown and great entertainers also were among those who basked in the Jersey countryside. Vacationing at a Jersey resort became fashionable.

When employers began granting workers a "week off" during the summer, middle- America began coming to spend it in "the country" or at "the shore." First, it was by train. When Ford invented the mass-produced auto, however, a new era opened. Highways built during the 1920's and 30's saw thousands flooding them for a weekend in the Jersey countryside. Before WWII, one-day trips became popular. The big hotels and boarding houses were the first to feel the brunt of the day-trip era.

Following WWII, a new trend became popular – building a "summer home," for those who could afford it and even many who could not. Burgeoning lakeshore and seaside communities, "locked-out" once-accessible lakes and shorelines. The less fortunate found their way on day trips to a dwindling number of public resorts. Eventually, it became necessary for the state to acquire recreational properties for the major portion on its citizenry who were deprived of places to go.

As prosperity increased, along with greater ease of transportation, these "summer homes" were transformed into year-round houses while people only worked in the cities. Jersey's countryside became crowded with permanent residents and its highways with commuters. As air transportation became more popular, vacationers had to go "somewhere else" to get away from it all. Density of people, which once only existed along New Jersey's corridor, had begun to seep into both of its sides.

The energy crisis of the late 1970's turned people back to rediscover amusement closer to home. The advent of the Green Acres and Historic Preservation programs and a regard for in-state tourism also led to the rediscovery of what interesting sites there are to see, what a great heritage there is to enjoy, and how many places there are to go right here along the trails of New Jersey.

Indian Trails

New Jersey's early roadways were once pathways followed by its "original People," the Lenape Indians—or Delawares as the British chose to call them. Drawn by dreams of mineral wealth somewhere in the black hill country, adventurous early Dutch settlers along the Hudson gradually winded west in the years both before and after the English takeover in 1664. From Esopus (now Kingston), they followed a combination of Indian trails that finally became a route of their own – first to Port Jervis, then south along the Delaware called Pahaquarry.

This route bore a series of names over the years. It was once known as "The Trade Path" because that is what it became. Believed to be built to haul minerals back to the Dutch port of Esopus, it also bore the names, "The Esopus Road," and "The Old Mine Road" as well.

Lest you conjure up thoughts of these Indian trails as modern highways – erase those pictures. Instead think of pathways through woodlands at times overgrown and practically impassable, but clear-cut enough to make you follow. Years of travel made these routes positively distinguishable and in time wide enough to accommodate horse and wagon. But do not ever imagine concrete or macadam strips suitable for a modern vehicle to negotiate.

By the time of the American Revolution, "the Old Mine Road" had been in use by settlers for more than a century. It was used for hauling grain and cider to market and in bringing back necessities. It was recognized by Washington's mapmaker, Robert Erskine, as a suggested route for moving troops and supplies north and south. It had already accommodated a number of forts along its route during the Indian raids of the French and Indian War.

In its early days, it was the only route in and out of the Minisink Country. Once the Delaware was established as a water route to Philadelphia it lost some of its value for transporting goods. But its continued use by hunting parties and varied land travelers was verified by the many Inns or "resting places" that remained to dot its pathway.

Other trails long in use by the Indians also led settlers in and out of New Jersey's northwestern frontier-lands. One that comes quickly to mind is the Minisink Trail. A combination of several trails originated by the Lenape of the Minisink Country eventually led to the Jersey Shore. You will remember that the woodlands Lenape of northern Jersey's hill country had a definite tradition of traveling to the Jersey seaside at least once each summer for seafood and shells. It was sort of an annual Indian "clambake."

This trail was actually a combination of routes bringing the various branches of the Lenape tribes from their year round locales all over north Jersey to key points along the route. At these points, they joined other paths, all of which eventually led in a southeasterly direction to their rendezvous. The route became known as the "Minisink Trail" because it originated at Minisink Island on the Delaware. The several joining trails converged upon present-day Elizabeth on the tidewater, and thence south to points along the Atlantic as far as Tuckerton. There, the Indians celebrated their annual summer respite, before returning to their woodland habitats in the backcountry for the remainder of the year.

From Minisink Island, the trail led through present-day Hainesville, past Culver's Lake, then Branchville and on to Newton. It cut across Morris County into Union County where it joined with others at Springfield. Then, reaching a common trail at Elizabeth, it led south along the shoreline.

There were other well-traveled Indian trails as well, leading eastward to the coast from the Delaware. All of them became settler's roads eventually. One of those originated near what is now Trenton. Known later as the "Old Dutch Road," it was originated as the "Assunpink Trail." Stretching from the Delaware, it passed through such present-day places as New Brunswick, Piscataway, and Woodbridge before converging upon Elizabeth. From there, it joined the Minisink to points south.

"The Naraticong Trail" was still another route that led first Indians, then settlers from the Delaware eastward. This path stretched from present-day Lambertville and ended in Elizabeth. Eventually known as the "Old York Road" it traveled through Mount Airy, Ringoes, Reaville, Three Bridges, Bound Brook, and Westfield before joining the Minisink. Thus the "Original People" guided the early settlers along the trails of New Jersey.

History of Roads

"The Old Mine Road," a familiar route through the Delaware Water Gap National Park, stretched at one time for more than 100 miles. It started at the Pahaquarry copper mines and winded through what later became Millbrook Village in Warren County, went up along the Delaware past Flatbrookville and the old village of Minisink, then on to Mackhackamack, now Port Jervis. From there, it wended north and then east through what are now Wurtsboro and Ellenville. It finally ended at Esopus, once a Dutch port on the Hudson River. Its journey took it through a wild, mountainous region of forests, waterfalls, and Indians. It bore a number of names during its long history. But "the Old Mine Road" is its most familiar. The road probably even preceded the Dutch in its origins, though they are credited with building it around the 1650's to bring copper out of the backcountry for shipment to the Netherlands.

Most of our early roads were built over long-trodden Indian trails. Of course, the footpaths used by the Indians were not adequate for horse drawn wagons, and much work had to be done to accommodate them. But the original path was a much-used Indian passageway for untold generations before the coming of the white man. Washington's official surveyor, Robert Erskine, included the road on his maps of the area, so its location and use during the period of the American Revolution is also well established.

The road was first used as a pathway for trade, carrying out ore and furs, then logs. When settlers arrived, foodstuff was hauled over this ancient trail. Though at first used only by those seeking the riches of ores and furs, the road later became a passageway west for pioneer Dutch farmers immigrating to the Delaware from the Hudson Valley. Once established, these farmers began shipping their apples eastward in the more profitable form of cider, as well as their grains. These were exchanged at Esopus for the goods they could not produce for themselves. In those days, shipments south via the Delaware were unheard of. By the time the Delaware's outlet became known, this "Trade Path," as it was also called, had become well established as a transportation route.

In a time when you did not travel very far in one day, guesthouses, or resting places were established along well traveled routes at regular intervals. Later known as inns, they became quite popular with local folk as well. I had mentioned earlier that "the Old Mine Road" eventually became part of an established route between New England and Philadelphia. As such, it came to carry many a notable traveler during the days when the separate colonies were trying to become a nation. One of those travelers during the period of the American Revolution was John Adams, when he was serving in the Continental Congress. In a previous article I had also added: "and at the Constitutional Convention." Well, of course, Adams was not at the Constitutional Convention since he was serving as our ambassador to England following the war, so scratch that.

One of the first white settlers recorded living in the Minisink region along this road was a blacksmith by trade, Wilhelm Tietsoort. He lived about two miles below Mackhackamack (Port Jervis) around 1690. In 1713, he sold some of his land to a Jan Decker. During the Indian rampages of the French and Indian War, Tietsoort was driven further south. By this time, there were pioneer settlers scattered on both sides of the Delaware. Some of the old family names that appeared in the Minisink, according to the ledger of Aaron Depue, a storekeeper in the area in the 1740's included: Thomas Brink, Daniel Brohead, Jan Cortrecht, Adam Dingman, Nicholas Dupui, John

Fryermuth, Jacobus Quick, Thomas Quick, Benjamin Shoemaker, Abram Van Campen, Isaac Van Campen, Jacob VanKuykendalls, Anthony Westbrook and Abel Westfall.

Another Westfall, Jurian, was reported on April 1, 1756, to have had his barn burned by marauding Indians. This occurred on his farm at the Minisink near "the Old Mine Road," and involved a considerable loss to him of livestock and grain. Two years later, on June 13, 1758, eight men were reported to have been massacred at his place.

The village of Minisink, which was located somewhat north of the Sandyston and Montague areas, along "the Old Mine Road" south of Port Jervis, is said to have been the oldest settlement in northwest New Jersey (Sussex County). It started as a resting place for the men who were carrying ore from the Pahaquarry mines along "the Old Mine Road," Sussex County's first grist mill, saw mill, general store, church, schoolhouse, blacksmith shop, and cemetery were all said to have risen there. Minisink was once an important settlement along the trails of northwestern New Jersey, and many of those old families became a prominent part of its heritage.

Transportation Systems

New Jerseyans, like most Americans, have enjoyed such a fabulous transportation system for so long that most fail to realize the important role it has played in their history - and continues to play in how they live. Poor transportation systems today have much to do with the poor-ness of the so-called Third World nations. The use of all our modern systems of production are of no value, for example, if you can not get your product to a marketplace. Our own colonial craftsmen could not have increased their production and competed with craftsmen in other communities, even if they had our modern assembly lines, in view of the poor systems of transportation with which they had to suffer.

Even in the early 1800's, overland transportation in New Jersey was so poor that it was cheaper for our West Jersey farmers to move bulky agricultural products down the Delaware by raft or flatboat, reload them on ships in Philadelphia and sail them to New

York City, than to move them overland by wagon. Is it any wonder then that they eagerly hailed the completion of our east-west canals – the Delaware and Raritan and the Morris – in the late 1820's and early 1830's.

The first consideration any industry made, agriculture or manufacturing, if they were to prosper, was the cost of transportation. In the case of manufacturing, it involved both getting the raw material to the factory and getting the finished product to a marketplace. Once New Jersey's forests were depleted and coal had to be hauled in from Pennsylvania, much of the state's iron industry was on its knees. Not until the canals made transportation cheap enough for them to operate profitably were they back in business. It was no accident that the tomato canning industry got started in south Jersey. It was easier and cheaper to transport large quantities of this product to market rather than the bulky, perishable tomato.

Before the advent of the automobile and our modern highways, large concentrations of people were located near the their jobs. Most were in the factory towns near the cheap transportation hubs – the harbors, and later the railroad terminals. They in turn drew others to provide for their needs – store clerks, barbers, shoemakers, lawyers, doctors, etc. Cities grew at these points. The history of New Jersey of the 1800's is the story of how new systems of transportation were continuously changing once rural, farm-based areas changed into quite different places. As we advanced toward, and then into, the 20th century, turnpikes, canals, steamboats, railroads and finally, highways with their autos, trucks and buses. Each in turn had a tremendous impact on the history of New Jersey.

The coming of the railroads in the mid 1800's also had its negative side. By the time the Civil War was over, rail transportation was so perfected that the whole nation was now in brisk competition for the marketplaces of New Jersey. Iron from the Great Lakes became too much for the many little northwest Jersey iron industries. Midwestern grain put New Jersey grain growers out of business. New types of farming and ways of making a living had to arise. Each changed the countryside

In the 1830's, New Jersey's coastline was dotted with small but important trading ports. Its maritime status was apparent for all to see. The small ships of that day found it profitable to move trade in and out of its many ports. Shallow bays and small rivers could accommodate them easily and profitably. Newark, Jersey City, Elizabethport, the Amboys, New Brunswick, Salem, and Burlington were just a few of the larger ones. But the coming of the railroads brought such a flow of materials overland that soon only larger ports could handle the size of the seagoing vessels required for them to stay in business. Seaport trade, shipbuilding industries, and wharf-side jobs were all affected. The coming of the railroads radically changed New Jersey's once dominant seaport trade – altering both its history and its character.

In their day, the canals, seaports and railroad terminals of the 19th century, New Jersey acted as magnets that drew people to certain population centers. It was important to be near them to prosper. In between these centers, there remained an abundance of open countryside. Farmers were thus enabled to take advantage of this plentiful, cheap land. Large, baronial estates were purchased for practically nothing by wealthy New York entrepreneurs. They prided themselves on their vast country manors in New Jersey with their own private hunting and fishing grounds.

The coming of 20th Century highways had the opposite effect. People were no longer tied to population centers. For better or for worse, they could now be strewn wherever their autos would take them. The dramatic transformation of the New Jersey countryside began after World War I, was accelerated by World War II, and in the 1980's is about to transform the trails of New Jersey into something beyond recognition – and again alter its history.

The Great Steamboat Disaster

There are many stories regarding the use of the Delaware as a carrier of both goods and people. The Lenape Whihituck (Delaware River) has served as an artery of transportation since man set foot in the valley. The Lenni Lenape undoubtedly traveled up and down this water highway from the time they arrived in the land they called Scheyechbi. Among the first Europeans, Captain Cornelius Mey navigated his sailing vessel up the Delaware as early as 1614. He later brought settlers up this river as far as Gloucester, where he established Fort Nassau for the Dutch in 1623.

A half-century after the first Dutch from Esopus trickled down into the Upper Delaware around 1650, someone realized the value of the trees in the area to the shipbuilding industry. By the early 1700's, lumber mills were sending their timber down the river on rafts manned by a tough breed of river-men. These adventurous river-men also carried down-river the fur pelts that were gathered by trappers along such tributaries as the Paulins Kill, the Pequest, and the Musconetcong. Throughout the 18th century, Dutch, German, and French Huguenot farmers in the Minisink shipped their produce to market along the river highway.

The powerfully built Durham boats were much in use along the Delaware at the time that Washington made his famous crossing on Christmas 1776, before the Battle of Trenton. It was on these boats, too, that cannonball and other iron products from the Oxford Furnace were shipped to ports like Philadelphia during the American Revolution. But there are two stories in particular upon which I would like to draw your attention. The first concerns a Trenton clockmaker who piled the waters of the Delaware with the world's first steamboat!

John Fitch's original model, built in 1785, had paddle wheels at the sides. But in 1786 he changed this to a series of connected oars. It was a boat built after this later model, which he finally launched on the Delaware on Aug. 22, 1787, near Cooper's Ferry (Camden). This first steamboat was 45 feet long and 12 feet wide. Though constantly plagued with the inability to raise the necessary funds, he nevertheless went on to build a second, and larger vessel, in 1788. By 1790, he had a passenger-carrying steamboat plying the waters of the Delaware at 8 miles per hour from Philadelphia north, first to Burlington and later to Trenton. The public, however, was wary of the safety of a steam engine on a boat, and his financial backers refused to continue their support.

In 1793, John Fitch left for France where he hoped to find financial help for his steamboat experiments. Unfortunately, the French Revolution interfered with his high hopes. Without funds, and very discouraged, he was forced to work his way back to America. He left his plans there with the American Consul, where Robert Fulton later saw them. In 1817, Fulton launched what was claimed as the first steamboat. Fitch, discouraged over repeated failure, committed suicide in 1798.

His vision of steamboats carrying passengers and cargo on the Delaware eventually did become a reality below Trenton. In 1859, a project was undertaken, which brings up to our second story – steam navigation on the Upper Delaware! A group of Belvidere businessmen at that time, envisioned steamboat transportation plying the waters from there, north, to Port Jervis.

In early fall of 1859, three men, Richard Holcomb, William Sharp and Alfred Thomas, all of Belvidere, undertook the steam-line project. They gave the job of tackling the ship's construction to an Easton shipbuilder. It was determined that a steamboat with a 70-ton capacity would be feasible. The "Alfred Thomas," 87 feet long and 15 ½ feet wide, was ready for launching in early March 1860.

The eventful day was set. The maiden voyage was to commence on the morning of March 6, 1890. A great gathering of people assembled to witness this momentous occasion. The "Alfred Thomas" steamed out of the boatyard along the Lehigh amid cheering crowds of onlookers and passengers. It puffed into the Delaware at the Williamsport out lock. Upriver she headed, its passengers engaged in excited conversation, and waving to bystanders along the shoreline. At about noon she stopped at the Northampton Street Bridge to allow those who had not planned to journey all the way to Belvidere to disembark.

About three dozen people chose to stay aboard to complete the trip. At Belvidere, great preparations were underway for the launching of the initial cruise to Port Jervis. This, of course, was to be the routine run. With the sounding of the ship's bell the boat started to continue its upriver journey. She was not getting up enough steam, however, so the ship's captain decided to bring her up-shore at an island above town. There she remained at anchor until the necessary power was generated. The captain then ordered the sounding of the bell as a signal to cast off once again.

Almost simultaneously, an immense explosion electrified the people on both sides of the Delaware. With a violent blast of black clouds and orange flames, the upper section of the boat was hoisted skyward, ripped into pieces, and thrown about like matchsticks, the

211

timbers fell into the waiting waters. The remaining hulk slipped away from the shore and floated slowly downstream. Eventually, trapped against one of the bridge piling, it swayed there helplessly.

Shrill screams of anguish were emitted from aboard ship almost at the same time as the blast. Bodies were seen brutally hurled into the river. Some of the more fortunate jumped overboard and swam ashore. Among those killed instantly were William Sharp and Richard Holcombe of Belvidere. Rescuers took off in boats while large crowds gathered along the banks. As the dead and injured were transported back to shore, the "Great Steamboat Disaster of 1860" apparently ended forever any visions of a steam-line on the Delaware between Belvidere and Port Jervis.

The Morris Canal

The "canal bug" hit America in the second decade of the 1800's. It started when a canal to link the Great Lakes with New York Harbor was begun in 1817. Eight years later, in 1825, the Erie Canal was completed.

The charm and the colorful life of the canal boat, the locks and gates and the horses or mules pulling the boats along towpaths took America by storm.

New York Harbor became of much greater importance than ever before. New York's governor DeWitt Clinton was an overnight American hero. Cities and towns, including one in Hunterton County, NJ were named in his honor.

The Erie Canal was a huge success. People from other areas watched, then, built their own canals. Canals began to bind the nation together. Songs, stories, even legends about picturesque canal boat characters began to make the rounds.

Thousands of pioneer families used canals to move "West" at low cost. Farmers were, at last, able to ship their produce to the New York marketplace cheaply. The canal boats in turn carried manufactured goods inland. Everyone prospered.

So, in 1822, when George Macculoch conceived the idea of linking Phillipsburg to New York Harbor via New Jersey's iron hills, the state was ready for him.

The story goes that Macculoch's brainstorm came to him while fishing one day on Lake Hopatcong. Why not make use of the lake's water supply to link Pennsylvania's coal, New Jersey's iron, and New York's marketplace?

To the east of Lake Hopatcong, he theorized, the Rockaway and Passaic Rivers could help in making the connection to the Hudson with a terminal in Newark and then Jersey City. To the west of the lake, it could make it to Pennsylvania by using the waters of the Musconetcong River, then on to the Delaware with a terminal at Phillipsburg.

The state legislature authorized a study to be made of the feasibility of Macculoch's plan. In 1823, after receiving a favorable report, construction was approved for a private company, the Morris Canal and Banking Company.

More than a thousand workers, many Irish immigrants completed the 106-mile canal in 1831 – all by hand. It measured 52 feet wide at the top (too narrow, they later found), 32 feet wide at the waterline and 20 feet wide at the bottom. It was about four feet deep (too shallow for profitable use, they later found out). Its locks were 75 feet and nine feet wide. There were some 25 locks built in all.

The real challenge of the canal was to the mountainous west. The elevation of the canal at Lake Hopatcong was 913 feet higher than at its terminus near what is now Liberty State Park in Jersey City.

In addition to the 25 locks to raise the water level, inclined planes had to be used. The canal boats were pulled up the steep hills on wooden frames by chains or cables on these inclined planes. They ranged from 500 to 1,500 feet long. The walls of the canal were of stone and lime mortar. Concrete was, as yet unknown.

The canal boats could carry 25 tons of coal or iron ore, hauled by mules or horses walking along towpaths. Pennsylvania coal soon replaced the diminishing Jersey timber to fire the iron furnaces and forges. The iron then moved east to the bustling new manufacturing centers at Paterson, Newark, and Jersey City. Busy, prosperous, and often colorful port towns dotted its route.

Names like Port Murray, Rockport, and Port Colden sprang up. Older places like Hackettstown, Waterloo, and Stanhope came alive. Dover, Boonton, and Rockaway became boomtowns. Newark and Jersey City saw tremendous growth. Newark's population alone doubled in the decade between 1830 and 1840.

Canal boat captains became centers of activity and news. Canal boats themselves took on their own character and were affectionately given special names.

Though the canal era reached its peak in the decade of the 1860's, its decline probably went unnoticed at first. But with the end of the Civil War and the growing importance of the railroads, its eventual doom was sealed. The railroads quietly began buying out the canals in the 1870's and discouraged their use.

For the original investors, the $3.5 million cost to build the Morris Canal was well worth it. It revitalized northwest New Jersey's iron industry and canal-port towns. It gave an enormous boost to the production of fruits, vegetables and dairy products, which now had a ready market. It brought growth and prosperity to the wharves of Paterson, Newark, and Jersey City. It set the stage for the coming of the railroads.

By 1930, a defunct Morris Canal was taken over by the state. It limped along for a few more years, too small to compete. In the 1920's, it was drained.

Unfortunately, its historic significance was not realized. Most of it was sold off piecemeal. In Warren County today, where much of its original route was left untouched, the county hopes to create a "canal pathway" – to remind us of that colorful canal era that once existed along the trails of New Jersey – so long ago.

The End of Canals

Once the Morris Canal was launched, connecting the Pennsylvania coal fields with the iron hills of New Jersey and the burgeoning New York marketplace, other areas looked on with envy.

The newly conceived Phillipsburg-to-Newark waterway was envisioned as the economic savior of the region through which its pathway would cut. This vision was soon a reality.

Little port towns, such as Port Colden and Port Murray, sprang up all along its route. Other older communities, such as Waterloo, came back to life.

The renewed prosperity which it brought to the iron forges and furnaces of Warren, Sussex, Morris, and Passaic counties was only the frosting on the cake. West Jersey farmers, now with a steady marketplace for the produce, also prospered. What is more, the financiers were overjoyed with the blossoming manufacturing centers of Paterson, Newark, and Jersey City, which the Morris Canal was creating. The canal enthusiasts were very pleased and old hopes were renewed.

Just as the Lenape Indians had created a number of important trails extending from their main encampments along the Delaware to the New Jersey coast, so the canal enthusiasts envisioned a number of canal routes along similar lines.

The old "Minisink Trail" somewhat paralleled the Morris Canal to the north. The more centrally located "Assunpink Trail" led from the headwaters of the Assunpink Creek, along the valley of the Millstone, and then along the banks of the Raritan.

Pressure had been mounting as early as the War of 1812 to launch a canal eastward from the state's capital at Trenton. Along the route of the "Assunpink Trail," it would utilize Assunpink Creek, the Millstone and Raritan Rivers, and finally link Trenton by water to New Brunswick. From there, ships could easily connect with New York harbor.

In 1829, while the Morris Canal was well underway to the north, advocates of the Delaware & Raritan Canal pressed their case. Though "canal fever" had captured everyone's imagination, a new, more spectacular means of transportation was now also screaming for attention – steam-powered railway cars. This railroad system was competing with the advocates for the state's second canal for a state charter to provide a service over approximately the same stretch.

But a canal enthusiast, Robert Stockton of Princeton, was convinced that New Jersey could utilize both. He envisioned railroads servicing the passenger and light freight trade, while canals would handle bulky cargoes, such as coal, iron, grain, and lumber. He joined forces with the railroad. Stockton convinced legislators that New Jersey could have the best of both worlds.

As a result, the state legislature approved the building of the Delaware & Raritan Canal and the Camden & Amboy Railroad.

215

Built with private funds, the Delaware & Raritan Canal made money for its financiers from the start. Its marriage to the Camden & Amboy Railroad proved to be a stroke of genius. Without the ravages of early competition from the railroad, which badgered the Morris Canal, the Delaware & Raritan became the busiest canal in America! In its peak years between 1859 and 1870, it carried a larger volume of freight than even the Erie.

Unfortunately, once the Camden & Amboy Railroad was taken over by the enormously competitive Pennsylvania Railroad in 1871, a whole new attitude prevailed.

Just as the canal boats had captured much of the commerce from the earlier four-horse wagons, so the railroads began taking away customers from the canals. Trains could haul freight in one hour that took the canals all day. They also did not have to worry about freezing over in the winter months. Though freight business on the Delaware & Raritan Canal dwindled away, as it did on the Morris, it hung on there considerably longer. Pleasure boats also used it long after it ceased to carry freight. The last canal boat carrying freight on its waters was in 1933, long after the Morris Canal had been drained.

Its enthusiastic supporters never gave up. In 1943, they urged its renewal as part of an inland waterway to escape German U-boats during WWII. For 50 years, canoeists have been paddling along its quiet waters and camping along its towpaths. It was never drained. It has been utilized as part of a water system as well.

In recent years, the state has been developing this historic waterway as a 60 mile "Delaware and Raritan Canal State Park," which passes through Mercer, Hunterdon, Somerset, and Middlesex counties. Canoe and canal enthusiasts, hikers and history buffs all are grateful for the preservation of this slow-moving waterway, still intact along the trails of New Jersey.

Along its route they can yet explore areas steeped in history and natural beauty, traversing beside what was once the ancient "Assunpink Trail" of the Lenape Indians – New Jersey's "Original People."

Trolley Cars

There is no denying the economic impact to New Jersey that came in the mid 1800's with the coming of railroads. But the truth is that whether it was the advent of the swift stage lines, better roads, the steamboat, canals, the railroads, or whatever, throughout history, improvements in transportation have always been followed by periods of economic growth.

An efficient and convenient transportation system is probably one of the most vital needs for any society in order to prosper. A society without the ability to efficiently transport people, goods, and services cannot prosper. If it loses that ability – it will begin to decline.

New Jersey's growth has always been closely associated with an improved means of transportation. The coming of both the Morris and Delaware and Raritan Canals, swiftly followed by the advent of the railroads, brought an unbelievable improvement in the state's standard of living.

But probably nothing has ever matched the dramatic change in New Jersey that was brought about by the coming of automotive transportation – cars, trucks, and buses, in the years following World War I.

The amount of automotive through traffic that now crosses the border between New Jersey and Pennsylvania is greater than that between any other two states in the nation, and that between New Jersey and New York is second highest. It is easy to see, therefore, why there is a developing transportation crisis in New Jersey that must somehow be met.

Those facts, coupled with New Jersey's highways having the greatest automotive density in the world, in a state with the densest population concentration in the nation, must create serious concerns about how the looming problem of congested streets and highways will affect New Jersey's economy.

It appears to many experts that a return to some form of mass transportation, such as railroad, is the only solution.

217

During a comparatively short period in the state's transportation history, New Jerseyans experienced probably their most colorful form of transportation in the electric trolley car.

The trolley, which began replacing the horse-drawn street coaches in the 1880's, eventually proved to be very popular. But, like many other innovations, the clanking trolley car was at first greeted with opposition, particularly by those who feared "the monsters' would spook their horse-drawn vehicles.

Once accepted, trolley service expanded from within cities to between cities. The period of the 1890's to the end of WWI was the "golden era" of the trolley car. At first a convenient means of transportation from and to their homes for workers and shoppers within the confines of any particular city, the trolleys soon were adopted for short trip family excursions as well. In fact, they played an important part in the growth of family-oriented recreational areas within New Jersey.

Throughout the summer months the breezy, open trolley cars were a welcome relief for city-dwellers seeking leisure at the beaches or at an amusement park out in the countryside. The trolley lines from downtown Newark, for example, to the Olympic Park Amusement Park in Irvington, were crowded with merry joy-seekers from Memorial Day to Labor Day.

The trolley car and some form of outdoor recreation soon became synonymous in many minds. In fact, to increase their profits, trolley car companies actually got into the business of establishing picnic parks, zoos, etc. out in the country. By the year 1902, rider-ship on trolleys had reached astronomical proportions!

So popular had the local trolley become that its expansion into lines connecting other towns was inevitable. One of the state's earliest inter-city trolley lines was opened in 1892. It ran between Bridgeton and Millville. That line lasted until 1931.

In western New Jersey, the first trolley line ran through Warren County. It began on Sept. 15, 1906, and went through Washington from Phillipsburg to Port Murray. It was run by the Easton-Washington Traction Co. The fare was 25 cents. That line lasted until 1925, when it was replaced by a motor bus. The Morris County Traction Co. ran a trolley line from Elizabeth, through Morristown, to Lake Hopatcong. It also had a number of branch lines.

By the end of World, War I Public Service Corp. was running a gigantic system of street trolley lines throughout northern New Jersey, and connecting a number of cities such as Newark, Jersey City, New Brunswick, Camden and Trenton. The inter-city, electric trolley lines were the first to be replaced by the cheaper motor buses in the late 1920's and early 1930's. Local trolley lines managed to survive longer.

By the end of World War II, the last of the trolley lines disappeared from the trails of New Jersey. As we enter the 21st century, however, there may have to be a reincarnation of the trolley car in some form, if New Jersey is to survive both its growing gridlock and pollution problems.

Battle of the Railroads

Much has been written about the great competition in the late 1860's between the Union Pacific and Central Pacific railroads in their race to complete the nation's first transcontinental line.

But I wonder how many are aware that bitter competition between railroads was commonplace all over America and that New Jersey also played out its role in the "battle of the railroads?"

The overwhelming ability of a few powerful lines to eventually gain monopolies by ruthlessly gobbling up their competition finally led an enraged Congress to pass the Sherman Anti-Trust Act of 1890.

In 1846, what was to become the mighty Pennsylvania Railroad received its charter to build a line between Harrisburg and Pittsburgh. By 1858, it had reached Philadelphia.

Its wealth and political power grew. By 1869, it had bought out or leased lines needed to secure its right of way through to Chicago.

In 1874, bitter wars between it and the New York Central and the Baltimore & Ohio railroads broke out. All three by them had extended their lines from the East Coast to Chicago.

The Penn line eventually stretched across New Jersey, linking Philadelphia to New York City. Their line from Chicago was extended to St. Louis. It connected the two most important ports on the Atlantic coast with the Gateway City to the West! Its power and influence was everywhere.

I gave you this background so you know what New Jersey's little Delaware and Bound Brook Railroad was up against when it tackled the might Pennsy line back in 1875-76. This new little New Jersey railroad was chartered to build a line over a right of way they had secured between Bound Brook and Philadelphia. The clash came in the little village of Hopewell.

Hopewell is in the northern end of Mercer County, just over the tri-county border with Hunterdon and Somerset. The problem was that the D & BB Railroad had to cross over the tracks of the mighty Penn Railroad at Hopewell, in order to complete its cross-state journey to the Delaware.

The violence came on the morning of Jan. 5, 1876. It was the year of the nation's 100th anniversary of the signing of the Declaration of Independence. Huge crowds were expected at the Philadelphia Centennial Exposition.

Workers for the D & BB Railroad had to lay on the "intersection" on the Pennsy tracks at Hopewell to complete their route to Philadelphia. The hard-nosed Penn Railroad board of managers had not gotten where they were by being "good guys" and they were not about to start now.

New Jersey had passed a law in 1873 making railroad monopolies illegal, but enforcement was another matter. Big money was to be made on the crowds expected to be pouring in and out of Philadelphia by rail in 1876, and the Penn managers were not about to share it with this upstart.

So a Penn locomotive was dispatched post haste to Hopewell. There, it maneuvered back and forth over the spot where the Delaware & Bound Brook Railroad "intersection" over their track would have to be placed. The only time it moved on to a siding was to allow a Pennsy train to pass by. The D & BB Railroad workers tried in vain to lay their "intersection."

On the morning of Jan. 5, 1876, they made their brash move! When the Penn engineer backed his locomotive onto a siding to let one of their early morning trains go by, a mob of some 200 D & BB Railroad workers swarmed up to it with rails, ties, etc. and a gigantic iron chain. They blocked the Pennsy locomotive on the siding with their debris, and then made doubly sure by securing it to the tracks with the chain. Frantically they worked to lay their "intersection" on the Pennsy track before the Penn Railroad managers got wind of what was going on and sent reinforcements.

Hopefully, to prevent the arrival of help from Trenton, they piled debris on the tracks leading from that city. Someone, unfortunately, telegraphed word of the incident to Philadelphia, orders were issued to their nearest locomotive in Millstone to race to the scene and "ram the barricade!"

A locomotive steamed out of the Millstone and covered the 31-mile journey in 30 minutes. As ordered, the engineer rammed both the stockpiled debris and a nearby D & BB Railroad locomotive that had been placed there to guard the work in progress.

The little New Jersey community of Hopewell was soon swarming with action. Word had reached the media and they were sending dispatches of the incident throughout the nation.

Between the news reporters, hundreds of battling railroad workers, and some 1,500 spectators who had gathered, the local sheriff was overwhelmed. He called on the governor to send out the state militia.

By Jan. 7, track had been ripped up, a locomotive overturned and a melee was underway. On the 8th, a court order was read by the colonel of the militia and the Penn Railroad admitted defeat.

By 2 p.m., Jan. 8th, the D & BB Railroad steamed across the mighty Penn's tracks on its way to Philadelphia! The trails of New Jersey were once again free for all to travel. New Jersey's David had won the fray.

Railroads and New Jersey, Perfect Together

Railroads and New Jersey, perfect together.

From its beginnings, New Jersey has played a major role in railway transportation.

Back in 1812, a New Jersey engineer, John Stevens, published a pamphlet in which he urged the United States government to back experiments promoting a system of railways over which carriages propelled by steam engines would run. It would be the perfect solution to the problem of joining this large nation together.

His first locomotive model was placed in operation on tracks built on his property in Hoboken in 1826. Railroads went on to play a vital role in the Civil War.

By 1870, one could reach almost every part of the state by rail. The concentration of rails grew steadily well into the 20th century. By 1960, 11 major railroads were operating some 2,000 miles of railway lines in New Jersey. The state by that time led the nation in railroad density.

New Jersey's rail trails actually got started in 1832 when the first railroad was built between Bordentown and Hightstown. In 1833, the first tracks of the Camden and Amboy Railroad were opened. By 1837, it was connecting Philadelphia with New York Harbor.

Throughout their history in New Jersey, the railroads' heaviest flow continued to be in the corridor between New York City and Philadelphia. Locally, the arrival of the railroad in the mid 1800's played a major role in the development of the Warren County region.

The Warren Railroad came in the 1850's, and was followed by the Morris and Essex. They later became part of the Delaware, Lackawanna & Western Railroad, which served the region by carrying both passengers and freight. A Warren County native, John I. Blair, constructed what became the DL&W Railroad, along with the Scranton brothers, and went on to become the greatest single owner of a railroad property in the world.

By the 1960's, the busiest stretch of rail lines in the world was operated by the Pennsylvania Railroad's mainline in Rahway. The Central Railroad of New Jersey began in Jersey City, ran south to Bayonne, crossed Newark Bay to Elizabeth, then split – one branch heading west to Phillipsburg and the other leading south along the Jersey Shore. It operated the most rail miles within the state. The Penn-Reading, Seashore Line, which began in Camden, extended out across the southern part of the state including the south shore from Atlantic City to Cape May. The Pennsylvania Railroad crossed the Meadows into Newark, then headed west to reach the Delaware at Trenton. The DL&W Railroad line began at Hoboken and headed west to the Delaware Water Gap. With its various branches, this line was once New Jersey's major commuter railroad.

The Lehigh Valley Railroad began at Bayonne, crossed Newark Bay, and swung first south then headed west to the Delaware at Phillipsburg. The Erie Railroad began in Jersey City, followed the Passaic River to Paterson, and then headed to the New York State line at Suffern. The New York, Susquehanna and Western Railroad started at Jersey City, ran north then went west into Sussex County.

The New York Central Railroad started at Weehawken then ran north, entering New York State at Tappan. The Reading Railroad ran from the Delaware at Trenton, northeast to the New York area at Woodbridge. Both the Lehigh and Hudson River, and the Lehigh and New England railroads cut diagonally across the state's northwest corner, avoiding the New York City area. Other rail lines included the Morristown & Erie Railroad, the Rahway Valley railroad, the New York & Long Branch Railroad, the Belvidere and Delaware Railroad and the Erie Lackawanna.

By the end of World War I, railroads had become, throughout the US as well as New Jersey, the greatest carriers of both people and goods. A large majority (75 percent) of the freight, and an even larger percentage (80 percent) of the people, moving from one place to another over any distance, went by rail. Presidential campaigns were largely carried on from the rear end of special trains hired to criss-cross the nation in what came to be called "whistle-stop" campaigns.

Transportation began a slow change with the development of the horse-less carriage.

When Henry Ford's low cost, mass-produced "tin-lizzies" began hitting the market in the 1920's, the handwriting began to appear in the wall. With the coming of buses and trucks, competition to rail travel was already felt in the 1930's. Even so, World War II brought rail transportation to its greatest height in 1944.

Though they never reached that zenith again, railroads continued to be the major carriers of both people and goods throughout the 1940's and into the 1950's. Diesels and electrics had replaced steam, but by the 60's people overwhelmingly preferred autos.

Some form of rail transportation may well have to be the wave of the next century, however, if the trails of New Jersey are to be saved from the traffic paralysis and choking pollution being created by the very vehicles that replaced the railways.

Time for a Train

Ever since railroads began to exert their influence on the life of the people of the Untied States in the 1850's, things just have not been the same. One of the results of the introduction of the railroad in America as a means of transporting both people and goods from place to place over large distances was the need to establish a uniform system for telling time.

Again, New Jersey was in the forefront.

If goods or people were to be scheduled to board a train at a given station and time, and that train was scheduled to both arrive and depart from that station at a certain time, then it would have to devise a system for telling time more consistently than each individual's interpretation of it by the sun. This was especially true in a nation as expansive from east to west as is the United States.

Over the centuries, people determined time by the sun. Time, of course, is related to the line of longitude at which you are located. As the earth revolves, these lines of longitude (or meridians) are brought into line with the sun.

The rate of motion we are dealing with here involves one hour for every 15 degrees of longitude you travel either east or west. That means one minute for each 13 miles.

So, if a passenger travels west, his watch would be continually ahead of time at the place he reaches. When it was noon by the sun in Newark, it would be 11:58 in Trenton, 11:56 in Philadelphia, etc.

In short distances, it might be enough to miss a train. It amounts to about three hours when traveling from Newark to San Francisco!

Before 1883, the people of the US had to put up with an endless amount of confusion as they traveled on the nation's railways in an east-west (or west-east) direction.

Rather than expecting conductors to adjust their watches every minute as they sped along the tracks, each railroad company established certain meridian points at which the time was determined. With the increasing number of railroads that had come into existence by the 1870's, each determining the time by their particular meridian point, people became confused. Missing trains became commonplace. Something obviously had to be done.

This is where New Jersey entered the picture, William Frederick Allen, both the son of a railroader from Bordentown and, since the age of 16, a railroader himself, stepped into the breach.

In 1872, at the age of 26, he was made editor of the official guide of timetable for both railway and steamship lines. He became very much aware of the growing time chaos. A solution was needed.

The General Time Convention was held for that purpose in 1875. Allen was made its secretary and diligently worked to find a new system.

From his home in South Orange, in 1880, Allen was still setting his watch ahead each morning as he commuted to New York City, via Hoboken and setting it back each evening. Five years had gone by, and still no solution.

Then in April 1883, he announced his plan for introducing a universal railroad time zone system. It was based upon a theory worked out by C. F. Dowd of Saratoga, NY in 1869.

It consisted of dividing the United States into four zones by meridians of longitude, each 15 degrees, or one hour apart. They were to be called Eastern, Central, Mountain, and Pacific Time. The lines, which divided one from the other, were placed about halfway between the meridians. Throughout the zone, only one time would be observed. In this way, the difference between sun-time and railroad-time would be off no more than 30 minutes. Railroad time was to be the only time used by all railroad schedules within that zone.

A joint announcement by the railroads stated that beginning Nov. 18, 1883, Mr. Allen's Standard Time Plan would be in effect. When a traveler journeyed in any direction within a given time zone, the time would be the same no matter where he was in that zone, or what railroad was used. When traveling into a different zone, time would change by one hour. This uniformity of time made rail travel more convenient. At an international conference held in Washington, DC, most of the world's nations agreed to adopt Allen's Standard Time Plan using Greenwich, England, as its base meridian.

As with any change in the norms, there were protests and accusations about "tampering with God's law." Even the nation's attorney general got into the fray by declaring the whole plan illegal unless approved by an Act of Congress. The powerful railroads, however, were unmoved. They adopted the system as announced.

On Sunday, Nov. 18, 1883, the nation had to conform to the railroad's system of time, or miss their trains. In places like Oxford, in Warren County, it made no difference. Sun-time and Standard time were exactly the same.

But William F. Allen, who spent most of his life along the trails of New Jersey, and the American railroads, did affect the lives of most people when they introduced this new standard plan for telling time.

Motor Vehicles and Roads

As far as we know, a French military engineer, Cugnot built the first self-propelled road vehicles ever, back around 1769 – two steam driven carriages.

The first American to patent such a device was Oliver Evans in 1789. His first operational vehicle was built in 1804. A series of such machines followed in England, France, and Germany in the 1800's. The first American gas-operated automobile was built by Charles and Frank Duryea in 1893.

America's love affair with motor vehicles ever since, and the fact that New Jersey's highways carry a density of motor traffic unparalleled by any other state in the Union, certainly deserve mention in any series of articles on New Jersey.

For years before gas-powered autos were finally settled upon, a controversy brewed over whether steam, electric, or gasoline was the best means of powering these new vehicles.

George Selden took out the first American patent on the internal-combustion engine in 1895. The Association of Licensed Automotive Manufacturers began manufacturing cars under his patent in 1905. In 1911, the Ford Motor Co. won a court suit for the right to continue to build its own gas-powered cars. The American field was then wide open. Ever since 1903, when Henry Leland introduced complete interchangeable parts on his Cadillacs, car building had become practical.

Races and tours remained the chief means of promoting car sales at the turn of the 20th century. Henry Ford established 92 mph as the world's speed record in 1904, driving his "Arrow" racer.

At first, autos were too expensive for all but the wealthy. Ransom Olds became the first mass producer with his "Oldsmobiles" in 1901. Not until Ford offered a one-model, stripped-down, black, mass-produced "Model T" in 1907, could the average man afford to own a car.

Though World War I interrupted the popularity of autos once the "Model T" hit the market, the 1920's saw their sales take off to unbelievable heights. Within several decades, auto making became one of the largest, most important industries in the United States, and New Jersey certainly had more than its share of that market.

New Jersey's highway traffic density, between being a "corridor state," carrying traffic elsewhere and having the nation's highest population density, is the highest in the nation. Road building was once the responsibility of local property owners. The first involvement of the federal government in helping build roads came with the modest Federal Aid Act of 1916. Its purpose then was better roads for carrying the US mail. To take advantage, you had to have a state road department, which New Jersey established in 1917. First an eight member commission, it was reduced to four in 1923. A single commissioner under the governor was established in 1935.

The first New Jersey Highway Department introduced three-lane highways in the late 1920's, the nation's first circle (in Camden) and the first divided highways. The Pulaski Skyway, also started in this period, was completed in 1932. It was a new concept in bridges that took the highway over the Jersey Meadows and two rivers – the Hackensack and the Passaic – and saved the motorist considerable time.

In 1927, New Jersey's new highway department drew up plans for 45 new state highways spanning the state. Though stopped by the crash of 1929 and the "Great Depression," it was later aided by the federal government's gigantic public works program to stimulate the nation's economy. As a result, most of New Jersey's state highways were completed by the beginning of the 1940's.

Though World War II again stopped all progress, its end saw a flurry of highway construction in New Jersey to keep up with the tremendous increase in truck and automobile traffic that followed the war. This ended with the New Jersey Turnpike and the Garden State Parkway in the early 1950's. These were a return to the user-paid toll road concept first initiated in New Jersey at the turn of the 19th century.

As a result of the influx following World War II, New Jersey now has the highest traffic density in the world, with seven times the national average!

Its biggest problem as a "corridor state" had always been that it was stymied on both ends by water. This was handled for years by a very active ferry service. The increase in vehicular traffic following World War II, however, led to studies of better ways to cross its rivers.

The "Holland Tunnel" under the Hudson River was authorized in 1919. It was finally opened to traffic in November 1927. In 1926, the Benjamin Franklin Bridge over the Delaware was completed. The year1927 saw the construction of the George Washington Bridge over the Hudson River, and it was completed in 1931.

The series of new bridges and tunnels that followed, practically destroyed the once-prosperous ferryboat system, though current traffic volume seems to be encouraging the return of some sort of improved ferry service, as the trails of New Jersey enter the 21st century.

Transportation in Warren County

The history of the transportation system of Warren County is a microcosm of that of New Jersey as a whole.

In the period before the coming of the turnpikes at the dawn of the 19th century, both road and river transportation were crude at best. Slow, difficult, and beset with many delays - usually the result of weather conditions - poor transportation kept people pretty much isolated.

Most West Jersey folk thus spent their entire lives within a 10-20 mile radius of their homes. The difficulty in moving goods to a market place also kept the economy practically at a subsistence level.

With the development of the large, flat-bottomed, Durham boat, the Delaware River was at last opened for the shipment of farm products to Philadelphia, and eventually by clipper ship to New York City, in the period of the American Revolution. Washington commandeered their use all up and down the river, for his famous crossing of the Delaware at the Battle of Trenton.

The coming of the Durham boats made it possible to ship goods of the river north of Trenton, where the water was often too shallow for the normal riverboats to navigate.

The river boatmen, themselves, were a colorful lot with a whole separate way of life. But even the Durhams were limited by season to periods of heavy rainfall or melting snow. And, you still had to get your produce to the river over poorly kept roads.

When the new turnpikes came in the first decades of the 1800's, a whole new world opened. The fast Concord Stages that used them at last made passenger travel a little more bearable between communities. The large "Jersey Wagons", similar to the Conestogas that took pioneers westward, made it possible to carry large shipments of goods for sale at the market places. The "teamsters" who drove the wagons were also a striking breed of men whose livelihood made them tough and often licentious.

By the third decade of the 1800's, the Trenton-Belvidere Stage line was passing through Washington along the two turnpikes that crossed where that little village was developing. So, too, did the Easton-New York Line, which also went through Hackettstown on its way over the Easton-Morristown Turnpike.

When the Morris Canal, which was originally chartered in 1824 to be built from Phillipsburg to Newark, began operating small sections in 1829, another way of life opened. When finally completed all the way to Jersey City about 1834, new little communities sprung into existence, and older ones came to life. More than 100 miles long, the Morris Canal carried farm produce, coal, iron, lumber, and even passengers between the western and eastern borders of the state.

The canal boat era ushered in what was probably the most colorful and memorable of transportation eras. Whole families were involved in the life of operating the canal boats.

By the 1850's, however, the coming of the railroads did more for the economic growth of Warren County, and the state, than any

229

other system to that date. In 1856, Warren County's native son, John I. Blair, built the Warren Railroad connecting the Delaware, Lackawanna & Western Railroad at the Delaware Water Gap with the Jersey Central at Hampton.

Around the time of the Civil War, the Morris & Essex Railroad came through Warren via Hackettstown and Washington on its way to its western terminal at Phillipsburg. In the post-Civil War era, both became part of the DL&W system.

In 1871, the Lehigh Valley Railroad decided that the best way to beat their competition was to join them. So they leased the Morris Canal. By 1922, they had completed the purchase of all of its stock. By 1929, they had drained it dry – thus ending the canal era for good.

For many years, the railroads had a near monopoly on transportation services for both passengers and freight through Warren County and the state of New Jersey.

In 1906, a transportation system strictly for passenger service, that had begun elsewhere in New Jersey in the 1880's, was introduced to West Jersey by the Easton-Washington Traction Co. On a single track from Phillipsburg to Port Murray its electric trolley cars carried passengers through the Warren County countryside until Feb. 6, 1925.

Both the railroad and the trolley, however, began to feel the impact of the cheaper, more convenient gas-powered automotive vehicles that started coming on the scene in even greater numbers in the post WWI period of the 1920's.

Though a motor bus service replaced the trolley cars on the Easton-Washington Line in 1925, the train service was not much reduced until about 1939. It then took until Oct. 6, 1966, for the last passenger train to pull out of Washington's railroad station.

Gasoline-powered buses, trucks and private automobiles had all but done in the once-powerful railroads along the trails of New Jersey. Today, the demise of the type of automotive transportation that replaced the railroads now also appears to be just over the horizon.

CHAPTER 10: FOLKLORE AND LEGENDS

History of Halloween

A common thread had made Halloween, that night of ghosts and goblins, a universally celebrated holiday among early New Jerseyans. New Jersey was settled by a diverse group-starting with the Dutch in the 1620's, the Swede's in the 1630's, the British in the 1660's, and the Germans, Swiss and French Huguenots beginning in the 1680's. For a time, it had been divided into East and West Jersey as well. West Jersey was originally set aside by the British as a refuge for the Quakers. But by the year 1702, both Jerseys had been reunited by Queen Anne into one Royal Colony under the British Crown. So by the 18th century, a common thread of "European heritage" was shared by all those living in what for many years afterwards came to be known as "the Jerseys."

Part of that common thread was a strong belief in the return of ghosts. It was a belief brought to America over the years by this varied group of immigrants. The belief, in fact, had remained strong among the people of New Jersey right up to the 20th century, when the skepticism of the scientific revolution dampened its ardor. Those early settlers had also come from a background that had in the past set aside Nov. 1 as the "Feast Day of All Saints." This day had been dedicated by the leaders of the early Christian church as a time to pay homage to the memory of all those good Christians who had previously departed this earth.

Since feast days were commonly also fast days, and therefore were not a very enjoyable celebration, the night before became used by early Europeans as the last chance for the "big fling"- before the day of fasting and reverence. Oct. 31 then became known as the Holy Eve, or "Hallow E'en." Big bonfires were lit on this night to guide the "good spirits" to the various local parties that were being held throughout the countryside. Heavy feasting became the order of that night, and much merriment. Needless to say, Halloween soon became the more popular of the two occasions. In fact, most of the early New

Jersey settlers ignored All Saints Day – and even before the coming of the 20th century, Halloween had become a strictly secular celebration in New Jersey.

The early church leaders had in mind that the memories of the departed "saints," as all good Christians were called, were to be honored on "All Saints Day." The superstitious European peasants, however, soon envisioned that many of the "evil spirits" were on the loose as well on Hallow E'en. Two of today's customs in New Jersey concerning this holiday had their origins, in fact, from this very real fear. One was the practice of donning costumes. Originally, it was done to change one's identity so that the evil spirits would not recognize them. The other custom was that of leaving "treats." Its purpose was to appease the evil spirits; hopefully so they would not harm you. Today's custom of "trick or treating" by costumed revelers can be directly traced to these older practices.

Because throughout the years a strong belief in the return of ghosts had been prevalent among New Jersey residents, Halloween was a natural. Many folk tales incorporated the return on this particular night into its threads. Stories of the "Jersey Devil" struck terror into many hearts - and became especially rife on Halloween night. Tales of the "Jersey Pirates," once quite common along our shores, told of a return on that night to seek out their buried treasures. Also widespread were local stories such as that of Tom Quick, "The Avenger of the Delaware." He would come out each Halloween to find that elusive 100th Indian he had promised to kill in his lifetime to avenge his father's gruesome death by scalping during the Indian Wars on the West Jersey frontier.

The ghosts of Jerry Mack, who died at the Oxford Furnace, and of John Linn, the Jersey "Samson," whose feats of strength at Oxford were once legendary, also returned to their old haunts that night. So too, did that of Jacob Harden, "The Murdering Parson of Pleasant Grove," who returned each Halloween to seek the one for whom he got himself hanged on the gallows at Belvidere. There was also the ghost of the "White Pilgrim," now buried in a graveyard near Johnsonburg, who always rode his white horse at night. Joe Milliner, the infamous bandit known as the "Robin Hood of the Jersey Pines," made his annual reappearance then as well.

The many acts of witchcraft, sorcery, and wizardry, which at one time or another prevailed on Halloween along the trails of New Jersey, make today's celebration seem pale, indeed, by comparison. But, I think for most, the absence of that chapter out of our past is a welcome relief.

Ghosts and Goblins

You probably would be hard-pressed to frighten the sophisticated generation of inhabitants now populating New Jersey with scary tales of ghosts and goblins. Even on Halloween, when tradition tells us that the spirits of those dearly departed saints who left this earth are allowed to return to their old haunts. Today's watered-down version of this once important date, with its "trick-or-treat" costumers, brings little more than tolerant smiles, but it was not always so.

New Jersey's past was replete with a whole array of assorted ghosts and goblins who couldn't wait for Halloween to scare "the living daylights" out of untold generations of Jerseyites. Probably the most noted goblin of sorts was the infamous "Jersey Devil." This frightening, yet pathetic creature, which came out of the Pine Barrens of South Jersey in the 1700's, has been seen for generations since in many parts of New Jersey, including the Delaware Valley. Its descriptions vary, but all seem to center on its looking something like a flying horse with horns - or was it a goat with a horse's head?

It was supposed to have been the 13th child of Mother Leeds, who in her agony at its birth, is said to have blurted out something to the effect that it could go to the devil. And in a wink, so it did! The Rivermen, who plied the waters of the Delaware for many years, repeated the tale of its appearance in the large walk-in fireplace, a favorite haunt of theirs along the riverbank. Tables were overturned and chairs were tripped over as these burly men beat a fast retreat out of that place!

Other tales hark back to the days when Jersey's coastal inlets were infested with a myriad assortment of pirates and other scoundrels. The most infamous were such as Capt. Kidd, "Blackbeard," and the notorious Capt. Tew. All of these characters became central figures in hair-raising tales of ghostly apparitions returning, to ward off possible "thieves" bent upon uncovering their cherished buried treasures. The stories always occur at one secluded inlet hideout or another.

Ghost stories that centered around Indian atrocities along New Jersey's northwestern frontier country also abounded for many years among residents of the backcountry. The most far-fetched probably concerned themselves with the return of the fanatical "Avenger of the Delaware," Tom Quick. Bizarre tales of his escapades, while living, in which he sought revenge for the bloody slaughter of his father by a band of angry Delawares, turned to almost hysteria when they related some of his ghostly antics. Others concerned themselves with the frightening periodic return of victims of Indian attacks. One such ghost story referred to the newlywed 18-year old son-in-law and daughter of Nicholas Cole. The boy's apparition always returned with a tomahawk buried in his head, and hers even revealed her ghostly figure agonizing over what to do with her severed scalp. Both served as constant reminders of that fearful attack on the morning of May 17, 1758.

Scenes of dreadful acts that occurred during the American Revolution also made their cyclical return to haunt the minds and bodies of local residents. The Massacre at Hancock's Bridge, which took place at the Hancock House near Salem in 1778, and the Massacre at Chestnut Neck, occurring in early 1776 below the Batsto Iron Works, are two that come immediately to mind. The bloody floorboards at the Hancock House are still visible today.

Time and space, of course, prohibit my relating details of the many ghost stories that abounded in New Jersey over the centuries. But I can assure you that every region had their share, and they usually related to some event that once shook the local folk of that particular countryside. Along the inland waterways of the Mullica River near Pleasant Mills, the wandering ghost of Joe Miliner, the Renegade Bandit of the Tuckerton Road, who was hung for his daring deeds, is still purported to be seen.

Some even claim to see the ghost of Jacob Harden, the murdering Parson of Pleasant Grove, roaming near the Belvidere Courthouse with the noose still around his neck. He was hung there on July 6, 1860, for murdering his wife, Louisa. The ghost of Bonnel

234

Moody, hung as a traitor in Morristown, often returns to Moody's Rock, near Newton. Who can deny reports of the return of the ghost of Jerry Mack, found dead one cold February at the Oxford Furnace? Or, what of repeated reports of sighting the ghost of Johann Printz, whom the Indians dubbed, "The Big Tub"? Or, of those who died at the Indian massacre at Paulins Kill in May of 1756? Some say Alexander Hamilton still frequents Weehawkin where he died in a duel with Aaron Burr on July 11, 1804. All of these, and many more, are still haunting the trails of New Jersey - but nobody seems to care anymore.

The Ghost of Jacob Harden

That which is agreeable, which gives us enjoyment, satisfaction or delight, which brings us a feeling of happiness or a source of sensual gratification - such as in seeing beautiful scenery - is termed as being pleasant.

New Jersey has number of places that are so described. If you look at a map of the state, you will find that there is a Pleasant Grove in the Schooley's Mountain section of western Morris County just across the Musconetcong River from Warren County. On the edge of the Wharton State Forest in the heart of the "Jersey Pines," there is a Pleasant Mills.

In the flat, coastal area between the Lakehurst Naval Air Station and Barnegat Bay in Ocean County is Pleasant Plains. On a creek in Hunterdon County south of Round Valley State Park is Pleasant Run. Off Route 57 in Warren County between two mountain ranges is Pleasant Valley. South of the Brigantine National Wildlife Refuge and east of Atlantic City is Pleasantville. Then there is Point Pleasant on the Atlantic coast and Mount Pleasant overlooking the Delaware. Obviously, what brings pleasure in natural settings is not always the same.

But what made me think about all these areas of New Jersey described by someone in the past as being pleasurable? It was not something very pleasant. One thought involved the pine barrens of Pleasant Mills, haunted for several centuries by the "Ghost of Joe Mulliner," an infamous pine robber of the Revolutionary period.

The other concerns the "Ghost of Jacob Harden," the murdering parson of Pleasant Grove. One would think that such fine-sounding names would bring forth, joyful thoughts to the senses. But it's October, and as we approach Halloween, it is appropriate to conjure up thoughts of ghosts and goblins.

Our first tale along the trails of New Jersey involves that of the Rev. Jacob Harden. Sometimes referred to as the "Murdering Parson of Pleasant Grove," Harden brought to the courthouse at Belvidere one of the most infamous trials in the annals of Warren County. And he left behind him a haunted heritage of gruesome circumstances ranging from a murderous deed to a horrible hanging. The ghoulish attitude of the public witnessing his hanging was no less revolting than the crime itself. In fact, it is one reason those who know about such things tell us that his ghost continues to haunt the Courthouse Square at Belvidere.

Jacob S. Harden was born near Blairstown. He first taught school in Stillwater. He roamed the hills of Warren, Morris, and Hunterdon counties selling Bibles. When he was about 21 he was licensed to preach by a Methodist group known as the Swartswood Society, and rode circuit among the little churches of the Clinton district. He was minister of the Anderson Church in Mansfield Township when he committed his heinous act, and was living there with his wife at the home of a parishioner; thus, the trial at the Warren County Courthouse in Belvidere.

He had been married to Louisa Dorland, also of Blairstown, when in traveling about in the Clinton circuit he encountered a buxom maiden at his church in Pleasant Grove who sent his head-a-spinning. He fell madly in love. Thinking to correct the mistake of his first marriage by slowly eliminating his wife, and then marrying this second woman, he conceived of what he thought was a foolproof method. He began bringing her apples. The apples he brought, however, were treated with doses of arsenic! In time, she died. Unfortunately, he was accused of her murder. Indicted in April of 1859, he was tried, convicted, and on a hot summer day in 1860, hung on a scaffold in the Courthouse Square at Belvidere.

But it was the ghastly circumstances of the hanging more than the sinister nature of her murder that brought about the ghostly hauntings of Belvidere by Harden's shadowy spirit. For you see, when a confession was obtained from him, arrangements were immediately made for its printing, along with the story of his life and courtship, to be sold to the crowds at his hanging!

Not only were these cheap exposes for sale, but tickets of admission to witness that hanging were sold as well. And to add to the circus-like treatment of this act of justice, special trains were run on the Belvidere-Delaware Railroad. These trains were to accommodate the throngs who were expected to pay to see him swing on brand-new gallows especially erected in the square for this event. And so the "Ghost of Jacob Harden" has for a century now haunted the Courthouse Square at Belvidere, still objecting to the carnival atmosphere that was promoted for his execution so long ago. It is just another of those tales haunting the trails of New Jersey.

Halloween's Ghosts of Schooley's Mountain

The evening of Oct. 31 will soon be upon us. Halloween, it has come to be called. In pagan times, various peoples were celebrating different festivals on Nov. 1. The early leaders of the Christian Church decided, therefore, that it would be wise to let these recent converts continue to observe their feast days only with a Christian connotation. So the idea was conceived that Nov. 1 be set aside to commemorate all those good Christians who had departed this earth. It would, from thenceforward, be known as the "Feast of All Saints." The evening before, on Oct. 31, would be the Holy Eve or "Hallow E'en." To guide the good spirits, huge bonfires were to be lit throughout the countryside. Feasting on the evening before would be followed by fasting on the holy day itself.

In time, Halloween became the more popular of the two among the common folk, and customs grew about its significance. Some of the pagan beliefs crept back. Superstitions about "evil spirits" on the loose that night were among them. And so an old custom returned about disguising yourself so these "evil spirits" would not recognize you. And leaving treats to appease them so they hopefully would do you no harm also resurfaced. It did not take much to leap from this to the present New Jersey custom of "trick or treat" by costumed youngsters. Basic to all, however, was the belief that on

237

this night the spirits of the departed returned to their old haunts, and vigils or watches were to be kept during this evening of feasting.

Over the years, those who came to America brought their customs of the observance of Halloween to these shores. A strong belief in ghosts and goblins and witches was prevalent in America. It is not surprising then that this holiday constantly rekindled thoughts of those ghosts that once were so common in New Jersey. And throughout all times, there have always been charlatans attempting to make personal gain from the weaknesses of their fellow beings.

Take the story of the secret buried treasure supposedly to be found in the wilds of the Schooley's Mountain, some 20 miles west of Morristown, and just across the border from Warren and Hunterdon counties. Ghosts were believed to be guarding these hidden riches. All that was needed was someone who could curry their favor when they came out on Halloween, and convince them to reveal its whereabouts. There were enough people of substantial means living in Morristown in those days who believed this poppycock to interest a charlatan in trying.

He soon convinced men of substance from the community that he held a supernatural power with ghosts. He performed acts of magic over a period of time sufficient to gain their confidence in his "gifts." Finally, he informed them that each would have to appease these spirits with a gift of gold or silver, which he would forward to them, before they would reveal the location of the treasure. Then on Hallowe'en he took them to a dark and desolate region in the Schooley's Mountain and scared them half out of their senses with contrived scenes of ghosts and goblins prancing about in wild anger on the wood's edge.

It was soon divulged that someone had talked about the secret rendezvous. The whole thing was off for the time being. Since it was a sure bet that one or more of them had indeed told family or friends about it and since no one wanted to admit publicly to being duped because of their greed, he got away with it. When he tried it again, however, he was arrested. He then mysteriously escaped before a public trial revealed any names. It has been told that he still engages in those secret meetings with the ghosts and goblins each Halloween. And, in different desolate spots of the Schooley's Mountain each year, he brings them to a wild frenzy on the edge of some wooded area.

Now Jacob Harden's lover also lived on that side of the Musconetcong River, in the little village of Pleasant Grove. It is not hard to imagine, therefore, why he sometimes leaves his haunts at the Belvidere Courthouse square, and returns to seek the woman for whom he gave his life at so early an age. Each Halloween, the ghost of the "Murdering Parson of Pleasant Grove" returns to seek the one for whom he got himself hanged so many years ago. Then there is the story of the "Ghost of Jerry Mack" of Oxford Furnace, and that of Joe Mulliner, the infamous bandit of Pleasant Mills. But, alas time has run out again, and those tales will have to wait for other times along the trails of New Jersey.

The Ghost of Bonnel Moody

Before the age of TV and radio, when even books were hard to come by, people had to create their own entertainment. One form of diversion was to sit about on an evening and retell the legends that they had heard. Legends about the exciting people who once roamed the countryside thereabouts. Those who were best at telling these tales were much sought out by the local folk. These storytellers, whose chief aim was entertainment, kept alive much of the folklore of an area. Some of the best-liked kinds of narratives were those spine-tingling tales of ghosts. So, if someone's death lent itself to a good ghost story, it did not take long before such a yarn was underway.

Early New Jersey was replete with many such accounts of ghosts haunting its waysides. One such tale is told about "the Ghost of Bonnel Moody," who still haunts the rocky country known as Moody's Rock in Sussex County. It seems that back in the period of the American Revolution, Sussex had its share of Tories. Tories remained loyal to the British crown. The Moody Brothers, James and Bonnel, were more than mere sympathizers, they were activists.

The Moodys recruited local boys to serve in His Britannic Majesty's Royal Army. They spied on the American Rebel Army, reporting its movements and whatever else might be of interest to the British authorities. They sought out, and then organized bands to destroy, those local ammunition stores which were secretly hidden in the area by patriots. The boys intercepted dispatches sent to or by Washington to detachments of American Troops sent through the region. Often these armies were headed over to Old Mine Road going north to New York or New England, or south to Pennsylvania. They helped "spring" Tories from the Sussex County jail at Newton that might have been imprisoned for loyalist activities. And they turned rebel sympathizer's over to the British authorities to be jailed for actions they may have committed against the King.

James Moody, in time, joined the British Royal Army. The time, in fact, was October of 1777. For the courage he showed in a brave venture he undertook in the spring of 1781, he was given special recognition. It seems that in a daring escapade he intercepted a message meant for Gen. George Washington. For this act, he was promoted to the rank of lieutenant. The Moodys lived in Newton. So when they plotted to rob the Archives of Congress in Philadelphia was betrayed, it was no surprise that they hid out in the rocky crags and caves south of Newton in the region of the Big and Little Muckshaw.

James eventually made his way to the Delaware River, and by May of 1782, he had escaped to England. There he wrote of his adventurous deeds to the delight of his English neighbors. But his brother Bonnel was not so fortunate. He was captured and thrown into prison at Morristown. There he was tried, found guilty, and as an example to others executed as a spy and traitor to the American cause. To Bonnel his loyalty to his King and the Royal Crown of Great Britain was an honorable act. He, therefore, loudly bemoaned his "unjust" sentence of execution as a traitor. And thus was set the scene for the "Ghost of Bonnel Moody." For Bonnel warned his executioners, that unless and until he was vindicated of this wrongful punishment, his ghost would return to haunt the rock crags of Sussex and its inhabitants would find no rest.

Moody's Rock, 2 miles South of Newton, has been the haunt of the ghost of Bonnel Moody for more than 200 years now. And, from what I have been told, this unsettled spirit has been bemoaning its unjust fate to anyone in the hill country from which he once operated. From Millbrook in the west to Milton in the east, from Augusta in the north to Allamuchy in the south, he has, as promised, been giving these folk no rest. And he will not, until they grant that his actions were those of an honorable man. So far, his moans of complaint have been received upon deaf ears. This man would have history as a hero had the tides of war gone differently. Just one of the many ghostly tales that have been heard haunting the trails of New Jersey there are still more just waiting to be told.

The Legend of Jonas Cattell

The Delaware River forms the western boundary of New Jersey. It separates the state from Pennsylvania for some 200 miles from just below Port Jervis, New York in the north, to Penns Grove, NJ in the south. After that, it separates New Jersey from the state of Delaware south to about where the Cohansey River empties into it, before it widens into the Delaware Bay. Though it is one river, no one region through which it passes could typify it. Its journey southward encompasses a variety of terrain and lifestyles. From the heavily forested, rock strewn, rugged mountains of the north, past city harbors, flat farmlands, and eerie pinelands, it ends in the swampy tidewater country of the south.

I would like to take you to that region around Woodbury, south of the Philadelphia area. Here we find both Jersey's "Garden Spot" and the edge of its "Pine Barrens." In 1638, the Swedes and the Finns were the first Europeans to settle there. They were followed in a generation or two by English and Scotch-Irish Quakers. The Quaker leader, William Penn, in 1681 considered establishing his "Philadelphia" on this side of the Delaware shoreline.

Because its rich farmlands were an excellent source of food, for both the British and Patriot armies, and because its location below the rebel capital of Philadelphia gave it strategic importance, it found itself deeply embroiled in the struggles of the American Revolution. It was here, in fact, that the new Republic purchased its first land. That was in July of 1776. In 1777, it built Fort Mercer at nearby Red Bank to protect the approach to Philadelphia from the south.

The British attack on Fort Mercer came suddenly in October of 1777. It was led by some 2,200 Hessian troops, backed by the cannonade of two British warships on the Delaware, the 64-gun

"Agusta," and the 18-gun "Merlin." Some 400-ragamuffin patriots under the command of Col. Christopher Green held their ground, though they were greatly outnumbered. Under a murderous close-range fusillade (the Americans withheld their fire until the enemy was almost on top of them), the Hessians attacked and withdrew twice before finally retreating in defeat. But not before losing some 400 dead and wounded, including their commanding officer. American guns mounted on barges in the river also sank both British ships. It was a splendid American victory. The Red Bank Battlefield is now part of Fort Mercer Park.

But it was to the legend of Jonas Cattell to which all of this was leading. Among the hunters that gathered in the local taverns to spin their tall tales about Jonas, he was the hunter's hero. Traveling only on foot, Jonas could outrun both rabbit and hound, fox or horse. He was by all accounts the swiftest, most cunning, most tireless man ever to take to the woods in pursuit of game. Jonas Cattell was a big man for those days, six foot, one inch tall. He was vigorous, athletic of build, and uncommonly strong as well. But it was the swiftness of foot of this dauntless hunter for which he was most renowned.

Born in Woodbury in 1758, Jonas lived for almost a century. He grew into manhood on his father's farm, and at the age of 18, enlisted in the army during the American Revolution. There he was soon assigned the role of scout and messenger. He raced long distances over difficult terrain, but his messages always got through. In October 1777, he was captured and then released by Hessian soldiers before their "surprise" attack on Fort Mercer. His swift run around the marching Hessians warned Col. Green of the impending attack. This advance warning is credited by many with the readiness that made the America victory possible.

Hunting, fishing, and cross-country runs kept Jonas Cattell in shape over the years. Married to Mary Stockton of Burlington in 1796 at the age of 38, Jonas and his wife raised six sons and five daughters. During all of this time, his eagle eye and swift feet were constantly in demand by local hunters for the tracking and pursuit of game in the surrounding Pinelands wilderness.

At the age of 50, he was matched in a 22-mile race from Mount Holly to Woodbury with the swiftest Indian in the state. Cattell beat him by 200 yards! At 83, he was still walking and hunting the woods with his dog and his rifle.

The legend of Jonas Cattell grew greater as he aged. His prowess seemed endless. Jonas Cattell died in 1854 at the age of 96, having enjoyed outsmarting the fox up to his 90th year.

Many more yarns of this hunter's hero await to be told, but for now this was just one more of those almost forgotten tales found so often along the trails of New Jersey.

Tom Quick – Avenger of the Delaware

Legends are what make one state different from any other and the trails of New Jersey have a sufficient number of those tales to set it apart. They tell us something about the place and its people in any given period of time.

In these days of enlightenment, the legends of "Tom Quick-Avenger of the Delaware" are not always appreciated. But we were not here to edit the state's history -cutting out what we do not like - but rather to report it. Not that everyone who writes doesn't add something of their own biases, consciously or unconsciously, anyway, but if you at least tell all, you allow others to make their own judgments.

Having said that, I will tell you of a legend that was once very popular in parts of New Jersey. That it gave vent to a definite bias against the native Americans only reveals a fact of life that existed at the time.

From about 1750 until the early 1900's, the legends of Tom Quick made the cracker-barrel circuit throughout northwestern New Jersey and, if not as often, in other parts of the state as well. It was a reflection during that period of a commonly held belief that "the only good Indian was a dead one." Not many were interested in the Indian's side of the story. They had, after all, at least heard about the blood-curdling tales, even if they had not experienced them. Stories of Indian raids, scalpings, kidnapping of women and children. All had affected their thoughts.

The pre-European period Indians of the Lenape Whittuck (we call it the Delaware) were a peaceable lot as humans go. They sought only to provide themselves with the basic necessities of food, clothing, and shelter. The heavily forested New Jersey countryside, interspersed with numerous clear, swift-moving streams, placid lakes and a 130-mile oceanfront to which they trekked at least once a year, gave them a satisfying life. So when the first Europeans arrived, they were generally willing to share it.

It was into such a setting that the Quick family found themselves when they first arrived in the Delaware Valley country. Living on the remote frontier of northwestern New Jersey, they too, had to wrestle with the challenges of providing the basic essentials in order to sustain life. The Minsi (people of the stone country) befriended them. The adults got along with each other and the Quick boys played with the Indian boys. They hunted, trapped, fished, and trod the many waters in harmony.

The Europeans, however, were obsessed with the idea of "owning the land." It is not clear to this day if the Indians ever did understand that concept. Even when they agreed to "sell," they were not both on the same thought wave. But one thing was clear. In the so-called "Walking Purchase of 1737" they had offered to "sell" as much land as could be walked over in one day. Instead, the Europeans hired professional runners to cover a terrain in 24 hours that was beyond anyone's wildest intent. The Indians never recovered from that deceit. Many incidents too numerous to mention here followed. Some years later, during the French and Indian War, the French exploited their festering anger. They incited them to revenge.

It was in this setting that the elder Quick, for years a friend of the Minsi, was attacked and mangled by a band of young warriors. He was scalped and left to die. His two sons, who were hiding in the brush, witnessed this brutal act.

Though the Quick brothers escaped physically unharmed, the psychological scars they bore were never healed. They were frightened, confused, and angry. Tom Quick made a personal vow with a venom for revenge unmatched in the annals of New Jersey folklore. He would spend the rest of his life avenging his father's cruel death. Thus, from that fact was born the legend of "Tom Quick - Avenger of the Delaware."

As the years went on, no tale of his cunning acts in getting even with the Indians was too tall to believe. There were, in fact, as many tales as there were people to tell them. He is said to have once spotted three Indians skinning a deer. Stopping to think, he realized that if he fired a shot he might get one, but the others would surely kill him. So he cleverly waited until they were all in a straight line. When he did fire, his bullet went clear through the first two and imbedded itself in the third. Tom Quick had cleverly done three Indians in with one shot! Everyone roared.

One time he was surprised by four Indians while splitting a log. His quick mind offered to give himself up without a fight if they would but help him finish. If they would put their fingers in the crack he created, and yank on his signal, they could do it. They agreed. Like a flash Tom knocked out the wedge. While they stood there helplessly trapped, Tom Quick did them all in! Everyone laughed.

And so the stories went on the "cracker-barrel circuit" along the trails of New Jersey about Tom Quick, the Indian Slayer.

The White Pilgrim

The belief in witches and ghosts that is often associated in America with New England, and more particularly Salem, MA, was in fact rampant throughout early America. New Jersey was no exception. Every community or region worth its salt had its ghost or witch stories to tell. Today it is necessary to get into the offbeat areas where the same families have been living for generations in order to "dig up" some of those famed ghost stories.

In Warren County out in the Johnsonburg area, for example, there roams the ghost of the "White Pilgrim." Those fortunate enough to have had ancestors in the region whose history goes back into the early 1800's know of this gentleman first hand. Those unfortunate enough to have keen imaginations as well are still plagued with his apparition. For those who know of his existence, this white specter may still be seen in the slippery mists that often rise up mysteriously out of the low spots or along the little creek bend of an evening. His spirit still slips up and down the roadways on a foggy night, haunting the woods and fields around Johnsonburg or Kerr's Corners or Ebenezer or Shiloh or perhaps anywhere in Frelinghuysen or

Allamuchy or other nearby townships where he once rode; always spooking those who pretend to be without sin.

Today in the Christian Church Cemetery in Johnsonburg lie the remains of Joseph Thomas. His grave is marked, appropriately enough, with a thin "White" spire or obelisk. He first rode into the area clad in white garments and mounted on a pure white horse, according to some accounts, back in the early 1830's. This itinerant preacher came to bring the gospel to the farmers and villagers of the region. He planned to stay a while, as was the custom of circuit riders of his day, and make some conversions, perhaps. If he was fortunate enough, even build a little church. Then he would move on to new pastures where he would repeat the whole process all over again.

This was not to be his destiny there, however. His lot apparently would be to remain in the Johnsonburg area until his judgment day. For he never left alive. His ghost still frequents this rolling countryside where an untimely death felled him at the age of 44. His restless spirit is particularly disturbed, in some versions of this tale, by those pious people who only pretend their virtuousness. For it seems that one evening, soon after his little church was built, and after having preached in it only once, he came riding back from one of his jaunts in the countryside to find lights on in the building.

Somewhat amazed that there was activity in the church at that hour, he peered through the window before entering. To his great shock and dismay there in the midst of this new sanctuary was an unholy group of men. The only one's his enraged eyes could focus upon, however, were those he had thought were pillars of this new church. They were sitting and standing around a table upon which were strewn piles of money and stacks of cards. "Blasphemy!" he exploded. Almost paralyzed with indignant anger, for gambling was considered a cardinal sin, he recovered to find himself surging furiously through the front door, and into their astonished midst. The thought of these men secretly using this House of God for this unholy purpose filled him with anger. He scattered the table, cards, money, and frightened men throughout the sanctuary!

A few days later the "White Pilgrim" was buried of the dread disease known as small pox. Being untouchable, no one was allowed to view the condition of his body. Even his remains were refused burial in the church cemetery by the church leaders for fear that others might be contaminated. His grave was dug instead in the forsaken burial grounds know as the "Dark-of-the-Moon" Cemetery. It was not for another dozen years that it was considered "safe" to dig up his body and rebury it properly in the church cemetery. Now, a white spire marks the earthly remains of this itinerant preacher who rode into this area on his white horse, dressed all in white, so full of purpose so many years ago. The spirit of the "White Pilgrim" has become just another of those interesting tales that haunt the winding trails of those bucolic hills of northwestern New Jersey around Johnsonburg.

Shades of Death Road

In journeying throughout New Jersey you can be intrigued by the names of its local roads. In Ocean County, for example, my curiosity is always aroused at sighting the one called "Double Trouble Road." I believe it was in Bergen County that I noted an artery named "Burnt Tavern Road." Near my Warren County home, there is one tagged "Fiddlers Elbow Road." The stories that abound behind these names fire one's imagination. But if you should inquire as to their origin, you will often as not, get a number of versions as to how they were so dubbed. Several months ago, an 84-year-old gentleman from Great Meadows named James DeLong volunteered his version of how "Shades of Death Road," where he resides, was named. Much of that which follows was taken from his letter.

"Shades of Death Road" lies in the northwestern part of Warren County. It wanders along the base of the Jenny Jump Mountains for about four miles, stretching from Route 80 to the Hope-Great Meadows Road. Originally an Indian Trail, and later a logging road, it remained a quaint dirt byway until the arrival of utility lines and macadam in the 1950's. Once providing the route, over which giant timbers from the Jenny Jump Forest were hauled to a sawmill, it now helps get its farmer-residents to their destinations.

It does not take too much creative genius to conjure up tales of violence and death relative to a highway that bears a name such as "Shades of Death." And so stories abound among local fold about Indian massacres, logging accidents, numerous baffling murders, and the mysterious disappearances of sojourners along this trail, including several itinerant salesman.

Perhaps a bit more inventiveness is behind those narratives concerning the preponderance of untimely deaths on this route due to such prevailing diseases as malaria, cholera, and diphtheria. Maladies such as these felled the early settlers of this region in great numbers. This is not surprising since the area around Great Meadows was once plagued with disease-ridden swamps. According to DeLong, between 1870 and 1884, the dredging of the Pequest River, which flows through the area on its way to the Delaware, did much to eliminate those swamps. And with the disappearance of the swamps so went their disease-borne deaths.

The gentleman from Great Meadows apparently chose to espouse an answer that harks back to the days of the American Revolution. It seems that one of the local boys of the region was attached to a unit under the command of Gen. Benedict Arnold, in the days before that esteemed officer turned traitor. They were stationed in upstate New York.

There, the British General, John Burgoyne, was heading south to activate the three-pronged British Plan of 1777. The plan was to split the American colonies. As part of the American action to foil that plan, Arnold was ordered to move to the defense of Fort Stanwix. To accomplish this he had to get his troops over a difficult trail.

The route went through a densely forested region infested with the death-dealing Iroquois. They were allied with the British at the time. The vine-hung trail provided the lurking Indians with a perfect cover. Death lurked at every shadowy turn. The hanging trees were thickly over-grown with wild grapevines. In a letter to his folks back home in Easton, which then, as now, was the metropolis for the western region of what is now Warren County, our local soldier wrote of this trail as a "veritable Shades of Death Road." The letter was published in the Easton paper which was apparently much read in the region. The account of this road was an apt description of the one in Warren County with its low-hanging, vine-covered trees. Having such a striking resemblance, the name was presumable, therefore, adopted by local residents.

Or so goes, at least, the evidence presented by Mr. DeLong. Now you have to admit that a road with an epithet like that has to evoke spine-tingling feelings of impending doom. It is one thing to travel over such an artery on occasion, but remember Mr. DeLong lives there! Is it any wonder, then, that he should take comfort in adapting the less ominous version of the road's name? For that is the one which he chooses to embrace. I do not doubt his choice mind you, but like so many others I find myself wanting to believe some of the more spell-binding accounts as I search about the countryside for more tales along the trails of New Jersey.

Some Jersey Tales - The Ghosts of "Blackbeard"

Being surrounded on three sides by water, no accounts of "Jersey ghosts" would be complete without a tale or two about the infamous Edward Teach. Originally commissioned as a privateer by Queen Anne of England in the early 1700's, Teach turned to piracy after Queen Anne's War ended in 1713. Ghosts stories related to Teach have been popular throughout the state ever since. In fact, he has become Jersey's favorite Buccaneer.

Captain Teach, like so many English pirates of that era, operated out of England's colonies in America. His piracy was with the blessings of the appointed Royal governors. The governors' protection, of course, had a price tag - a share of the loot. Though his hideaways were in the Bahamas and the Carolina coast, New Jersey's coastline was an important base of operations. From Sandy Hook to the Cape on the Atlantic side, around Cape May along the bayside, into the mouth of the Delaware River, and up as far as Foul Rift to present-day Belvidere, his name brought terror to the eyes of those who heard it mentioned.

Commonly known as "Blackbeard," Capt. Edward Teach cut such an impressive figure that he was believed to be the embodiment of the Devil himself. After his death, "Blackbeard's" ghost continued to scare the living daylight out of those who dared occupy his old haunts. His sense of humor saw comedy in acts of violence. It was with great amusement, for example, that he severed fingers or arms to gain access to valuable rings or bracelets worn by his hapless victims. He never ceased to take keen delight in the terror-stricken faces of those who watched as he drank a flaming concoction of gunpowder mixed with rum to which he had set fire.

One of the "Blackbeard" tales centers on the time he sailed up the Delaware River in a ship loaded with booty plundered along the Jersey coast. He and his men were hoping to find a secluded spot along the riverbank. The location they sought would have to be little traveled, but with sufficient landmarks to guide them on their return. Stories ranged that the site was anywhere from Burlington to Belvidere.

The men decided that they would locate their loot at the base of a tree. Burlington has such a tree, which they have since dubbed "The Pirate Tree." Other towns had made similar claims. The pirates allegedly dropped their stolen treasures - locked in a heavy chest - into a large hole. To safeguard it from thieves one of the crew would have to remain as a sentinel. He would be released to divvy up the bounty upon the return of the others. The chosen sailor, unfortunately for him, was shot through the head and buried upright over the treasure chest. For it was believed in that day that the ghost of a dead body would make a far more effective guard than any mortal being.

The story told on many a dark and foggy night in select little towns along the banks of the Delaware from Burlington to Belvidere is that no one has yet found that buried treasure. But the ghost of "Blackbeard's" faithful guard has been seen haunting the riverside. He is said to roam the shoreline bemoaning his ill fate. It is told that he calls to his shipmates with anguished wails. His ghostly whimpers remind them that he still stands vigil awaiting their return.

"Blackbeard" himself met an untimely end in 1718. Caught by surprise, the fierce pirate, nevertheless, blasted away at the royal ship that challenged him with all eight of his cannon. Lt. Robert Maynard of the Royal Navy hurried most of his men below deck. Seeing only the dead bodies as he neared Maynard's vessel, "Blackbeard" ordered his men to board ship and cut the remaining crew to pieces. As he boarded, the hidden crew poured out of the hold and a wild fray followed. It took a slash of his throat from behind, five gunshot wounds and some 20 slashes to his body before "Blackbeard" finally fell to the deck dead. Maynard, fearing the Devil would not die, ordered the pirate's head removed and hung from the bowsprit. He had his body chucked overboard.

Since that fateful day Blackbeard's headless ghost has been sighted haunting many of his favorite hangouts. Fishermen have spotted the phosphorescent glow of the beheaded specter on the waters. Others not far inland have seen his spirit vainly searching for its severed head along the edge of the water. Many a tale of this decapitated ghost carrying a lantern has made the rounds of the three Jersey shorelines. "Teach's Light" became the answer to numerous unexplainable "night glows" along the trails of New Jersey.

CHAPTER 11: FAMOUS PEOPLE

Captain Kidd

Ever hear of the Jersey Pirates? No, I am not referring to a baseball team. I am talking about the real thing, pirates that once infested the New Jersey shoreline and molested legitimate shipping.

New Jersey's broken coastline, containing many inlets and broad bays hidden by shifting sandbars, made the ideal setting for these marauding sea thieves.

Piracy was very much a part of New Jersey's nautical heritage, and some of the world's most famous, such as Capt. Kidd and Capt. Teach, better known as "Blackbeard," once roamed its waters.

Even the more legitimate pirates - called privateers, existed along New Jersey's coastline during the American Revolution, encouraged by the young nation to prey on British shipping.

Yes, pirates swarmed the Jersey coastline from Sandy Hook to Cape May. What they did and what treasures they supposedly hid continue to live on in folk tales and legends passed along by those whose ancestors along the shore communities go back for generations.

The pirates themselves knew that the mere sight of the pirate's flag, with its skull and crossed-bones, made most men's blood run cold. So they eagerly fostered the savage image that it portrayed. Piracy, after all, was a very profitable industry.

Starting as a sea captain, and later as a respected New York merchant, Capt. William Kidd, the legendary arch-pirate of them all, was originally employed by the British government. He was actually commissioned to capture the then-infamous pirate, Capt. Thomas Tew.

His investigations, however, led him to discover the close connections that had been made between pirates and governing officials. Because he knew too much about official misdeeds, he was framed for some alleged crime and sentenced to hang on the gallows!

Capt. Kidd, however, was somehow able to escape. It was then that he decided that since he was now a fugitive anyhow, he might as well take up the profitable act of piracy himself. Having discovered that the key to a long life as a pirate was to unite his endeavors with those of greedy government officials, he boldly made his connections.

Capt. Kidd became the most scandalous of them all! Depending upon what emotion was gripping him, fed by his own past mistreatment, he alternated the treatment of his victims between extreme savagery and an unusual gentleness.

Capt. Kidd's original attempts to capture one of the most famous pirates of that day, Capt. Tew, led him to the dinner table of a man appointed governor by the crown. Capt. Tew made no attempt whatsoever to hide his nefarious deals with the king's representative in the colonies.

He appeared regularly as the governor's dinner guest. He even had the gall to ride with him publicly in his coach! This so-called public servant was selling "pirate protection" at the equivalent of $100 per man.

As long as they paid their protection money, notorious pirates were always welcomed guests at the governor's home.

Kidd's own pirating adventures along the Jersey coast took him to its many small islands. Tales of his "buried treasures" have lured many a person on treasure hunts up and down New Jersey's coastline over these many years. Stories of a "Kidd's Tree" someplace, where he is supposed to have planted a secret treasure, once were rampant. According to these reports, only some $50,000 of the estimated $250,000 in today's currency that he was alleged to have buried, has ever been recovered.

Another of the more renowned pirates who once operated off the Jersey coast, among other places, was Capt. Edward Teach, better known as "Blackbeard." He was an abnormally tall and well-built man with a coal black beard that hung to his waist. His appearance led his men to believe that he was an embodiment of the devil himself.

According to legend, the Delaware Bay and lower Delaware River are literally bulging with his supposed buried treasures! And at those places, also, according to these same tales, are the ghosts of the men he cold-heartedly had buried in order to stand permanent guard over his ill-gotten loot.

Some of the pirates that operated off the Jersey shore, not satisfied with what bounty they could extricate from those unfortunate passing ships, also left their ships to raid houses located along the nearby beach.

A brash French pirate once pillaged homes regularly in the Navesink Highlands until he was finally driven off by the Monmouth militia.

At times, organized attempts were even made by fleets of private ships to drive these sea marauders away. Such was part of the nautical heritage found along the trails of the New Jersey shoreline.

Naval Heroes

New Jersey could aptly be called "the Peninsula State," since it is a piece of land almost totally surrounded by water. With some 127 miles of its east coast bordering on the Atlantic Ocean and a southern cape whose western boundary is the extensive Delaware Bay, it's no wonder that the state has a strong maritime heritage.

It should come as no surprise either that some of the nation's most famous naval officers also have their New Jersey connection. Richard Somers, for example, comes immediately to mind at this particular time of the Libyan crisis. He was born at Somer's Point (named after his family), on Sept. 15, 1778. He died at the Battle of Tripoli, North Africa, on Sept. 4, 1804. This was a time in history when the bandit nations of North Africa were exacting tribute from the nations of Europe for the "privilege" of using the waters of the Mediterranean.

Aware that the more you paid these international bandits, the more they demanded, the young United States was the only nation that stood up to them. Declaring its rights to "freedom of the seas," our country declared that it would rather spend "millions for defense than pay one penny for tribute." New Jersey's young naval officer, Richard Somers, for gallant service in the war with Tripoli, was promoted to commander. During an especially dangerous engagement of that war, he was killed at the very early age of 26. He became one of the new nation's youngest naval heroes.

In a recent mini-series on television, you heard the name of still another noted American naval hero from New Jersey. Robert Field Stockton was born on Aug. 20, 1795 at Princeton, where he also died on Oct. 7, 1866. Though Stockton's most notable claim to fame was probably his seizure of California during the War with Mexico, he also served valiantly in the War of 1812 and the Algerian War of 1814-15. At the latter, he secured the territory that now makes up the Republic of Liberia, which was founded by freed, former, American slaves.

Still another New Jersey naval hero was James Lawrence, born in Burlington on Oct. 1, 1781. Fatally wounded during the War of 1812, he also fought for freedom of the seas. The battle was between his ship, the "Chesapeake," and the British "Shannon." It was at that time he uttered his immortal words, "Don't give up the ship!" It became the motto of the US Navy. Lawrence, too, had first become a national hero for his actions on the night of Feb. 15, 1804, when he destroyed that captured American frigate "Philadelphia" during a daring raid in the harbor of Tripoli, North Africa. It was being held prisoner there for ransom money.

A more recent American naval hero of New Jersey was born in Elizabeth on Oct. 30, 1882. William Frederick "Bull" Halsey became a full admiral in November of 1942, and was noted for distinguished service in the naval battles of the Pacific during World War II. But the man I'm leading up to, because he has a prep school named after him at Pine Beach within sight of my mother's home, is Admiral David Farragut. Farragut won his most noted fame for his command at the battles on the Mississippi River and the Gulf of Mexico during the Civil War. The Admiral Farragut Academy, however, is his only New Jersey connection.

In the early 1930's a young naval officer, Jackson Lahn, and a Spanish-American War veteran, Capt. Frederick Patten, searched the East Coast from Maine to Florida, seeking a site suitable for establishing a naval training prep school. They finally settled on a once-fashionable 75-room resort hotel overlooking the Toms River. It was called the Pine Beach Inn. Originally built in 1910 on the site of what turned out to be an old Indian burial ground once called Eagle

Point, it had fallen into disuse during the early 20's because of Prohibition. It became the new academy's main building. Its doors opened in September 1933, with 56 cadets enrolled.

Admiral S.S. Robinson, former superintendent of the US Naval Academy at Annapolis, Brig. Gen. C.S. Radford of the US Marine Corps, and Capt. W. Kable Russell of the US Navy, were the founders of America's first naval prep school at Pine Beach. Honor cadet graduates receive nomination from the headmaster for admittance to the U.S. Naval Academy. Many outstanding naval officers have been among New Jersey's Admiral Farragut Academy graduates over the years. Included among its roster are 12 admirals of the US Navy and two generals of the US Air Force. Admiral Alan B. Shepard Jr., America's distinguished astronaut, was among them. Lorenzo Lamas, who plays Lance Cumseth on the CBS TV show "Falcon Crest," is also an alumni of the Academy at Pine Beach - along the trails of New Jersey.

Lt. Richard Somers

As we visit in and around New Jersey's South Shore, the Queen of Seaside Resorts is the prime jewel around which all else revolves. Since we have devoted a previous column exclusively to this world famous convention city, however, we will look now at its outskirts.

Those of you who are interested in horse breeding will, of course, want to take the Atlantic City Expressway northwest to McKee City. Once at the Atlantic City Raceway, you will immediately take the opportunity to view its fine thoroughbreds in action. For the wine connoisseur, the finer arts of grape fermentation may be observed at Gross' Highland Winery in Absecon. Located off Route 9, north of the city, this winery offers daily tours of its operation with the opportunity to tempt your palate with wine testing as well.

Traveling south to Margate City will bring you in full view of a unique six-story wood and tin structure built in 1881. Lucy, the Margate Elephant, was a public relations gimmick that has become a South Shore landmark. Used now as an observation point, it contains a museum, gift shop and nearby eating facilities. You certainly should not visit in this area without having taken the time to pursue this unusual site.

Continuing still further to the south of our "City by the Sea," we will reach Somers Point. There, on the Shore Road, is the Somers House, birthplace of the American naval officer and hero, Richard Somers. Somers, who was born there in 1778, died in action during the Tripolitan War in 1804. The Somers House was built about 1720 by his great-grandfather, a harbormaster, after whom Somers Point was named. It now houses the Atlantic County Historical Society headquarters. The Society's large museum there, in addition to Somers' family memorabilia, contains many exhibits relating to the nautical history of Jersey's South Shore. The house itself is furnished with period furniture, some of which belonged to the Somers family.

Richard Somers, who joined the US Navy in 1798, was first assigned to the warship, the "United States." During this period, our nation became involved in a naval war with Tripoli. This Tripolitan War was fought because the ruler of Tripoli was demanding tribute from a number of nations, including the United States. This extortion money was paid "for protection" from pirates while trading in the Mediterranean Sea region. While older nations were paying the so-called Barbary Pirates their extortion money, the young United States refused. The United States adopted the slogan, "Millions for defense, but not one cent for tribute!"

During the War on the Barbary Coast, Lt. Richard Somers was placed in charge of the "Nautilus." While in command of that ship he was sent to the harbor of Tripoli in North Africa. A small flotilla of US ships had assembled there to take action against the arrogant Sultan of Tripoli who had in fact become an international extortionist. The Sultan had taken prisoner another Jerseyman, a Captain William Bainbridge, commander of the US warship, the "Philadelphia," and he was holding him in chains for ransom money.

Somers volunteered to take part with 12 others in a daring attempt to blockade the harbor of Tripoli by sneaking in and sinking the captured "Philadelphia" in the middle of the harbor. Turning a smaller ship, the "Intrepid," into a floating mine, the plan was to float it in under cover of darkness and then blow it up alongside of the captured ship. This action would then render the pirate's harbor useless. The volunteer crew, with Somers in command, was to make their escape in two small boats, after setting the explosive-loaded "Intrepid" afire!

While the small boat was stealthily plying the harbor waters late on the night of Sept. 4, 1804, she was apparently spotted by the Sultan's shore battery. Before the crew could complete their task and make their escape, she was fired upon by guns from the shore and blown up. Thus the young naval officer from Somers Point became an American Naval hero. Six US naval vessels have since borne his name.

Leaving Somers Point, we travel southward along Ocean Drive, after taking Route 52 across the bridge over Great Egg Harbor Bay. This easternmost route will take you through many of Jersey's quaint South Shore resort towns from Ocean City all the way to Cape May. En route you view the Atlantic Ocean to your east, and Inland Waterway to your west. But let us save that journey for another week.

William Newell,
Founder of the US Coast Guard

At this time of the year our minds often turn to thoughts of the "Jersey Shore." Aside from swimming and beach lounging, that also conjures up pictures of the boats that are plying the waters off the coastline.

Today we take for granted that vital role, played out by the US Coast Guard - its lifesaving service. The man who was originally responsible for this very important activity certainly deserves the accolades of us all, but especially those of his fellow Jerseyans. Unfortunately, all too few even know his name.

William A. Newell, a young graduate of the University of Pennsylvania Medical School just a few months before, was also making one of those regular visits to the Jersey shore on the late summer night of Aug. 13, 1839. In fact, he was a guest there at the home of his uncle in Manahawkin when a summer storm came up.

Newell was standing on the dunes at Long Beach Island that night as a brig hit a shoal just offshore.

The newly graduated medical doctor, whose just-completed training had left him imbued with the high purpose of bending every effort to save human lives, stood helpless on the shore, while the cry of drowning human voices rang in his ears, amidst the pounding of the wildly roaring waves.

On the morning of the 14th, less than 300 yards from where the young doctor had stood the night before, that boat appeared stuck on a sandbar. The bodies of its 14 crew members lay strewn about the beach-dead. They were the victims of an ill-fated attempt to swim ashore.

The young doctor was haunted with the helplessness of his situation and the resulting horrible loss of lives due to his inability to do something. Some means must be invented for preventing such disasters in the future, he thought. Perhaps the presence of lifelines that could somehow be propelled from shore to ships in distress could be devised.

Five years later, in 1844, Dr. Newell had set up a medical practice in Allentown, NJ. He made many friends there. Still determined to do something about establishing an offshore lifesaving service, he ran for, and was elected to, the US Congress.

Dr. Newell had, in the meantime, been trying a number of different methods for propelling lifelines from shore to ship. At last, he believed that he had found such a means. Eagerly he sought help from his fellow representatives. Not one member of the Congress, however, was interested. He sought out famous national personages, such as Henry Clay and Daniel Webster, in the hope that they could influence others. No one would sponsor his lifesaving plan.

Within an 18-month period in his first term, between 1846 and 1848, Newell had counted 122 ships that had been battered along the New Jersey shore. On one night alone, in February of 1846, 10 boats were wrecked and 45 people had died.

Clearly, something had to be done. Newell finally, in desperation, found out how congressmen often got things passed in which they alone were particularly interested. So he attached a "rider" to a sure-bet lighthouse bill. Congress, almost to his surprise, passed it unchallenged!

His rider authorized "the expenditure of $10,000 for providing surf-boats, rockets, cannonades and other necessary apparatus for the better preservation of life and property from shipwrecks along the coast of New Jersey between Sandy Hook and Little Egg Harbor." Newell's rider had, in fact, created a new naval unit, the US Lifesaving Service!

In Dr. Newell's long life, he served for two terms as governor of New Jersey in the 1850's, was re-elected to Congress in 1865, was elected president of the New Jersey State Board of Agriculture in 1875, and in 1880 was appointed governor of the Washington Territory, by then-President Rutherford B. Hayes.

In 1884, he finally settled down at his home in Allentown, NJ, to resume the practice of medicine. He continued this practice until 1901, when he died near his 84th year.

The trails of New Jersey have been home to many a pioneering person. The efforts of Dr. William A. Newell in creating the US Lifesaving Service should certainly be remembered among them.

In 1790, the United States Congress had created the US Revenue Cutter Service with the specific purpose of enforcing the new nation's custom laws. It was, therefore, made a part of the Treasury Department.

In 1915, that service was combined with Newell's US Lifesaving Service and renamed-the US Coast Guard! Since then, it assumed the US Lighthouse Service in 1939 and the Bureau of Marine Inspection and Navigation in 1942.

As a direct result of Dr. Newell's persistent concern for saving lives, the coast of New Jersey and the nation is a far safer place today. New Jersey should be proud of this contribution of its native son, William A. Newell.

Peter McGuire, Father of Labor Day

As I sit here writing this article on Labor Day weekend, my thoughts naturally turn to how this American holiday came into existence. An investigation of its origins once again turns up, you guessed it, a New Jersey connection!

Peter J. McGuire, who is buried in Arlington Cemetery in Pennsauken, is credited with being both the father of "Labor Day," and one of the original organizers of the American Federation of Labor (AFofL).

Though born on the lower, East Side of Manhattan in 1852, Peter McGuire moved to Camden in 1880 and spent the remaining active 26 years of his life there. He was at his home in Camden in 1894, in fact, when he was notified that Congress had finally approved of his pet project, the establishment of "Labor Day" as a national holiday.

To solidify the New Jersey connection, the only president to be born in New Jersey, Grover Cleveland, interestingly, issued the proclamation designating the first Monday of each September as "Labor Day."

Peter McGuire, the son of Irish immigrant parents, was familiar with labor from an early age. He quit school at age 11 in order to help with the family income. He sold newspapers, was a bootblack, swept shops, cleaned streets, ran errands, and did just about every other chore imaginable to earn money to help keep his family from starving.

There were none of the federal social programs at that time with which we are so familiar, and so dependent upon, today.

Throughout it all McGuire found the time to attend night classes at Cooper Union in order to acquire an education.

McGuire is supposed to have first met Samuel Gompers at this early age in 1866. Both later became leaders in the American labor movement. He is said to have proposed a "Labor Day" holiday as early as 1872, when in one of his many speeches promoting the causes of labor, he suggested that a day be set aside as a national holiday to honor, "those who from rude nature have delved and carved all the grandeur we behold...the common man, the workingman."

Finally, after thousands of speeches, which McGuire doggedly made before probably millions of people over a period of 22 years, President Grover Cleveland in 1894 declared his "Labor Day" as a national holiday. It was a personal triumph for the unceasing efforts of this legendary New Jersey resident who would not accept defeat.

Peter McGuire, who became an apprentice piano-maker at age 17, soon became an active cabinetmaker unionist. At age 19, he was already a strong advocate of the 8-hour workday. He became a labor organizer, and as such fought labor's battles not only figuratively, but in those days in the streets as well.

While in St. Louis in 1879, he agitated for a "national" union of carpenters and joiners. He established his home in Camden the year before he helped organize the "Brotherhood of Carpenters and Joiners" in 1881, with offices across the Delaware in Philadelphia. He became its first secretary.

Constantly at work promoting the cause of organized labor, McGuire was in the forefront of the "American Federation of Labor (AFofL)" in 1886 when it came into existence. But always he fought as well for a holiday commemorating the role of labor in the building of America.

A fervent pitch he made at a labor rally on May 8, 1882, in New York seems to have been the turning point. It should be a day to honor, "the industrial spirit, the great vital force of this nation," he said. He envisioned it as co-equal, and lying between those two other great American holidays, Independence Day and Thanksgiving. Only the parades, the picnics, the speeches would all be to extol the virtues of America's great labor force.

On September 5, 1882, the first great "Labor Day Parade" was held in New York City. Some 10,000 workers marched in it. It was organized by the "Knights of Labor," one of the first national labor unions.

When it was held again in 1884, it was followed by a resolution by the "Knights" that such parades be held all over the nation on an annual "Labor Day." Oregon became the first state to declare such a state holiday on Feb. 21, 1887. Following Oregon's example, four more states declared it to be a state holiday that same year: Colorado on March 15; New Jersey, April 8; New York, May 6; and Massachusetts, May 11. They had set the first Monday in September as the date of the holiday following the suggestion of Peter McGuire. Oregon, which had at first observed it in June, changed it to September in 1893.

McGuire never made any financial gains from his efforts on behalf of labor. When he died in Camden on Feb. 18, 1906, though he was not penniless, he was close to it. Here, again, we see how the trails of New Jersey played a prominent role in another facet of America's heritage.

Presidents in New Jersey

Because of what had happened there, the whole world heard of this little seashore community on Sept. 19, 1881. But did you know that this famous New Jersey health and pleasure resort once served as the summer capital of the United States under the administrations of two US presidents, U.S. Grant and Woodrow Wilson?

Some seven presidents, in fact, and many other notables, spent at least part of their summers at this once-plush, Monmouth County, New Jersey, seashore resort.

It was, however, the one president who died there, victim of an assassin's bullet several months before, who brought to it world-wide attention in that first year of the 1880's.

One of the oldest seashore summer resorts in the US, this New Jersey location took its name from a brook which passes through it. The brook is a branch of the South Shrewsbury River. The Lenape Indians, who had a summer fishing village there, referred to it as "land's end." The first known European to establish a summer home at this place was a British officer stationed in New York City before the Revolution, a Col. White. After the American Revolution, his property was confiscated by the new American government.

In 1788, a Philadelphia financier, Elliston Perot, who pioneered building boarding houses along the Jersey shore, took over Col. White's summer home and converted it into a resort hotel. It soon attracted wealthy families from both New York City and Philadelphia. In time, the area became a well-known resort for the rich and the famous. The notorious "Diamond Jim" Brady was one of those who cavorted there in his heyday.

What was destined to turn the attention of the world to Long Branch, NJ, however, occurred on the morning of July 2, 1881. President James A Garfield was at a Washington, DC railroad station. He was bound for New England to deliver the commencement address at his alma mater, Williams College.

Out of the blue came a disappointed office-seeker. He aimed and fired the shot that was to leave the nation stunned, and the president lingering in agony for months. His bearing during that trying period won him worldwide sympathy and admiration. His doctors thought about the healing affects of the sea breezes. Perhaps the salt air would be of benefit to him, if he were to be removed from the stifling heat of Washington, DC. They settled on the little seashore resort community of Long Branch.

Immediate arrangements were begun to have the wounded president moved to the summer home of a friend. On the morning of Sept. 5, 1881, US Attorney General Wayne MacVeigh asked officials of the Jersey Central Railroad at Jersey City to build a spur by the next day from their Elberon Station to a Long Branch beachfront cottage. The intention was to transport the seriously ill president there directly from the White House. The impossible task was undertaken immediately. Hundreds of railroad workers labored around the clock to lay the more than half-mile of track.

The 49-year-old president had, since the attempted assassination on July 2, lost more than 70 pounds. He was hovering between life and death. It was hoped that the believed curative effect of the salt air would turn the tide in bringing about his recovery.

Word of the imminent arrival of the wounded president soon spread throughout Long Branch. Crowds from numerous hotels and summer homes in the area began arriving on the scene. Everyone who could, pitched in and in some way helped with the proceedings. Women and girls served refreshments to the workers. Men and boys helped move ties, rails, spikes, etc.

President Garfield's train arrived at the Elberon station at 1:09 p.m. one Sept. 6. Unfortunately, the heavy locomotive that pulled it was too much for the spur, and a lighter one had to be brought in. This engine, however, failed as it tried to make a slight grade. Instantly, the hundreds of workers still on the scene pushed it over the incline manually. It finally made it to the seaside cottage which had been readied for the president. Soldiers held back the throngs as the wounded man was carried inside.

Out of his bedroom window, Garfield had a beautiful view of the Atlantic Ocean from the Jersey shore. He, at first, seemed to rally. But the president had not been moved from the stifling, muggy summer air that plagued the nations' capital at that time of the year soon enough.

On Sept. 15, blood poisoning set in. The president struggled valiantly for life. But at 10:30 p.m. on the night of Sept. 19, 1881, James A. Garfield, the 20th president of the United States, died along the trails of New Jersey. At a summer cottage in a little seaside resort know as Long Branch, a brief funeral service was conducted. The man, whose life from farm boy to president had epitomized so well the "American Dream," was then brought home to his final resting-place in Cleveland, Ohio.

As so often in the past, New Jersey once again played out its vital role in an American drama.

The Sam Colt Connection

Most people have heard of the "Colt .45." Credited by many with the "winning of the west," it was dubbed, "the great equalizer," because of the role it played in making each man equal to his neighbor - no matter how big or small he was.

But did you know that it was first produced by Sam Colt right here in New Jersey back in the year 1836?

Samuel Colt, who was born in Hartford, CT, on July 19, 1814, was a restless young man who was sent to sea in 1830 at age 16, "to settle him down," according to his father. By his own account, it was while he was at sea that Sam first conceived of the idea of a "revolver."

Always interested in firearms, Colt was sailing in the Far East as "foremast hand" when he was watching the ship's wheel turn. It was then that the idea of a "revolving breech firearm" came to his head. He is supposed to have whittled the first wooden model of his famous "Colt .45" revolver while he was on that seafaring journey.

In order to raise the funds he needed to produce his "revolving breech" firearms, Colt set about, after his sea journey was over, on a lecture tour which took him from Quebec to New Orleans. Pretending to be a "wizard of practical chemistry," known as Dr. Coult, late of London and Calcutta, he gained notoriety by making people look ridiculous on stage. The secret was his use of nitrous oxide, or "laughing gas."

Sam Colt received his patent on the "revolving breech" from the US Patent Office on Feb. 25, 1836. Designed for use on pistols, rifles, or shotguns, it featured an automatic rotation of the cylinder during cocking.

Securing a group of financiers from the New Jersey area, Colt first obtained an old mill in Paterson, where he began the manufacture of all three firearms in a stock company he organized. Colt ran the Paterson business almost single-handedly, not only as the superintendent of the shop, but as the publicity agent and sales manager for his new invention as well.

Colt soon introduced his backers to build a four-story gun factory in Paterson in order to produce his new weapons more efficiently. Always the showman, his "Gun Mill" was topped with a weather vane designed in the form of a gun. He also built a white fence around it with pistol-shaped pickets!

While there, Colt worked on machines that would adopt Eli Whitney's mass-production method of making interchangeable parts on an assembly line. He produced beautifully engraved barrels on his Paterson-made Colt weapons with silver or gold handles. He then sent them to the world's leaders - including President Andrew Jackson.

Unfortunately, Army officials, always difficult to admit to change, called his weapons useless and refused to give him the large orders he needed to both establish his "Colt .45" as an accepted weapon and insure its financial success.

To make matters worse, during an exhibition he had arranged at the Capitol for the new President, Martin VanBuren, the loud crack of his revolvers panicked the team of horses on the President's carriage. The driver lost control, toppled off and was killed. Everyone's attention was diverted to the unfortunate accident and the whole purpose of the demonstration was forgotten. Obviously, no sale was made.

During the fierce Seminole Indian War (1835-1842), in which Florida's Indians waged a tremendous fight against the US Government's attempt to remove them to the Indian Territory, Colt's guns were first introduced to battle in 1838. The war, conducted by the famed Indian Chief Osceola, was considered to be the fiercest of all Indian campaigns. The army bought 50 of Colt's revolvers in a desperate attempt to gain greater superiority over the obstinate Indian residence.

Though small numbers of Colt's weapons were sold throughout the West, including to the "Texas Rangers," its sales were not sufficient and Colt's Gun Mill in Paterson folded in 1842.

After several other ventures in New Jersey in the early 1840's with submarine batteries, underwater explosive mines to protect New York Harbor, and submarine telegraphy, Colt moved back to Hartford, CT. While there in 1846, the US Army ordered 1,000 of his revolvers for use during the Mexican War.

Because of its success in that war, hundreds of thousands were manufactured at the Colt Patent Fire Arms Co. of Hartford during the Civil War. He had to build an immense new armory to keep up with the demand. He was on his way to tremendous prosperity when he died on Jan. 10, 1862.

Following that war, the Colt .45 gained enormous popularity. Once again, the trails of New Jersey had played a vital role in another bit of Americana. Colt's Paterson "Gun Mill" was destroyed by fire in 1863.

Seth Boyden, "one of America's greatest inventors"

New Jersey, throughout its history, has been a leader in the field of science and technology. A surprisingly large number of new inventions and technological advances in agriculture, manufacturing, and medicine have been given birth in this state. When one considers that in both size and population it has for many years been one of the smallest in the nation, the number of its achievements becomes truly remarkable. Remember, too, that its present rank as the most densely populated state in the nation was not always so.

Tanneries began appearing in such places as Elizabethtown and Newark as early as the late 17th century. But it took until the early 1800's for a mechanical wizard, named Seth Boyden, to come on the scene in Newark with first a leather-splitting machine and then, in 1819, a process for turning out "patent leather." Both of these established Newark and New Jersey as a leader in the nation's leather-making industry for many years thereafter. Boyden, in fact, came up

267

with so many different products in his lifetime that another New Jersey innovative genius, Thomas Edison, referred to him as "one of America's greatest inventors."

In 1826, Boyden produced malleable cast iron. The US Patent Office granted him a patent for the process in 1831. The United States at least was enabled to become a leading iron manufacturer in its own right, with New Jersey in the forefront. This new process made it possible for pig iron to be easily stretched, shaped by hammering in the forges or pressured with rollers. For the first time, the nation was totally free of Europe in this field, and soon took off to unprecedented heights as a leading manufacturing nation.

From leather manufacturing and then to iron, Boyden's never-satisfied mind soon moved on to steam engines. By 1837, he was designing new and improved ways for moving locomotives across the state's and nation's new fascination - the railway. Boyden gave Newark's fledging industry another economic boost when he came up with a new hat-forming machine, thus putting that growing town into the forefront in another field - the manufacture of hats.

But Seth Boyden's inventive mind, which has sadly been practically ignored by the state and nation to whom he gave so much during his lifetime, was far from exhausted. He was constantly investing his profits from one industry into new research, which led to developments in totally different industries.

New Jersey's Seth Boyden was the embodiment of the kind of person who made this nation great. His hunger was not for ever-growing personal wealth but for new ideas and new ways of doing things. As soon as one industry prospered, he sold it and put his energies and money into some other challenge.

In time, he got into the field of metallurgy, and soon developed a method for producing an imitation gold alloy for decorative purposes. In the 1840's, he turned his attention to still another new and fascinating field - photography. A Frenchman, L.J.M. Daguerre, had come up with a method of producing pictures on a silver surface sensitized to light by iodine, and then developed by mercury. His pictures came to be called daguerreotypes. Boyden worked on his process in Newark until he devised a way to increase the light with a reflector, and thus improve the pictures. He was the first to produce them in America. Again, it all happened right here in New Jersey.

In 1848, another New Jerseyan, James Marshall of Lambertville, discovered gold while erecting a sawmill on John Sutter's land in California. The world went into a gold rush "tizzy" the following year the likes of which had not been seen before, nor since. The most unlikely people were included among those "forty-niners" who dropped everything, from every corner of the earth, and headed for the gold fields. New Jersey's most prolific inventor, Seth Boyden, was among those bitten by the fever. He returned to New Jersey, however, the following year. Boyden was not one to waste his time with something that was not producing results.

After a few years back in New Jersey, Seth Boyden, at the age of 67, purchased a farm in Clinton Township (now a part of Irvington and Maplewood) in 1855. There he began to dabble in growing "bigger and better" strawberries. The whole area soon became the "strawberry capital" of the state. Boyden, who shared his ideas with local farmers, had developed a giant hybrid strawberry noted for both its size and sweetness. Though a statue was erected to this uncommon inventor in Newark in 1890, it is disheartening how few people along the trails of New Jersey today have ever heard of Seth Boyden. He died in 1870 at the age of 81 on his beloved farm in what is now Maplewood, New Jersey.

Alfred Vail and the Telegraph

New Jersey and technology - perfect together. Many events will be celebrated in the near future to bring this fact home.

The 150th anniversary of the invention of the telegraph back in 1838 by three men, including New Jersey's Alfred Vail, at what is now called "Historic Speedwell Village" in Morristown, is one of them.

So, too, is the 100th anniversary of the opening of Thomas Edison's "Invention Factory" at the "Edison National Historic Site" in West Orange.

Edison, who was born on Feb. 11, 1847, was introduced to science and technology, interestingly enough, when he was taught telegraphy as a young teenager out of gratitude by a station agent whose boy he rescued.

In 1864, his creative mind came up with an automatic telegraph repeater, his first invention. This was to be the beginning of a lifetime that would find the US Patent Office granting him more than 1200 patents for a variety of inventions and improvements that revolutionized the world.

To commemorate what has been proclaimed by Gov. Thomas Kean as a yearlong, "New Jersey, the Invention State, Celebration," a traveling sci-tech exhibit will begin its appearance first at the Morris Museum.

Later, it will be on display at the State Museum in Trenton, then at the Steadman Art Galley on the Camden Campus of Rutgers University. Its final stop will be the Terminal Building in Liberty State Park. It will remain there until the opening of New Jersey's brand new, multi-million dollar science and technology museum - the crowning glory to New Jersey's commitment to be tops in the nation in the fields of science and technology.

More than 100,000 square feet will be devoted to various "hands-on" science and technology exhibits. This new state-of-the-art museum is expected to represent the latest approach in science exhibits by having all sorts of things "going on" and by encouraging people participation.

Getting back to Alfred Vail, his example looms as even more important to New Jersey today because it represents the kind of atmosphere that will hopefully be created by design in New Jersey.

Samuel F. B. Morse, Leonard Gale, and Alfred Vail had formed a partnership that operated out of a building at Vail's father's ironworks in Morristown. Each of these men brought to that partnership a different, but necessary aspect, of what it takes to come up with a new, workable invention. This is the very type of partnership being promoted by the state today - as we stand at the threshold of the 21st century.

Gale's contribution was the brilliance of his scientific knowledge. Morse represented that inventive genius so vital to developing something new and different. Vail had the mechanical skill needed to put the first two together and come up with a workable product. His father had the money to finance it. It is the same kind of partnership that is needed today to bring science and technology together. In their case, it enabled the bringing into the world a brand new communications system that was to become only the beginning in a long series of inventions that would remake the world.

Morse's mind originally came up with the idea of an electrical signal causing an electro-magnet to activate a pen on a piece of paper. Gale's knowledge of the scientific principles involved in Joseph Henry's electromagnet and Vail's skill in improving upon the mechanics of an instrument that could be practically used for sending messages were combined.

Together they were able to produce the new telegraphy device that was firs demonstrated on Jan. 6, 1838. This historic event took place, in an upstairs room, in one of the buildings at Vail's father's Morristown ironworks. Through some three miles of wire strung throughout the place, Vail sent this message, "A patient waiter is no loser." Morse received the message and was able to repeat it correctly. The device worked!

Although Alfred Vail of Morristown created the contraption born in the mind of Samuel F. B. Morse, based upon the scientific principles set forth in Joseph Henry's electromagnet, and so fully understood by their partner, Leonard Gale, only Morse won the recognition of the public.

This instrument, which was first demonstrated along the trails of New Jersey, went on to be presented to the world, and the US Congress, over a wire stretched between Washington, DC, and Baltimore, MD. In 1844, it carried this dramatic message, "What hath God wrought?"

Thomas Edison, "The Wizard of Menlo Park"

New Jersey has a reputation as the "Invention State," and the governor has proclaimed this year as a commemorative year to help celebrate that fact. In this column, we can do our share by bringing that aspect of our state's heritage to your attention. In addition to having myriad of inventors and inventions to which it can lay claim, the State of New Jersey was home to probably two of the most productive and creative men of all time - Seth Boyden and Thomas

Edison. It is to Thomas Edison that we perhaps owe the most for the enjoyment of our present lifestyles. The man was an untiring inventive genius.

"The Wizard of Menlo Park" was one of the names by which Edison became known before he moved his operation from Menlo Park (Now Edison) to his new "Invention Factory" in West Orange - now a National Historic Site. He was a man of his times. Americans 100 years ago were possibly at the height of their delight and support of the new scientific technology that was just beginning to open the doors to a whole new world of the future. Americans of that day, still in the age of innocence, were enthralled and amazed with all the "miracles" making their appearance in this dawning new age. Thomas Edison was their hero.

Because he was, in a sense, a folk hero, and because he had such fantastic approval by the public, Edison was able to gain financial support for almost every creative idea with which he set his mind to involve itself. In this sense, he was the right man for the right times, and his success was therefore guaranteed. Not every inventor had that luck.

Edison was also the gap, so to speak, between the individualistic inventors of the past, and the corporate inventors of today. He brought into the world the idea of bringing together a team of workers into an "Invention Factory." Together they would work on new ideas. Thomas Edison was the first to recognize the need for teamwork on a large scale in the highly technical and financially competitive world that was emerging. Today, big corporations employ their own research and development departments. They work around the clock just to keep ahead of the competition. Today's inventors are, for the most part, nameless.

For 50 years, between the 1880's and the 1930's, however, Thomas Edison's name was a household word, not only in New Jersey, but also throughout the world. Edison's start in New Jersey came at the age of 22, while living in Elizabeth with the family of Franklin Pope, his partner as an engineering consultant on telegraphic problems. He worked out of a building in Jersey City. This was in 1869. An improved stock market ticker was his first commercial enterprise. By 1871, he had set himself up in his own plant in Newark where he made his new "tickers," financially backed by Western Union.

While manufacturing his tickers," Edison developed an automatic high-speed telegraph with another company he helped organize in Newark. They made his new telegraph devices in competition with Western Union! These two companies and a third he organized, provided the financial backing, while Edison provided the inventive genius. They also took over the patents on his many improvements in the field of telegraphy, and most of the profits, but they did help Edison to make a name for himself. This was to prove very helpful to him when he decided to make the move to his next stage, that of a full-time inventor.

By 1876, Thomas Edison felt ready to begin inventing as a full-time business enterprise. To do this, he started putting up a series of buildings on a plot of ground he bought in Menlo Park. It soon gained the public's acclaim as Edison's "science village." He hired a variety of men, ranging from skilled mechanics to different types of scientists. He became the "father" of today's corporate research and development "think tanks." His "Invention Factory" supported his attempts at new research, and the development of new products. He continued to make profits from previously successful inventions, and by hiring itself out to corporate giants to work on their pet projects.

Thomas Edison had thus established along the trails of New Jersey the first such enterprise in the United States - the forerunner of today's highly organized corporate research and development laboratories. From his "science village" in Menlo Park, and his later "Invention Factory" at West Orange, Edison spent the next 50 years revolutionizing the communications industry we now all take so much for granted. The telephone, phonograph, lighting, and motion pictures all were to be guided by the hand of this inventive genius.

Edison and the Recording Industry

New Jersey's heritage in the field of communications spans many years. Thomas Edison was in the forefront in this field throughout his long career.

He began in New Jersey in 1869 as a consulting engineer on telegraphic problems. In the mid-1870's, he made the telephone a commercially practical device.

His crude phonograph, developed in 1877, first used tinfoil wrapped around a hand-cranked cylinder. He began production with the Edison Speaking Phonograph Co. in 1878.

It was much improved upon in 1885, when it was replaced by a wax cylinder. Other refinements soon followed and it eventually became a profitable source of commercial entertainment.

With the growing popularity of the radio in the 1920's, however, recording soon became a dying industry. Not until new refinements brought about its rebirth in the years following WWII did it begin its rise to the heights it has achieved today.

Edison had "imprisoned sound" in 1877. In 1949, a current resident of Warren County, Clair Krepps of Franklin Township, then chief engineer with Capitol Records, working with Frederic March, released some of those sounds when they produced the recording "Hark! The Years."

This record reproduced the actual recorded voices of more than 50 celebrities whose lives spanned the two centuries since Edison's first records were produced. Krepps has played an important role over four decades in the growth and advancement of the modern recording industry.

His outstanding work as an engineer in this field was recognized in 1975 by the National Academy of Recording Arts and Sciences when it awarded him a place in its "Hall of Fame." This coveted award was received for the part he played in the 1946 Capitol Records' recording of Nat King Cole's "The Christmas Song," the industry's second biggest all-time hit record. "Chestnuts roasting in an open fire" still rings familiar after 42 years.

Krepps, who was born and raised in the little coal-mining town of Kiesterville, in southwestern Pennsylvania, had been intrigued in his youth by that wonder of the day, radio. He and his brother, Edgar, were repairing and installing them in cars in the 1930's when WWII broke out.

After Pearl Harbor, the US Navy sent out an urgent call for anyone with the slightest knowledge of radio. Clair and his brother responded. It was to be his introduction to an industry that would engulf his life for the next four decades.

He was assigned to a "hush-hush" school by the Naval Air Force. There he was to learn about a secret weapon developed by the British called "radar." He soon became project engineer - designing, installing, and flight-testing a "Flying classroom" - teaching its use to pilots and aircrew men of carrier-based planes. It was this project that brought him into contact with Commander Birkenhead.

After the war, back in California, Birkenhead met an entertainer named Johnny Mercer and a businessman, Glen Wallachs. They had just started a recording company, Capitol Records. It put out Ella Mae Morse's hit record, "Cow, Cow Boogie." They needed an engineer to set up a recording studio in New York City. Birkenhead contacted Lt. Ollie Summerlin in North Carolina and Chief Petty Officer Clair Krepps in Sunbury, PA. Krepps moved to Bergenfield, NJ, across the Hudson from New York City, and went to work for Capitol Records. There he remained as chief engineer for the next five years.

During that time, such famous stars as Stan Kenton, Ray Anthony, Paul Weston, Peggy Lee, Jo Stafford, Margaret Whiting, Roger Williams, and the jazz trumpeter, Miles Davis, were among those he recorded. Also, there was the Barnum and Bailey Circus Band, the Vatican Boys' Choir from Rome, Charlie Barnett and his orchestra, Benny Goodman, Les Paul and Mary Ford, Nellie Lutcher, Sarah Vaughn, Maurice Chevalier, and many more.

"Fired with the idea of carrying Edison's banner to its logical conclusion," Krepps and a group of engineers, each working for different studios, founded the Audio Engineering Society of America. A multi-millionaire industrialist, Sherman Fairchild, was enticed into becoming its president. Krepps served on its board of governors.

The group published papers on new ideas and inventions in the field of recording. Their efforts brought about advancements in know-how and equipment that led to the development of "hi-fi." Other innovations mushroomed into all sorts of improvements, including "stereo." The recording industry was given a whole new lease on life.

Krepps introduced a piece of equipment known as an "equalizer" for improving tone-control of a recording. Today, it is used in all recording studios. Krepps eventually went on to open his own recording studio in New York City before retiring to his home in Warren County's Montana section 14 years ago.

His story is another chapter in the role that communications played along the trails of New Jersey.

John Roebling, Bridge Builder

I am sure that you have all heard of the Brooklyn Bridge. It was, at the time of its completion in 1883, the largest suspension bridge ever attempted. But I wonder how many are also aware of its New Jersey connection?

That's right, the first chief engineer for the Brooklyn Bridge was the famous American bridge-builder, John A. Roebling of Trenton. After his death in 1869, one of his sons, Washington A. Roebling, succeeded him and then supervised its construction until its completion in 1883.

John Roebling was born in Germany in 1806. He graduated from the Royal Polytechnic School in Berlin in 1826, where he wrote his thesis on suspension bridges. In 1831, he came to America and settled in Pennsylvania.

In 1841, he became the first person to manufacture "wire rope" in the United States. After building a suspension bridge across the Monongahela River at Pittsburgh in 1846, he moved to Trenton, where he began the manufacture of his wire cables. In 1851, he built a suspension bridge across the Niagara River connecting the United State with Canada.

Between 1856 and 1867, his New Jersey-based company built bridges throughout Pennsylvania and Ohio. They won a national reputation for their excellence in the building of suspension bridges.

Because of this reputation, John Roebling of Trenton was chosen to be the chief engineer in 1868 for what was to be, at that time, the largest suspension bridge ever attempted. Unfortunately, he was injured on the job a year later and died in Brooklyn on July 22, 1869, of complications resulting from that injury.

One of his three sons, Washington A. Roebling, also a civil engineer, supervised the Brooklyn Bridge's completion, which took 14 years.

Washington Augustus Roebling, who was born in 1837 in Saxonburg, PA, graduated from Rensselaer Polytechnic Institute in 1857. After graduating, he was employed with his father's Trenton firm until he joined the Union Army during the Civil War in 1861.

Following his mustering out as a colonel in 1865, he returned to the Roebling Co. He had been the assistant engineer on the Brooklyn Bridge project at the time of his father's death.

Though he went on to become president of Roebling and Sons, his health gave out during the 14 years the Brooklyn Bridge was under construction.

In the meantime, he became fascinated with the field of mineralogy. He became an expert in that pursuit and, as a result of his expertise, a yet unnamed white mineral found at the mines in Franklin, NJ, was named "Roeblingite" in his honor. His large and valuable collection of minerals was presented by his son to the Smithsonian Institution in Washington, DC, after his death at Trenton on July 21, 1926.

John A. Roebling's third son, Charles, who took over the Roebling Co. in 1904, founded a New Jersey community 12 miles south of Trenton - named "Roebling." This "company town" was at one time considered the best of the once-numerous, planned-industrial towns of that day in America.

Charles Roebling built this community to house the workers for a new mill he constructed in 1906 for his growing wire and cable company. The new mill produced products ranging form chicken wire to 36-inch steel cables. The community housed some 4,000-mill workers and their families in about 750 brick houses. Each had slate roofs, neat lawns, gardens, and fruit orchards. Most of his mill workers at that time were recent immigrants.

Roebling's village also had wide macadam streets lined with trees. He also had several parkways built, leading to a centrally located community hall where plays, movies, and dances were held. A recreation center was also built with bowling alleys and pool tables, and a field with a 1,500-seat grandstand in which company-sponsored football games were held.

This planned "company town" also had a commercial center including a general store, drug store, bank, hotel, bakery, barbershop, and even a small hospital. Roebling was determined to provide a happy, complete community for his workers. He even set up a large park along the Delaware with picnic groves, nature walks, and a grandstand for holding concerts. Hailed by authorities of that day as a model "company town," Roebling, NJ, was the pride of both its founder and its residents.

The Roebling Mill was sold to another company in 1952 and the community that surrounded it became a part of Florence Township. This little section, however, remains as a reminder of how the trails of New Jersey once played a role in the life of the New Jersey family that helped build the Brooklyn Bridge.

This family, by the way, also went on to build the George Washington and the Golden Gate bridges. The New Jersey connection, you see, extends to suspension bridges nationwide.

The Two Claras: Barton and Maas

New Jersey has had its share of women who have made their mark in the world because of their social concerns. The two that come to mind immediately because they so symbolized those many pioneering women who have defied traditional concepts of what should be their role in life, were the two Claras. One, Clara Baton, lived a long and fruitful life, which ended in her 90th year. The other, Clara Maas, came to an untimely death in Cuba in the spring of her life - at age 25.

Clara Barton began her career in New Jersey as a schoolteacher in Bordentown in 1851. It was a period in time when one, men dominated that field, and two, free, public schools were still the exception not the rule. Seeing a need for educating the less fortunate, Clara opened a free, one-room schoolhouse. It was one of the first free public schools in the nation.

In a way, it was somewhat fortunate for the rest of us that Clara's New Jersey neighbors of that day did not consider it seemly for a woman to run a school. She defied them for a time, but when they persisted in demanding that a male principal be place over her at the school, she handed in her resignation.

The year was 1854. Clara's one-room schoolhouse still stands in Bordentown today as a reminder of her pioneering efforts in education here in New Jersey. It was what she did afterwards, however, that made her mark in the world at large.

Clara Barton was working as a clerk in an office in Washington DC when the Civil War broke out.

She resigned her position, again, to defy tradition. She chose to enlist in another area that many of that day considered unseemly for a woman - nursing men in army hospitals and on the battlefield. In 1864, she was placed in charge of hospitals for the Army of the James. In 1865, she was assigned the task of searching the battlefields for the bodies of men of the Union Armies that were missing.

When the Franco-Prussian War started in Europe in 1870, Clara Barton joined with the Red Cross Society in organizing military hospitals in Baden, Germany and in Strasbourg and Paris, France. In 1881, she became the first president of the American Red Cross. From that time on, her life became one of leading that organization in the relief of victims of floods, earthquakes, famines, pestilence, and war, both in America and worldwide. Finally in 1904, after a long and fruitful career in the service of humanity she resigned at the age of 82!

Our other Clara, was Clara Maas. She was the first of nine children born in East Orange to a poor hat-maker and his wife. She took a job at an early age in exchange for her bed and board so that she could finish high school. Unfortunately she had only gotten through three years when at the age of 15 she had to take a money-paying job at the Newark Orphan Asylum to help support her family. In 1893, she heard that at the Newark German Hospital she could be trained as a nurse for nothing. So at 16 Clara became a "probationer." She was proudly graduated from the Newark German Hospital at the age of 18 as a full-fledged nurse.

When the Spanish-American War broke out in 1898, Clara Maas volunteered to serve in the American Army's Nursing Corps. After brief stints in Army Camps in Jacksonville, FL, and Savannah, GA, Clara was sent with units about to engage in battle against the Spanish in Cuba. The ravages of the dreaded yellow fever were plaguing both civilians and soldiers alike. She never forgot the suffering of the yellow-skilled victims.

When the Spanish-American War ended in 1898, Clara was discharged from the Army Nurse Corps. A short time later she heard that there was a need for nurses in the Philippines. In 1900, she volunteered to serve there, and was on the next ship out. Yellow fever was again running rampant. In 1901, she contracted that dread disease. Fortunately she fought it off and recovered. Considering herself immune, she volunteered to return to Cuba to participate in experiments with mosquitoes. Dr. Walter Reed and Gen. Wm. Gorgas suspected that they were the culprits. She contracted a mild case in June, recovered, and volunteered to be bitten again.

On Aug. 24, 1901, Clara Maas, who had come down with a violent case of Yellow Fever, became the only American and the only woman to give her life in the search for a cure for Yellow Fever. She was returned home to be buried at Fairmont Cemetery in Newark. In 1951, Cuba honored her with a postage stamp marking the 50th anniversary of her death. Her only memorial in America is found along the trails of NJ. The Newark German Hospital was renamed in her honor in 1952. The Clara Maas Memorial Hospital now stands in Belleville, as a monument to her life and work. That is the story of New Jersey's two Claras - long may they be remembered.

VanCampen Family

New Jersey's Dutch heritage spans a period of some 380 years. Warren County's VanCampen family can trace their roots in America back 330 of them. The Dutch claim to New Jersey resulted from its discovery and exploration by Henry Hudson in 1609. Its settlement took longer.

The loss of one of his crew, John Colman, to an Indian arrow through his neck and the wounding of several others did not encourage lingering. The Dutch East India Co. also was not interested. Their concern was trade with the Far East.

The New Netherland Co., however, did see its value for the fur trade and began sending merchant ships. Hendrick Christiaensen was one of those merchants. On one trip in 1619, he was killed by hostile Indians. There were a number of other Dutch fur traders as well, men such as Adrian Block, Jan DeWitt, Hans Hunthum, Cornelius Mey, Thijs Mossel, and Cornelius Rijser.

A first attempt at settlement was made in 1624 by the Dutch West India Co. Capt. Mey, for whom Cape May was named, arrived in March with a boatload of Dutch settlers - about 30 families. They were scattered in three settlements, two along the Hudson and one along the Delaware.

In 1630, a second settlement in New Jersey, Ft. Nassau, was also made along the banks of the Delaware, near the present city of Gloucester. Both settlements never became more than small trading outposts for the main Dutch settlement in America, New Amsterdam.

From there Dutch families would move north up the Hudson Valley or west into New Jersey. Some of those who moved north to Esopus later traveled west along the "Old Mine Road" into the Delaware Valley, eventually settling on the northwestern New Jersey Frontier.

It was in one of the Hudson River settlements that Abram VanCampen was born in 1698. The VanCampen family was to become prominent in the settlement of northwestern New Jersey. He was the fifth child of Jan VanCampen, whose father, Gerritt, had emigrated form Holland in 1658, while the Dutch were still in control.

In 1732, Abram made his appearance in what was then western Hunterdon County and purchased from the West Jersey proprietors 1,666 acres in the mountainous wilderness near the Water Gap.

Sometime in that period, Abram built his house near what is now Calno in Warren County, thus becoming one of Warren County's earliest settlers. In time, he became a justice of the peace and a colonel in the local militia. When the French and Indian War broke out in 1753, this West Jersey frontier became a hot bed of Indian attacks, instigated by their French allies.

With the Indians on a rampage, New Jersey Gov. Jonathan Belcher was pressed into sending a detachment of militia into the region. A number of forts between Phillipsburg and Mahackamack (near Port Jervis) to protect the scattered frontier settlers were then constructed.

Col. VanCampen was in charge of one of the detachments garrisoned at his home and nearby fort. Many hair-raising stories came out of that era in New Jersey's history - including the legend of Tom Quick, the Avenger of the Delaware.

In 1754, Abram's nephew, Isaac, bought a house that his father-in-law, Harmon Rosenkrans, built earlier. Because of its location on the road between New England and Philadelphia, it was designated an "Inn." Travelers could stop there, rest, and eat before continuing.

The VanCampen Inn became famous. John Adams was one of those said to frequent the place on his many trips between home and Philadelphia while serving both in the Continental Congress and at the Constitutional Convention.

Reinforcements to aid Washington at the Battle of Trenton also encamped there in 1776. Gen. Casimir Pulaski spent three months at the inn in 1778 with his cavalry regiment encamped nearby. Isaac was serving in the state legislature when the treaty ending the American Revolution was signed in 1783.

Abram's youngest son, Moses, built a farmhouse just north of his father's house. It has since been moved to the recreated historic Village of Millbrook. All three of these homes and several family cemeteries provide for us today a visual picture of 250 years of American history in northwestern New Jersey.

An old Chinese proverb once noted that one picture is worth a thousand words. In that vein, these old houses have become priceless depositories of our heritage.

In the words of Cervantes, they are…"the depository of great actions, the witness of what is past, the example and instruction of the present, the monitor of the future."

Now a descendent of those early pioneers, Stephen VanCampen of Independence, is engaged in a tireless effort to ensure that these great pictures of America's past, still found along the trails of New Jersey, might be preserved for posterity. His valiant efforts on their behalf cry out for the support of all who value heritage.

John Fitch and the Steamboat

The recent attention given by the current governor to the importance of New Jersey's concentration on scientific research and development, if it is to move successfully into the 21st century, reminds me of the past role of the state in this field.

New Jersey and its people have been laggards in this respect. But I do recall a New Jersey metal smith who visualized back in the 1780's that this nation could lead the world in shipping and trade if it would support his new approach to water transportation. It would not be the kind of shipping other nations had dependent as they were upon the wind. John Fitch saw us moving into the dawning 19th century traveling over the waters in boats that would be moved by the power of steam.

Fitch had a prosperous brass and silversmith business going in Trenton in the years before the American Revolution. During this conflict, his business fell off and by the early 1780's, he had become a surveyor instead. He was captured by the Delaware Indians while engaged in surveying out on the frontier, and was turned over to the British, with whom they were then allied. They threw him in prison. He was later returned in an exchange of prisoners to gain the release of some British soldiers but he had time while being held to think about this new invention.

Fitch did not invent the idea of using steam as a source of power. Steam was already in use to move stationary engines. What he did visualize was placing this engine on boats in order to move them across the water with steam-driven paddles. Fitch's first demonstration boat was launched on a stream in Pennsylvania. It was not a success. His second attempt was with a side-paddle wheel launched on the Delaware in 1786. It made a successful trip with passengers between Burlington and Philadelphia.

In 1788, he launched an improved model with a steam-driven paddlewheel at its stern. For two years, he operated a successful business there, carrying both passengers and freight. Unfortunately, he lost several of his boats in storms and finally his financial backers refused to build any new ones. Numerous attempts to gain new backers for his venture eventually brought his ideas to the attention of Robert Fulton, who took them and built his own steamboat on the Hudson. In the meantime, Fitch had become thoroughly depressed, took off for the wilds of Kentucky, and reportedly committed suicide there in 1798.

It was Fitch's inability to get financial aid either from the government, commercial ventures, or any of several scientific societies, all of which he sought, that led to his eventual demise and delayed the successful use of this new invention for several more decades. It is this type of weakness which out present governor hopes to avoid in our state today by bringing those necessary elements together to convert new scientific ideas into practical ventures.

The state of New Jersey in 1786 did grant Fitch exclusive rights to use steamboats on state waters for 14 years to help him launch his new enterprise unimpeded, but without financial support.

Another New Jersey inventor, John Stevens, was encouraged by Fitch's work with the steamboat to visualize still another means of steam-powered transportation. Stevens, who grew up in Perth Amboy, saw Fitch's boat launches on the Delaware and, after getting his own ideas on paper, got powerful friends in congress to pass the federal patent laws in 1790 to protect him before he went public. In 1791, he obtained a patent on a new steam boiler. Then he joined forces with a foundry owner in Belleville, Nicholas Roosevelt, and a financier named Robert Livingston. Together they launched a business, building and operating steamboats. Science, technology, and finance, along with government, had finally joined forces. Experiments on the Passaic River led to other improvements, including the first twin-screw propeller, which was not perfected, however, until 1839.

Stevens started a boat-line in 1800, carrying both passengers and freight along the Raritan River from New Brunswick across the bay to New York City. But in 1807, his partner, Robert Livingston, joined Robert Fulton, obtained a monopoly on the Hudson, and put Stevens out of business. In 1809, he moved his operation to Trenton where he opened a successful run to Philadelphia. He then began thinking of ways he could use this engine for land transportation.

His first attempt to get a franchise to operate a railway service between Trenton and New Brunswick was denied as a pipe dream. In 1815, however, the New Jersey Assembly agreed. For 10 years, he sought financial backing. Finally, in 1825 he built a rail-line on his own estate in Hoboken. By 1830, he had drawn enough attention to enable him to charter the first railway line along the trails of NJ - the Camden and Amboy Railroad. He thus opened a whole new chapter in New Jersey transportation.

Thomas Nast - Cartoonist

Between Election Day and the Christmas Holidays is an appropriate time to call your attention to New Jersey's most famous cartoonist. Though born in Landau, Germany, in 1840, Thomas Nast came to America at the age of six. He spent his early years in New York City. During his most famous period, however, he was a resident of New Jersey. He made his home and had his office in Morristown for more than three decades.

Nast studied at the National Academy of design in NYC, and by 1855, at the ripe old age of 15, he was working for Frank Leslie's Illustrated Newspaper drawing sketches. In 1860, at 20, he was sent to Europe to sketch prizefights, and was soon in Italy drawing pictures of Garibaldi's Revolution. In 1861, he was back in America where he married Sarah Edwards. It was not until 1862, however, as a cartoonist for "Harper's Weekly," that Nast's talent first began to attract attention.

Photography was a new art during the civil war. Though the first was photos appeared at that time, artist's sketches were still the main means of depicting its events. Thomas Nast's drawings, which appeared regularly in "Harper's Weekly," won him national acclaim. In fact, one of his cartoons attacking those who wanted to end the Civil War in 1862 attracted the attention of President Abraham Lincoln, who called him, "our best recruiting sergeant." It was in the period soon after that war, in 1871 to be exact, that Thomas Nast moved his family and drawing board to a big house in Morristown. While living in Morristown, where he remained for the rest of his life, Thomas Nast became a truly national figure.

Nast's clever political cartoons staring in 1871, and directed against Boss Tweed in NYC, brought him into the national limelight. Because of his opposition to the Tammany Hall gang he also opposed the next three Democratic presidential candidates, Greeley in 1872, Tilden in 1876, and Hancock in 1880.

It was Thomas Nast who first typified the Republican Party as an elephant and the Democratic Party as a donkey. Other editorial cartoonists soon began employing those same symbols. Though not originally meant as compliments, both parties have since adopted them as their party emblems. The elephant was first used by Nast to portray the Republicans as huge, spread-out hulk, trying desperately to please everyone and instead lumbering on the brink of disaster. His donkey symbolized the Democrats as a political "jack-ass," kicking about destroying everything, including good government.

Nast became a friend with President Ulysses Grant during this time, and the president often visited with him at his Morristown home. When the republicans indicated that they would not nominate Grant for a third term, for fear that the Democrats would say that he wanted to become another Caesar, Nast Lampooned both parties in a caustic cartoon which appeared in "Harper's Weekly."

It was Nast's determination to put an end to Boss Tweed's Tammany Hall political machine in NYC that eventually gained him some powerful enemies. His cartoons were more effective than editorials, according to Tweed himself, because his constituents could not read, but they sure could look at the pictures. An attempt was made to bribe him into taking an extended European tour, with an offer of half-a-million in gold to drop his cartoons. It was an indication of just how effective he was becoming. Tweed was finally destroyed politically, and it was he in the end who fled to Europe. Nast supported Cleveland, the only president born in New Jersey, in the election of 1884. This support cost him his post at "Harper's Weekly."

Nast probably became most famous for his depictions of Santa Claus around Christmas time. It was the Nast cartoon of Santa Claus as a fat, jolly old fellow, who became the familiar American symbol of a gift-giving saint visiting children's homes with a sack full of toys. His cartoons of Santa were also used in the later publications of Clement Moore's popular poem, "'Twas the Night Before Christmas." Though Moore published this poem in an anthology of poems that first came out in 1844, it was not until its later publication separately with Nast's illustrations that it really gained its popularity.

Because of Nast's fame as a cartoonist, many prominent people, including one of America's most beloved authors of that day, Mark Twain, beat a path to his home along the trails of New Jersey. His national acclaim led President Theodore Roosevelt to appoint him as the American Consul to Ecuador in the early 1900's. While there, he contracted the dread yellow fever, and died a short time later.

The cartoons of this famous New Jerseyan, however, remain with us as a reminder of his life and times.

Jonathan Belcher, Royal Governor

One of the Royal Governors of New Jersey who reigned during the period when the colony had a separate governor from New York, was Jonathan Belcher. He served in the ten-year span between 1747 and 1757. He became governor after the death in 1746 of Lewis Morris, who was the first of the royal governors not to have share in governing New York as well. Belcher also came to power at a time when the English Parliament was demanding more and more of its colonial governors, while the colonists were insisting that they do less and less. New Jersey was primarily an agricultural colony at the time. Though parliament's increasingly restrictive trade and manufacturing laws were not as injurious to New Jersey as they were to the more commercial colonies, New Jerseyans, nevertheless, became rebellious of any English power.

It was a period, too, when the colonist of New Jersey, as elsewhere in America, were becoming increasingly demanding of their rights of self-government. Belcher by temperament was probably the right man for those times. Executive power was on the decline, and Jonathan Belcher did not crave power. He also had come from Massachusetts and was anxious to be accepted by the people. There were land riots still going on from Gov. Morris's term, and he worried about having his salary cut. He and his wife had, after all, eleven children. And so it was that Gov. Belcher became a conciliatory governor - eager to please.

He was, when he arrived at Burlington, also 66 years of age and not in particularly robust health. His once great wealth had diminished, and he was forced to live in a manner less than that to which he had become accustomed. Not having had any ties with the Proprietors of Jersey's lands, the new Governor was also immediately looked upon with favor by the rioters who objected to the "quit-rents" being demanded of them. The facet that he was also a Presbyterian, rather than an Anglican, which most English ruler were, was also in his favor.

When Gov. Belcher moved from Burlington to Elizabethtown in 1751, three years after becoming Governor, he was caught up in the teachings of the great evangelist of that day, Jonathan Dickinson, who also lived there. It was a period of the "Great Awakening" in America and Dickinson was one of its leaders. Gov. Belcher was not only a deeply religious man, but also had a great concern for learning. It was Dickinson who in 1745 had founded in Elizabeth, and become the first president of the College of New Jersey, now Princeton University.

Belcher was accommodated in the Ogden-Belcher House upon his arrival at Elizabeth, which still stands today. It has become a State Historic Site. When the Governor came to town, Elizabethtown had already become a settled community of between 700 and 800 people. Most of its 150 or so buildings were still of wood frame, but a few were of brick and stone. Each home was surrounded by four to six acres with wooden fences to keep out roaming animals. Each had gardens and orchards. The town center was located around the courthouse and the First Presbyterian Church. There was a landing place for ships nearby where merchants had built wharves. Close by they had located their shops and stores. A parade ground for the militia to train was in front of the courthouse. The usual stocks and whipping post had been installed there.

A number of tavern were well placed in town. They served a variety of purposes in that day. The most important of them usually was the stage stop where mail and newspapers were received and read. Business was carried on at them, as well as political activities, auctions, dances, or any other community affairs. The larger gatherings were accommodated in a great hall on the second floor. Elizabeth of that day also had a number of mills. A gristmill, a sawmill, and several fulling and cider mills were among them. Many craftsmen had also set up their shops in town by that date.

Jonathan Belcher was also the Gov. of New Jersey at the outbreak of the French and Indian War, and as such played a large role in supporting the Crown in that struggle with France. Elizabethtown itself provided privateers for that war, as well as a detachment of militia, the "Jersey Blues," under Capt. Elias Dayton. About 1,000 men served from throughout New Jersey. He constructed forts along the northwestern frontier and built barracks to house British troops. The one at Trenton still stands as a State Historic Site. Belcher, who died in 1757, served an enlightened reign along the trails of New Jersey. He set the tone for what was expected of future governors.

Philip Freneau, Poet of the Revolution

Traveling along Route 36 in Monmouth County, beyond Raritan Bay and on up to the area of Sandy Hook, you'll be reminded of the state' maritime heritage. There you will first pass the little fishing port of Belford, and then the busy State Marina at Leonardo, as you approach the wharf area at Atlantic Highlands. I bring you to this region because it was there that the famed Jersey "Poet of the Revolution" of whom I want to speak, Philip Freneau, was inspired to write his poem, the "Hills of Neversink." On this scenic drive at Atlantic Highlands, atop Mount Mitchell, the highest point on the eastern shore of the United States, you can see not only Sandy Hook, Manhattan, and Long Island, but the ocean-going vessels coming in and out of the Hudson River Harbor as well.

Moving northwest on Route 36 to 516 and on to Main Street in Matawan, you will find the Burrowes Mansion. There, Margaret Burrowes, sister-in-law of Philip Freneau, moved with her husband Major John Burrowes Jr. During the American Revolution, he organized the First Jersey Company of militia.

At the Mount Pleasant tavern on Route 79, one-half mile from Route 34, called the "Poet's Inn," Philip Freneau often met with his revolutionary friends. They had formed the American Whig Society while he was a student at Princeton (then called the College of New Jersey). Freneau had been stimulated to a patriotic fervor by the president of Princeton, the Rev. John Witherspoon. A portrait of the

"Poet of the Revolution," as Jefferson called him, hangs in the lobby of the Inn.

Also off Route 79, about a mile south of Route 34, is the lifelong Philip Freneau homestead, Mount Pleasant. There, Freneau, whose poems inspired Americans to fight against British tyranny, is buried beneath a huge sycamore tree alongside his mother. He is in a grave married by a granite shaft surrounded by an iron railing about 50 yards from his farmhouse.

Freneau's father, Pierre, was of a prominent New York French Huguenot family, who married Agnes Watson of Freehold in 1748. Philip, their first son, was born in 1752. Pierre then bought 1,000 acres about a mile south of Matawan and built their country mansion, which he called Mount Pleasant. In 1765, Philip began his studies under the Rev. William Tennent, pastor of the Old Tennent church just outside of Freehold. This church had been converted into a military hospital during the Battle of Monmouth.

In 1766, he was sent to the Latin School at Penolopen, 7 miles west of Freehold, to prepare him for Princeton where he immediately gained notoriety for his writing. His earliest known work was a poem about Jonah and the Whale. Freneau's roommate at Princeton, James Madison, later became the fourth president of the United States. Another classmate, Aaron Burr, was to become vice president under Thomas Jefferson.

Freneau's ardor for the rising new nation was exhibited in the commencement ode, "The Rising Glory of America," which he wrote for his graduation exercise from Princeton in 1771. By the summer of 1775, he was busy in New York writing long lines of satiric verse supporting the cause of American independence. On May 25, 1780, while sailing from Philadelphia to the West Indies, his ship was attacked at a thrilling battle off Delaware Bay and Freneau was captured. He was later transferred to the prison ship, "Scorpion." After his release at Elizabeth Port, he arrived home in wretched condition and there wrote his invective poem, "The British Prison Ship," about the inhumanities of British treatment of captives.

For a time after this, he went to Philadelphia where he wrote many poems for the "Freeman's Journal." These showed his ardor for freedom and his opposition to tyranny of whatever source. Freneau's works after the war gave Americans poems which revealed for the first time the sounds and sights of their own countryside. In 1791, he was encouraged by Jefferson to come to Philadelphia to publish the "National Gazette," in opposition to Hamilton's "Federalist Papers."

In 1795, he began publications of his "Jersey Chronicle" back at Mount Pleasant. He wrote some timely poems during the War of 1812, but most of his poetry thereafter concerned itself with the imaginative themes gained through his long walks in his beloved Navesink Hills. Still hearty at the age of 80, he was engaged in one of his long walks along the road to Freehold when he died in a freezing blizzard on Dec. 18, 1832. Just another of those interesting tales along the trails of New Jersey.

Walt Whitman, Poet of the Civil War

Back in 1681, William Cooper came across the Delaware from Philadelphia and built a home on the Jersey side, which he called "Pyne Point." In 1688, William Royden obtained a license to run a ferry service from the Jersey shore to Philadelphia. Cooper bought him out, and for the next 140 years Cooper's Ferry is what they called the present city of Camden. A descendent, Jacob Cooper did attempt to have the town dubbed, "Camden," just before the outbreak of the American Revolution.

Cooper tried to give the name to a real estate development of some 40 acres, which he had laid out with six streets back in 1773. The name seemed appropriate in view of the thoughts of liberty that were on many minds at the time. The first Earl of Camden, Charles Pratt, was after all a noted champion of constitutional liberty back in England. Cooper felt that such a name would be a monument to the ideals here in America. Cooper's Ferry is what it remained, however, throughout the Revolution. Not until 1828 did the then town of 1,140 inhabitants officially adopt the name of "Camden."

It was the coming of the Camden and Amboy Railroad in 1834 that really gave life to this once little river village. It soon became the transportation hub for Jersey farm produce and bog iron products headed for the Philadelphia markets. Its Ferryboats were busier than ever. In the Civil War Period, it was also a "Station" in the nation's illegal "Underground Railroad," helping escaping slaves find their way north to points in New England and Canada.

It is to this period of the Civil War that I have been leading you in order to call your attention to another of New Jersey's famous poets. It was Walt Whitman's poetry relative to the Civil War that finally brought him recognition. And Whitman spent his last two decades, the most prominent of is life, as a resident of Camden.

Born in 1819 at West Hills, Long Island, Whitman spent his formative years in Brooklyn. He became a drifter. He worked on and off as a schoolteacher, a printer, a newspaperman, and a carpenter. He spent years wandering about Long Island, New York, and New Jersey wharves and shorelines between jobs talking to America's workers. Longshoremen, fishermen, river pilots, farmers were constantly sought out. Finally, in 1855, he published his detailed portrait of the American citizen of that day. He called it "Leaves of Grass." It was to be America's first national poetry. It was a new sort of poetry without the usual rhyme. Its lines were different. He called it free form. He was at first denounced.

During the Civil War, he went to Washington to nurse his brother back to health. He had been wounded while fighting with the Union Army. Whitman stayed among the wounded and wrote of their tribulations in a volume called, "Drum Taps." After Lincoln's assassination, he produced his now most famous poems, "When Lilacs Last in the Dooryard Bloom'd," and "O Captain! My Captain!" At last, he was accepted.

In 1783, he moved to his brother's home in Camden after suffering a stroke at the age of 53. His life during the next two decades as a resident of New Jersey proved to be the most rewarding period of his life. At last receiving recognition for his works, his "Leaves of Grass" was added to, and reprinted in, several new editions. In 1884, he bought his own home on Mickle Street, and later he received many noted visitors from throughout the world. He had intense feelings concerning the destiny of America, and the role to be played by its workers. His fame, by now, had spread far and wide. As a speaker for American Democracy, his works were translated into many languages.

Whitman felt that his soul would transcend this life, and often spoke in his old age about this "sparking" soul being overburdened with his great lummox of a corpse-body, which he was forced to drag about in his dying years. He died in 1892. His vault bears the inscription, which he wrote, "For that of me which is to die."

To visit Whitman's Tomb in Camden, you can get off of Route 30 at Memorial Avenue, then to Kaighn Avenue where you will turn right on to Park Avenue, and thence to Park Boulevard. His tomb is at the Harleigh Cemetery. At one end is Pyne Point Park where the Cooper House is located. The Camden County Historical Society Museum is at Pamona Hall, a Georgian Mansion built by Joseph Cooper Jr., also on Park Boulevard. Walt Whitman's house on Mickle Street, near Third is now a State Historical Site, commemorating another one of those interesting people who once roamed the trails of New Jersey.

Joyce Kilmer, Poet of the WWI Era

Back in 1681, John Inian led a group of English colonists to the south bank of the Raritan River in New Jersey. They came form earlier settlements in Long Island. At first, it was called Prigmore's Swamp. But by 1686, when John Inian began operation of a ferry service, for which he obtained exclusive rights in 1697, they began calling the place Inian's Ferry.

Seeking favor with the House of Brunswick, the new royal family of Britain, the name New Brunswick was adopted by the town fathers in 1724. The House of Brunswick became the British royal line with the ascension of the German Elector, George of Brunswick (Braunschweig in German), to the throne of Great Britain and Ireland in 1714 as King George I. His son, George II, granted New Brunswick its charter in 1730, just as a large group of Dutch settlers moved down from settlements in the Upper Hudson Valley of New York State, and practically took over the place.

These Dutchman established a Dutch Reformed Theological Seminary in New Brunswick in 1766. A charter was granted them by King George III, through the Royal Governor of New Jersey, William Franklin, son of Benjamin Franklin. It was called Queen's College. In 1825, it was renamed Rutgers College in honor of Col. Henry Rutgers, a financial benefactor of considerable importance. "Old

Queens," a fine example of Georgian Colonial architecture still standing, was erected in 1809. When the British occupied New Brunswick during the American Revolution, classes were held at Millstone and at North Branch.

The city of New Brunswick became an important stop on the colonial Post Road between the cities of New York and Philadelphia. During the Revolution, George Washington stayed there for a short time on his retreat from Ft. Lee across New Jersey to Delaware and safety in Pennsylvania. His British counterpart, Gen. Howe, followed him into New Brunswick on his pursuit, and subsequently set up a vital British outpost there for the remainder of most of the Revolution. A notable home of the period to visit there is the White Farm House in Buccleuch Park. But more of that place will have to wait for another time.

Cornelius Vanderbuilt was a New Brunswick resident form 1818 to 1829 when he was captain of the steam line he owned, running between New Brunswick and New York. His boats made connections at what is now Johnson Park with the stagecoach line bound for Philadelphia. He later became a multi-millionaire through his many steamboat enterprises and later his railroad interests. But perhaps its most famous resident was the American poet of the World War I era, Joyce Kilmer, who was born in New Brunswick in 1886. Camp Kilmer, a major embarkation point along the Atlantic coast during World War II, was named in his honor.

Kilmer, who was born Alfred Joyce Kilmer, dropped his first name when he began publishing his poems. His most famous, "Trees," first appeared in print in 1913. But it was after publication in 1914 by the George H. Doran Publishing House under, "Trees and Other Poems by Joyce Kilmer," that it became popular as a required memory poem in many schools (for those older than 50). "I think that I shall never see a poem as lovely as a tree," is still engraved in my head. Kilmer was educated at Rutgers and at Columbia in New York.

From 1908-09, he taught Latin at Morristown High School, and then served in various literary capacities on a number of publications. His first published work was, "summer of Love" in 1911. He had succeeded in publishing a number of subsequent works when in 1917 he enlisted in the 165th Infantry during the First World War. Kilmer was sent into battle with the US Expeditionary Force in

France. A brave and daring soldier, his promising career ended, when he was killed in action near the Ourcq, on Aug. 1, 1918. His memory was honored with the establishment of his birthplace in New Brunswick, on what is now Joyce Kilmer Post of the American Legion.

"I think that I shall never see A poem as lovely as a tree, A tree whose hungry mouth is prest Against the earth's sweet flowing breast; A tree that looks at God all day, And lifts her leafy arms to pray; A tree that may in summer wear A nest of robins in her hair; Upon whose bosom snow has lain; Who intimately lives with rain, Poems are made by fools like me, But only God can make a tree."

Just one more tale to be found for those who would but seek them out, along the pleasant trails of our great state of New Jersey.

New Jersey's Poets

There is something "poetic" about a summer thunderstorm atop Scott's Mountain in Warren County. Its dramatic lightening bolts and loud thunderclaps reminds one that New Jersey's physical environment has been the backdrop for numerous poets that the state can claim as its own. One can define poetry as a literary work in measured form, whether written or spoken, for the purpose of exciting a person's feelings - by beautiful, imaginative, or elevated thoughts.

Everyone is capable of being "poetic" when expressing their reactions to their surrounding, incidents in their lives, thoughts about life in general, love, politics or whatever. But some are more talented than others in the eyes of those who make such decisions, or chance focused attention upon their works. At any rate, New Jersey's literary heritage includes the poetry of such recognized poets as Philip Freneau, Francis and Joseph Hopkinson, Walt Whitman, Bret Harte, Richard Gilder, Henry VanDyke, Stephen Crane, Joyce Kilmer, A.M. Sullivan, and William Carlos Williams.

Either born, raised, or matured, or all three within New Jersey's borders, these men are considered literary products of three centuries of New Jersey history. Freneau, though born in New York in 1752, was graduated from Princeton, edited a rural New Jersey newspaper for a time, lived a good part of his life in the state and died in New Jersey in 1832. He is buried on his estate in what is now Matawan in Monmouth County. Considered America's first national poet and an ardent patriot, Freneau was called, the "Poet of the American Revolution."

Another poet of that era, Francis Hopkinson, was born in Philadelphia in 1737 and died there in 1791, but resided for many years in Bordentown. He was, in fact, one of the state's representatives to the Continental Congress, and a signer of the Declaration of Independence. He wrote both humorous and political poems. His son, Joseph, also a poet, and a lawyer began the practice of law in nearby Easton, PA, in 1791. He, too, lived for a time in Bordentown, and once represented that district in the New Jersey legislature.

Walt Whitman's glimpses at man and nature were set down in an uncongenial poetic style that for many years brought him great criticism. Though born in Long Island in 1819, and educated in Brooklyn, his mature years were spent in Camden, where some of his greatest poetry was written. He died there in 1892. His Camden home is now an historic site.

Bret Harte, though noted for his writing of the American West, once lived in Morristown. Richard Gilder and Henry VanDyke are known as the "Garden Poets." They wrote of the open fields, trees, streams, brooks, and birds of Burlington, Mercer, and Middlesex counties. Gilder was a native of Bordentown. His family home, Belle Vue, is now an historical site there.

Born in Germantown, PA, VanDyke was nevertheless a descendant of a long line of Jersey Dutchmen. VanDyke's fame came while at this home in Princeton, called Avalon. He was probably American Presbyterianism's most famous minister-teacher and inspirational poet. An ardent fisherman, his book of poems, "Little Rivers," is an established work of art on a sport. His inspirational poetry was rated among the giants of the period between 1890 and 1910. VanDyke probably is noted most, however, for his Christmas story, "The Other Wise Man," published in 1896. It sold millions of copies, in many languages, and is still in print.

Both Stephen Crane, born in Newark in 1871, whose most noted work was not poetry but a Civil War story, "The Red Badge of Courage," and Joyce Kilmer, born in New Brunswick in 1886, and most famous for his poem, "Trees," passed thorough life barely making 30. Crane tried to cram too much of life into a short span and died of tuberculosis in 1900. Kilmer met his fate on a French battlefield in 1918.

A.M. Sullivan, "The Poet of the Musconetcong," was born just after the turn of the 20th century in Harrison. He captured praises of New Jersey's woods and streams in many collections of verse. Sullivan came closest to being a native son of not only New Jersey, but of Warren County as well. His father ran a country store in rural Oxford, where he was raised. Though he later resided in Montclair, it was through the years that he spent at the family home along the Musconetcong near Hackettstown that his most noted works were inspired. His "Songs of the Musconetcong and Other Poems of NJ," published in 1968, explores the rural New Jersey landscape he loved so well.

William Carlos Williams, born and died in Rutherford, 1883-1963, concentrated his works on facets of the history and life of nearby Paterson. He rounds out the three centuries of noted American poets who lived and worked along the trails of New Jersey.

Henry F. Skirbst

UNIT 3: PAST OF NEW JERSEY

This unit explores the historical heritage of the state of New Jersey and its influence on the nation's development.

Chapter 12: Indians
Chapter 13: Colonial Period
Chapter 14: Revolutionary War
Chapter 15: People and Places of the Revolution
Chapter 16: Civil War Era

Henry F. Skirbst

CHAPTER 12: INDIANS

Indian Heritage

The people of New Jersey have a rich natural heritage in their northwestern counties that I hope present and future generations will never let slip away to the over- development that has engulfed much of the state.

If you want to return, in body and spirit, to an oasis of our natural past, where wooded mountains and plateaus are interspersed with peaceful river valleys, and where the many mountain streams come tumbling down in the waterfalls from glacial lakes through splendid gorges, and where other natural wonders await you, return to the former hunting grounds of the Delaware - the Minisink.

That stretch of the upper Delaware River, from just south of the Delaware Water Gap, north of Columbia in Warren County, and encompassing the Worthington State Forest, Delaware Water Gap National Park, Stokes State Forest, High Point State Park, and lands in between, through Sussex County, and on into Port Jervis in New York, is called the Land of the Minisink. It stretches for about 40 miles, and includes both the Jersey side just described, and the Pennsylvania side as well. The Woodland Indians, who inhabited this region since prehistoric times, knew nothing, of course, of our political boundaries, and so occupied the lands on both sides of the river as one entity.

Along the Jersey-side is the interstate hiker's highway, the famed Appalachian Trail. It takes you through the Land of the Minisink past those now well-known natural landmarks, the two glacial lakes, Catfish and Sunfish ponds in Warren County, and Buttermilk Falls in Walpack Township, Sussex County. It travels along the entire length of New Jersey's Kittatiny Ridge. Three fourths of the region is still forested, just as it would be remembered by those residents of that bygone era, who were known to the white settlers as the Delaware Indians.

The Delaware Indians called their river the Lenape Wihittuck, and themselves the Lenni Lenape. For the most part, they lived in harmony with their natural surroundings. Their forefathers had come east in prehistoric times, according to their Legend of Migration, or Walum Olum. They fought fierce wars with the previous inhabitants, the Allegewi, to gain these beautiful lands. To do this they had to ally themselves with another band of Indians that had been coming east also, just north of their path. The French called these people the Iroquois, by which name they are better known, but they called themselves the Mengwe. The Mengwe, or Iroquois, kept mostly to the north after the wars, remaining in what is now New York State. Generally, they maintained a sort of kinship with the Lenape, but occasionally they also sought control over the Minisink.

The Land of the Minisink gets its name from the particular tribe or clan of the Lenape that inhabited it. Many others went further south. It was the Minsi, or Wolf Clan of the Lenape, and the most aggressive of the three living in New Jersey, that remained in the Minisink. At least until the white settlers succeeded in driving them out. These Indians put up repeated struggles to keep their beloved Minisink. But the first successful white encroachment finally came with the Walking Purchase of 1737. It was an agreement that the Delaware Indians apparently little understood. But the English, with the help of their fierce allies, the Iroquois, forced them to adhere to it, and their land shrunk.

They remained peacefully in their now smaller area, however, until the famed Indian Wars of the 1750's. At that time, Teedyuscong, who was named Chief of the Delawares, led bands of warriors throughout those lands of the Minisink that had been lost by the infamous Walking Purchase. Egged on by the French, settlers were killed, homes were burned, and prisoners were taken. Contrary to popular belief, the English government offered bounties for Indian scalps. It was a time that naturally popularized the legend of Tom Quick, famed Indian Slayer of the Delaware.

The massacres at Montague caused bitter feeling with the Delawares, and the tribe eventually was forced to withdraw from the Minisink altogether. During the Revolution, sporadic fighting broke out there, encouraged by the British who allied with the Iroquois, between small tribes of Lenapes living in Pennsylvania and the

Iroquois from New York, and white settlers. By the end of the Revolution, however, even the warlike Iroquois had been subdued and were forced to move west. By that time, the Minisink saw the last of its Indian inhabitants. What a wonderful tribute we could now pay to this once proud people by establishing at Worthington Forest a center for the Study of Eastern Woodland Indians in their old hunting grounds.

The Lenape, New Jersey's "Original People"

The remnants of New Jersey's once proud Indian tribes – the Lenni Lenape, as they called themselves, or the Delaware, as the English knew them – are now scattered throughout North America. Settlements are known to exist in Canada and parts of Oklahoma and the Great Lakes region of the United States. These scattered people can still trace their lineage to New Jersey's "Original People." The last of the Indians left New Jersey soil as tribes in the early 1800's. A much larger exodus took place in the late 1700's. A few scattered individuals remained.

The campus of Trenton State College is located on the site of what was once an ancient Lenape Indian camp. Excavations at the Abbott Farm, an old village site south of Trenton, have turned up many interesting artifacts of this once mighty people of New Jersey. Collections of these specimens may be seen at the New Jersey State Museum in Trenton. The Library at Rutgers, the States University of New Jersey in New Brunswick, also has a large collection of written materials about the Lenapes. Much of the Rutgers' data was donated by the late Charles Philhower, to whom we owe a great debt for his lifelong interest in New Jersey's Indians.

Of course, like all of our ancestors, they too were once immigrants according to what the experts have been able to deduce. But, as their name implies, the Lenni Lenape were the "Original People" to inhabit the region we now call New Jersey, as well as eastern Pennsylvania and the area of New York around Port Jervis. They also belonged to a much larger nation of Indians known as the Algonquins – an Eastern Woodland Indian, many of whom were fierce warriors.

But the New Jersey branch of the Algonquins, the Delaware, were mostly hunters, fishermen, and farmers who preferred to be left alone in peace. The Delaware were also broken up into smaller clans (families) and then still smaller tribes, each with their own lifestyles according to where they lived. Those who inhabited the rocky, wooded mountains of what are today's Sussex and Warren Counties in New Jersey, as well as nearby New York and Pennsylvania, were known as the Munsee or Minsi clan. The symbol on their family crest was that of the Wolf. They were the most warlike of the Delaware Indians. Perhaps it was because of the hostile nature of their neighbors, the Iroquois. Perhaps it was their greater struggles with the forces of nature.

Those in New Jersey's central region were perhaps the most peaceable. They were often the arbitrators of disputes among the others. Their symbol was that of the Turtle, and they were known as the Unami. To the south of this clan was the land of the Wild Turkey, the Unilachtigo. All were described by early Europeans as a handsome people, bronze colored in skin, black hair and eyes, well built bodies, and generally friendly in nature.

As with all people, one's ability to get along has limits. One of the causes of problems that the early Europeans encountered with these Jerseyites came about because of their differences in culture. The Indians worshipped Manito or Manitoba, the god of nature. They loved the land, and believed that it belonged to everyone. It was, after all, the giver of food, and thus life itself. They did not abuse it or misuse it. They had long ago learned to live with it. They traveled freely on it, either over land or by water, in search of food.

Annually, they made summer pilgrimages to the Jersey shore. There, mounds of seashells remain as stark evidence of their annual trek. These shells were also used to make wampum (money), or pretty decorations for body or homes. When Europeans talked of selling their land to them for their exclusive use, they were dealing in terms with which the Indian had absolutely no concept. This clash in cultural differences, along with the European's introduction to them of "alcohol," led to unending disputes.

First driven from their lands to the east, tribes from that region soon were crowding those already settled in northwestern Jersey. In time, conflict with European settlers in the Land of the Minisink led to bloody battles of a nature previously unheard of along these trails of New Jersey. Tales of warfare that inevitably followed, and the swooping, surprise Indian attacks that preceded them, eventually led to the call for removal by force of these once proud "Original People" from the trails of New Jersey. Some of these tales I have already told. Others still wait to be heard.

The Walking Purchase

Though Sussex County (which then included the land we now call Warren) was created out of a large chunk of Morris County in 1753, the erupting Indian Wars that followed along New Jersey's northwestern frontier soon, temporarily at least, drove its county government back to Morristown.

You remember that part of the French strategy in America during the French and Indian War was to stir up the Indians against Britain's colonists in her American settlements. The French fur traders and trappers had been living among the Indians as their equals. They had as a result, succeeded in winning many of them over as their allies in the struggle between these two European empire builders for control of North America. Their strategy had proved to be quite successful all along the Delaware Valley, and its heavily forested bordering hill country. The reason it bore such good fruit there was rooted in the history of the area. Everything had been going along fine between the local Lenape tribe and the original early settlers until the associates of William Penn thought up the idea of the "Walking Purchase" back around 1735. Under terms of that agreement, it was understood by the Indians that the settlers would be permitted to "use" the Indian's lands unmolested for as far as a man could walk in any one day from a given point.

The first problem arose from the fact that there seemed to have been a difference of opinion as to what each meant by a "purchase." The Indian's view of a land ownership, it seems, was quite alien from that of the colonists. The Indians apparently viewed land "ownership" not from an individual, but rather a tribal viewpoint. It, however, was permanently "owned" in their view by no human. It was "used" temporarily by whatever tribe could control the region at any given

305

time in history. Each individual in the tribe was permitted to hunt, fish, and build their homes with as little disturbance to its natural features as possible. So they were, in their view, granting permission for settlers to "use" a given area of the lands over which people had been exercising "control" for many generations.

This apparently did not mean that they themselves could no longer hunt or fish in it as well. So when they were being harassed, and even shot at, by settlers for such innocent activities as "stealing" fruit from orchards the settlers had planted, or chickens from their barnyards, they had no idea what this was all about. It seemed to them to be merely an act of unfriendliness, and possibly even an attempt to forcefully gain "control" over their rightful domain by people to whom they had peacefully granted permission to use these lands.

The second problem centered upon a deception the Indians felt had been foisted upon them in the terms of the "Walking Purchase." They were under the impression that they had agreed to allow this "use" by the settlers over a stretch of terrain as large as an ordinary man could "walk" in one day. It was an agreement in which both parties pretty well understood about how much of an area an average human could walk in one day.

Craft, cunning, and treachery were not considered an acceptable part of these terms. So when persons specifically adept as runners were brought in to swindle them out of far more land than had been intended, they were enraged. The ruse that had bilked them became a source of constant friction over the ensuing years.

Though their ruling elders had decided to let the agreement stand, rather than bring needless death to both sides through wars, a festering discontent continued to brew under the surface for decades. As a result, when the French sought to stir up animosities in the mid 1700's, they had a ready-made source of ferment.

The provoked Indians eagerly struck out at the settlers in 1755, releasing years of pent-up emotions. Such savagery was exuded that the alarmed colonial governor called upon the provincial Assembly for money to build 10 forts along the Delaware to protect the settlers. The ruins of some still remain.

In May of 1756, the killing or capture of members of the family of Anthony Swartswood, in the area of what is now Swartswood Lake State Park, led to further action by Gov. Belcher.

He offered rewards for the bodies of Indian males 15 or older, dead or alive.

The legend of Tom Quick, the Avenger of the Delaware, was thus born. His boasted escapades of his single-handed acts seeking to avenge his father's brutal killing, made him a legend not only in the backcountry of Warren and Sussex, but all along the trails of New jersey for generations to come. Long after the bloody Indian Wars had ended, and the newly elected President Gorge Washington had sent Gen. John Sullivan to drive the Indians out of the Valley, tales of the adventures of Tom Quick persisted.

Woodland Indians

When the Europeans and the Minsi Indians first met in Jersey's Land of the Minisink in the mid-1600's, both seemed happy with one another. For Europeans, there was expertise to be gained from the Indians in the ways of the forested mountains. For the Indians there were new tools of metal and new materials for clothing. In time, however, misunderstanding arose, particularly regarding the different concepts each concerning land rights. When the Delaware Chiefs (Lappawinso, Tisheekunk, and Nutimas) signed the agreement in 1737, later known as the Walking Purchase, they were probably unaware they were putting their approval to a document that permanently removed their people, the Lenni Lenape, from their ancient hunting grounds – The Land of the Minisink.

Perhaps it was an act of destiny that so much of their former hunting grounds were not engulfed in industrial development, but have been preserved instead in state and national forests and parklands in Jersey's northwest. How appropriate it would be, then, if 250 years after the signing of that ignominious document, in 1987, the State of New Jersey could invite the descendants of those once proud "Original People" to return to their ancient homeland in the Minisink, and therefore find a portion of it rededicated to a study of their heritage.

It would seem a small repayment indeed, if the state's Division of Parks and Forestry were to undertake such a project in the natural setting of say, the Worthington Forest in Warren County.

Experts of the Algonkian people, such as Dr. Herbert C. Kraft of Seton Hall University, might be persuaded to assist in the reconstruction of a typical Village of the Eastern Woodland Indian. Kraft spent many years in the Delaware Valley gathering evidence of the Lenape Indians' previous existence in the region.

People could go there to see and learn about the Woodland Indians in a live setting. Excavations in the new area have uncovered evidence of the types of bark-covered long houses, wigwams, and sweathouses that were typically used in the Minisink Villages. Further diggings have uncovered information concerning the types of furnishings and tools used, and other artifacts that reveal characteristics of the kind of lifestyles led by those Lenape Indians, whose culture is now an integral part of New Jersey's heritage. The material exists for the recreation of such a village and the natural setting is available. What is needed is the expertise to put it together, and then to man it, once created.

To complete the value of such a center, a Museum of Natural History would need to be constructed nearby, where lectures, displays, dioramas, as well as films, would make the center a truly significant repository of information concerning New Jersey's Indian heritage. How exciting it would be if New Jersey were to become a focal point for such an attraction. Woodland Indians now living elsewhere might descend upon the state annually for a gigantic powwow.

The Lenni Lenape of the Minisink, who were basically a peaceful people, were slow to react aggressively to the Europeans' invasion of their land. Such a center could present the Indian viewpoint of Teedyuscong, chief of the Delaware's attacks of 1755-56 on the settlers of the Minisink. Walking in the Indian's moccasins, for example, one might take a different view of the European's fraudulent acquisitions of their lands, depletion of their natural resources, and what was worse, the altering of their lifestyle and their subjection to new diseases and alcoholism which all but destroyed them. A whole new understanding might arise as to why those fierce Indian uprisings in the Minisink recurred in the spring of 1756 and again a year later. Perhaps the legend of Tom Quick, the Indian Slayer of the Delaware, would then be seen in a new light as well.

More could be learned also, from the Indian's eyes, as to why the constant raids occurred in the Minisink during the years of the American Revolution. These Indian raids, viewed at the time with terror by settlers, at first led George Washington to dispatch Gen. Casimir Pulaski and his cavalry unit to guard the Minisink. Continuing in their severity, he later sent Gen. John Sullivan on a campaign to destroy any existing Indian Villages remaining in the area, and to drive those Indians who had retreated to Pennsylvania's Wyoming Valley, out of the region forever. But more tales of New Jersey's Woodland Indians will have to wait until another time.

Preserving New Jersey's Indian Heritage

Recently revealed plans to establish, eventually, a life-size Indian settlement on land being cleared along the banks of the Musconetcong, across the river from the historic restored Village of Waterloo, are like a dream coming true.

The American Indians have held a special place in my heart ever since I was a little boy. I think it is because I perceived them to be an inseparable part of the wilderness, nature lore, and the great outdoors, which embrace my whole being. Part is probably also because they are so intrinsically entwined in my mind with another great love-our American heritage. Whatever, I have maintained for years that New Jersey (Lenapehoking) ought to do something of this nature in northwestern New Jersey to promote its rich Indian heritage. And now at last I see those seeds about to bear fruit.

The founders and operators of Waterloo Village in Byram Township have decided that they are the ones who will do it. They are going to make a start at least this year toward the major goal of establishing on the outskirts of their already well-known restored village, an outstanding live museum of the New Jersey Indian. In keeping with this goal, they have hired John Kraft, son of Herbert Kraft, director of the Archeological Research Center at Seton Hall University, and one of the state's foremost experts on the New Jersey Indians. John, who like his father is an archeologist, will be the curator of the new Indian museum and exhibits.

The Lenape, considered members of the great Algonkin Nation, is the main branch of the Eastern Woodland Indians, which inhabited our state, along with eastern Pennsylvania and probably southern New York State, for some 10,000 years. The Minisi, Munsee, or Minsi tribes – people of the stone country, known as the Wolf Clan, were the main band of Lenape Indians occupying what is now Sussex and Warren Counties and nearby Hunterdon and Morris. Being neighbors to the fierce Iroquois of New York State, they were the buffer clan. So they had to be on guard more than their southern counterparts. Consequently, the tribes of the Minsi were the more warlike of the three main Lenape Clans.

The Turkey Clan, inhabiting central Jersey, was considered the peacemakers. The Turtle Clan of south Jersey was the most peace loving often derisively dubbed, "old women" by their neighbors.

The upper Delaware region had been the quiet site of a number of archeological digs, over the as, among the professionals. But little has been revealed to the general public. So, with the establishment of this currently modest, new Indian Museum and Exhibit, and the eventual, planned opening of a much larger museum of the New Jersey Indian, and of a life-size Indian Settlement on the banks of the Musconetcong, much more of our rich Indian heritage will become public knowledge.

Perhaps at last New Jersey residents will come to appreciate still another facet of their unbelievably unique heritage – that of the Indians of Lenapehoking. And the rich culture of these once proud people will be moved back into the mainstream of public knowledge in our state – where it rightfully belongs. We can learn much from their culture today. How to live with – rather than in opposition to, our natural surroundings is a much -needed lesson to be learned in our ever-burgeoning state.

The current exhibits and model of an Eastern Woodland Indian's long house will be temporarily housed in Waterloo Village's Carriage House this year. Unlike the plains Indians, the Lenape lived in bark-covered structures with log-poled frames – not the skin-covered teepees so typically thought of because of the more popularized stories of our western Indians. This is just one example of how this settlement and museum will clarify many misconceptions so many of today's inhabitants have of the American Indians. They tend to lump them all into one mold.

A New Jersey resident who is a descendant of the Lenapes, James "Lone Bear" Revey, has been hired to demonstrate Lenape crafts at the village. A search is currently being made of Indian reservations in our American West and Canada. It was to these places that our native Jersey Lenapes were driven starting some 200 years ago. It is hoped that through this search the real Lenape culture – through legends, music, tools, utensils, and clothing, can be brought back to this New Jersey site where it all began.

The success of this venture, of course, will depend upon the public support, through attendance and funds, which it receives from the people and officials of New Jersey. A fascinating new door is about to be opened concerning old tales that once stalked the trails of New Jersey. Be there!

"Wampum"

I never cease to marvel at the vital roles played by our little state of New Jersey in the vast panorama of America's heritage. Many American Indian tribes used strung shells, called "wampum," extensively for ornamental purposes. They were made into belts, necklaces, bracelets, scabbards, etc. The Dutch and English colonists used them as a medium of exchange. Clam and oyster shells were cut into discs and then strung like beads.

Though not actually money, they were so highly valued by the Native Americans because of their beauty, their symbolism or as a badge of wealth and position that as a result they became an important means of exchange. As such the colonists considered them to be "Indian money."

We have all heard of it and its extensive use by the many Indian tribes. But I wonder how many are aware of the New Jersey connection. It will probably come as a surprise, to many, to know that much of the "wampum" that was produced in the United States from 1775 until 1889 came from five generations of the Campbell family, who "minted" it at their Pascack Trading Post at Park Ridge in Bergen County.

Of course, before that time it was the Indians themselves who began the practice of exchanging various items they possessed for the valued beaded shells they had assembled.

Our own Delaware (Lenape) Indians had for generations made their annual treks from the hills and forests to the Jersey shore. There, in addition to their "clam bakes," they gathered shells and carried them back to their "villages" in the forests and hill country of western New Jersey to be worked into "wampum."

These beads were made of the interior of the shells. They were then arranged into various significant designs. The black or purple beads, which were the more highly valued, were made from the dark "eye" of the shell. The white or tinted ones came from the outer parts.

The beads were little shell cylinders about one-eighth of an inch in diameter and one-fourth of an inch in length. By rubbing then against stones, the Indians were able to achieve a highly polished finish. With a flint awl they bored a hole through them in order to string them.

Eventually used universally among all North American Indians, "wampum" first became a medium of exchange among the Indians along the Atlantic seaboard. Its possession was also believed to be in some degree a passport to the "happy hunting grounds" by using it to gain favor with the "Great Spirit."

The Lenape exchanged their "wampum" not only among themselves, but also with the Iroquois of New York State and the various tribes to the west in Pennsylvania. Each, in turn, carried them further west to exchange with their neighbors. Its use became an important bond between the various Native American tribes.

When John Astor began his fur-trading business, he used "wampum" bought at the Pascack Trading Post in northern New Jersey. This Jersey "wampum" eventually found its way to the Indians of Oregon, where Astor had established fur-trading posts in the early 1800's. Though Johannes Stoltz of Hawthorne was a major supplier of wampum in northern Bergen County before they came, it was the Campbell family who gave New Jersey its reputation as a major "mint" of Indian money.

The five generations of New Jersey Campbells began with the arrival of William Campbell from Scotland in 1775. Though the use of wampum for trade in New Jersey had diminished by that time, those Lenapes who had migrated westward beyond the Kittatinny Mountains carried their "wampum" with them, and its popularity spread among western Indians. William Campbell was a shrewd businessman and in time gained control of this wampum market.

New Jersey's seashore shells eventually made up only a small part of this business. Negotiating with West Indian trading ships, Campbell was soon importing cheaply the beautifully colored shells their ships were bringing into New York Harbor as ballast. They became extremely coveted among the western Indians.

When his son, John, took over the business, Campbell wampum was being used extensively throughout the US. It was apparently John's sons, Abraham and William Jr., who made the connection with the Astor Trading Co. of Oregon. By then the Campbell wampum business in New Jersey was a million-dollar industry. By the time John Jacob Astor died in 1847, he had become a close personal friend with Abraham Campbell of Park Ridge.

Abraham's four sons, Abram, David, James, and John all got into the wampum-making business, which had become the largest industry in northern Bergen County. James invented a water-cooled drill, which helped increase production.

In 1889, when the Oklahoma Territory was opened, and the last Indian was driven onto reservations, the trails of New Jersey saw the last of its "wampum" manufactured. Once again, New Jersey had played out its role in another bit of our heritage.

"Purchasing" Property

Living in the nation's most densely populated state, many residents today find it hard to believe that west Jersey was at one time part of the American frontier. That Indians were once on the rampage there, and that forts had to be erected to protect the few lonely pioneer farmers who had dared to encroach upon their primeval woodlands, seems far-fetched today.

However, those who lived, fished, or hunted in the rugged, heavily forested hill country of Jersey's northwestern counties, even a decade B.D. (before development), would not have too much difficulty imagining this once pristine wilderness. One would hope that before it completely succumbs to the suburban sprawl that has engulfed much of the state, there would be at least one more last-ditch fight, on the part of those who appreciate its value, to preserve what is left of what many would choose to call "God's country."

When pioneer farmers were moving into what at the turn of the 1700's was known as Hunterdon County (first Morris, then Sussex, then Warren became separate counties), the Indians greeted them in friendship.

The Minsi Indians (a people of the Lenape nation) had been occupying these lands for perhaps thousands of years by that time. Their ancestors had come east to this place in search of better hunting grounds. They were living in peace and harmony with a land of deep forests and fertile valleys with abundant game and fish for all, much natural foodstuff and plentiful water. They saw no harm at first in welcoming the newcomers to their land of plenty. The Dutch had been there earlier, mostly to mine copper in the Pahaquarry. Some trapped fur or traded with the Indians. Some had even stayed to farm. Life was good.

The Minsi (people of the stone country) lived off the land. They hunted, fished, gathered edible wild plants, nuts, and berries, and even carried on some primitive farming at the time of the arrival of these pioneer farmers. It was only as the peculiar (to the Indians) concern about "property rights" arose, that this tranquil life gradually transformed.

Eventually it became a nightmare. First came the constant bickering about trespassing. Indians always had eaten wild fruit from trees. Only now, they were on some farmer's orchard. They were "private property." This whole concept of not being able to live off the land as they had always done because it was now someone's "private property" was foreign to them. They saw no harm in sharing nature's abundance. Eventually the bickering increased in intensity. Tempers flared. Shots were fired. People died. In time, the woods were too deep. Warfare broke out.

Treaties were made and treaties were broken. In the so-called "Walking Purchase," a treaty by which the Indians believed they were tricked, much of the Minsi lands were "purchased" by the white man. At any rate, the wounds never healed. When the French and English were engaged in a worldwide struggle over "property rights" in the

1750's, the French saw an opportunity to use their Indian friends in America. This ember of flame was blown upon in northwestern New Jersey.

The French were aware of the festering wounds over broken or misunderstood treaties. They encouraged the Indians to join them in driving out the English. The French had always lived in America as hunters, trappers, and fur traders. They did not come in droves and demand "property rights." They mingled and intermarried. They lived in America much as the Indians did. They were natural allies. Encouraged by these powerful friends, the Indians began open warfare upon the pioneers of New Jersey's frontier lands. Lonely farmsteads along the Delaware Valley and Ridges burst into flame. Whole families were slaughtered or taken into captivity.

To combat this new turn of events, constant demands were made upon the Governor of New Jersey for protection. The Assembly finally approved construction of 10 forts along the Delaware into which local residents could flee for protection in the event of attacks. The forts were also to be maintained by detachments of militia to come to their aid. One of the local commanders of these militia was a longtime resident of what is now Warren County, Col. Abraham Van Campen. His strongly built stone house became part of one of these fortifications.

The father of one of the residents of the area was scalped brutally while on a fishing expedition in sight of his two sons. The one boy, Tom Quick, never forgot that sight – or the treacherous act of those who had once been their friends. He vowed to avenge his father's death in the years that remained to him. Thus was born one of the many colorful folktales that arose along the trails of New Jersey – that of "Tom Quick – Avenger of the Delaware."

"Clambakes" at the Jersey Shore

As once again we enter that annual period variously described in folklore and ballad as those "hazy, lazy days of summer," my thoughts inevitably turn to two apparently unlike images – the Lenape Indians and the "Jersey Shore." What makes me so apt to reflect upon these two images at this season is their historical connection. The trip to "the shore" is not just an act conceived in modern times by 20th century admen. This annual trek to the Atlantic Ocean in New Jersey seems to have endured the test of time. The fascination of it seems to have its roots somewhere in mans' very inward being. Though the mode of travel, the time involved in both getting and staying there, and, the very nature of the activities engaged in once arrived, may vary over the years, the fact of the going remains intact.

That its roots trace back to the state's aborigines is what so fascinates me. New Jersey's native inhabitants, the Lenapes, lived simple lives. They hunted game in its deep forests and fished in its clear, pure rivers and streams. They gathered nuts and berries and raised certain crops. And each summer, almost like a natural clock, they migrated from all over the state to the "Jersey Shore!"

Living in harmony with nature they took from its waters and woodlands only what was required to survive – ever mindful of leaving for future generations what had sustained them. Seashells became both ornaments and wampum. In the process of raising crops, they burned woodlands to clear space. Because of their small numbers, however, this practice did little damage to their environment. But wherever in the state they lived, when summer came, they dropped everything and headed for "the shore."

The various tribes and sub-tribes of the Lenape were generally of a peaceful nature. They were never in any great numbers in their occupancy of this land. They were also but a small branch of the much larger Algonquin family. In the course of their movement into the land of New Jersey they had to fight members of the Iroquois family. In so doing, though they won the right to live in the land between the two big rivers, they also gained a traditional enemy among the Iroquois.

Tradition has it that the various tribes of the Lenape nation that occupied the northernmost New Jersey region at the time of the coming of the Europeans, were of the Minsi, the people of the stone country, the wolf clan. Living nearest to the Iroquois, the Minsi tribes had to defend themselves more often, and so had the reputation of being the most warlike. Those Lenape, who lived in the southern part of the state near the ocean, were of the Unalachtigo tribes, the turkey clan. They were the most peaceful of the Lenapes, and the host tribes for the annual "clambake." In between, in central New Jersey, were the Unamis, the turtle clan. They were the arbitrators of disputes and their chief Sachem was considered "chief" of the entire Lenape nation.

The route of the great, annual migration of all the various tribes from their permanent homes in northern New Jersey to their summer place along the "Jersey Shore" was the "Minisink Trail." It began in northwestern New Jersey at Minisink Island in the Delaware – a short distance below the modern town of Port Jervis, NY. As it passed through the various regions around the present-day towns of Newton, Andover, Netcong, and finally Dover, each particular sub-tribe moved along it. At Dover, it divided for a time. One branch continued through Whippany, Hanover, and Livingston, crossed the Passaic River and headed for Springfield. The second branch went from Dover through Morris Plains, Morristown, Madison, Chatham, across the Passaic River into Summit, and then rejoined the first trail at Springfield. The "Minisink Trail" became one again at Springfield. From there, it headed south through Westfield, Metuchen, and Matawan to various points along the "Jersey shore." Mounds of seashells such as at Tuckerton are attributed to these summer Indian "clambakes."

Usually this annual trek left a small cadre of "old folks" behind to tend to crops and watch the permanent villages. They had their days at "the shore" for many years before. Those times would now be but memories. But for the majority, it was a great time for fun and fellowship and a time to meet with other members of the Lenape nation to exchange tales and promote their folklore. But it was also an important time for gathering food and wampum. Fish was gathered not only for immediate use, but for the long winter's food supply.

The return journey home would always be in the late summer, just in time to harvest another crop. And so the seasons passed along the trails of New Jersey. But the annual trek to the "Jersey Shore" seems timeless.

The Last of the Lenape

At first, the Indians of the Delaware Valley and those settlers who gradually invaded their territory lived in comparative harmony.

As early as 1737, the Presbytery of New Brunswick was sending missionaries to the "Forks of the Delaware" to preach to the Indians of that region. In the period from 1740 to 1744 the Rev. David Brainerd, who was known as "the Apostle to the Indians," preached to both Indians and settlers alike in the Phillipsburg area. He is said to have used Moses Tatamy, a Delaware Indian, as an interpreter. In 1742, Joseph Shaw, a Moravian missionary, preached to a variety of both Indians and settlers in the Minisink Country.

Often in the early years of settlement along New Jersey's northwestern frontier, hunting parties of both Indians and pioneers went out together. The streams contained much fresh fish, the forests much wild game. There was abundance for all. But as the bear, deer, wild turkey, and other game animals became diminished, encroachment by the settlers in Indian hunting grounds aroused increasing resentment. As farms and farm buildings expanded and fences were erected, the tensions grew. When the Indian "stole" fruit from the settlers' orchards they were increasingly shot at by irate farmers. Retaliation became the order of the day on both sides.

In 1754, the tensions that had been building up over the years were used by the French to stir up the Indians. The French were hoping that Indian warfare would drive out settlers from English territories. Throughout the remainder of the 1750's, the entire upper Delaware Valley erupted into a series of frightening Indian raids and massacres. Forts were built on both sides of the Delaware by the governments of both New Jersey and Pennsylvania. War had changed the lives of both Indians and settlers alike. Constant tragedy replaced a once peaceful coexistence.

Orders were issued by the colonial legislature for arrest of any Indians "skulking about" the countryside friend or foe. When captured, these "peaceful" Indians were herded into jails in such places as Easton, Trenton, and even as far away as Elizabethtown. Both sides began to realize the futility of the situation. In October of 1758, they met in Easton to see if they could not come to some kind of amicable agreement. Teedyuscong represented the Indians as their chief Sachem. Gov. Francis Bernard represented the New Jersey colonists.

A wampum place belt was presented to Bernard by Teedyuscong. Bernard, for his part, offered the Lenape Sachem a treaty that would last "as long as the sun shall shine." The terms of the treaty gave the once-proud Delaware 3,258 acres in the Pine Barrens of Burlington County, where they could remain forever in return for the rest of western New Jersey. The Lenape, who once roamed at will from the banks of the Delaware to the waters of the Atlantic, from the Kittatinny Mountains to the Cape May marshlands, were to be relegated to an Indian reservation in the Pines.

The younger braves resisted such an arrangement. They became renegades. Other nearby Indian nations insisted that the Lenape abide by the treaty – perhaps in the hope of taking pressure off themselves. In the end, as the spring of 1759 came, the people of the Lenape nation began trickling out of their beloved forested hills all up and down the Delaware Valley region into the pinelands that Bernard had named, "Brotherton." Freedom had been exchanged for security, but the strong braves wanted no part of this "captivity." Those who came were mostly the old or very young.

None of the promises of help in establishing an Indian "community" in the Pines was kept. John Brainerd, an Indian missionary, came to do what he could. He helped to build a log church. When he left in 1744, they were without direction. Some of them tried making it the white man's way. The Edgepillock River was dammed up to run a saw and gristmill. The place came to be called "Indian Mills." Some worked in nearby iron or glassworks. Nostalgia for the freedom of the forests in the days of yore, however, enveloped them like a sickness. Their main goal became death, and return to their "happy hunting grounds." A sedentary life, disease, and alcoholism overcame them.

Indian tribes from upstate New York and the Great Lakes region continually called upon their Lenape brothers to come live with them. As their condition gradually worsened, they inevitably gave in. Finally, the last sad vestige of those once noble Lenapes asked permission of the State Legislature to sell their pinelands and move. In 1801 the state agreed. By the summer of 1802 they loaded their few belongings on 12 rented wagons and crossed the trails of New Jersey for the last time. The "Original People" had left the land of their ancestors in the custody of the white man.

CHAPTER 13: COLONIAL PERIOD

New Jersey's Colonial Heritage

For years, New Jersey has stood by and idly watched neighboring states capitalize on their history – thus capturing the lucrative trade. Our own people have rushed off to Massachusetts, Virginia, New York, and Pennsylvania, for example, to ooh and ah over their historic landmarks – while ignoring their own state's rich heritage. I am delighted to say, however, that it is at last beginning to come out of its cocoon, and slowly but steadily parade with pride some of its own unique past.

New Jersey, for example, is the only state whose origins can be traced to three of the competing sea powers of 17th century Europe – Sweden, The Netherlands, and Great Britain. All three sought and gained footholds in the then "New World" by establishing colonies in what we now call New Jersey. New York shares our Dutch heritage, since both were part of New Sweden. But no other state can claim to have been settled by all three nations. And none of the Original 13, save those, was settled by nations other then the English.

I was reminded of this unique heritage when it was brought to my attention recently that a group in the southwestern New Jersey community of Salem was finally planning to exploit their Swedish legacy. Elaborate plans are underway to commemorate the 350th anniversary, in 1988, of the first landing of the Swedes in the United States during the reign of King Gustavus Adolphus. He was the last of Sweden's monarchs to seek overseas colonies – and New Jersey was his choice. He was also probably Europe's principal military figure of that day. What makes these plans so much more exciting, however, than the usual short-lived pageantry, parades, etc., is the permanency of their proposed celebration plans.

The Swedes are credited with introducing to America, in New Jersey's wilderness, the type of log cabins that came to typify life on our frontier throughout the nation's westward movement. What this 20[th]century New Sweden Company hopes to accomplish is the reconstruction of an authentic replica of a 17thcentury Swedish settlement on the banks of Salem Creek, a few miles upland from where it empties into the Delaware River. The Swedes called this river Varkins Kill at the time. The proposed recreated Swedish village will actually be several miles north of Fort Elfsborg, the first documented Swedish settlement in the United States.

Fort Elfsborg eventually came to be known as "Fort Myggenborg," which means the Mosquito Castle. It seems that the famed Jersey mosquitoes plagued the inhabitants of the Swedish fort more than the coming of the Dutch. They, rather than the Dutch force, are credited by some historians with eventually driving the Swedish settlers to move elsewhere. Lt. Sven Skute was in command of the completed fort. The two principal Swedish investors in the original settlements were Klas Larson Fleming, head of the Swedish Naval Office, and Axel Oxenstierna, the king's Prime minister.

The leader of the expedition, which brought this first Swedish settlement to America, was actually a Dutchman Peter Minuit. His excursion set sail from Sweden in two ships – "The Kalmar Nyckel," which meant the Key of Kalmar, and the "Fogel Grip," which was the legendary Griffin, half-lion and half-eagle. They arrived at the banks of the Delaware River in mid-March, 1638. Minuit set sail back to Sweden after seeing his first settlers situated. Unfortunately, for Sweden's colonizing efforts, he was lost in a storm at sea. His energetic plans were sorely missed.

As a result of this loss, Peter Ridder, rather than Minuit, became the first governor of "New Sweden." He arrived in America in April of 1640. Like Minuit, he too was a Dutchman, but a long-time resident of Sweden. Ridder proceeded to buy up large tracts of lands from the Indians along the banks of the Delaware. He did not get along too well with settlers, however, and was replaced in 1643 by the colorful Johan Printz. The Indians of the area called him "The Big Tub." He weighed more than 400 pounds. Printz ruled the colony well from 1643 to 1653.

The proposed 8-acre recreated Swedish Village will include typical houses, a church (the Swedes were ardent Lutherans), a boat shed, a forge, and a small working farm. It will be modeled after Skansen, an open-air museum in Stockholm, and named New Skansen. Promoters hope to attract about 1,000 visitors a day. A new era is thus about to open, giving rebirth to old tales along the trails of New Jersey.

Henry Hudson and the Dutch

In September of 1609, Henry Hudson and his crew, sailing for the Dutch East India Co., anchored off the coast of New Jersey at Sandy Hook in their ship, the "Half Moon." They thus became the first known Europeans to explore the region we now call New Jersey. By their own account, it was described as a wonderful place to see, "pleasant with Grasse and Flowers, and goodly Trees." And the people there were a handsome and friendly group. Unfortunately, the behavior of the crew, which had been made up of about 20 unruly men of many nationalities, aroused the anger of the Native Americans.

Though the American Indians they met at first welcome these strangers warmly, and many goods were exchanged, it did not last. Only a few days later, the Indians attacked a small ship sent ashore to do some further exploring. John Coleman became the first fatality, and then, the first European to be buried on New Jersey soil. He had been mortally wounded when an Indian arrow pierced his body. The previously boisterous crew, now cowed, refused further explorations. Hudson and his men left New Jersey, explored the river now bearing his name, and then returned to Europe in November of that same year.

Fabulous descriptions of the bounteous lands they had explored spread. Reports of abundant furs, which were quite popular for both men and women in the Europe of that day, were especially quick to be noted. The Dutch were not slow at spotting an excellent trade opportunity. They were a rising merchant nation of that day, and furs were in great demand. It must be supposed that a number of smaller, private trading companies began to set out for the New World to establish fur trading posts. However, the first we have been able to find recorded were those of the United Netherlands Co. in 1614. It was probably because this wealthy group of merchants sent out an especially large expedition with a number of ships. The commanders of these sea craft were captains whose names were to become familiar – Block, Mey, and Christiansen. One had an island, another a Cape named after them.

But it was not until newly chartered Dutch West India Co., of 1621 decided that colonization was a good means of setting up a profitable trade venture that the Dutch impact on the New World was really made. Because trade, and not Dutch Colonization, was the main purpose, the Dutch enlisted whomever they could recruit for their first colonies. Since too few Dutchmen were at first willing to leave the comfort of their native land, these early "Dutch" settlements contained a variety of discontents of other nationalities.

From the area we now call Belgium, came Flemings and Walloons, French Protestants known as Hugenots, fleeing persecution in France, were also early willing immigrants. Rhineland Germans of varying religious sects, who were seeking the freedom to worship as they pleased, saw this opportunity in the new Dutch colony. So too, did a number of Englishmen also seeking the religious toleration offered by the Dutch. In time, though, more and more Dutchmen did take advantage of the generous land "grants" offered them under the "Patroon system." This system was developed by the leaders of the trading companies in order to encourage Dutch settlers to come to the New World by offering large land grants to those who got others to come.

One thing stands out about these first Dutch settlements. Their people all reported with awe the great stands of timber they saw. A seafaring people, they immediately saw the possibilities for a great shipbuilding enterprise on these new shores. Being in the trading business also made them keenly aware of the tremendous fur-trading possibilities offered there. The abundance of bear, beaver, deer, elk, fox, mink, otters, panthers, raccoons, skunks, weasels, wild cats, and wolves never ceased to amaze them – and whet their appetites. It was, of course, a partnership with the Indians that made the first Dutch fur trading enterprise in New Jersey so lucrative. The Indians bartered their many fur pelts with the Dutch in exchange for things they did not have and valued – trinkets, cloth, guns, and liquor.

Those lands on the west side of the Hudson, which we now call New Jersey, were known by local Indians as "Hobocan." They were probably the first in New Jersey to be settled by the Dutch. Fort Nassau was established by them along the Delaware in the area

323

around Gloucester. Small attempts at settlement were also made at Cape May. Copper Mining led to the building of the Old Mine Road, and some settlement near the Delaware Water Gap. Farming, fishing, fur, trading, and lumbering occupied the lives of most of those early colonists who settled along the trails of New Jersey now so long ago.

The Swedish Start

Perhaps the key to the puzzle of why the Dutch allowed the Swedes to settle along New Jersey's South River lies in the make-up of the Swedish Trading Company. I say "puzzle" because the South River, as the Dutch called the Delaware, was considered Dutch territory in the early 1600's. And yet no opposition was made when the Swedes first moved in. Considering how aggressively the Dutch protected their commerce, one would have expected at least some attempt being made to prevent these early Swedish settlements.

Let us look for answers in how Sweden got its start in New Jersey. A Walloon businessman, Wilhelm Usselinx, was a major power in the Dutch West India Co. He was dissatisfied, however, with its lack of aggressiveness in establishing trade in the Americas. So, while he was in Gothenburg, Sweden, in 1624, on business, he got himself an audience with the Swedish King, Gustavus Adolphus.

This king was quite the military figure in Europe of that day. Swedish power was being felt along the Baltic Sea, where he was in constant battle with the Danes and Germans, and at the moment with Poland and the east Prussians. The Russian Czar had only recently also been stung by his military prowess. Is it any wonder, then, that he would be all ears at the prospect of perhaps expanding his exploits into the Americas?

Usselinx convinced King Gustaf II to grant him a charter for a Swedish trading company. After all, England and the Netherlands were already using that technique to establish their colonies. The energetic Usselinx had visions of a vast personal trade empire not only in America, but also throughout the world. He was now seeking similar ventures among both the Swedes and the Germans. He was, in fact, off to Danzing next.

The New Sweden Co. would be one outgrowth of all of these endeavors. Getting a charter was only the first step. Selling stock in it was time-consuming. Dutch businessmen were among his first takers. Many were already living in Sweden. Two Swedish officials, Klas Fleming, chief of the Naval Office, and Axel Oxenstierna, the king's Prime Minister also became major investors.

With that kind of influence in the Swedish Court, Usselinx next sought both Swedish ships and military protection for his venture. The Swedish government would eventually provide two ships, "The Kalmar Nyckel," and "The Fogel Grip." Because it was supposedly easier to enlist sailors in the Netherlands, not only the officers of these Swedish ships were Dutch, but so was most of the crew. We can now begin to see some answers to our puzzle. But that was not the whole story. The Dutch West India Co., under Peter Minuit, attempted, in 1623, a Dutch settlement along the Delaware River. It was destroyed by an Indian massacre. Usselinx now enlisted this same Dutchman to lead a "Swedish Expedition" back to this same spot along the Delaware, this time to establish a Swedish trading settlement.

Matters, in the meantime, got a little complicated when King Gustaf, who was an on-the-field commander in his military escapades, got himself killed at the Battle of Lutzen in one of the many German states of that day. His daughter, Christina, succeeded him.

Fortunately for Usselinx, she vowed to complete her "father's plans" for the establishment of Swedish trading colonies in America. I am sure Usselinx must have had some frightful moments about the fate of his long-planned-for venture until Christina's vows were made public.

The next problem was getting sufficient Swedish colonists to establish a settlement in the New World. Unfortunately, there were few takers. They ended up either inveigling or forcing a small number of army deserters, prisoners, or individuals who had gotten into financial problems to join the detachment of Swedish soldiers assigned to protect this new Swedish colony in America. It was not a good beginning.

When they left Gothenburg, Sweden, in early November of 1637, they ran into fierce storms. It took a month of bouncing about on rough seas before they landed, not in America, but in the

Netherlands. After sustaining serious repairs, they finally set sail again for America on Dec. 31, 1637. Not until mid March 1638, would this first ""Swedish Expedition" limp up the Delaware River to plant a Swedish colony in America.

On the way up the river, they stopped at the Dutch Fort Nassau, and, according to Dutch accounts, told them they were just going to stop to take on needed water and wood before journeying on. So they let them pass. This, then, was the beginning of the puzzling establishment of the colony of "New Sweden" along the trails of New Jersey in what was generally regarded as Dutch territory almost 301 years ago.

New Sweden

We often think of Minnesota or Wisconsin when we conjure up thoughts of Swedish immigrants to America. Yet it was to New Jersey's Lower Delaware Valley that many of these sturdy pioneers came as early as 1638 – long before the first Swedes set foot in the North Central part of the United States. "New Sweden" was established first on the Delaware's west bank in present-day Delaware and Pennsylvania. It was not long, however, before Swedish settlers were crossing that river to farm the Jersey side. Since they were mainly farmers, their settlements were really scattered farmhouses.

Though the Dutch were already in southwestern Jersey when the Swedes came, they tolerated their Swedish settlements until 1655. Then they decided to make them a part of "New Netherlands." When the English, in turn, took the area from the Dutch for the first time in 1664, it was the tolerant English Quaker's turn to permit the Swede and Dutch settlers to remain. In fact, the region continued to attract even more Swedish settlers than before.

The settlement of present-day Swedesboro, originally called Rackoon, took place under English rule, and soon became the predominant Swedish settlement in America. The mixture of Dutch, Swedish and English Quaker influence that soon descended upon the region is best illustrated by the establishment of Gloucester. At first a Dutch settlement in 1623 called Fort Nassau, the town later became Swedish, and finally was renamed Gloucester City when the Quakers moved in. The Swedish settlers continued to farm there, however, no matter who ruled it.

Such other present-day places as Repaupo, Greenwich, Paulsboro, Mullica Hill, Finns Point, and Elsinboro were once centers of Swedish life in southwesters New Jersey. The first Swedes to live in the area built low log houses. A log cabin built in the 1640's by Anthony Neilson still stands between Paulsboro and Gibbstown. It is of great interest to both historians and architects. The "Jersey Swedes" were said to have first introduced to America the typical log cabin associated with the American frontiersmen. Swedish immigrants would have been much more familiar with that type of stricture than would those who came here from Britain.

Present-day Elsinboro was the site of the original Swedish fortification known as Fort Elfsborg, which was built there in 1643 by Johann Printz, a 400-pound man who was then governor of New Sweden. This gigantic man was referred to as the "Big Belly" or the "Big Tub" by local Indians. Because of the terrible problem the Swedes encountered there with mosquitoes, the fort was soon nicknamed, "Myggenborg," or Fort Mosquito.

In Swedesboro stands "Old Swedes Church." Originally built by the predominantly Lutheran Swedes, it was once the most important Lutheran congregation in the Jersey portion of "New Sweden." The last clergyman sent to America by the King of Sweden was its pastor Nicholas Collin. The celebrated Swedish naturalist, Peter Kalm, once attended there. Though hardly readable, gravestones of early Swedish settlers are still visible scattered throughout the ancient church cemetery. One of the many southwestern Jersey Swedish cultural heritages that succumbed to English rule was the conversion of this once Lutheran Church to the Episcopal faith in the late 18th century.

Swedish settlers are said to have established themselves as early as the 1630's, along the banks of the Maurice River where it empties into the Delaware Bay. Such unlikely current name-places as Port Elizabeth, Leesburg, and Dorchester were once Swedish settlements before assimilation by English Quakers. The Maurice River was named by the Swedes after the ship that first brought them there, "The Prince Maurice." The Mullica River, Mullica Inlet, and the town of Mullica Hill were named after Eric Palsson Mullica of

Halsingeland, Sweden, who settled the region with his family around 1697 – long after "New Sweden" had been swallowed first by the Dutch and then by the English. Many Swedes were working as lumbermen in that heavily forested region during the mid 1700's when the Swedish Lutheran minister, Carl Magnus Wrangel, toured the area and reported his findings.

Swedish names on old tombstones, old churches, a few towns and rivers with Swedish backgrounds, a log cabin, a few stones of old Fort Elfsborg and some family names still borne by residents are all that remain of a once-predominant Swedish tradition of New Jersey. Perhaps someday, someone will reassemble the many tales that must lie just below the surface. And once again all will see and enjoy another part of that diverse heritage that in New Jersey.

Colonial Period – Dutch & Swedes

Lest you get the impression that "New Sweden" was solely a New Jersey colony, I must hasten to tell you that it was not. Just as the Dutch of "New Netherlands" settled on both sides of the Hudson, so the Swedes of "New Sweden" also colonized both sides of the lower Delaware.

And, just as the Dutch colony later was divided into the two English colonies of New York and New Jersey, so the Swedish colony later became a part of the three English colonies of Pennsylvania, Delaware, and New Jersey. Both also saw their rivers as the centerpiece of their colony, rather than as a dividing line.

Several other interesting comparisons are worth noting as well. Both, for instance had greater numbers of settlers come from their homelands after their own nations lost control of the territory. Also, both, when challenged, surrendered without a fight. Apparently, their colonists were not particularly interested in what nation claimed sovereignty over the wild lands into which they had come to settle.

They were obviously far more concerned with taming the surrounding wilderness in order to make a living for themselves and their families, than they were about which sovereign claimed to rule over them. They also continued to speak their own languages, and observed their native customs and religious beliefs regardless.

In time, they both were assimilated into the English colonies, although, other than language, both groups probably influenced their English neighbor almost as much as the reverse.

I had mentioned earlier that the Dutch also had begun to settle along the Delaware Valley as well as along the Hudson. In fact, they had built Ft. Nassau, around what is now Gloucester, NJ, as early as 1626 – a dozen years before the Swedes first came to the lower Delaware. In their minds, there was no question but that this was Dutch country.

In 1648 – 10 years after the Swedes moved in, the Dutch also built Ft. Beversrede on the west side of the Delaware, now a part of Philadelphia. The Swedes had earlier built their first stronghold guarding the entrance to the Delaware at what is now Wilmington. It was called Ft. Christina, after their new young queen. She actually was not even old enough to rule, and, in fact, did not become full sovereign until 1644, when she became 18.

In 1651, however, the Dutch finally decided that they would have to challenge the Swedes, who had two more strategically located forts than they. This they did building a Dutch fort even further south than the Swedish Ft. Christina. They built Ft. Casimir near what is now New Castle, Delaware. The Swedish governor, Johan Printz, did nothing. The Dutch governor, Peter Stuyvesant, therefore decided that he had successfully outmaneuvered the Swedes, and let it go at that. Apparently, neither side felt the need to engage in battle.

Then in 1653, Gov. Printz was recalled. He was replaced by a young Gov. Johan Rising. He arrived in May 1654. Rising was determined to let the Dutch be aware that they were not to be tolerated on Swedish territory. He demanded and got the surrender of Ft. Casimir. He hoisted the Swedish flag and renamed it Ft. Trinity, since all took place on Trinity Sunday. This act turned out to be a fatal mistake for the Swedes.

Gov. Stuyvesant was now enraged! He felt obliged to take positive action against these interlopers. After seething for months, he sent a large fleet and a detachment of soldiers in September of 1655 to recapture Ft. Casimir. This was accomplished without firing a shot. Not satisfied with rectifying this insult, however, the Dutch decided to remove the Swedish colony entirely. So they sailed further north and captured Ft. Christina as well. The surrender of this Swedish stronghold led to the relinquishment of all Swedish rights to New Sweden. Who knows what might have resulted had King Gustaf II of Sweden been still alive!

Oddly enough, a Swedish ship loaded with new settlers and supplies arrived after the colony surrendered to the Dutch. They also reported that many more new settlers were waiting back home to come over with the next ship. It seems that the idea of American colonization, slow in getting started, was just beginning to catch fire back in Sweden. The Dutch, having had enough problems of their own getting colonists to come to America, decided to let the Swedes enter, if they would swear allegiance to the Netherlands, which they did.

So ended the rule of Sweden along the trails of New Jersey. The Swedish culture, however, remained along the lower Delaware for many years to come. Last year, in commemoration of the 300th anniversary of the first Swedish settlement in New Jersey, a permanent replica of a Swedish farm village on the New Jersey frontier was built in Bridgeton as a reminder of those early Swedes.

Hopefully it will become a popular tourist attraction, continuing to remind us of that unique era of our heritage.

Quaker Colony

You will recall when Great Britain finally wrested "New Netherlands" from the Dutch in 1664, the king's brother, the Duke of York, received title to those lands.

He, in turn, gave two old friends, Sir George Carteret and John Lord Berkeley, the lands between the Hudson and Delaware Rivers that we now call "New Jersey."

Though the Dutch took it back briefly between 1673 and 1674, and rebuked those land titles, the Duke hastily restored them again in June of 1674, just as soon as England recaptured the area.

Berkeley and Carteret had, in the meantime, informally divided New Jersey between them, so they could sell off shares as they saw fit. Berkeley's half was called, "West Jersey" and Carteret's half, "East Jersey."

For the next century, therefore, the people of the American colonies became accustomed to referring to that region as, "the Jerseys." George Washington, during the Revolution, in fact, constantly referred to "the Jerseys" when making reference to his activities there.

At any rate, that was the setting that led to the next step – the settlement of "West Jersey" as a separate Quaker colony by William Penn and his associates.

This was to occur even before he was granted the better known tract on the west side of the Delaware as a refuge for Quakers. That came to be called, "Pennsylvania."

Berkeley, who had been given title to all the lands of "West Jersey," got himself mired down in all sorts of financial problems back home in England. He had to sell his American lands quickly in order to bail himself out of his embarrassing money problems.

He, therefore, made a hasty deal in 1674 with John Fenwick, who represented a Quaker named Edward Byllynge. Berkeley's lands in New Jersey were sold to these Quakers for the sum of 1,000 pounds. So Fenwick kept the deed to the lands as payment for that debt.

This is where, in 1675, William Penn gets into the New Jersey land picture. The two men got into a public argument over this deal. Since this type of behavior was against the teachings of their church, the Society of Friends now stepped in. Their purpose was to settle, amicably, this "family" dispute among their members.

William Penn and two others were selected to mediate the problem. Their ruling was that Fenwick could keep one-tenth of the West Jersey tract for himself.

The remaining "tenths" were to be sold among members of the Society of Friends in order to establish West Jersey as a haven in America for the persecuted Quakers of England.

Fenwick was angered at the outcome but decided that he would be the first to establish a Quaker colony in West Jersey. After advertising the place in glowing terms, he set sail for America in the summer of 1675 with a boatload of 48 hopeful Quaker colonists, including his three daughters. His wife refused to come.

They reached these shores in November of 1675. There, along the Delaware, they established their Quaker haven. They called it "Salem" from the Hebrew word for peace.

But peace was far from what they got. Fenwick started off on the right foot by "buying" the site from the local Lenape Indians. Then he went about setting up his community with streets and building lots, each with houses quickly put up on them in preparation for winter.

Where he went wrong, however, was declaring himself governor of the colony. It seems the Fenwick-Byllynge deal with Berkeley was never fully accepted by the Duke of York. For one thing, Carteret had not agreed with Berkeley as to the exact boundaries between East and West Jersey. For another, the Duke was not ready to give up his right to manage the political government of this territory, especially to the Quakers!

By the "Quintipartite Deed" in 1676, Penn and several other Quakers representing West Jersey, and Carteret for East Jersey, agreed to legally divide the colony of New Jersey into two separate colonies. The line was to run from Little Egg Harbor along the Atlantic coast diagonally to the northwestern tip of the colony. Though the exact line remained in dispute until 1743, when the West Jersey holdings were extended further to the east, it did give the Quakers control of the entire reach of the Delaware River from the New York border south.

But Fenwick refused to give up his right to govern, and stubbornly insisted he was governor.

On September 25, 1676, Gov. Edmund Andros of New York, who also claimed that right, ordered his arrest. On December 8, he was hauled off to jail screaming and in chains.

While he was still there, William Penn began to pursue his goal in earnest of establishing a Quaker settlement along the trails of West Jersey. He secured Fenwick's release and dropped him off at Salem, while he sailed further up the Delaware with a boatload of new settlers. Thus did Quaker settlements become a part of the heritage of West Jersey.

West Jersey Province

The establishment of the "Province of West Jersey" as a haven for Quakers in 1676 in no way limited that area to its settlement by people of that faith alone. In fact, the Quakers brought a document with them that gave to those who settled among them more freedom than those found anywhere else in America.

It was called by the cumbersome title of: "The Concessions and Agreements of the Proprietors, Freeholders, and Inhabitants of the Province of West Jersey in America." I suppose, considering its valuable contents, it deserved such a big name.

It was written by William Penn and Edward Byllynge. It guaranteed to all who would come to their Quaker haven in the Province of West Jersey the most freedom to govern and the most civil liberties to be found anywhere.

"We put the power in the people," they said in their document, for perhaps the first time.

Individual rights were guaranteed. The secret ballot for annual elections was established. Free speech, freedom from illegal arrest or imprisonment for debts, trial by jury, complete religious freedom, all were assured.

Much of what we today consider the rights of Americans were first found in that early Quaker document in New Jersey.

Fenwick had established the first Quaker settlement, you may recall, at Salem, NJ in 1676. But it was Penn's much larger group that arrived along the banks of the Delaware in August 1677, that really began in earnest the Quaker settlement of the west Jersey Province. They arrived on the ship, "Kent," some 230 strong.

The province was then divided into 100 sections. Ten of these went to Fenwick, who had been promised one-tenth of the whole province when he agreed to settle his argument with Byllynge.

We read much, in our history books, about Penn's settlement of Philadelphia and Pennsylvania in 1682 as a Quaker refuge. I wonder how many realize that the Province of West Jersey, six years earlier, was actually the first such venture in America?

Anyway, the remaining 90 sections of West Jersey were offered for sale to any Quaker desiring to invest in this new haven. By 1683, all of them had been purchased. Only a small number of those purchasers were wealthy. There were only nine purchasers of more than one section. Those who bought even an entire section only numbered 23 out of the original 120. Many had to go in together and split a section, in order to raise the needed money.

Most of those early Quakers were small businessmen or craftsmen. The majority were English, less than a handful were Scots. A dozen and a half were Irish Quakers who bought that tenth found in the area of present-day Camden and Gloucester counties. It came to be known as the "Irish Tenth."

The first boatload that sailed up the Delaware in the "Kent" stopped at the Swedish settlement of "New Stockholm." It was located near where Raccoon Creek emptied into the Delaware. The Swedes they met there were friendly. They helped those Quakers who chose to stay with them to get through that first winter, both with food and makeshift shelters.

Another group, however, chose to move further upstream. This second group named the new settlement they founded Burlington, after a place in England. The nearby Lenape Indians with whom they came in contact were also a friendly people. They got the new settlers through that first winter with both wild game and Indian corn.

By the time William Penn had founded his "City of Brotherly Love" on the Pennsylvania side of the Delaware, many more Quakers had come to settle their haven in West Jersey. Almost 1,500 of them were living in the Burlington and Salem settlements alone. All along the valley of the Delaware, and up its inland waterways, new Quaker settlements were coming into existence. Their relations with the Lenape were, for the most part, good.

The Quakers were a very enterprising group. One of their members, Mahlon Stacy, took off with his family up the Delaware as far as he could sail. When he reached the rapids and the falls, and could go no further by boat, he stopped, erected his home and built the first mill constructed in West Jersey.

In time, a settlement grew up around Stacy's mill. One of his sons later sold a large tract in it to a Philadelphia merchant named William Trent. We know that place today as Trenton, the state capital.

Now, more than 300 years since this first Quakers settled along the Eastern banks of the Delaware, we can still find traces along those particular trails of New Jersey, of the sturdy homes, meeting houses, and farmsteads that were once such an important part of the state's early Quaker heritage. May we have the wisdom to preserve at least some of it.

East Jersey

While the Quakers under John Fenwick and Edward Byllynge were reasonably successful in creating a "Colony for the Society of Friends" in the new Province of "West Jersey," attempts to promote settlement by New Englanders in "East Jersey" were practically at a standstill.

Two events were mainly responsible. One was the constant controversy between East Jersey proprietors and the citizens of the six townships already established there. They were mainly arguments over the required payment to the proprietors of quitrents by those who purchased lands. The second was a Dutch re-conquest. This latter was followed by a period of confusion over land title rights – even after the British retook possession. Add to this the confusion in the land titles created as a result of the original grants given by the Duke of York's first governor, Col. Richard Nicolls, and you can see why people for a time shied away from settling in East Jersey.

To add to the woes of those who would settle in "the Jerseys," both East and West Jersey were subjected to a constant barrage of challenges by the New York Governor, Edmund Andros.

Andros insisted that he alone had the power to govern "the Jerseys," twice he threw West Jersey's John Fenwick into prison for his insistence that he had the right to govern in that province. Repeated arguments with East Jersey's Gov. Philip Carteret eventually resulted in his arrest by Andros. Gov. Carteret was finally brought to trial in New York City. Though the humiliated New Jersey governor was acquitted by the New York jury, the court, before setting him free, warned him no to try governing there again.

Compounding his problems in the midst of all of this was the death of his cousin, the Proprietor, Sir George Carteret. Philip wrote letters to powerful friends in Britain while Andros ruled East Jersey with an iron hand, arresting those who dared to protest.

Andros was finally recalled to England by the Duke of York. Philip who remained as a private citizen of Elizabethtown, resumed his duties. But his actions did him in. His victory over Andros apparently went to his head. First, he challenged New York over the rights to Staten Island. Then he dissolved the East Jersey Assembly over a dispute as to their powers. A new group of 24 proprietors had purchased Sir George Carteret's land grants from his heirs after his death. They recalled Philip Carteret and replaced him temporarily with a new governor, Thomas Rudyard. Rudyard was a prominent and popular Quaker.

Under the 24 Proprietors, most of whom were Quakers, the settlement of "East Jersey" soon turned into a Scottish undertaking. Most English Quakers, it seemed, opted for West Jersey or the new Quaker Colony of Pennsylvania. A drive to arouse interest in the purchase and settlement of East Jersey in Scotland was organized.

A leading Quaker, Robert Barclay, who played a prominent role in the recruitment of Scottish purchasers and settlers, was named as the new Gov. of East Jersey. He arrived in January of 1684. A new town and a new capital were created for him at Amboy Point, located at the mouth of the Raritan River. It was soon called Perth Amboy in honor of one of the Scottish Proprietors, the Earl of Perth.

Most of the disappointingly few Scots who eventually did come to East Jersey were not Quakers. They came from Aberdeen, Edinburgh, Kelso, and Montrose. An ambitious expedition of Scottish Quakers from Leith, led by George Scot, ended in the tragic death of him, his wife and half of the settlers from a fever contracted on the way over. This, coupled with a decline in religious persecution in Scotland, practically ended Scottish emigration to East Jersey.

In 1690, Gov. Barclay died. Migration from New England and Long Island had practically ceased. The once insatiable demand for land sales in East Jersey suddenly went begging. The hoped-for brisk trade at the new port of Perth Amboy did not materialize. New York captured the market for the export of even Jersey-grown provisions and livestock. Most of the Scots settled in Perth Amboy as craftsmen. Others took up farming on lands at Cedar Brook (Plainfield) and along the foothills of the Watchungs and the banks of the South Branch of the Raritan River.

Since the majority of these Scotsmen were not Quakers, but godly Calvinists instead, they soon begged for ministers of their own faith to be sent from their homeland to serve them in their new land. Thus, what started as a hoped for Scottish Quaker refuge, ended in the beginning of a strong Presbyterian movement along the trails of New Jersey. It was the movement that by the time of the American Revolution was to play a prominent role in the fight for independence.

"The Revolution" of East and West

The reunion of the Provinces of East and West Jersey under one royal governor came about in 1702, after a series of uprisings against "the proprietors." It was known as "the Revolution."

The settlers of both Jerseys became increasingly dissatisfied with the way they were being ruled by these individual landowners. Dissentions grew into riots, and riots into open revolt.

The dissenters were basically sick and tired of the expected payment of "rents" to agents of what had often become the children of essentially absentee landlords. They saw no sense to what appeared to be becoming a perpetual and arrogant proprietorship of their lives.

The Quakers of West Jersey first began expressing their independence when, in 1685, they elected their own governor.

One of the proprietors, Edward Byllynge, not only claimed the right to name their governor himself, but he had also denounced the "Concessions and Agreements," by which they had been governed since 1676, as no longer in operation.

Dr. Daniel Coxe, who was not a Quaker, became governor of West Jersey in 1687 with a promise to protect the colonists' fundamental rights. This quieted them temporarily.

When Gov. Andrew Hamilton came back to New Jersey in 1700, where he was serving as governor of both Jerseys, he found he had an open revolt on his hands.

New Jerseyans were definitely becoming a very independent lot. They cherished the personal liberties they had won. Leaders of the East Jersey Province had petitioned King William III for the right to a governor who was not prejudiced toward the proprietors. No action was forthcoming from London.

On March 4, 1700, a band of revolutionaries stormed the Middlesex County Courthouse. They would not go unheard! They nailed shut doors against agents of the proprietors seeking court orders to collect rents or take property. The same action spread to Essex County on March 11. By July, Monmouth was having equal problems. In September, Essex rioters were dragging judges off their benches, beating them, and tearing up the courthouse. The citizens were determined they would be heard!

Back in July, some 60 horsemen had descended upon Justice Pierson's home in Newark and demanded the release of a "political" prisoner. When refused, they went down the road, seized the keys from the county sheriff, and freed the prisoners themselves. This sort of "revolutionary" activity by the Jersey colonists against the proprietary authority continued throughout the remainder of 1700 and into 1701.

Another mob in Monmouth County did essentially the same thing as those in Newark, except that they had to beat the sheriff in order to gain the jailbreak they sought.

When Gov. Hamilton arrived with a force of militia, he found himself being beaten back by armed citizens twice that size. Townspeople also disrupted sessions being held at the courthouse by holding loud militia drills outside at the same time court was in session. By the spring of 1701, they went still further. They seized the entire court, including the Governor, and held them prisoner for a week until they got concessions.

About the same time, in the spring of 1701, West Jersey colonists rebelled against a heavy tax imposed by their Quaker proprietors. Some five dozen irate citizens broke into the Burlington jailhouse in late March. The county officials fled in terror.

The power of the people seemed invincible. After it became apparent that the citizens of New Jersey were not going to be silenced, the proprietors decided that, if they were going to hang on to their land titles, they had better give up their right to govern. They voted to yield.

In late 1701, their board of trade back in London petitioned the king for a reunion of the Jerseys under royal rule.

When William III died childless in 1702, and his sister-in-law, Anne became queen of Great Britain, she reunited New Jersey as requested. William Penn protested loudly for the West Jersey Quakers. The queen, however, went ahead and appointed Edward Hyde, the Lord Cornbury, to be New Jersey's first royal governor. About all he had going for him was that he was Queen Anne's cousin.

Much to the disappointment of New Jersey's proprietors, Lord Cornbury was also made governor of New York. When he arrived in August 1703, he, as expected, chose to live in New York City. There too, would be given his main attention. New Jersey's role as second fiddle to New York had begun.

His main interest along the trails of New Jersey was to make the most profit from the land deals there as possible in the shortest period of time. The "Cornbury Ring," as it was called, is another whole story of corruption and abuse that made the proprietorship look tame by comparison.

Land Riots

In January 1738, New Jersey was finally assigned a royal governor who was to govern only New Jersey.

Since Queen Anne had taken over the responsibility of governing the province in 1702, the governorship of New Jersey had been shared with that of New York.

As could well be imagined, most of that governor's time and concern was directed not to New Jersey, but to the larger, more active New York colony. After many years of protesting this arrangement, the man who spent most of his adult life in this protest was appointed to the post

Thus did Lewis Morris become New Jersey's first full-time royal governor.

One of Morris's first acts as governor was to call for the popular election of an Assembly. This body had not been elected by the people for the past eight years under previous governors.

Because Lewis Morris had been a prominent New Jersey figure for half a century prior to his appointment, and because he had gotten along so well with people in all walks of life, his appointment was greeted with much applause.

To show their appreciation of this man, in fact, the new county that was created in 1739 by slicing off the northern part of Hunterdon was named Morris in honor of the popular new governor. Its county seat, furthermore, was named Morristown. The Morris County of that day also included present Sussex and Warren counties as well.

Lewis Morris was already 67 years old when he was made governor of New Jersey. Born in New York City in 1671, he had practiced law there and was made a judge of the Superior Court of New York and New Jersey in 1692.

He had served both on the appointed Governor's Council and as an elected member of the New Jersey Assembly that had called for the surrender of proprietary government to the crown.

In fact, Morris was prominent in that Assembly which had also drawn up the complaint against Gov. Cornbury that was presented to Queen Anne, resulting in his ouster. He had called for a separate governor for New Jersey at that time as well.

From 1710-1738, he served as the chief justice of New York and New Jersey. He was holding that post when he was made New Jersey's first full-time royal governor.

Unfortunately, Lewis Morris' honeymoon with the seemingly inevitable opponents of any governor – the elected legislature – soon ended. Money seems to be the universal divider. They quarreled over his salary, and their right to enact any laws concerning money. In 1745, Gov. Morris, in a harsh criticism of the Assembly's lack of cooperation, publicly called them a bunch of idiots. From that time on, it was over between them.

To compound matters, the governor's son, Robert, was one of three proprietors, which included James Alexander and David Ogden, who in 1745 began legal proceedings against "squatters" on their lands. The proprietors claimed that anyone who refused to pay their required "quit rents" was a "squatter."

The "squatters" claimed that they had purchased their land directly from the Indians and that, at any rate, they owned it by right of possession, since they had been tilling it for a given number of years.

Land – its use and its rightful ownership – was again to become a source of trouble in New Jersey. Strangely enough, Lewis Morris, who fought because of previous "land riots" to take the right to govern away from the proprietors, and then to get New Jersey its own governor, was now to find himself in the odd position of being the first royal governor to again have to deal with the "land riots" issue.

"Squatters" throughout the colony were threatening to kill any agents of the proprietors who came snooping around their lands.

The judge who would have to try the first case to come before Chancery Court was Gov. Morris.

When, in the summer of 1745, no appearance was made by those in the Horseneck Section of Essex County first charged with being illegal possessors, eviction notices had to be served. This section included the present Caldwells, Fairfield, Livingston, and Roseland.

The first of the new series of "land riots" occurred at the Essex County Jailhouse in Newark. A band of 150 horsemen arrived on September 9, 1745, to break Samuel Baldwin free. Baldwin, of Camptown (now Irvington), had been arrested as a "squatter."

These "land riots," which grew worse and soon spread into Morris, Somerset, Hunterdon, and Middlesex counties, caused the trails of New Jersey to shake once again with the seeds of revolution.

In the midst of this disorder, the 75-year old Gov. Morris died a broken and disheartened man. He had become a victim of the same disorders over land that had brought him power in the first place.

New Jersey's Tea Party

The first permanent settlements in New Jersey were made by the Dutch, near what is now Jersey City across the Hudson from their main trading post at New Amsterdam. Dutch fur trappers and copper miners had been in the Delaware Valley in northwestern New Jersey since the 1650's. Some Swedish and Dutch trappers were found along the same river in the southwestern part of the state as early as the late 1630's. Only a few lonely farm families were part of what could be called permanent settlers along the east bank of the Delaware.

After the first English takeover in 1664, scattered fishing villages on the lower shoreline appeared. Some small Quaker settlements arose to the west, near Pennsylvania. Several religious-oriented communities sprang up at Newark, Elizabethtown, and Woodbridge. By the late 1600's, William Penn, who had sent agents into several provinces near the Rhineland, invited groups of Germans seeking religious asylum to come to his lands in the New World. He offered lands not only in Pennsylvania to these immigrants, but lands he had purchased from John Fenwick on the Jersey side of the Delaware as well.

Most of Jersey's original families were farmers who had been unhappy with their lives in Europe. They sought the freedoms offered in the New World. They were poor folk who raised their own food, made their own clothing and furniture. They built their homes from the abundant wood and stone found on the land. They produced a large crop of corn and wheat. A self-sufficient people, they grew their own vegetables, raised cattle, hogs, poultry, and sheep. There was also ample fish and wildlife for their needs to be found in Jersey's forests, streams, and fields.

For many years, they lived simple and hard lives, but free from tyrannical government rules and regulations. They wanted only to be left alone. The Swedish farmers did not object when the Dutch took over, nor did the Dutch with the coming of British rule. Most of the early settlers – whether Swedes, Finns or Danes, Dutch or Flemish or French, Germans, Swiss, English, Scotch, Irish or Welsh – remained loyal to the British Crown when, in 1702, New Jersey was made into a Royal Colony.

By the mid-1700's, a valuable iron industry had been added to the Jersey economy. Shipbuilding, lumbering, and a growing merchant class were also becoming important.

During the decade of the French and Indian Wars, from 1754 to 1763, all were happy to receive the protection of His Majesty's troops. Along the Jersey frontier, Indian raids and uprisings were constantly being instigated by the French monarchy. France was in a worldwide struggle with Britain for control of Empire – and its rich trade.

The British had built some half-dozen barracks in New Jersey to house their troops. Only the one at Trenton remains as an historic site to this day. They also urged the royal government of the colony to build a number of forts along the upper Delaware to protect the farmers along New Jersey's northwestern frontier – in what is now Sussex and Warren counties. The struggle was fierce and often bloody. Out of it, a new folk-hero arose: Tom Quick, Avenger of the Delaware. Stories of the exploits of Tom Quick, the Indian Slayer, became greater than life itself among the yeomen farmers, trappers, and woodsmen who lived in the Jersey wilderness.

Unfortunately, when the wars ended, the tax burden on the people of England became so tremendous that they sought relief in the colonies. Instead of working with the colonists' representatives, however, the British government began imposing harsh taxes and restrictive regulations on its trade and manufacturing. All in the hope of gaining needed funds, the British trampled on Jersey freedoms that the colonists had grown to expect. The fiercely independent Jerseymen grew restive and rebellious.

In the struggles against the domineering British rulers, new heroes arose in all sections of the Jersey countryside. There was, for example, that busy port in southwest Jersey called Greenwich. When Captain J. Allen brought his ship, the Greyhound, into harbor there, carrying a cargo of tea with the hated tax, trouble arose.

Word spread, and the Howell Brothers, Richard and Lewis, called a meeting at their home. A gathering of "Indians" was led by Fighting Phil Fithian, plotted Jersey's own tea party. It took place on a night late in November of 1774.

The popular tea-burner, Richard Howell, went on to be elected governor of New Jersey. Fighting Phil Fithian died of camp fever in 1776 while serving as a chaplain in the Revolutionary Army. A monument erected to the Jersey Tea-burners stands in the center of Greenwich. The Daniel Bowen House, where the infamous tea had been stored, is now an historic site. Just a few reminders of that rich heritage to be found along the trails of New Jersey.

Colonial Life

It sometimes does the heart good to look back into the past and see how those who came before us coped with the struggles of life. People who have moved from other regions may have some inkling, at least, of what it was like for New Jersey's early inhabitants when they first arrived. They too, had left familiar surroundings, either in the "old country" or in another developed settlement, in order to launch a new life. But for them, it was to be an untamed wilderness. They too, left relatives and friends behind. But for them, there were no new neighbors nearby to befriend. How well they adjusted was entirely up to them. Their abilities and their characters were put to the extreme test. They had none of the security that comes from the knowledge that nearby are those with whom they might share their problems and joys.

Those first families to previously unsettled regions of New Jersey had to break the ice, so to speak. They were totally dependent upon their own skills and stamina. The houses in which they would live had to be built entirely by each pioneer farmer – sometimes with family help, sometimes without. Usually it would be temporary shelter of un-squared logs with a bark and twig roof and a dirt floor. It most likely contained two openings for windows covered with greased paper and a doorway draped with canvas. Indoor life was always in a state of semi-darkness.

While a more "substantial" home was gradually being constructed, these pioneer families lived in those crude huts for as long as three years. In this period they also had to clear some fields for growing crops – for New Jersey was then a heavily wooded wilderness. And they had to construct some type of shelter for their farm animals, who in the meantime were running wild without protection from the elements. Larger log cabins with great stone fireplaces were usually their second homes. As they prospered, this often was incorporated into their larger, permanent homes as the kitchen area. Their first furniture, with the exception of what little they might have brought along, was made by the farmer himself. Depending upon his skill, it was usually crudely constructed.

344

Water for cooking, bathing, and only rarely drinking had to be hauled regularly indoors and heated over the fireplace in large iron kettles. Drinking water was generally considered unsafe, and apple cider was the most favored daily beverage.

At first, the water came from nearby springs. Later crude wells were dug and hand pumps installed. Bathing was most often done (by men and boys only) in the nearby streams and creeks. As time went by, bathing by the fireplace (and later the kitchen stove) was a weekly ritual for the entire family.

Refrigeration, as we know it, was non-existent. The preservation of food was difficult. Drying poles were hanging from beams over the fireplace all year. Apples, other fruits, herbs, peppers, and strips of meat were hung to dry. Smoked and salt-cured meats came with time. The former was prepared in specialty built "smokehouses." Most farmers eventually built little stone and frame or sod "spring-houses as well." Milk, butter, and whatever could be kept cool was placed in crocks sitting them, deep in the cold spring or stream water over which they were built. Hunting and fishing, along with the slaughtering of their domestic animals, particularly hogs, provided much fresh food for the table.

A lug pole at the fireplace, upon which could hang iron and sometimes copper or brass pots, was the housewife's cooking place. Later, an iron crane was installed on the sidewall that could be swung over the fire or out away from it. Roasting had to be done on a "spit" until a tin-roasting oven was obtained. Most people were using some tin utensils by about 1820. With New Jersey's abundance of iron foundries, iron frying pans with a three-foot handle, gridirons, pots, and three-legged skillets were much in use in fireplaces, throughout the 18th into the 19th centuries. Tin reflector ovens first began appearing in town houses as early as the second half of the 18th century. Ladles, spoons, dishes, pails, chopping bowls, molds, etc. were all made of wood. Wooden trenches about a foot square and three inches deep were the first dishes and had to be shared with others.

The arduous task of washing clothes was at first a seasonal chore. In time it was done monthly and finally each week. Nearby streams soon were replaced by tubs with wooden poles and washboards. Homemade "washing machines" were devised in time.

Rainwater was collected in barrels. Dryers were bushes and later hemp-rope strung between trees. This, then, gives us only a brief glimpse of some aspects of what life was like along the trails of New Jersey in those "good 'ole days" gone by.

CHAPTER 14: REVOLUTIONARY WAR

New Jersey in the American Revolution

In view of this being the 208th anniversary of the Battles of Trenton and Princeton, considered by many to be pivotal victories for the American cause, I thought I might devote this article to a quick overview of New Jersey's overall role in the American Revolution. It might help put New Jersey's key part in this historic American event into better perspective.

Because of poor "PR," New Jersey's important position in the War for Independence has never been fully appreciated. A state that saw five major battles, a number of winter encampments of the Continental Army, and hundreds of minor battles and skirmishes deserves much more recognition as a "Crucible of the Revolution" than it has received.

Even before the start of the American Revolution, New Jersey had its active "Committees of Safety" and "Correspondence," just as did Massachusetts, though to read the history books you'd never realize it. After the Boston Tea Party in March 1774, in which the partisans protested a British tax that refused to go away, New Jersey had its own Tea Party! I have yet to see a history text in our schools, however, that ever made mention of it. Again, it is all in your "PR" men. That is the stuff of which history is recorded. I am not going into detail on any of these events at this time; suffice it to say for now that New Jersey's "Greenwich Tea Party," on the night of December 22, 1774, was probably more dramatic, and certainly took as much guts, as did the one that was held in Boston.

And what about the Declaration of Independence? You could easily get the impression that only Massachusetts and Virginia were represented from what your usual history tells you. But New Jersey sent some pretty high caliber delegates in Francis Hopkinson of Bordentown, who later designed the Great Seal of the United States, as well as Abraham Clark of Elizabeth, John Hart of Hopewell, and Richard Stockton and John Witherspoon of Princeton. All pledged their lives, their fortunes, and their sacred honor. Some of which was lost to them.

Nothing in the war anywhere was more disheartening either than was Washington's retreat across New Jersey in November of 1776, which led to the writing of Tom Paine's "The Crisis" right here on Jersey soil! Nor was there a more dramatic event anywhere than his re-crossing of the Delaware on Christmas Day of 1776. Nor was there a more exhilarated triumph than his victories at Trenton and their follow-up rout of the British in Princeton a week later in early January of 1777. We hear a great deal about Valley Forge, but Washington also spent several winter encampments of note at Morristown. Though the winter of 1777 following his two victories wasn't bad, that of 1779-80 proved to be the most bitter of the century, and a far worse experience than that suffered at the more publicized in Pennsylvania.

The spring of 1777 saw battles at Spanktown (Rahway) and Quibbletown (Metuchen) before Washington moved his troops back to the Delaware River in order to prevent the British capture of the rebel capital, Philadelphia. There was another major Battle of Red Bank fought there in defense of Fort Mercer on October 22, 1777. The fort had been built to help keep British warships and supply ships away from the capital. Though they won that first battle, later the fort was lost, as was Philadelphia. That was when Washington spent his cruel winter nearby at Valley Forge.

With the spring of 1778, the British attempted to move back to New York. This time, Washington pursued THEM across New Jersey and engaged them in the war's longest battle - on probably the hottest day, June 28, 1778. The Battle of Monmouth, the state's fourth major engagement, was also the first at which American forces faced the British, European style, in the open field, and drove them from the state!

The following winter of 1778-79 was spent in Somerset County with Washington headquartered at the Wallace House in Somerville. There, Martha joined him and many a prominent American came to the most celebrated stay the Washington's had during the war. Then came the most sufferable winter at Jockey Hollow in 1779-80.

When the British again invaded New Jersey in the spring of 1780, we witnessed first the Battle of Connecticut Farms (Union) in early June, later followed by the state's fifth major battle at Springfield on June 23, 1780. There, the British were prevented from taking Washington's Military Headquarters, then located at Morristown. These few highlights barely scratch the surface of the many tales of American bravery and intrigue that traversed the trails of New Jersey. However, they should help you to get a firmer grasp of the big picture within which the many other tales can then be fixed into place.

"Loyalists," "Neutrals," and "Rebels"

The actual fighting of the American Revolution had begun in mid April of 1775 in the little New England hamlets of Lexington and Concord. By July of that year, the Royal Government of His Majesty's colony of New Jersey had been removed with the arrest of its last Royal Governor, Wm. Franklin. It was replaced by the Provincial congress of New Jersey. Committees of Correspondence and Observation had already been in operation since the punishment, which the British government had meted out to Boston as a result of · the Boston Tea Party. New Jersey had even had its own Tea Party in 1774 at Greenwich, the little port at the mouth of the Cohansey River where it emptied into the Delaware.

Events leading up to the Revolution, in fact, had stirred up considerable patriot enthusiasm throughout the colony. General Washington was greeted with gusto when he rode through on his way to assume command of the Continental Army outside of Boston. Church bells rang fervently when in the following July of 1776, a "Declaration of Independence" was proclaimed by the Continental Congress meeting in Philadelphia. But one must not lose sight of the fact that there was still a large Loyalist sentiment throughout New Jersey.

Once the British had driven the patriots from Long Island and NYC, and had taken Fort Lee, the preponderance of Loyalists increased. Particularly in those regions lying near the great British armies and fleets of warships in and about NYC and Staten Island.

There were also considerable numbers of "neutrals" in West Jersey, or wherever large bodies of Quakers were living. After Washington's army retreated across the state with the British in pursuit, new pockets of "loyalists" arose wherever British troops were stationed, such as at Perth Amboy, New Brunswick, and Princeton.

Through the "rebel" population of the Jerseys often rose and fell with the success or failure of Washington's army, there remained a strong base of middle-class citizenry that were patriot to the core, and sustained the Revolution through bad times as well as good. Staunch Loyalists decreased in time, by either leaving or remaining silent. Patriot activity was particularly strong along the Jersey shore where privateering, which the British considered piracy, centered at Little Egg Harbor.

New Jersey sent Abraham Clark, John Hart, Francis Hopkinson, Richard Stockton, and John Witherspoon to represent them at Philadelphia. There, on July 4, they voted for Independence.

The state then adopted a new constitution renouncing its loyalty to the Crown.

On July 18, the state government became the Convention of the State of New Jersey. Resulting Loyalists uprisings in Hunterdon County had to be subdued by the new state militia. Armed Loyalists in Monmouth County outwardly aided the British and mad life miserable for patriots. Six battalions of New Jersey Loyalists were recruited. They continued to serve in the British army throughout the war. In time, however, those remaining outward "loyalists" were often arrested and deported. Sometimes they were "tarred and feathered" out of town.

Before the British took NYC, Washington had set up a "Flying Camp" outside of Perth Amboy under Gen. Hugh Mercer. Its purpose was to protect his southern flank. Supplies and reinforcements had to come from New Jersey. Gen. Howe's troops had arrived at The Narrows from Canada on July 3, 1776. By mid-July, some 10,000 American militia from Pennsylvania, Maryland, and Delaware, as well as New Jersey, had assembled at the Perth Amboy encampment. Regiments of continentals up from the south passed through it before joining Washington in New York City.

On July 18, 1776, Gen. Mercer led his first raid of Continentals from his "Flying Camp" on those British garrisons under

Gen. Howe that had gathered on Staten Island. He was attempting to weaken them before they had a chance to launch an attack on Washington. A strong gale, however, prevented a successful landing.

Throughout July, more British troops arrived. On Aug. 1, Sir Henry Clinton and Lord Cornwallis disembarked with large armies from South Carolina. On Aug. 12, a fleet of 30 warships convoyed 400 transports loaded with both Hessian and British soldiers- the largest expedition ever sent out by England. Gen. Howe was now poised for the attack with some 32,000 men under arms. Gen. Washington waited for the onslaught with a defense force of 20,000. Unknown to both sides, the impending battles were destined to spill over on to the trails of New Jersey, and drag the revolt to its lowest ebb. These were to become, in the words penned in Newark by Thomas Paine, "the times that would try men's souls."

The War in June

June always reminds me of the American Revolution. During those bygone years of our nation's history it was the custom to call a halt to military operations with the onset of winter, and to resume, once again, those activities only when the coming of spring weather permitted. As a result, by the time June rolled around, the opposing forces were always in full swing. Such major battles as Connecticut Farms, Springfield, and Monmouth all occurred on New Jersey soil during the month of June.

It was on June 29, 1776, along the shore of Cape May, that the episode of the American brig, "Nancy" took place. She had been hotly pursued all the way home from St. Croix and St. Thomas by six British men-of-war. The Continental Congress had previously purchased a goodly amount of arms and powder there, and the "Nancy," laden down with her cargo of military supplies, safely reached the southern coast of New Jersey. Once there, she was run ashore by her captain in a heavy fog. Most of her cargo was landed and turned over to patriot forces before the ship was abandoned, and the heavy fog lifted. But before her captain left the brig to be taken by the enemy, he lit a mine in her cabin - set to burn slowly. When the British fleet discovered the "Nancy" in the lifted fog, they hastily sent a boarding party to capture their prize. No sooner had they boarded the vessel to claim their victory, when she blew up and hurtled her captors "40 or 50 yards into the air," according to the excited reports of the watching Patriots.

June 29, 1776, was also the date that ships transporting Gen. Howe's main British army to the New York area for the attack on New Your City arrived from New England, and dropped anchor off of New Jersey's Sandy Hook. This incident, of course, was the prelude to the collapse of New York, and Washington's subsequent retreat across New Jersey.

It was also in June of 1776 that outbursts of violence occurred against the Patriots by bands of local Loyalists throughout Hunterdon County. They had to be subdued with special detachments of militia sent to the Hunterdon hills by the Provincial Congress of New Jersey. Tories in Shrewsbury also defied Patriot demands to form Committees of Inspection that June. They had to be forced to do so by local patriots from the Freehold area.

On June 11, 1777, Gen. Howe advanced toward Washington's forces then entrenched in strong positions north of Bound Brook. Washington had moved his troops there, after a rough winter encampment in Morristown, in anticipation of heading off an expected British attack on the new capital at Philadelphia. The British, with 11,000 well-trained troops, were harassed so badly by parties of armed farmers on horseback, that it took them two days to get 3 miles beyond Somerset Court House.

Unable to lure Washington out of his strong entrenchments, and battered by Morgan's riflemen and the patriot farmers, Howe finally had to give up his march toward the Delaware and the capture of Philadelphia. So on June 19, he began his return to New Brunswick, then Perth Amboy, and finally he ferried his embarrassed command back to Staten Island - his plans for an attack across the Delaware on the rebel capital having been foiled.

Again in June, on the 17th in 1778, after having taken Philadelphia the previous fall in an attack by sea, the British burned its shipyards, and under cover of darkness ferried its troops across to the Jersey shore.

The new British commander, Gen. Henry Clinton, had orders to evacuate the city and get his army back to New York. The plan now was to hold New York City as a base of operations while concentrating on the conquest of the South, Morgan's Riflemen and Warren County's Gen. William Maxwell and his brigade, had the job of sniping the British flanks. Cadwalader's Pennsylvanians were to harass their rear. By the time they reached Monmouth Courthouse (Freehold), they were softened for the attack. On June 28, 1778, Washington ordered an attack, which began the longest, hottest, and most controversial battle of the war - the Battle of Monmouth. The British were routed after Washington reversed an uncalled for retreat by Gen. Charles Lee.

In June of 1780, news was received of the British defeat of Gen. Lincoln's Continentals at Charleston, SC. The British under Knyphausen at Staten Island decided to end the war by taking Washington's Headquarters at Morristown. Enraged local farmers routed him with the support of Maxwell's regulars at the Battle of Connecticut Farms. Clinton, hoping to reverse this humiliation, on June 23, led another invasion which was stopped at the Battle of Springfield. It was to be their last incursion along the trails of New Jersey. And it was June.

The Crisis

On this dreary November day as I sit here beside my window to write today's column, my mind drifts back to similar November days in New Jersey over 200 years ago. With Washington in the midst of his bitter retreat across the state, the cause of Independence, which had risen to such dizzy heights just the summer before, was now at the lowest ebb it would reach throughout the entire conflict. In a moment of weakness, Washington spoke sourly of the "infamous conduct of the Jerseys" during this trying period.

Writing to his brother back in Virginia, a despondent Washington had "guessed that the game was pretty nearly up." Thomas Paine, who had done so much to stir the patriot fervor with his booklet "Common Sense," was now in the midst of writing another. This one was entitled "The Crisis." While sitting at various campfires with Washington's army in its flight across New Jersey,

Paine penned his immortal words. "These are the times," he said in his opening remarks, "that try men's souls."

Though much of Jersey had risen that July of 1776, the four disastrous months since August had brought a turn about in its fervor for liberty. Long Island had fallen first. Then followed the loss of Manhattan, the defeat at Fort Washington and the near escape of Nathaniel Greene's forces at Fort Lee across the Hudson in New Jersey. With Fort Lee's fall, there was irreparable loss of its great stores of artillery and other much-needed supplies. The British onslaught toward the rebel capital at Philadelphia was next. It was this humiliating chase of the patriot army across New Jersey that really frightened her citizens, and thus created the panic to sign those British loyalty oaths.

Washington's small remaining army united with Greene's on the other side of the Hackensack River at the village that bore its name. The weather was typical of November. The loss of needed supplies and equipment as a result of their hasty evacuation was sorely missed. Cornwallis kept up the pursuit. Washington's attempt to use the Passaic River at Newark for a stand failed. He withdrew his troops from Elizabethtown and Perth Amboy as well as in his flight southwestward. Panic spread among the people, many of whom hastened now to sign the British oaths of allegiance. Even the state government fled from Princeton, to Trenton, to Burlington, and finally broke up. Its key figures went into hiding to escape capture and possible execution.

A similar stand at the Raritan River was equally impossible. After destroying more of his much needed supplies, Washington abandoned New Brunswick as well. With enlistments running out, desertions mounting, clothing ragged, and food practically non-existent, Washington's little army, and with it the cause of Independence, was all but destroyed.

Fortunately, an act of Divine Providence saved the day. Howe sent word to Cornwallis to halt his pursuit so that he could catch up. Washington had thus found, once again, the needed time to make his escape secure.

Moving on to Trenton, the Commander of the American Revolt had enough boats gathered up to take most of his men across the Delaware to Pennsylvania. He then returned to the area around

Princeton, where, with a small detachment he had left behind, he delayed the British advances further by felling trees on the main highway. He dispatched the Hunterdon Militia up and down the river for miles to round up any boats that the British might use to cross it. He then left Trenton just as the British moved in!

When Cornwallis searched the Delaware for boats to pursue the Americans, he could find not one. He occupied Pennington and Bordentown and Burlington as well as Trenton. Howe, who had caught up, gave orders to his troops to prepare for winter quarters. He himself went back to the comforts of New York. Cornwallis made preparations to visit his sick wife back in England. Disease, discomfort, and despair seemed destined to destroy the small rebel army on the west side of the Delaware without anymore help from the British.

Towns and villages through which the British passed that dreary November, as well as lonely farmhouses on the outskirts, felt the plundering and looting - whether they had signed the loyalty oaths or not. Hopewell and Lawrenceville (then called Maidenhead) were especially poorly treated. Princeton was sacked. Throughout the state, Tory bands victimized known patriot farmers. The reaction was swift. Patriot bands began reorganizing out of Morristown to attack Loyalist farms and British outposts. British messengers and patrols had increasing difficulty in getting through. Thus the tide was turning once again along the trails of New Jersey as November gave way to December more than 200 years ago.

New Jersey's Northwestern Frontier

While in retreat across New Jersey in November of 1776, Washington sent a constant stream of orders to Charles Lee to move his troops out of White Plains, NY into New Jersey to join forces with him in a desperate attempt to save their sinking cause.

As time elapsed, he became mystified as to Lee's whereabouts. By early December of 1776, the American commander had been forced to retreat across the Delaware into Pennsylvania. Lee still had not arrived. Washington hoped to gain time and the

355

reinforcements necessary to regroup and reactivate the collapsing Revolution.

The former British officer, Charles Lee, who had been commissioned by Congress as a major general, was still expected to arrive momentarily with the 5,000 troops under his commend. But Lee, who treated Washington with disdain, dragged his feet. He chose a route that took him through Morristown, and then crossing the mountainous terrain of Morris, Hunterdon and Warren (then Sussex) counties, would bring him to the Delaware at Easton. He would then turn south and join up with Washington.

On the night of December 12, he stayed at Mrs. White's tavern in Basking Ridge, while his troops were scattered around the neighboring countryside. About 10 o'clock the next morning, he was aroused by the cries of one of his sentries. A force of British cavalry was approaching. Lee was captured!

A fighting Irishman, Gen. John Sullivan from New Hampshire, quickly took command of Lee's remaining, scattered troops and marched them westward into Warren (then part of Sussex) County. Arriving opposite Easton, he turned south along the river. He joined forces with Washington on December 20. He was, however, 3,000 short of the 5,000 men Washington was expecting.

Another army under Gen. Horatio Gates, who had also received urgent orders from Washington, had moved south from their headquarters at Ft. Ticonderoga in upstate New York. They arrived about the same time. His 6,000 troops were also disappointingly small.

Gates had come down from that northern outpost via the "Old Mine Road." Along the way, he had stayed at VanCampen's Inn while his troops encamped nearby.

Other than activities of the local militia, the movement of these two armies was the first outward signs of the American Revolution witnessed by the people of what is now Warren and Sussex counties, since the opening shot was fired in April of 1775.

The back route was to be used often to avoid British scrutiny of their movements. Local legend has it that Washington himself came through the area on his way to West Point in November of 1779.

Just as the French had earlier stirred the Indians against the then English-controlled settlers, so during the Revolution the English used the same tactic. The British frontier commander stationed at Ft. Detroit, Col. Henry "Hair Buyer" Hamilton, gained notoriety by offering a reward to any Indian on the frontier who delivered an American scalp to him.

The Indians throughout New York and Pennsylvania were in such a state of agitation because of his instigating, that pioneer farmers in New Jersey's present-day Warren and Sussex counties were once again subjected to sporadic Indian attacks.

The chief culprit in this area was a half-breed named Chief Joseph Brant. At first, Washington, in 1778, sent the dashing Polish volunteer, Gen. Casimir Pulaski, with his cavalry unit to protect the settlers. Pulaski is also believed to have spent some time at VanCampen's Inn during the three months he served in the area. When he finally withdrew, claiming inaction, Brant's raids in Pennsylvania's Wyoming Valley, New York's Mohawk Valley and the New Jersey frontier mounted. The pressure was increased for Washington to do something.

He finally offered command of an expedition against the Indians to Gen. Horatio Gates. Gates, however, declined on the basis of age (he was then 50), and poor health (his rheumatics were acting up). The fiery Gen. John Sullivan (then 38) was delighted to accept the assignment.

A number of places in both nearby Pennsylvania (Sullivan's Trail) and New York (Sullivan County) now bear his name. Sullivan carried out his orders with his usual gusto. A slaughter of the Indians then living in the Wyoming and Mohawk Valleys totally destroyed some 40 of their villages.

The savagery that ensued on both sides was unbelievable. A Lt. William Barton of the 1st NJ Regiment described the skinning of two Indians "from their hips down" in order to make "boot legs" for himself and his captain. Another American Lieutenant, leading a detachment of ambushed soldiers, had his head cut off.

In retaliation, that same Indian band was chased, "tomahawked, scalped, and butchered." Within the year, however, peace reigned once again on the trails of New Jersey's northwestern frontier.

357

Henry F. Skirbst

Ten Crucial Days

In the period between Christmas 1776 and New Year of 1777, George Washington was participating in what has since come to be known as "the Ten Crucial Days" of the American Revolution. And you guessed it; New Jersey played a key role.

Let us look at some of the incidents that took place here during that critical time so long ago. Washington's little army of half-starved, poorly clothed and sparsely equipped troops really deserve our undying gratitude. It is hard for today's Americans to begin to imagine how anyone could have endured such hardships. Not only did this rag-tag little army continue to fight after retreating across New Jersey to Pennsylvania, but also went on to achieve important victories once back on New Jersey's soil. These victories were to become turning points of the struggle.

It was truly a time that was "to try men's souls." And, as people have done so down through the ages in the approaching days of a New Year, a review of the past, and an assessment of the prospects for the future was being made. If the New Year of 1777 was not to see the American hopes for independence completely shattered. Washington would have to come up with a strategy for victory, and soon.

To add to his woes, enlistments were running out and rumors were running rampant concerning his ability to command. The events about to take place in New Jersey during the last days of 1776, and the beginning of 1777, were to clinch both Washington's right to command, and the nation's confidence in its ability to achieve independence.

Washington had decided that his prime responsibility at this point was to protect the young nation's capital, Philadelphia, from British advances. His first act upon crossing the Delaware River into Pennsylvania, therefore, was to order the confiscation of all boats along that river, both north and south of Trenton. In addition, all ferries and fords were reinforced with special guards and artillery units hopefully to prevent his being out-flanked.

Coryell's Ferry (Lambertville) was of special concern both because his main encampment was located just north of there, and because his spies had warned that the British under Cornwallis were headed in that direction. He thus sent the Hunterdon County Militia to collect all boats on the Upper Delaware and Lehigh rivers. This move was designed to both provide his own troops with transportation back to Jersey, and to deny their use to the British.

Washington's denial of the British crossing led to their setting up Winter Headquarters along the Jersey side of the Delaware from Burlington to Trenton. To make matters worse, Gen. Charles Lee, who coveted Washington's command, was captured by the British while under orders to move his troops across New Jersey in an attempt to reinforce Washington.

In view of his questionable loyalty to the commander, however, this turned out to be a fortunate bit of ill luck. A much more dependable man, Gen. John Sullivan, assumed his command, and led some 2,000 veteran troops to Easton, PA. From there they began their march down the Delaware, joining Washington outside of Trenton.

In order to deceive any British spies, who might be watching his movements prior to his planned Christmas Day crossing, Washington had been drilling his troops daily, fully equipped for a three-day engagement.

Then, at about 4 p.m. on, the appointed day, instead of dismissing the units as usual, he marched them to the embarkation point at McKonkey's Ferry. Using the Durham boats the Hunterdon Militia had rounded up, he began crossing.

Assembling on the Jersey side in the midst of a bitter storm, they then divided and took different routes south to Trenton. One American unit mistakenly engaged a unit of the British Army in a skirmish at about 8 o'clock that evening. Having taken place before the appointed time, much to Washington's annoyance, this action served to warn the enemy of their presence. As it turned out however, the Hessians assumed that this was the much-heralded attack that they had been warned. So after repulsing it, they relaxed their alerts.

As a result, what appeared to have been a bad stroke of luck actually helped ensure the American victory on the morning of Dec. 26, 1776. A young officer who was seriously wounded at the Battle of Trenton, near what is now the Battle Monument, later was to become the nation's fifth President. His name was Lt. James Monroe. Just another interesting tale along the trails of New Jersey.

Second Battle of Trenton

The year 1777 started out on an upbeat note in New Jersey for the patriots of the American Revolution.

The demoralizing rout across the state that had ended 1776 was definitely behind them. The British army in New Jersey was, without a doubt, now on the defensive.

When those cavalry units that fled Trenton arrived in Princeton with the news of the American victory, the British commander there, Gen. Alexander Leslie, felt a sudden weakness in his legs. They were so certain of taking the state, capturing Washington in the spring, and ending the whole bloody affair, that they were completely taken aback by this sudden change of events.

On New Years' Day, the British force in New Brunswick, under Maj. Gen. Sir James Grant, left only a rear guard and marched to assist Leslie at Princeton. News had reached them that Washington was planning an attack there next! Col. Karl Von Donop, of the Hessian Brigade, was ordered to move there also from Allentown, NJ. The British commander in America, Gen. Lord Cornwallis, arrived that same day from his New York City headquarters 50 miles away.

The following morning, Cornwallis moved out to head off Washington outside of Trenton, before he could move on Princeton. He was there, commanding about 8,000 troops and had 28 cannon.

By promising to guarantee them a $10 bounty, personally if necessary, Washington had gotten some 3,000 men to re-enlist for another six weeks beyond their current enlistment, which had ended on Dec. 31. Mifflin and Cadwalader, after an all-night march on Jan. 1, arrived with several thousand more men to assist. He now had some 4,200 men and 40 cannon at his disposal. His spy networks kept him well informed of what the British were about. He spent two days fortifying the east bank of the Assunpink Creek, where his men were "dug in." On Jan. 2, he sent a strong detachment ahead on the road to Princeton to meet up with Cornwallis and play a delaying game with him.

When the advance guard finally returned, they were under British fire. These British troops, however, had already "spent" themselves. They had been delayed and harassed to the point where they had been able to move only 10 miles in the past 10 hours!

The engagement that followed when the two main armies clashed came to be known as the Second Battle of Trenton. After sustaining three attacks, the British losses were reported to have been some 500 killed and wounded. American losses were reported as "small." The direct attacks at the bridge, plus one further down stream, had all been repulsed by the entrenched Americans along the Assunpink. Cornwallis decided to call it quits for the night and bag the "Old Fox" in the morning. Again he was sure he now had Washington "trapped."

That night, Washington left a small group behind to keep their campfires burning. The rest then wrapped their feet in rags to silence their movement. Anything metallic was treated in the same way. They circled the sleeping British army ahead, and marched silently past them into the night.

Washington hoped to take the British garrison at Princeton totally by surprise before daybreak, wipe them out, and go ahead to do the same at New Brunswick the next day. A British gold chest awaited them there!

The next morning Cornwallis awoke to empty trenches ahead of him, and the muffled sound of booming cannon in the distance behind. The "Old Fox" had outwitted him again! Mercer's brigade had been kept back to delay any pursuit by Cornwallis.

Suddenly, part of the force Cornwallis had left at Princeton with orders to join him in the morning appeared in view. A battle ensued in which Hugh Mercer was mortally wounded. His men panicked. Their retreat also panicked a group of Pennsylvanians led by Gen. Greene, who had come to their rescue. Hearing this, Washington came back from his forward position to rally them. He succeeded, and the British force was now sent running.

The American main army under General's St. Clair and Sullivan attacked the remaining British force at Princeton. When the British heard that the other part of their army was being routed on its way to Trenton, they too, broke ranks and fled. Some sought refuge in

Nassau Hall, where a well-placed shot from Alexander Hamilton's cannon led to an early surrender.

Some 100 British were killed and 300 prisoners taken, plus badly needed blankets, oxen, sheep, horses and two brass cannon.

Another strong British force had been defeated.

A detachment of Pennsylvanians left to guard the rear made contact with Cornwallis. Now leery of more trickery, he avoided them, giving Washington time for his escape.

Another glorious day had dawned along the trails of New Jersey that early January 1777. The future now looked bright and rosy.

The Battle of Princeton

Nothing illustrates New Jersey's key role in the outcome of the American Revolution more clearly than those 10 crucial days between Trenton and Princeton.

When word of the American victory at Trenton in Late December, 1776, reached the nearby British stronghold at Bordentown, the enemy withdrew their forces from that Delaware River station as well. These troops set up new positions further to the east—first at Crosswicks, then at Allentown, and finally reinforced their Princeton outpost.

A sort of panic that had spread throughout British helped positions in west Jersey. Their counter-spies were working overtime feverishly trying to determine where the next American, surprise attack would be felt. British intelligence reports, doctored by Washington's own system of counter-spy activity, mistakenly had Washington gathering increasing strength. Word of imminent rebel attacks began filtering in. In a maddening crescendo, the British command heard reports of possible strikes in strength by American revolutionaries anywhere from Rocky Hill, north of their Princeton force, to Mount Holly, southeast of their Delaware River stronghold at Burlington—just across the river from the American capital at Philadelphia. They broke into a state of nervous apprehension.

In the meantime Washington, who had returned to Pennsylvania with prisoners taken in the Trenton campaign, was sweating out the expiration date of large numbers of his weakened army. In order to take full advantage of this successful Trenton campaign, drive the British back all along the Delaware, and thus save the American capital at Philadelphia, he had to gamble on still another successful attack. And soon! If he failed, he could lose not only Philadelphia, but his entire main army, and with it, the cause of independence itself. He decided to risk everything in a hazardous gamble for another quick victory. His next moves could place all hopes in jeopardy. The scene for this perilous action would again be New Jersey.

The New Year, 1777, had dawned on brightened hopes for eventual triumph of the American use. He again crossed the Delaware. The ice packs made this second crossing even more difficult than the first. He hoped for a victory that would lead to the withdrawal of all British forces from west Jersey, and thus relieve the pressure of Philadelphia.

British outposts north of Lawrenceville, almost directly east of what is now Washington's Crossing, were the first to feel action. American riflemen carried on an harassment campaign. Shooting from houses and along fencerows they gradually drew the British toward Trenton. By nightfall they were wading across Assunpink Creek. Washington had a force of infantry and artillery established on the south side of this stream, between the British advance and the Delaware. Cornwallis stopped his attack, planning an assault upon the Americans in the early morning hours. Then he would pin their backs to the Delaware!

Washington, however, planed a daring night march around the British. He kept a small detachment behind to deceive Cornwallis into believing that his troops were still encamped on the south side of the Assunpink. By dawn of Jan. 3, his army was on its way to Princeton! Cornwallis' force, to his rear now, was relishing an attack on him in the other direction! Washington' spies had provided him with excellent intelligence concerning British movements. He felt confident that his plan would succeed.

After engaging various units of the British army at Princeton in intense fighting, Washington's army was able to pull off another notable victory. The British retreated to their stronghold in New Brunswick via Hillsborough. Washington himself headed up the

Millstone Valley, camping for the night at Griggstown. Cornwallis, realizing he had been tricked, now raced to New Brunswick thinking that Washington was headed there to capture a War chest full of gold—sufficient to carry on the Revolution for another year. Washington, however, took his exhausted army north via Pluckemin for a winter encampment behind the protective Watchungs in Morristown.

The British had been driven from west Jersey, and were now left holding only two remaining stronghold in the state, New Brunswick, and Perth Amboy. Philadelphia had been saved. Washington's actions that winter along the trails of New Jersey probably had a more lasting effect on the outcome of the young nation's history than any other during the war. A visit to the Princeton Battlefield site will help you relive those exciting days when New Jersey was indeed the "Crucible of the American Revolution."

Winter at Morristown

After Washington's brilliant victories at Trenton and Princeton at the end of 1776 and the beginning of 1777, the British braced for another attack. This time they were certain he would go for their store of gold at New Brunswick! As the Americans headed north on the road toward Kingston, the British pursued. Washington's rear-guard kept the enemy busy with harassment tactics while his main army, slowed as it was with prisoners and captured contraband, marched toward New Brunswick—as expected.

Washington had his men destroy the bridge when they reached Kingston to slow down the British pursuit. Then, after holding a council of war, the majority of the American officers voted to forego the New Brunswick campaign. It was agreed that the men were in no shape for another battle, particularly since Cornwallis was in hot pursuit at their rear. Instead of continuing on the road to New Brunswick, therefore, they took a left fork and headed for Morristown!

Cornwallis, in the meantime, was totally fooled once again. He continued on the road to New Brunswick, thinking the Americans were ahead of him. Worried about suffering still another defeat and losing his gold and more supplies to boot, he marched his troops throughout the night in order to get to New Brunswick by morning. When he got there, he found his garrison poised for the attack, and his stores cached safely along the banks of the Raritan. Washington, however, had eluded him. The "winter campaign" had obviously ended. He would now "settle in," and get the "Old Fox" in the spring—as originally planned.

While the British concentrated their New Jersey forces in quarters at Perth Amboy and New Brunswick for the remainder of the winter, Washington marched on to Morristown. After several nights on the road, they reached their destination on Jan. 6, 1777. Washington set up his military headquarters at Freeman's Tavern, with his immediate guard and their officers camped along nearby streets. His main army, however, encamped in the Loantaka Valley, three miles from the village. Gen. Greene, in the meantime, kept his army guarding the approaches to Morristown at Basking Ridge. The more Washington studied his position at Morristown, the better he liked it. It would be a place to which he would return many times during the course of the war, and a permanent guard would be established there.

It was a deeply devoted patriot section of the state for one thing. The topography was excellent for defending their position for another. They were near both iron works for military supplies and rich farmlands to feed the troops. They were at an excellent altitude for spying on British movements to the east. He was well placed to move an army either southwest to Philadelphia, if attacked, or to his forts on the Hudson, if need be.

Washington's biggest problem at the moment was the ever-expiring enlistments of his troops. The various states were more concerned with raising militia to defend their own turf than in supplying men for the Continental Army. Recruitment was an ever-present necessity. New Jersey's militia, which was at his disposal while in the state, was worn out from the continual engagements in which they had been involved since the British moved their headquarters from Boston to New York City. He was constantly writing Congress to press for more troops.

Aside from rowdyism produced by the boredom of camp life, Washington's main problem that first winter at Morristown was sickness. To everyone's dismay, the much-feared "smallpox" broke out in camp and soon spread to the village. Washington ordered his whole army inoculated for the first time. It was a new technique and much feared, both for the pain inflicted by the methods in use, and by the fact that it also might result in death. It eventually checked the epidemic, however, and Washington's insistence upon its use proved right in the long run.

There was another and not-often-mentioned outcome of Washington's decision to set up a permanent headquarters at Morristown. The little New Jersey community became quite the center of concentration for distinguished families of wealth from both throughout New Jersey and New York City.

They fled to it not only because they felt safe there. This enclave along the trails of New Jersey also afforded them the contact they craved with those in seats of power; not only in the blossoming new republic, but from those capitals of Europe who were lending it their support. Morristown became a center of trade, commerce, and high society partially as a result of Washington's decision that January in 1777.

Headquarters at Morristown

After his glorious victories at Trenton and Princeton, Washington took his war-weary troops up New Jersey's Millstone Valley. He was headed for Morristown in one of the most patriot-inhabited areas in New Jersey. Morris County could count among its residents probably one of the largest proportions of ardent rebels of any in the state. Washington could not only depend upon the natural protection of the mountainous terrain and the Great Swamp in his new winter headquarters, but the politics of the people as well.

In the little village of Morristown, which had about 50 houses all told at this time, Washington made his first winter quarters that January of 1777 in the Jacob Arnold Tavern, across from the county courthouse. The Baptist and Presbyterian Churches were available for use as hospitals. Not only did Washington have the comfort of knowing that he was among people who supported the American cause, and in a natural protective setting, but he was ensconced among vital war provisions as well.

Nearby was Ford's Mill, where rebel gunpowder was made. The village itself contained a large cache of patriot war supplies. He was also in the heart of the iron country with forges that were supplying cannon ball and other necessities for the American revolutionary army. Needed foodstuffs and iron, both ore and bars, were constantly being transported to Morristown overland through the rugged terrain from as far away as the Warren and Sussex hills (which were then all part of Sussex County).

So favorable were the conditions there that Morristown was to become Washington's military capital throughout the remainder of the Revolution. Though officers and special honor detachments were housed nearby, the main part of Washington's Continental Army that first winter were encamped about 2-1/2 miles to the south and east of Morristown in the Loantaka Valley. Huts for the soldiers were built there, as they were to be later at Jockey Hollow. Nearby farmers were also more than willing to sell food to the troops. Unfortunately, that plague of the 18th century, smallpox, raised its ugly head that winter and soon was found in epidemic proportions among the troops. The arrival of that dreaded disease had spread terror among populations for some three centuries, and Morristown was no exception. Washington had to take desperate measures. He therefore instituted the first mass inoculation of a full army. Though the soldiers feared this solution, Washington refused to back down.

In spite of these problems, Washington sent for his wife, Martha, to come up from Virginia and be with him at Morristown, along with the wives of other officers. Washington soon captured their hearts by his way with ladies. Riding parties, dances, and dinners helped take the rough edges off the harsh winter weather as well as the problems of the war.

But Washington was a stickler for observing routine military detail. Assemblies, drills, and marches on the parade ground continued daily. An elaborate system of signal stations was also instituted in the wooded hills surrounding the headquarters and far back into the north and west, and into the hills and villages to the south and east. Washington worried constantly about a surprise British attack. Both the Morris County militia and various local patriot groups kept an ever-watchful eye out for any signs of an approaching enemy.

It was at Morristown that winter that many patriot Germans living in the surrounding iron hills of Morris, and the nearby Somerset hills of what was then called German Valley, found justifiable pride. They witnessed the arrival of their beloved former Lutheran pastor, the Rev. John Peter Muhlenburg, in the uniform of a brigadier general. Many Germans were embarrassed that the Hessians were aiding the British. Muhlenburg's arrival with the command of a regiment that he had organized in Virginia of patriot Germans from the Shenandoah Valley gave them cause to hold their heads high once again.

Several other dashing new officers, aside from Muhlenburg, joined Washington's army that winter at Morristown. Pennsylvania was also justifiably proud of its spirited Gen. "Mad Anthony" Wayne. He arrived with a regiment of lusty backwoods Pennsylvanians, which he also raised himself and put into topnotch fighting shape.

Another lively addition was Col. Dan Morgan. He arrived with two regiments of Virginia sharpshooters, whose accounts were soon to become legendary. Morgan is believed to have been born in New Jersey's Hunterdon County, where the family lived before migrating to Virginia.

The trails of New Jersey were busting at the seams with a new spirit of revolutionary vitality as it waited out that winter of 1777 in those zealously patriotic hills of Morris County.

Rallying the Troops

Washington lost his cool, Lee was suspended from the Army, and Lafayette marveled at how superbly the American commander regained his self-control and rallied his confused troops to a victory in what turned out to be the longest battle of the Revolution. And it happened right here in New Jersey

The heart of the Monmouth Battlefield now lies within some 1,000 acres of a state park, which is closer to its exact appearance during the time of the Revolution than any other Revolutionary battlefield site. Its fields and orchards are right out of the scene in

1778 when George Washington, while riding down the Englishtown Road, was startled to find the American forces under the command of Gen. Charles Lee in a full panicky retreat.

Entitled "Washington Rallying the Troops at Monmouth," this famous painting by Emanuel Leutze now adorning the Visitor's Center at the Monmouth Battlefield State Park in Freehold exemplifies the role the American commander-in-chief played so often during the course of the War for Independence.

After the fall of Philadelphia, the nation's capital, in the early autumn of 1777, Washington tried unsuccessfully to retake it. Failing that, he retreated to winter quarters at nearby Valley Forge on the Schuylkill River to await spring. In the meantime, France recognized our independence in February of 1778 and promised military intervention. Britain, fearing a French attack on divided English troops, decided to give up Philadelphia voluntarily and move its army back to its main base in New York before the French arrived.

When Washington's spies related this intelligence, he made preparations to attack the Philadelphia force before it could reunite with the army in New York. And where would this battle take place? You guessed it. The cream of both the British and American armies were destined to clash right here in New Jersey. It would be a drama not to be exceeded anywhere in the Revolution.

Clinton, the British leader, finally crossed the Delaware into New Jersey at Gloucester on June 18, 1778, more than a month after he arrived in Philadelphia to replace Howe. Brig. Gen. William Maxwell of Greenwich Township was ordered by Washington, still at Valley Forge, to take his New Jersey Brigade of Continentals and harass the British on their march through New Jersey. Brig. Gen. Philemon Dickinson was sent with his New Jersey militia to assist Maxwell. The British force of 15,000 rested first at Haddonfield and then headed towards New York, planning to travel via Mount Holly, Allentown, and New Brunswick. Gen. Benedict Arnold assumed command of Philadelphia the day after the British moved out.

By June 21, Washington and his main army had crossed the Delaware at what is now Lambertville. He was marching through New Jersey parallel to, and some 30 miles north of, the British force. Once the British army left Haddonfield they were constantly molested by not only Maxwell and Dickinson, but by Daniel Morgan and his famed riflemen as well. Roads were blocked by felled trees, bridges were destroyed, and Morgan's riflemen kept up a constant sniping at both marching columns and resting bivouacs. By June 26, through scorching sun, drenching downpours, and constant harassment, the wilted British army had only gotten 60 miles. Switching their original route eastward, they arrived at Monmouth Courthouse (now Freehold).

In the meantime, Washington's cocky army of 11,000 was well uniformed and fresh from Von Steuben's stiff military training at Valley Forge. It was the best force fielded by the Americans to date. At Hopewell, he had stopped for a Council of War. He offered two alternatives - either force Clinton into open battle, and, possibly with an American victory, end the war, or keep wearing him down all the way to the coast. General Green, Wayne, and Lafayette led the group in favor of taking the initiative. Gen. Charles Lee was violently opposed. His will moved the majority, impressed by his previous military experience.

Washington was disappointed with Lee's stand. Contrary to the decision reached, he decided to lead his main army into a position to block the British advance, which was still aimed toward New Brunswick and finally Amboy on the coast. Sending Maxwell and Morgan to continue their harassment, Washington headed for Kingston. Lafayette led an advance guard on to Cranbury. Clinton, having received intelligence of Washington's move, decided to change his route to Monmouth and Middletown. Washington attempted to head them off at Hightstown, but was stalled by a fierce cloudburst. The British made it to Monmouth Courthouse unscathed. Washington then took off for Englishtown with Lafayette's force to his south.

The stage was now set for the longest and most dramatic battle of the Revolution - the Battle of Monmouth. But time and space will force that tale to await another week.

The Battle of Monmouth

The Battle of Monmouth Courthouse was replete with the vicissitudes of war. From dishonor to heroism, it saw the extremes.

On June 30, 1778, Maj. Gen. Charles Lee was put under arrest. On July 1, Gen. George Washington ordered his court-martial. On July 4, he was charged on three counts. The first was disobedience of orders in not attacking the enemy at the Battle of Monmouth on June 28. The second count was misbehavior before the enemy on the same day by making an unnecessary, disorderly and shameful retreat. The third was for disrespect shown to the Commander in Chief. On August 12, he was found guilty of all three counts and suspended from any command for one year. Lee never again saw service, and died on his farm in dishonor on October 2, 1782.

During that same battle, while the meadows of New Jersey's Monmouth Battlefield were steaming with heat on that late June day in 1778, and the American troops were withering in anguish, the other extreme was being acted out by a young woman called Molly. As cannon roared and muskets cracked, she was busily hauling water to relieve the parched throats of those fainting men. Various eyewitness accounts have come down to us concerning the actions of this brave woman during the cannonading the troops were both giving and receiving on that sweltering day. One common thread running through them all, however, was that this Jersey battle did indeed give birth to a new national folk heroine, Molly Pitcher.

One private's diary, that has enlightened us on many aspects of the American Revolution from the eyes of an enlisted man, was that of Joseph Plumb Martin of the 8th Connecticut Regiment. Martin in his account also told of another incident involving Molly. While she was aiding her husband at his cannon, she stretched her legs to hand him a cartridge. At that very moment, an enemy artillery shell passed between them, severing the entire lower part of her petticoat. Molly coolly went about her job.

There is some disagreement as to Molly's origin. One story states that she met and married John Hays in Carlisle, PA where she had gone to be employed as a servant girl when she was 15. During the Revolution, her husband enlisted in the 1st Pennsylvania Regiment of Artillery and eventually ended up manning an artillery piece at the Battle of Monmouth. Most accounts say that Molly was born Mary Ludwig on October 13, 1754, on a farm outside of Allentown, NJ. While her husband was on duty, Molly went back to visit her parent's farm. This explains her presence at the Monmouth Battlefield. He came through Allentown in pursuit of the British and Molly joined him, a practice not uncommon in those days.

Because of the unusually hot and humid weather Jersey was experiencing in June of 1778, more men on both sides were collapsing of heat stroke than bullet wounds at the Battle of Monmouth. When Molly's own husband fell from his post as a cannoneer, he had been overcome by heat exhaustion. Molly is said to have manned his cannon at that point and kept it in service until relieved. But it was for her role while under fire in saving many an American soldier from death by dehydration that Molly became a true heroine.

Another uncertainty surrounding this story was where Molly was getting the water. Based upon the fact that eyewitness accounts that told of Molly's deeds were from outfits under Maj. Gen. William Alexander's command, there are a number of possibilities. McGelliard's Brook, Weamaconk Creek, and a well near an 18th century farmhouse were all nearby that battle hill commanded by Alexander. Some say the well, which is still in use, was the most logical location. So Molly's Well had for years been marked as an historic site.

When Molly died in 1833 at the age of 79, she was a widow named Molly McCauly. She, by then, had buried two husbands. Her second also lived in Carlisle. A foster son, Wesley Miles, finally arranged for a monument to be erected at her grave by the citizens of Cumberland County as part of the nation's Centennial Celebration on July 4, 1876. The monument is inscribed, "Molly McCauly Renowned in History as Molly Pitcher, The Heroine of Monmouth."

In Freehold today you may want to visit the County Historical Museum on Court Street and the Battle Monument on the Green opposite it. On the West Main Street is the restored Gen. Clinton's Headquarters, as well as St. Peter's Church, which served as a temporary hospital. At the Monmouth Battlefield State Park, in addition to the Visitor's Center, there is the Craig House, which stood near the center of the battle, and a plaque identifying Molly Pitcher's Spring. The Tennent Church, which also served as a temporary hospital, is nearby. In Englishtown is the Village Inn where Washington is believed to have first convened the court-martial of Gen. Lee. A tour of the area will help you recapture these days.

Winter Trials

During the comparatively quiet winter of 1778-79, George Washington made his headquarters at the home of John Wallace, while his troops were encamped in the hills around Middle Brook. It was a fun time for the general and his staff, and many parties were held at the Wallace House in Somerville. Even his wife, Martha, came up from Virginia. Now a state historic site, it is worth visiting this place to absorb some of the 18th century Americana so prevalent along the trails of New Jersey.

With the coming of spring and summer in 1779, New Jersey remained unusually quiet. So Washington and one of his aides, Maj. Henry "Lighthorse Harry" Lee, used the time to plan for ousting the British from Paulus Hook (Jersey City). Since Paulus Hook served so often as a jumping off point for British marauders who plagued the Jersey countryside, it seemed like a good time to eliminate that thorn in their side.

The original plan envisioned an attack from troops based in Newark. Instead, a more unexpected route was conceived. On the afternoon of August 18, 1779, Lee moved his troops from their encampment near Paramus to a position at New Bridge. After a miserable march across marshes in waist-deep water, the surprise attack on the British force at Paulus Hook was launched in the pre-dawn hours of August 19.

Approaches to the British position were well protected. Three sides faced water while the fourth looked out onto a salt marsh. The attack was, therefore, a complete shock and 159 British prisoners were taken. But Lee failed to complete his mission by destroying the fortification and making off with its supplies. Because he also did not rendezvous when scheduled on the Hackensack River, the boats awaiting him there were gone. As a result, his men were faced with another exhausting march across the marshlands.

Because of these apparent errors in judgment, Lee faced a court martial. He was exonerated, however, and later praised instead by Congress. On September 24, 1779, Congress paid tribute to Lee's attack on Paulus Hook with these words, "Notwithstanding rivers and entrenchment's, he, with a small band conquered the foe by warlike skill and prowess, and firmly bound by humanity those who had been conquered by his arms."

As winter again approached, Washington moved his headquarters back to the hills of Morristown. This time he stayed at the home of the late Col. Ford, while his army encamped at Jockey Hollow near Loantaka Brook, a tributary of the Passaic River. It was to be one of the fiercest winters of the century. Snowstorm followed snowstorm beginning in early December and lasting well into March.

Much has been written about the suffering at Valley Forge. Much more could be written about the afflictions endured at Jockey Hollow. Furious winds, bitter cold, lack in supplies of food and clothing and, until huts could be built, living in tents, made life almost impossible for Washington's half-starving troops. As in all of history, only that which is made public receives its mark in the history books. Valley Forge seems to have had a better "Public Relations" team.

In writing his diary concerning those months of privation, Private Joseph Martin wrote, "I did not put a single morsel of victuals in my mouth for four days and as many nights." He also noted of his winter outside of Morristown that "I saw several men roast their shoes and eat them." Dr. James Thatcher, a surgeon in Washington's army, wrote of this winter that it "is the most severe and distressing which we have ever experienced...Our soldiers are in wretched condition for the want of clothes, blankets and shoes...accompanied by a want of provisions."

With the news reaching him by spring of the mutinous discontent running rampant at Morristown, the Hessian commander of British troops at Staten Island decided that this certainly sounded like a good time to move out and capture the troublesome rebel outpost with its stores of supplies. And so it was that on the night of June 6, 1780, some 5,000 British troops moved from Staten Island to Elizabethtown.

Burning buildings and farms along the way, they marched to Connecticut Farms (now Union). From there, they would take the road to Springfield, which was the outpost guarding Morristown. At Connecticut Farms the wanton "murder" of Johanna Caldwell, wife of the Rev. James Caldwell, while she sat in the parsonage, so aroused the countryside that it became a virtual "hornets nest" of militia. It was such an enraged atmosphere that the British troops were repulsed and turned back at the Battle of Connecticut Farms, along the trails of New Jersey.

Colorful Characters

In June of 1780, as the result of a double invasion by the main British army in America, New Jersey was again to be the scene of an American victory that boosted patriot spirits and crushed British hopes for a much needed victory in the north. Washington could not speak highly enough of the valiant role, played by the Jersey militia in that decisive campaign. A Massachusetts artillery officer hailed it as another "Battle of Lexington." Sir Henry Clinton, remembering a year later how Jersey's amateur soldiers stood up to his powerful regulars, rejected the idea of tackling them again. As a result, an attempt to stop Washington as he rushed through New Jersey on his way to engage Cornwallis - in what was to be the decisive Battle of Yorktown - was overridden.

The roll call of colorful characters surrounding New Jersey's decisive Battle of Springfield was seemingly endless, but it is necessary, at least partially, to relate these names in order to appreciate the story of that engagement. Surrounding it all, of course, was that mysterious element of leadership provided by the central figure of the American Revolution himself, George Washington. His cool countenance seemed time and time again to rescue the wavering spirits of the patriots at crucial moments.

Then there was Washington's opposite, the overly suspicious and dangerously secretive British commander-in-chief in America, Sir Henry Clinton. His inability to confide in his subordinates probably cost Britain the war. The second highest British officer in New York was Maj. Gen. William Tyron, who was not at all fond of his commander. Backing him up was Maj. Gen. James Robertson, who openly detested Clinton. Clinton's second in command, and the acting commander in New York during his brief absence in Carolina at the outset of the Jersey campaign, was the professional Hessian soldier hired by the British, Lt. Gen. Baron Wilhelm von Knyphausen. His inability to speak a word of English not only hampered his usefulness,

375

but added to the confusion that surrounded both the Battle of Springfield and its prologue, the Battle of Connecticut Farms.

Lurking in the dark shadows of Morristown, the American military capital during that period in 1780, was the mysterious "Mr. Moore." Morristown was the main objective of the British invasions that brought on the Battle of Springfield. "Mr. Moore" was better known to Maj. John Andre, then the head of British intelligence in America, as Maj. Gen. Benedict Arnold. "Mr. Moore" was busily trying to wrangle a field command out of the unsuspecting Washington. At the same time, he was feeding the British information as to the condition of the American forces in Morristown.

Then there was Benjamin Franklin's ardent loyalist son, William. A former popular British governor of New Jersey, William Franklin was determined to play a key role in rallying the state's substantial number of loyalists into a British citizen's army. His hope was to make the state the first northern colony to return to the arms of the British crown. He too lost face after the catastrophes at Connecticut Farms and Springfield.

On the scene was that cool and competent native of Rhode Island, Gen. Nathaniel Greene. The veteran Greene, though given complete charge for the first time, handled his regulars with brilliant poise. And leading Jersey's own regulars, the New Jersey Continentals, was the man rumored to be the toughest, hardest drinking army commander Washington had, Warren County's own Gen. William "Scotch Willie" Maxwell. The troops loved to fight under his command.

The most colorful participant in the Battle of Springfield was not in the military. He was the man the British called "The High Priest of the Rebels." The patriots knew him as "The Fighting Parson." The Rev. James Caldwell, pastor of Elizabethtown's Presbyterian Church, went down in history, as the folk hero of the Battle of Springfield. As he rode up and down the battlefield, Caldwell roared, "Give 'em Watts, boys," while flinging hymnals retrieved from the Springfield Presbyterian Church at the waiting infantrymen. The paper from the songbooks was used to cram down the barrels of their weapons for wadding.

Because of his ardent patriotism, Caldwell was wanted by the British. As a result, he had his family moved to the parsonage at the

Connecticut Farms Presbyterian Church in what is now Union. During the battle there, a British soldier shot his wife, Hannah, who was a patriot in her own right, while she was shielding her children in a back room of their house. Her death aroused the citizen-soldiers of the area to a fever pitch, and may have been part of the reason for their excellent performance. The Caldwell House is only one of the many historic sites in the area. An account of the battle itself will have to await another time.

Battle of Connecticut Farms

Under cover of darkness, the first of what would be two invading armies crept ashore at Elizabethtown Point from Staten Island on the night of June 6, 1780. The objective would be the capture of Washington's main army and commissary at Morristown, then the military capital of the Revolution. The battle that followed the first invasion was at Connecticut Farms (now Union). The second invasion came on June 23. The entire campaign would go down in history as the Battle of Springfield, one of the turning points of the American Revolution, and the last major attempt of the British to defeat the rebels in the north.

Washington had moved his military headquarters back to Morristown in December of 1779. There the troops endured the worst winter of the century. Incredible snowstorms and severe temperatures, coupled with an inability to provide sufficient food and clothing, led to a flood of desertions. Both the Hudson River and Long Island Sound had frozen over for several weeks. The Raritan River was frozen for at least several months. In the spring, just after suffering from three full days without food, two regiments of the Connecticut Continentals mutinied. Rumors of the deplorable condition of Washington's army made recruiting next to impossible. His hopes of raising an army of 25,000 men to join forces with their new allies, the French, to defeat the British in the south were all but shattered.

In the meantime, British armies had captured Savannah in Georgia, and Gen. Clinton decided to lead part of his main army form New York south to take the port city of Charleston as well. It was during Clinton's absence that his subordinates, Major Generals James

Henry F. Skirbst

Robertson and William Tyron, decided to capture some glory for themselves and embarrass Clinton, whom they detested, by defeating Washington at Morristown and ending the war on their own. Clinton, however, had left the Hessian officer, Lt. Gen. Baron von Knyphausen, in command of his New York garrison and as usual left no hint of his future plans. To bring their plot to fruition it would be necessary to convince von Knyphausen, who spoke no English, that it was vital to attack Washington immediately.

To add fuel to the fires of mischief surrounding Clinton, Benjamin Franklin's son, William, was vehemently promoting the idea that New Jersey's loyalists were on the rise. He was certain, he said, that they needed only the presence of the British army in New Jersey to encourage them to seize control. Robertson and Tyron kept feeding this kind of date to von Knyphausen, who insisted that leading an invasion without Clinton would be exceeding the bounds of his temporary command. Compounding the pressure on the Hessian officer, however, was word from a "Mr. Moore," one of the pseudonyms used by Gen. Benedict Arnold, that a blow struck at Washington now might well end the war. Knyphausen finally acceded to these varying pressures, and on the night of June 6, led his army of 6,000 troops, aboard a 60-boat fleet for the invasion of New Jersey.

When sight of the invasion was spotted, fire signals and alarm guns atop South Mountain in the Oranges sent the signal that had been pre-planned for such an attack. Two regiments of the Jersey Brigade, under the command of Warren County's Gen. William "Scotch Willie" Maxwell, raced from their campsites at Camptown (now Irvington) and Elizabethtown to block the advance. Jersey militiamen raced from their farms throughout the countryside. The combined British-Hessian army on the march to Morristown found itself at Vauxhall (now Union) fighting off assaults from all sides. Farmers took shots from their houses and barns. Militia fired at them, Indian style, from behind trees and fence rows. Maxwell's Brigade of regulars had never seen such magnificent local support as they fought to stem the advance, and give Washington time to block the road to Morristown by Short Hills.

Where were Franklin's loyalists? What had happened to those half-starved disgruntled, rebellious regulars "Mr. Moore" spoke of? The brunt of the battle was to settle in at the little village of

378

Connecticut Farms. Knyphausen was determined to throw up fortifications within the village that night and resume fighting in the morning. Washington decided on a midnight surprise assault. In the meantime, word reached the Hessian that Clinton was on his way back from Charleston, and was planning an invasion of New Jersey and an assault on Morristown. With that stunning information, he decided on a fast retreat back to Staten Island where he would await Clinton's arrival. To keep the Americans busy while he escaped; he set fire to the little village. Thus ended the Battle of Connecticut Farms, prelude to the main Battle of Springfield. In addition to the Caldwell House you might want to visit the graveyard of the Connecticut Farms Presbyterian Church where Hessian and patriot soldiers lay side by side in Jersey's battle-scarred soil.

Battle of Springfield

After their defeat at the Battle of Connecticut Farms (now Union), the British lay in wait at Staten Island, licking their wounds. On June 23, 1780, having learned that Washington had taken his main army north to defend a probable attack on West Point, the British moved on Morristown again. This time Gen. Nathaniel Greene was in charge of the American defense force at Springfield.

The alarm guns sounded at 6 a.m. Warren County's own senior officer, Gen. William "Scotch Wille" Maxwell, led the advance attack. Maxwell's Brigade, assisted by local militiamen, were out on patrol, and became the first to spot and engage the enemy as it moved toward Springfield. Though outnumbered 4 to 1, Gen. Maxwell's troops stubbornly held the enemy back. Then, retreating slowly to high ground outside of the village, he was able to hang in there until reinforced by Gen. Stark's Brigade.

It was during the fierce fighting at the Battle of Springfield that the "Fighting Parson," the Rev. James Caldwell, gained his fame as a national hero. As the patriots exhausted their supplies of paper wadding for packing the cannon, Caldwell stepped into the fray. Dashing in and out of the nearby Springfield Presbyterian Church, he grabbed handfuls of Watt's hymnals. He repeatedly returned to the men on the firing lines in the heat of battle with the admonition,

"Give 'em Watts, boys!" This daring act, at risk of his own life, enabled the patriots to keep up a steady bombardment of the enemy, and gained the Parson the endearment of the American troops.

The Battle of Springfield cost both sides dearly. Though the British advance on Morristown was halted once again by the brave defense of the outnumbered patriots, they did not leave the village without first inflicting great devastation. The Springfield church and more than several dozen homes and other buildings were set afire. With most of the town's citizens now homeless, one can appreciate the emptiness with which the victorious local militia returned to their families. By nightfall, the British troops retreated back to Elizabethtown. The next day they had returned to their headquarters on Staten Island. Though they had not gained their objective - Morristown - they had made its defenders pay an awful price!

I might mention here that Warren County's contribution to Washington's Army of the Revolution, Gen. William Maxwell, of Greenwich, had first appeared as a representative of New Jersey's military officers in the war as a colonel participating in the Battle of Quebec. Among other engagements where he appears as a noted participant are such Jersey actions as those at Amboy, Westfield, and Metuchen, the pursuit of Clinton across New Jersey, and the Battles of Monmouth and Connecticut Farms. He had moved to the defense of Connecticut Farms when aroused by "Old Snow" while at an outpost in Camptown (now Irvington). Maxwell also played important roles in the defense of Philadelphia at the Battles of Germantown and Brandywine.

After the Battle of Springfield, Washington moved his army to the Sincack (now Preakness) Valley, and the area around Paterson, in early July. There he awaited reinforcements for his expected defense of his important outpost on the Hudson, West Point. By early August, he moved his troops closer, into the Hudson Valley at King's Bridge. That September he was to receive his greatest shock of the war - news of the treason of his trusted commanding officer at West Point, Gen. Benedict Arnold. Though Arnold's accomplice, Maj. Andre, was captured, and on October 2, 1780, executed, Arnold himself escaped and deserted to the British. Washington had great difficulty accepting Arnold's treacherous deed.

During early October and throughout November of 1780, General Washington returned to his headquarters at the Theunis Dey Mansion in Preakness. His troops were encamped all along the nearby Passaic Valley from Wagaraw (now Hawthorne) in the north to Little Falls in the south. The main body of his troops was near the Great Falls. The Dey Mansion is now an important historic site run by the County of Passaic, and is well worth visiting. Most of the time, in the summer months at least, it is manned by volunteers dressed in colonial costumes performing various colonial crafts. It vividly portrays life, as you would have found it along the trails of New Jersey during those anxious days in the nation's War for Independence.

While at his headquarters of the Dey Mansion, Washington and Maj. Henry "Lighthorse Harry" Lee plotted a daring capture of Benedict Arnold.

The Dey Mansion and the Plot to Kidnap Washington

On the morning of July 1, 1780, Gen. George Washington arrived at the home of his friend, Col. Thuenis Dey, in what was then Bergen County. The Dey Mansion was to serve as his temporary military headquarters because of its strategic location in the upper Watchung Hills. Dey had become fast friends with Washington, both because of their common interests, and because Dey, as commander of the important Bergen County militia, had many contacts with the American leader.

It was there on July 14 that Washington received the news of the French army's arrival under Rochambeau at Newport, Rhode Island. Many important American military and political leaders busily moved in and out of this historic New Jersey home during Washington's stay, but the one visitor who affected the dramatic story about to unfold was the American general, Benedict Arnold.

That story ended on October 2, 1780, when Maj. John Andre's promising British military career came to an untimely halt. For it was on that day, he was executed as a spy just across New Jersey's northeastern border in Tappan, New York at the age of 29. As an aide to the British commander in America, Gen. Henry Clinton, it became

381

Andre's unfortunate responsibility to act as the go-between when the American general, Benedict Arnold, sent word that he wanted to get in touch with the British commander. The meeting would involve Arnold's proposed treasonous betrayal of the American fortifications at West Point.

Arnold assumed the code name "Gustavus" in his contacts with Andre, who took on the pseudonym of "John Anderson." On September 19, 1780, "Anderson" traveled up the Hudson on the British sloop, the Vulture, for his rendezvous with "Gustavus." He went ashore on the night of September 21, meeting "Gustavus" on the riverbank near Haverstraw. The two men then moved to the nearby home of Joshua Hett Smith, and American loyalist. During their extended meeting, the Vulture was forced to move downstream under American fire. Cut off from his planned retreat, Andre had to arrange to return to the British lines by horseback. Arnold arranged for a horse, persuaded Andre to disguise himself as a civilian, and hid the treasonable papers in his boots.

Accompanied by the loyalist in whose home he had met Arnold, Andre re-crossed the Hudson on a ferryboat from Stony Point, and slept at another loyalist farmhouse that night. He then began to proceed to the nearby British lines. He was stopped, however, by American sentries near Tarrytown on the morning of September 23. They turned him over to the local American commander, a Lt. Col. Jameson, who unsuspectingly notified Gen. Arnold of their find. Arnold, thus warned, was enabled to make his escape. The unfortunate Andre, however, was sent to Gen. Washington's current headquarters at Tappan on September 29, 1780.

Accused of sneaking behind the American lines with an assumed name under cover of darkness, and of being caught in disguise with details of American defenses concealed in his boots, a board of officers presided over by Gen. Nathaniel Greene tried and found him guilty of spying. He was sentenced to death by hanging. Gen. Clinton wrote to Washington that Andre had been invited under a flag of truce by Gen. Arnold, with passports guaranteeing his safe return, and asked for his release.

Washington wrote back that the circumstances of his capture could hardly be considered normal for one carrying a flag of truce, and added that Andre had confessed to his act. Though Washington was sympathetic to the young officer's being subjected to the full penalty for gallantly performing his duty, while the traitorous Arnold got off scot-free, Andre was nevertheless hung. Clinton was enraged, and rumors spread that he plotted the capture and execution of Washington as a traitor to the Crown.

Such rumors, in the midst of Arnold's defection to the enemy, could not be treated lightly. A safe headquarters had to be found. New Jersey's upper Watchungs came to mind again, and the 600-acre estate of Col. and Mrs. Theunis Dey, in what is now Passaic County, was chosen. A personal guard of 150 select men accompanied the American commander-in-chief to the Dey Mansion in the Preakness Valley. Shortly afterwards, a daring attempt to kidnap Washington was indeed made by the bold and ruthless cavalry officer, Col. John Simcoe, with his famous Queen's Rangers. They were repulsed, however, by American forces at the Totowa Bridge.

New Jersey's Dey Mansion is today one of the great colonial houses of the northeast, and can be visited in its beautiful 367-acre setting at Preakness Valley Park in Wayne Township. There, with authentic herb gardens, furnishings of the period, and the colonial garbed students demonstrating colonial crafts, you may feel the spirit of those days in colonial New Jersey when great Americans were fighting this nation's War for Independence.

The Yorktown Connection

Much has been written about the final major battle of the American Revolution fought at Yorktown, Virginia and the surrender of the British Gen. Cornwallis on October 19, 1781. Little, however, has been said of the ruse that had been played out back in New Jersey, which made that victory possible. Though the triumph at Yorktown marked the end of any significant fighting among the British and American forces, it should be remembered that the articles of peace ending that war were not ratified by the Continental Congress for almost two years - On April 15, 1783. While Congress was in session at Princeton, word of the end of the conflict finally came on September 3, 1783, with the signing of the Peace Treaty at Paris. Only then had the new nation won its independence, and its recognition as the United States of America.

The year preceding the Battle of Yorktown was a trying one for the Americans. On January 1 of that year, the Pennsylvania Line, encamped at Morristown under Gen. Anthony Wayne, mutinied. Marching off to Princeton, it reached that community by the evening of January 3. There it negotiated for a redress of its grievances. A settlement was finally reached on January 7. It then marched to Trenton where the terms would be carried out. The success of the revolt soon spread to other troops. Washington's army was then deployed in a semicircle surrounding New York City. It extended from an area in the north along the Hudson above West Point, south through Paramus, and ending at Jockey Hollow outside of Morristown.

The New Jersey Line was encamped at Pompton. Word of the Pennsylvanian's successful revolt reached it. On the night of January 20, they, too, mutinied. Defying the orders of their officers, they marched off to Chatham. At Chatham, a conference was held with Col. Elias Dayton and the Rev. James Caldwell addressing their complaints. They, too, were promised relief. Upon returning to their encampment at Pompton, however, they were met by a detachment of 500 troops sent in the meantime by Washington, who was unaware of the settlement at Chatham. Their ringleaders, Sgt. Gilmore and John Tuttle, were captured, court-martialed, and shot by a firing squad as an example to other troops.

The British commander, Gen. Clinton, was headquartered in New York City with the main British army in America. But a large segment had been detached and into action in the south where the British were having some important successes. Gen. Cornwallis had moved his victorious army into Virginia. There, however, he found himself being pressed by the Americans under Lafayette, Wayne, and VonSteuben. Word received by Washington was that if he could move his army south, and get the French fleet to move in by sea, a trap might be set for Cornwallis from which he could not hope to escape.

In order for Washington to move his army south, and at the same time keep Clinton from sending reinforcements and thus preventing the planned capture of Cornwallis, some contrived deceptions on Washington's part were required. His initial hoax was a pretense at moving his army into action on the Hudson. His troops instead were quickly reversed at the last minute and sent marching at double-time southward across New Jersey. Crossing the Delaware they headed for Virginia. He then let "secret plans" for a major attack on Staten Island fall into British hands. All indications that such an attack would be conducted were undertaken.

Among the ruses carried on when Washington was heading south were the construction of storehouses and powder magazine's at key locations in New Jersey, which seemed in preparation for a major attack. Another pretext involved the building of a bakery at Chatham with sufficient ovens to provide for supplying a large army. In late August, he had some 3,000 men hastily moved into Chatham, one of the outposts guarding Morristown, with a flurry of activity indicating something big was up. These preparations showed that the attack on Staten Island must be imminent. Under cover of darkness, they then moved out on the night of August 28, 1781. By the way of Green Village Road, they reached Bound Brook overnight, and from there on to the Delaware and points south. They would join Washington in Virginia.

Before Clinton became aware of the ruse, taking place along the trails of New Jersey, the snare to trap Cornwallis in Virginia had been set. Before Clinton could muster his troops for a rescue, the entrapment had been completed. Before Clinton could recover from the shock of what had happened to him, the "Old Fox" had outfoxed him once more. Even in that faraway battle, New Jersey continued to play a vital role in the outcome of the Revolution. News of the stunning victory brought great rejoicing throughout the New Jersey countryside.

CHAPTER 15: PEOPLE AND PLACES OF THE REVOLUTION

George Washington

I could hardly let February slip by without bringing your attention to the particularly close connection that existed between New Jersey and the nation's first president and hero of the American Revolution, George Washington. This is, after all, Washington's birthday month, and New Jersey does have a closer tie to our most honored man than any other state, save his native Virginia.

I grew up in an era when it was quite the fetish for places in this state to boast that "Washington slept here." There was also much ridicule that if Washington did indeed sleep in all of the places that it was claimed he did, he must have slept through the entire Revolution. Well it is a fact that Washington did spend more time in New Jersey in the eight-year span between the opening round of the Revolution in 1775 and the peace treaty ending it in 1783 than in any other state. And since you do sleep 365 nights in a year, that does give you quite a large number of places where you could have slept.

Washington made a considerable number of close acquaintances within the state during the war, and he not only communicated with them, but also visited some of them after the war, particularly en route to his inauguration in New York in 1789 as the nation's first president.

He also had excursions into New Jersey during the Constitutional Convention, which he chaired in Philadelphia in 1787. He enjoyed riding his horse across the Delaware in pastoral New Jersey.

Time and space prohibit mentioning all of the places within New Jersey where Washington stayed. A brief overview of his activities during the Revolution, however, will provide some insight.

New Jersey first witnessed Washington after he had been named commander-in-chief of the Continental Army in Philadelphia. Dressed in his attractive blue and buff uniform, Washington made brief appearances at that time in both New Brunswick and Princeton, while en route northward to Boston to assume his new command.

Washington's next appearance in the state would start early in November of 1776 when he was maneuvering his forces across the Hudson in an attempt to prevent the British from gobbling up New Jersey, after his defeat in New York City. The loss of his position at Fort Lee led to his desperate retreat across New Jersey's countryside between Hackensack, Newark, New Brunswick, and Princeton. He finally crossed the Delaware into Pennsylvania near Trenton in December of 1776. Quite a few places could claim "Washington slept here," after that rout.

His return to New Jersey on Christmas Day of 1776 led to a brilliant double victory at Trenton followed by the defeat of the British at Princeton in early January of 1777. Those victories were later touted as "turning points" of the war. It was after Princeton that Washington decided to march his troops through still more of the New Jersey countryside. This time up the Millstone Valley he went. His destination was to be his first winter stay at what was to become his permanent military headquarters, Morristown.

In late May of 1777, Washington moved his encampment over the Watchungs and along the banks of the Raritan to settle at Middlebrook in the Somerset hills. From there, he hoped to keep the British bottled up in New Brunswick, preventing a move on Philadelphia. Engagements against the British in this area, in which Warren County's hero, Gen. Willie Maxwell, participated, finally drove the frustrated British out of New Jersey and back to Staten Island. Washington then moved back to his headquarters in Morristown to celebrate the first anniversary of the signing of the Declaration of Independence.

After the British returned to capture Philadelphia by sea, Washington had a series of forts built on the Delaware to harass shipping and starve them out. The British decided to get out and concentrate their forces in New York City. As they began their retreat across New Jersey in the spring of 1778, Washington followed them to harass, engage, and finally defeat them. This came at the Battle of Monmouth at the end of June. The British rout ended in their escape to Staten Island.

Washington returned to Middlebrook in December and headquartered at the Wallace House in Somerville. Suspecting an attack on West Point Washington moved north in the spring. He engaged them at Stony Point and then moved back to Morristown for the worst winter of the century. The following spring he repulsed two attacks on his headquarters. One was the Battle of Connecticut Farms, the second the Battle of Springfield. They were to be the last major engagements along the trails of New Jersey. But not the end of Washington's activities in the state!

Washington's Spy Network

Every war has had its share of secret weapons to help one side gain a greater advantage over the other. One of George Washington's "secret weapons" was his uncanny ability in the field of espionage. Washington was a master at the art of recruiting individuals to serve directly as spies, or as operatives in the far more complicated role of double agents. But little was known of the exploits of a great many of Washington's spies until comparatively recently. Nothing is kept from the public more carefully than the identity of a nation's spies. In obtaining money for these operations from Congress, Washington even acted as his own Chief of Intelligence. Thus, he kept the operations more secretive.

Spy stories make intriguing novels, and James Fennimore Cooper's, "The Spy," was one of this nation's earliest. Based upon an actual, though unidentified, spy of Washington's time, Cooper heard the true account of the man's exploits from John Jay. But his identity, even 40 years after the war, was not revealed. A nation's people are quick to forget a spy's service after a war, and often are ungrateful for his sacrifices. In fact, in times of peace, there is even a tendency to regard the former agent's activities as distasteful. Its no wonder then that men like John Honeyman, soon became our unsung heroes.

I am sure there are a number of houses throughout the State of New Jersey where clandestine activities took place at various times in our history. Such places, when known, have been dubbed as "The Spy House." One that was given that title is in the vast Wharton Tract in the Pine Barrens near the shore of Batsto Lake. During the American

Revolution, you may recall that Batsto was an important producer of iron for munitions and military supplies for the Americans. The Spy House in this case, therefore, was in the employ of British Intelligence. That activities in the village, and the movement of supplies, was carefully reported by spies for the English, has recently been uncovered by a search of British Archives.

In Port Monmouth, commanding a view of Sandy Hook, Raritan, and Lower New York Bays, stands an American Inn that has been officially named "The Spy House." Originally built along the Jersey shoreline as the Shoal Harbor Plantation Homestead in 1663 by Thomas Whitlock, it was occupied by his descendants until the early 1900's. Now a museum depicting the heritage of the Bayshore area of Jersey, it is open on weekend afternoons.

During the American Revolution, the resident of that day, a Mrs. Seabrook, turned the home into an inn partly to save it from being burned by the British. In those days, inns were often respected as neutral "watering places" by both sides, and thus left unharmed. Whoever occupied the area at the time felt free to occupy it as well and enjoy its refreshments. However, one of Washington's spies, a Col. John Stilwell, saw the value of the place as a base for clandestine activities.

British packet boats, in the business of bringing supplies to His Majesties troops quartered nearby, often anchored in Shoal Harbor. And, often as not, the crews of these British ships came ashore to partake of the refreshment of the Inn and perhaps even to enjoy the pleasures of sleeping ashore for a night or two. Stillwell and his agents kept watch at the inn. When a British ship was found to have left only a skeleton crew aboard, because too many had gone ashore to the inn for an evening's merriment, the word went out.

A crew of patriots was soon dispatched from nearby whaleboats. Its orders were to sink the under-manned British packet boat with its valuable military supplies aboard. It soon became known as Washington's "Whaleboat Warfare." Over a period of four years, this special Jersey Campaign led to the destruction of some 39 British supply ships. The supplies that did not reach British troops were sorely needed. So one can easily see that the "Whaleboat Warfare" operating out of the Jersey Shore's Spy House in Port Monmouth greatly aided Washington in the winning of the war.

That the British became suspicious of "The Spy House" activities became obvious when they, against all established precedence, attempted to burn the Inn down. Before setting fire to the Inn, in order to keep it from being saved, they destroyed all of its water buckets. But good luck was with the Americans again, for the fire was set on a wash day. The Seabrook women were thus able to smother the flames with loads of wet clothing that had been soaking in tubs in the wash shed! Just another of those interesting tales that abound along the trails of New Jersey.

John Honeyman: An American Spy

Having served as a special agent in counter-intelligence for the Defense Department more years ago than I care to remember, I perhaps have a unique place in my heart for stories about spies and counter-spies. So I might be accused of showing partiality when I sympathize with those many unsung heroes whose deeds in that very specialized form of serving one's country go unnoticed.

It is to one of these unsung heroes in New Jersey that I would call your attention today. He is a Jerseyman whose role as a double agent for George Washington during the American Revolution may very well have saved our young nation from collapse before it was fully born.

I find it sad that his somewhat neglected grave in Lamington, where he died at age 93, has only a weather-beaten headstone and alongside that, a small Revolutionary veteran's marker. The people of New Jersey, much less the nation, have indeed little noted nor long remembered what this man did here. Rupert Hughes, an historian who wrote of Washington's role in keeping alive the flame of independence, lamented how the name of Nathan Hale, whose spy-mission failed, has nevertheless become a household word in America and how he has a "splendid monument" erected to glorify his unfinished deed. Yet, Hughes says, "For John Honeyman, who made the first great (American) victory possible, there is oblivion."

On Dec. 18, 1776, George Washington, having lost New York City and Fort Lee and having fled across this state with the British hot upon his tail, wrote a heartrending letter home to his brother John

Augustine, while hovering with his remaining troops on the Pennsylvania side of the Delaware. In it, Washington himself admitted, "I think the game is pretty near up." But something exciting happened during the week following the writing of that letter, changing the course of history. And it was John Honeyman, the Griggstown cattle dealer, who made it happen.

John Honeyman, a 46-year-old Scotch-Irish immigrant who was living in that little village 10 miles north of Princeton, had been acting as Washington's personal spy ever since Washington had been appointed at Philadelphia as commander-in-chief of the Continental Army. Both had served as colonials in the British Army during the French and Indian War more than a dozen years before. It was, in fact, Honeyman's discharge from the British Army and his letter of commendation from the British hero of that war, Gen. James Wolfe that gave him his perfect cover as an ardent Tory who was fiercely loyal to the British Crown.

Honeyman had been practicing his trade as a waver in Philadelphia, where he married his Irish-born wife, Mary, when he offered his services to Washington as a double agent. Pretending to spy for the British, he would instead by spying for Washington. A very dangerous game to play, Honeyman's Scotch-Irish blood was so on fire for independence from English domination that he was willing to gamble his life for a chance to outsmart them.

As the two men discussed Honeyman's possible role as an American spy while pretending loyalty to the British, it was decided that he could be most useful as a butcher and dealer in livestock. He had some experience in such a role back in Ireland. The British were anxious to make contacts with colonists of that trade in order to gain meat supplies more easily for their army. The die was cast. His first act was to gain the confidence of the British. He moved his wife and four children to the village of Griggstown in New Jersey, which had a large loyalist population. There the John Honeyman House still stands on Bunker Hill and Canal Roads.

Under their contrived plan, Honeyman, acting in his role as a Tory, provided livestock for the British Army, and eventually offered them his services as a spy. Having access to the countryside in his trade allowed him to come in contact with both sides. He was to keep his eyes and ears open, and report back any information that might prove useful. As a double agent, he had to allow himself to be captured from time to time by American outposts. After realistic and body-battering struggles, he would be taken prisoner by unsuspecting Americans who were instructed by Washington to bring the Tory in. To protect his cover, only Honeyman, and Washington ever knew of his double-agent role as an undercover agent throughout the war. The only exception was his wife.

Once Washington had been able to see him alone, he arranged time and again for him to make daring escapes. It was to one of these daredevil escapades that Washington referred when he wrote to his brother that December day. That "no man...had ever had a greater choice of difficulties" as he had to make, to try and "extricate himself" from the predicament he and his battered army found themselves in across the Delaware. How he used Honeyman in these crucial days will have to wait another time along the trails of New Jersey.

Crossroads of the American Revolution

New Jersey has often been dubbed the "Crossroads of the American Revolution." Over and over again, George Washington, as commander-in-chief of the Continental Army, crossed and re-crossed the state - being either pursued by or in pursuit of His Royal Majesty's British Armies. Or, he was headquartered there, encamped there waiting for, planning on, or licking his wounds after an attack. Or he was taking refuge from a plot on his life, or just sitting out a winter waiting for better weather, or eventually writing his farewell address to his troops. Whatever the purpose, George Washington spent more time in New Jersey during those trying years than in any other state save his own native Virginia.

But battles, skirmishes, or incidents involving the American War for Independence were not always played out with George Washington as its central figure. In every war, there are hundreds of battles in which the commander-in-chief is not directly involved. So it was in New Jersey during those struggling years of the late 18th century. More than 100 documented engagements took place between American and British troops during those trying years. Many more incidents occurred between foraging parties of both armies and citizen-patriots as well as Tories.

Remembering, during the next of the nation's heart-wrenching wars, which like the Revolution, often pitted relatives and friends against one another, New Jersey feared it would once again become such a "crossroads."

In the early days of the Civil War, in late April 1861, Gov. Charles Olden recalled those tragic years of less than a century before. Noting that New Jersey was the "natural highway from North to South," and fearing a repetition by the armies of the Union and Confederacy, Olden made a special plea to the state legislature. He urged that it take steps to "resist invasion, should circumstances again threaten it" by placing detachments of the state's militia at key positions in the southern sector of the state - where such an invasion might likely occur. After all, he said, only the Delaware Bay separated New Jersey from its southern enemies.

In the ensuing years, much occurred, and New Jersey, caught up in its expansion and growth in trade, industry, and commerce, forgot about its rich Revolutionary heritage. A stalwart few organizations in lonely vigil insisted upon its preservation.

Washington's Headquarters in Morristown and the Trenton Barracks were two such historic sites that stood almost alone. They were jealously preserved by struggling private groups for many years. Only recently have the people of New Jersey - and the nation - begun to recognize the many other places in the state worth protecting in order to perpetuate for present and future generations the memory of those stirring years in our nation's history.

Today, you can visit Fort Lee Historic Park, south of the George Washington Bridge, where Washington's heartbreaking retreat across New Jersey began that bleak November day in 1776. Go on from there to the Von Steuben House at New Bridge, near where some 2,000 troops heading southwest crossed the Hackensack River. Then race across the state to Washington's Crossing State Park along the Delaware where on Christmas Day in 1776, he reentered the state after a short hiatus in Pennsylvania. View the Battle Monument and Old Barracks museum in Trenton and the Princeton Battlefield State Park to be reminded of victories in January of 1777 that rekindled American hopes for independence.

From there go on to Morristown, where the nation's first National Historic Park commemorates Washington's Military Capital Headquarters, starting in January of 1777, and the harshest winter of the century spent at Jockey Hollow in 1779-80. Witness, the site at the Red Bank Battlefield State Park back on the banks of the Delaware where the British began their offensive against Philadelphia in late 1777, which led to the dreadful fall of the nation's young capital.

Then travel to Freehold where on June 18, 1778, in the longest battle of the war, victory was declared by the Americans on a retreating British Army. Having been pursued and harassed since they left Philadelphia, they were finally engaged in battle at what is now Monmouth Battlefield State Park. The Wallace House in Somerville served as Washington's Headquarters from December 1778 to June 1779. The Dey Mansion in Wayne served as both Washington's Headquarters in the summer of 1780, and as a haven when his life was threatened in the fall. Finally, at Rockingham in Rocky Hill Washington wrote his farewell to his troops while awaiting the Peace Treaty.

All these and more have many tales to tell about the state's vital role in the Revolution - along the trails of New Jersey. Visit them!

The War in Northwest Jersey

I have been asked from time to time what of significance happened in northwest Jersey during the Revolution.

Made up mostly of what is now Sussex and Warren Counties, this area was primarily an off-beat location, sparsely settled and not containing the kind of targets that British generals considered vital. Its conquest could hardly bring the expectation of gaining some important military objective. Not that the pioneer folk living there were oblivious to what was going on, however. Both loyalist and patriot elements were represented, as well as large numbers of "neutrals," especially among its Quakers who were opposed to any violence.

By the eve of the Revolution in 1775, the Sussex County freeholders (Warren was then a part of Sussex) had begun to show their defiance of the crown by refusing to pay the salaries of royal appointees.

A Committee of Safety had been organized at the county seat in Newton in August. A quota of two regiments had been set for Sussex by the Continental Congress. One of Washington's trusted officers was Brig. Gen. William Maxwell of Greenwich Township in what is now Warren County. He played important roles in battles fought both inside and outside of the state. For most of the war, he commanded the state's "Jersey Brigade."

Its farms, as well as its iron foundries, played important roles in supplying food and fodder to keep the rag-tag American armies in the field. And, the funds it was assessed to pay its "fair share" for winning the war created havoc among its people. Maj. Hoops' Slaughterhouse in Belvidere, along with his gristmills, is said to have sent vital foodstuffs overland by wagon on treacherous trails to Washington's army in Morristown. And, down the Delaware in Durham boats to supply troops in the Philadelphia area.

Though the Shippens of Philadelphia were operating an iron business in Oxford that greatly aided Washington's army, Dr. Shippen's niece, Peggy, was among the aristocratic set in that Pennsylvania city with strong Loyalist leanings. In fact, it has long been rumored that her marriage to Gen. Benedict Arnold played a large role in his later betrayal of Washington.

One of the regions most notorious Loyalist, Bonnell Moody, operated a spy network and haven for British sympathizers outside of Newton. A Sussex farmer, James Moody, led a band of 73 neighbors into British service in 1777. The isolated Montana region of Scott's Mountain had been a hotbed of Tories; many having sought refuge there from other regions. The loyalist West Jersey Volunteers sent out many foraging parties to obtain food for the British armies.

The Committee of Safety of Newton on July 9, 1777, found it necessary to prepare a list of those persons from the area considered dangerous to the cause of liberty. Margaret "Peggy" Vliet Warne, became a heroine, of a sort, riding her circuit of mercy on horseback as a substitute country doctor when the regular area doctors went off to war.

The coming of the Revolution also brought back the frightening Indian attacks along the Jersey frontier. Only this time it was the British who were stirring them up. Col. Joseph Brant, a half-Indian in the British service, was one of their most notable leaders, particularly in the very northern sector. Most of the attacks once again centered in the Minisink country - on both sides of the Delaware, and into neighboring New York state around the Port Jervis area.

One of the earlier forays occurred April 25, 1777, at Montague. There a band of about 25 Indians led by two Tories attacked and captured the Brinks family and destroyed and plundered the young Westrook and Jobs home. At the latter, they killed the men and took the women and children captive. Attempting the same thing at the home of Capt. Abram Himer of Millbrook, however, they were rebuffed by the captain and his slaves. They fought them off until a detachment arrived from the fort. The soldiers drove this band away, but other attacks were repeated all along the frontier. Major Moses VanCampen of Walpack, a noted Indian fighter, was involved in many such hair-raising events.

During the fall and winter of 1778, Gen. Casmir Pulaski was in command of a Continental army detachment of about 600 sent into the Minisink country by Gen.. George Washington to protect the frontier. Coming up from Trenton to Easton, he headquartered first in Newton before moving throughout the area.

Gen. John Sullivan, who had marched through the area in 1776 with reinforcements for Washington at the Battle of Trenton, returned in 1779 with orders to drive the Indians west of the Wyoming Valley, and thus put an end to their atrocities in the Minisink. For the most part his expedition ended Indian problems along the trails of New Jersey from that time forward. Most Indians moved further west, some into the Ohio Valley, some into Canada.

The Morristown Encampment

New Jersey has the distinction of having the first National Historical Park in the nation. Though it began back in 1873, under the auspices of the Washington Association of New Jersey, it was not until 1933, however, that an Act of Congress officially constituted the

Morristown National Historical Park as a unit of the National Park System.

Administration by the National Park Service of the US Department of the Interior, this reservation has three units - the Washington Headquarters Area, the Fort Nonsense Area, and the Jockey Hollow Area.

The Headquarters Area contains the Ford Mansion, which was built by ironmaster Jacob Ford Jr. in 1772-74. This house served as the nation's military headquarters during the horrible winter of 1779-80. It also has an historical museum of Revolutionary War memorabilia to its rear, constructed in 1935. The Fort Nonsense Area contains reconstructed earthworks at the top of a steep hill known as Mount Kemble. Washington ordered its construction while in Morristown for his first encampment during the winter of 1777, following the battles of Trenton and Princeton. He had it built in order to better protect the military stores being cached at Morristown. The most extensive area is that known as Jockey Hollow.

Jockey Hollow was the site of Washington's main army encampments while he headquartered in the Ford Mansion during the devastating winter of 1779-80. That winter, as it turned out, was the worst of the entire 18th century. This area also served as the site for the encampments for the Pennsylvania Regiments and the New Jersey Brigade in the winter of 1781, following their participation in the Battle of Yorktown, VA, through the end of the summer of 1782.

The Jockey Hollow area is, to many, the most interesting. It contains, in addition to the several thousand acres of woodlands and picnic facilities, the sites of various brigades of Washington's Main Army, along with log replicas of an army hospital and officers' and enlisted men's huts. There, too, is a comparatively new Visitor's Center, where you can view slides and pick up pamphlets of Washington's Morristown activities. Also, on that site is the Henry Wick Farmhouse. Built around 1750, its yards, gardens, and barn have been reconstituted so that you may experience them as they might have been in that day. This house served as headquarters for Gen. Arthur St. Clair, commander of the Pennsylvania Line. It was also the home of Tempe Wick, who legend tells us, hid her horse in her bedroom to prevent its capture by mutinying soldiers. This house has been furnished to give you a feel for what the home of a fairly prosperous Jersey farmer of that period was like.

After his victory at Princeton in the early days of the New Year of 1777, Washington had several options open to him. The one that was most enticing was to hit the British with a third lightening bolt at their New Brunswick stronghold. Washington knew that he could have seriously crippled the British war effort by this triple blitzkrieg. Possibly, he could have ended the war there. Valuable stores of supplies, plus a cache of gold sufficient to keep the Revolution going for another year, were to be had by the storming of New Brunswick. It was the move that the British commander, Cornwallis, finally awakened at Trenton to what was going on, feared was coming next. He broke out into a cold sweat as he raced to meet it.

A quick conference with his officers, however, advised against taking on another major battle, much to Washington's dismay. His troops were in a state of exhaustion after the two previous campaigns. Further action now might instead end in disastrous defeat. New Jersey was to be denied its Battle of Yorktown. He heeded their counsel and instead headed up the Valley of the Millstone. Stopping first at Somerset Courthouse (now Millstone) for the night, he next marched them to Pluckemin. On Jan. 6, he headed for Morristown and the first main encampment of the Continental Army in that Morris County community of about 250 people. Containing some 50 or 60 buildings, Morristown was well situated for his needs. Secure behind a series of mountains and swamps, the center of an important iron industry, and inhabited by an extremely patriotic citizenry. Morristown was to prove an ideal setting for the tales that were about to follow along the trails of New Jersey. But they will have to await another week.

Artillery Park

Somerset County's "Artillery Park" in Pluckemin is a good example of how an historic site is sometimes born. It can disappear into the wilderness after years of disuse and live on only in someone's memory. Old timers may talk about it in moods of reminiscing. After several generations have gone by it is often relegated into a local myth - believed by some, and disregarded as only hearsay by most. Then something may occur. That old tale is suddenly and dramatically regenerated. It blossoms forth as an exciting new historical find.

So it was with Gen. Henry Knox's "Artillery Park." Rumors of the old campsite were recently brought to the forefront by a court order demanding that Bedminster Township zone a cornfield next to the mythical site for some 1,000 housing units. Before the wilderness area was completely decimated by developers, a non-profit community group, the Pluckemin Archaeological Project, was created to study the place that had long been reputed to have been the Revolutionary campsite of Gen. Knox's artillery back in the years 1778-79.

Fortunately, some time before, a resident of Pluckemin, Clifford Sekel, remembered hearing those tales about a supposed Revolutionary War campsite being "somewhere up on the hill," and decided to research it for a graduate thesis while he was a student at Wagner College. He eventually discovered long-buried materials on the rumored Knox encampment at Bedminster in the National Archives. His paper, "The Continental Artillery in Winter Encampment at Pluckemin, NJ, 1778-1779," was the basis for a stir of local pride and interest during the celebration of the nation's bicentennial.

In fact, in 1979, as a bicentennial celebration of the historic occasion, the residents of Bedminster held a recreation of "Gen. Knox's Ball" at the campsite at which he celebrated the French Alliance of 1779. Local folk dressed in 18th century costumes for the affair, brought in 18th-century music, had a field demonstration by the "Brigade of the American Revolution," and even invited the French consul general to attend the celebration.

So, when the court order came, the citizens of Bedminster Township were ready for it. In addition to Sekel, another resident, John Seidel, who was an archaeologist and a doctoral candidate in American Civilization at the University of Pennsylvania, led the move to undertake the immense project of trying to relocate the actual site. Financial support was forthcoming from local businesses and individuals. As the "dig" got underway excitement mounted.

Somerset County College created a course in archaeological field studies and named Seidel its instructor. The Artillery Park site was to be its location. Before long the "dig" had created statewide interest. Ten archaeologists and other professionals arrived on the scene. Soon students from Rutgers, Drew and five colleges from out-of-state were on hand at the Knox campsite. Much of the area had been first cleared of brush, mapped and photographed in preparation for the "dig."

Thousands of artifacts have since been recovered, analyzed and catalogued on this once remote Watchung slope. Thirteen mounds of stone - the remains of fallen-in chimneys, were located. The site of what was once an "Academy" for instructing officers was found. It was also determined to be the building in which Knox had held his "Ball" celebrating the French Alliance so many years ago. An industrial portion of the camp was also revealed - where the manufacture and repair of military equipment obviously had taken place. Officer's barracks and probable site where the enlisted men camped were also under study as the archaeological "dig" in New Jersey's Pluckemin Village continued.

The noted New Jersey historian, John Cunningham, described the Pluckemin "dig" at what had previously only been the rumored site of Gen. Knox's military encampment as "the most exciting historical venture ever undertaken in this area of New Jersey." He described the Artillery Park as "a historic site of major national importance."

New Jersey has long been known by such terms as "The Crossroads of the Revolution" and "The Crucible of the Revolt." But as time goes on even more information works its way to the surface about this state's vital role in those exciting times. From old tales, sometimes no longer believed, new finds of historical significance are reappearing along the trails of New Jersey.

The Von Steuben House

Events of the past few months add further proof of New Jersey's prominent role in the era of the American Revolution. In November, New Jersey officials participated with representatives from the Netherlands, Great Britain, France, and Spain in celebrating the anniversary of the recognition of the United States as a free nation, in ceremonies held at Princeton.

This December marks the 200th anniversary of the presentation of the Zabriskie House in River Edge, Bergen County, to one of the nation's leading foreign volunteers, Major Gen. Friedrick Wilhelm Ludolf Gerhard Augustin Von Steuben. This fine example of a Dutch, stone farmhouse, which came to be called the "Steuben House," was presented by New Jersey to that German-American officer in appreciation for his service to the cause of freedom during the American Revolution.

The house was given to him on Dec. 23, 1783, shortly after congress, which was convened at Princeton, officially had received word of the signing of the Treaty of Paris ending the war. This was the treaty that also recognized the United States as an independent nation.

The state of New Jersey had hoped to be honored by Von Steuben's presence as an active citizen when it made the gift. Von Steuben, however, resided there only a short time after he was discharged from the army in March of 1784 and became an American Citizen. In 1786, the state of New York gave him a 16,000-acre estate in Oneida County which he could not afford to refuse. He became a member of the University of the State of New York's Board of Regents, and one of the founders and president of the Society of Cincinnati. He died at his Steuben, NY, home on Nov. 28, 1794.

Steuben, who was born on Nov. 15, 1730, in Magdeburg, Prussia, served with distinction under Frederick the Great during the Seven Years' War, which in America was known as the French and Indian War. He was later knighted as a Baron in 1769. Von Steuben volunteered to serve in the American army through the inspiration of Benjamin Franklin, who was then serving as our representative in Paris. Franklin recommended him to Congress. He sailed for America in late 1777, presented himself to congress, then assembled in York, PA, in 1778, and immediately reported to Gen. George Washington at Valley Forge. He was made inspector general and given a commission by Congress with the rank of a major general.

Washington gave Steuben the task of training his troops. As drillmaster, Von Steuben soon had the American army equal in skill and discipline to the best British regulars. He was with Washington when he crossed into New Jersey in pursuit of the British army, which was moving from Philadelphia to its main headquarters in New York City. Steuben saw his first action at the Battle of Monmouth, at what is now Freehold.

It was there on that Jersey battlefield, now a state park, that the peculiar action of Gen. Charles Lee almost let an American victory slip by with his call for a retreat. Washington, in a fit of unusual anger, reversed that order and saved the day. It was there, too, that the legendary Molly Ludwig Hays became the American Revolutionary heroine, known thereafter as "Molly Pitcher." It was she, you recall, who kept the troops, many of whom, were dying of a treacherous Jersey heat wave, supplied with pitchers of water.

The "Steuben House," now a state Historic Site was built around 1695. An addition was added in 1752. A Dutch colonial farmhouse of brick and fieldstone, it was confiscated by the government during the Revolution because its owners, the Zabriskies, were active loyalists. The house was occupied at various times during the war by officers of both sides. There is a fine example of a colonial kitchen on the first floor, and colonial bedroom furnishings as well as a museum on the second.

Decorated for the holidays in the Lutheran and Dutch Reformed traditions of the Hackensack Valley, the Von Steuben House holds special "Christmas Candlelight Tours." In the Dutch Christmas custom, a line of wooden shoes stuffed with straw and carrots for Santa Claus' reindeer, will appear at the fireplace. The house is decorated for the season by the Bergen County Historical Society, which also arranged an exhibit of 150 years of children's toys and games. An 1881 printing of the famous "Twas the Night Before Christmas" is also on display. This features that other well-known Jerseyite, Thomas Nast, and his rendition of what has come to be the modern concept of Santa Claus. Just another bit of Americana to be found along the trails of New Jersey.

CHAPTER 16: CIVIL WAR ERA

New Jersey Before the Civil War

We often think of the Mason-Dixon Line as the dividing point between the Northern and Southern states. New Jersey was in the peculiar position of having the southernmost 40 miles of its 166-mile north to south length lying below that famous line. Whether that had anything to do with the pronounced "southern" sentiment to be found in the state at the time of the Civil War remains to be seen. It is a fact, however, that many of its seashore resorts were also "playgrounds of the southern plantation aristocracy" in pre-civil War days. Cape May was a summer extension of the Southland.

Probably a very important element of New Jersey's sympathetic attitude towards the South in that period, however, had to do strictly with the economics of the two sections. Southern cotton was important to New Jersey Industries and New Jersey's manufactured products were much in demand by southern customers. There is nothing like financial dependency to attract two sections to each other.

The early Dutch and Swedish settlers, at first, had little interest in slavery, but when Queen Anne established New Jersey as a royal colony the picture changed. She encouraged the slave trade by establishing a monopoly for a royal slave dealer, the Royal African Company of England. It might be noted also that, with the exception of New York, New Jersey's slave population in the colonial period was the largest of any of the northern colonies.

In a population of some 47,000 in 1737, there were more than 3,900 slaves in New Jersey. That number gradually increased. By 1745, the number of slaves in New Jersey was listed at about 4,600 in a population of about 60,000. Many of those early slaves were treated harshly and severely punished even for the most minor crimes. Severe whippings were common. They were often substituted for hangings or burning at the stake for more severe crimes, so the owner would not lose his slave.

From the beginning, it was the Quaker settlers of New Jersey who took the strongest stands against slavery. The early Puritan settlers would have nothing to do with the practice. As early as 1714, an organized attempt was made to return all slaves to their African homelands. Though some early Quakers held slaves, they seem to have been the first to renounce the practice.

Newspapers were constantly carrying advertisements offering rewards for escaped slaves. Jacob Armstrong of Johnsonburg, for example, offered a six cent reward in the "Warren Journal" on September 3, 1844, for the return of his runaway slave, 17 year-old Andre Barnes. As you can see by this date, slaves were still held in New Jersey into the mid 1800's. This particular paper was sent to me by a former Warren County resident, William Young.

One early New Jersey Quaker leader in the movement to abolish the institution of slavery was John Woolman of Mount Holly. He was also a leader in the effort to educate slaves. His efforts are partially responsible for the adoption in 1786 by the new state of New Jersey law forbidding the importation of any new slaves into the state, and of the manumission law of 1804, providing for the gradual freeing of the state's slaves. Though one of the nation's earliest abolitionist societies was established in New Jersey in 1793, the number of slaves had reached almost 12,500 by 1800.

There were, of course, other abolitionists in New Jersey who were not Quakers. A Presbyterian minister from Basking Ridge, the Rev. Robert Finley, comes to mind as one whose sermons on the topic aroused a great deal of controversy. Though the denomination advocated the abolition of slavery, still, it was a source of deep division among local congregations. Some ministers avoided the issue by classifying the topic as "too political" to be discussed in sermons. Some who did not do this found themselves without churches.

As the mid 1800's approached, the number of slaves in New Jersey gradually declined. Requiring the freeing of those slave children born after July 4, 1804, when females reached 18 and males 21, was the key, rather than a falling out of belief in the institution. By 1840, the number of slaves was down to 674. It officially ended in 1846 when the state's remaining slaves were reclassified as "apprentices." As an "apprentice," they could not be bought and sold.

By 1860, on the eve of the Civil War, there were still 18 "apprentices" remaining in the state.

Though the trails of New Jersey had definite pro-southern leanings in 1860, and did not give its electoral votes to the Republican candidate, Abraham Lincoln, there was no doubt about its pro-Union sentiment when the South withdrew. New Jersey was the first state to answer the call for volunteers, and Warren County sent the first volunteer contingent under Capt. Edward Campbell of Belvidere. Patriot fervor ruled once the war was underway.

Slavery and the Underground Railroad in New Jersey

In the early days of New Jersey's history, as with every other colony in America, the holding of bonded servants and slaves was considered to be perfectly proper. Even the early Quaker inhabitants, though they were among the first to discourage this "institution," were slaveholders. The first Dutch and English settlers of New Jersey held both indentured servants and slaves, and records indicate that they continued using slave labor on farms right up through the first decades of the 19th century. Native Indians as well as Negroes were among those used in this manner.

The earliest record of slaves being held in the state was a report of more than 60 being used on a plantation in Shrewsbury in 1690. One hundred years later, the 1790 census listed 11,423 slaves throughout the state. The first attempt by New Jersey to move toward the abolition of slavery came in February of 1821. At that time, it was declared that any slave children born in the state before July 4, 1804 would become free, if they were females, when they reached age 21. If they were males, they were to be set free at age 25.

Slavery was not finally abolished entirely within New Jersey until an act of the legislature declared it so in April of 1846. An indication of how slavery gradually declined after 1790, however, is revealed in the following census figures for Sussex County taken each decade thereafter. In 1800 there were 514 slaves listed in the Sussex census; in 1810, 478; in 1820, 378; 1830, 51; 1840, 13, and by 1850, only one. Since slavery was no longer permitted after 1846, you might wonder why the 1850 census still listed one. It seems, however, that

405

the aged slave, Caesar Soults, living on the farm of Peter DeWitt of Walpack, refused to accept his freedom. He died 10 years later at the estimated age of 100.

After about 1820, the Quakers began to become more outspoken in their opposition to slavery and soon participated avidly in what came to be called the "Underground Railroad." This "railroad" contained no locomotive cars, tracks or other features expected of an ordinary railroad. The names of its "passengers," "conductors," "main lines" and "stations" were kept secret. It traveled only by night. Though there were no tickets, the cost of its operation was tremendous and had to be paid for by soliciting contributions.

The "Underground Railroad," in fact, was no railroad at all, but rather a term used in the United States before the Civil War for the process of conducting slaves in their escape to freedom. Its "main lines" ran from the so-called "Border States," such as Maryland, Delaware and Kentucky, through the northern "Free States," and then on to where no fugitive slave laws could touch them - Canada. The many abolitionists who aided and abetted the escaping slaves offered their homes as shelters or "stations" along the secret routes.

Untold hundreds of fleeing slaves between the 1820's and the opening of the Civil War entered New Jersey on their way to freedom. A dozen branches of the mainline passed through the state, but most ended at Jersey City. The dedicated Quakers of South Jersey aided escaping slaves across the Delaware Bay and from there into "stations" in Burlington, Camden, Cumberland, Gloucester, Mercer, or Salem Counties. Wagons over, often rough, roads then carried them to a north Jersey "station." Those who aided these fugitives were breaking the law. As a result, they were risking their own freedom. They also often gave freely of their meager savings to aid the cause. It was a daring and sometimes costly enterprise.

Since New Jersey did a brisk business with the South, however, many business men were sympathetic to the southern slave holders who sent "chasers" to recover their "property." The philosophy of "states rights" also had many advocates in New Jersey, who therefore tended to identify with the southern states' slaveholders, who believed they had a right to recover their fugitives. As a result, the "Railroad" did not have a smooth track through the state. It is said, however, that a slave chaser coined the term,

"Underground Railroad," in frustration when he declared, after much fruitless searching in the state, that they must be "running a train underground."

Following the election of Abraham Lincoln in November of 1860, a group of southern states seceded. The die was now cast. When the shot was fired upon Fort Sumter, indicating that the very existence of the "Old Union" was threatened; there was no greater unity than that to be found along the trails of New Jersey. Many a young Jersey man volunteered, was wounded, crippled for life, or paid the supreme sacrifice for his country in the terrible four year ordeal that was called by some "The War Between the States."

Antislavery Movement

It was 121 years ago this month, in July of 1863, that the twin Union victories of Gettysburg and Vicksburg took place. These were important to the eventual outcome of the Civil War. Their anniversary reminds us of the role that New Jersey and its citizens played in that very significant conflict in this nation's history, conflict that was vital to its growth along the road of democracy.

But we should also remember, before we point the finger of guilt, that New Jersey during its early history was also a slave holding state. When Berkeley and Carteret were granted the lands we now call New Jersey, 150 acres of additional land were offered to those who first came to settle here for every full-grown male slave they brought with them. For each child slave brought into New Jersey, they would be entitled to an additional 75 acres.

Slavery was encouraged by Queen Anne of Great Britain to help develop the new lands more rapidly. In fact, her appointment of the Royal Governor of New Jersey in 1702 stressed that she was to encourage a direct slave trade with Africa. This royal encouragement of slavery was designed to gain the necessary labor needed in order to tame its wild lands as quickly as possible. The end result, of course, was more profits for the royal treasury.

Though the slave trade itself was outlawed in the early 1800's, the practice of keeping small numbers of slaves continued in this state well into the 19th century. To Jersey's credit, however, it was a native born and raised in Hardwick Township, a Quaker settlement in Warren County, who began one of the earliest antislavery societies in the nation back in 1815. Benjamin Lundy, who was born to Quaker parents on January 4, 1789, in Hardwick, first became disturbed at the practice while apprenticed to a saddle-maker in Wheeling, in what is now West Virginia. Lundy left Hartwick at the age of 19 to learn the saddle business in a place that was at the time the center of slave trading.

His "Union Humane Society," formed to combat this practice, soon gained a membership of some 500 in Virginia. He later began writing articles on the subject at Mount Pleasant, Ohio, in a journal entitled "The Philanthropist." By 1821, he had started publication of his "Genius of Universal Emancipation." In 1824, he moved this publishing operation to Baltimore. In 1825, he began arranging for the settlement of freed slaves in Haiti. By 1828, he was aligned with the famous abolitionist, William Lloyd Garrison. Though he did not live to see the abolition of slavery, Lundy continued his antislavery activities throughout his lifetime. He died while engaged in the delivery of antislavery lectures in Lowell, Illinois on August 22, 1839.

The Society of Friends, or "Quakers," had been advocates of the abolition of slavery since it was instituted in this country, and were among the earliest leaders in the causes of emancipation. So it is not surprising that they were deeply involved in the 1850's in activities to aid runaway slaves in their attempts to escape to the North. The village of Quaker Settlement in Warren County was, in fact, an active station of the so-called "Underground Railroad" during that period.

Though New Jersey still had many southern sympathizers in the dark days preceding the Civil War, they were quick to answer the call to arms once Lincoln issued his challenge for volunteers. Three days after Confederate guns fired upon Fort Sumter, Lincoln sent out his call. New Jersey was the first state to respond. Warren was the first county within the state to answer that call. A company, led by Captain Edward Campbell of Belvidere with seven officers and 50 recruits, was on its way to Trenton almost immediately. Four regiments of the Jersey Brigade were the first fully organized brigades to reach the nation's capital.

When the Jersey Brigade marched through the White House grounds on that beautiful spring day in early May, President Lincoln received them personally with the remark that considering their population New Jersey had done better than any other state. All told, New Jersey supplied 88,305 men, approximately 10,000 more than had been requested of them. Forty regiments of infantry, three cavalry and five batteries of light artillery from New Jersey fought on every major battlefield of the Civil War. More than 6,000 enlisted men and more than 200 officers made the supreme sacrifice at the altar of freedom - that all men might be free.

Call to Arms

It is hard to believe today, the wave of panic that began to sweep through New Jersey back in late April 1861. The consequences of the Confederate attack on Fort Sumter in Charleston Harbor off the coast of South Carolina finally began to sink in. This singular act had opened what was to be the most physically and emotionally devastating war this nation had as yet faced. The immediate reaction, of course, was a wave of patriotism. It is said that the price of American flags rose 400 percent!

On April 17, 1861, President Abraham Lincoln called for some 3200 men to be sent from the tiny state of New Jersey to help fill the ranks of the newly organized Union Army. Though New Jersey had not supported Lincoln in the recent election of November 1860, and though the state had definite pro-southern sentiments, such a challenge to the unity of the nation was another matter. The response was overwhelming. Some 10,000 volunteers were recruited within a week!

Gov. Charles Olden, a Quaker with definite antiwar sentiments, immediately issued a proclamation activating four regiments of the State Militia. They were to be manned strictly by volunteers, and would serve for a term of only three months in the Union Army. This was sufficient time, according to the belief in the north at the time, to subdue any rebels who harbored thoughts of dismantling the greatest Union of States this world had ever seen.

There was to be no doubt as to where New Jersey citizens stood when it came to protecting the Union.

By the next day, April 18, 1861, Capt. Edward Campbell of Belvidere marched off to one of several camps hastily erected outside of Trenton with a contingent of seven officers and 50 men. Warren County thus became the first county in the first state of the nation to answer the president's call to arms. Two days later old Commodore Robert Stockton, hero of the War of 1812, sounded the alarm from his home in Princeton when he reminded Gov. Olden of the potential Confederate enemy began only a few miles away across the Delaware Bay. It still had not been determined exactly which states would eventually make up this new Rebel nation.

The fact was that New Jersey had recently been a slave-holding state itself, and much sentiment existed for the southern cause among its citizenry. Some of it was strictly economic; however, there was much lucrative trade taking place between New Jersey and the South, which would be lost in the event of a prolonged war. This financial loss would be felt not only by the barons of industry, the state was reminded, but by their many employees as well.

In view of the nearness of the potential threat to the state's safety, Commodore Stockton urged the Governor to post troops at vital locations within the state, and offered his services to that cause. Within 10 days, Olden, on April 30, 1861, called upon the state legislature to act to protect New Jersey from invasion. Noting that the state of New Jersey had been from its birth a natural highway linking North and South, and that it had been a "crucible" of the Revolution, suffering much devastation during that war, he called upon the legislators to prepare the state for the worst. He urged the selection of several locations in the state's southern sector for the manning of a suitable defense should an invasion occur.

By May 8, 1861, all four regiments of the New Jersey Brigade were in full parade along Pennsylvania Avenue in the nation's capital. Lincoln himself, in viewing the New Jersey contingent on the White House grounds, remarked that considering its small population, New Jersey had presented a fuller and more completely equipped body of men than had any other state in the nation. Before this tragic Civil War had ended, New Jersey would supply 40 regiments of infantry, three regiments of cavalry and five batteries of light artillery.

New Jersey units would see action on every major battlefield of the war. More than 6,000 of the state's citizens would sacrifice their lives on the altar of the Civil War. Warren County's own Capt. Joseph J. Henry, who was born at the Shippen Manor in Oxford, became the first New Jersey officer to lose his life in that war.

When the Confederate Army did invade nearby Pennsylvania and clash in one of the bloodiest battles of the war at Gettysburg in the early summer of 1863, the worst fears along the trails of New Jersey finally appeared imminent. Gov. Joel Parker on June 29, 1863 called upon the president, immediately, to name Gen. George McClellan of Orange to head an army of New Jersey, New York, and Pennsylvania troops to defend the middle states. The President wired back "I think you will not see the foe in New Jersey."

Lincoln in New Jersey

Though, unlike the American Revolution, New Jersey was not a battleground of the Civil War. A wide variety of its people participated in some way, and the war's effects were felt in many ways before this traumatic four-year conflict ended. That tragic event was over 125 years ago this spring, but its impact is still being felt in the life of our nation.

As I mentioned before, New Jersey was for many years a slave-holding state. Its southern counties were below the Mason-Dixon Line. Its northeastern sector had a pleasant and profitable trade relationship with the South. Its Atlantic Ocean resorts, particularly the Cape May area, were for many years, a playground for the southern aristocracy. Its most famous institution of higher learning, Princeton, was for all practical purposes, southern oriented - a good part of its student body coming from wealthy southern families. It was considered by many southerners to be a "Border State."

Within this context, New Jersey had definite pro-southern sentiments. It generally favored the doctrine of "state's rights," which southerners supported vehemently, and did not support the candidate of the newly formed Republican Party, Abraham Lincoln, in the election of 1860. But it also had a strong Quaker population, . particularly in its western counties, who were, like the Republicans, definitely antislavery. They were also pacifists, however, opposed not only to a war with the South, but any war as a means of settling disputes.

On February 21, 1861, the newly-elected Republican President of the United States, Abraham Lincoln, made an extended stop in the politically hostile state of New Jersey on his way from his home in Springfield, Illinois to assume his new duties in Washington, DC. He was determined to let New Jersey's people know exactly what he was going to have to do, if the "secessionists" of the South insisted upon leaving the Union. There was a definite concern for Lincoln's safety in New Jersey. Meanwhile, its Quaker governor, Charles S. Olden, had, after all, extended the olive branch to Lincoln in inviting him to come to the state and speak to its state Legislature at Trenton.

From his train in New York City, Lincoln and his retinue's first stop in New Jersey was a cool welcome in Jersey City. From there, he went on to a very warm reception in Newark, where he participated in a mile-long parade lined with cheering mobs of thousands. Newark's population in 1861 was about 80,000. If estimates were true, most of them witnessed Lincoln's visit to the city.

The president stopped again to a great cheering crowd at Elizabethtown, where he was given a cannon salute. Next, stops were made at the railroad stations in Rahway and New Brunswick. At Princeton, they merely slowed his train to loud salutes before stopping at its destination, Trenton, where he was to make two speeches, one before each legislative body. Lincoln spoke first to a cool reception before the New Jersey State Senate and then to a rude one before the General Assembly. At both, he was courteous and appreciative, but stated his position. The next time Trenton, New Jersey, would see this Presidential train was in 1865, when it bore the body of the assassinated President on its way back to his home in Springfield, another victim of this tragic war. In the meantime, four long years had passed, slavery had ended, and the Union was restored.

After Fort Sumter, New Jersey's people had responded to Lincoln's call for volunteers with great patriotism. All animosities against him were forgotten in an outpouring of support for the "Old Union." All told, New Jersey sent 88,305 men in 40 regiments of infantry, three of cavalry, and five batteries of light artillery into that conflict between 1861 and 1865. Many would return crippled for life. 6,082 New Jersey enlisted men and 218 officers never came back.

Some of New Jersey's citizens, such as Sam Cooper and Sam French, gained fame as officers in the Confederate Army. Others, such as Philip Kearny, Judson Kilpatrick, George B. McClellan, and Percy Wyndham became national heroes for their roles in the Union Army. Still others played out their dramatic roles in a variety of ways and places. Washington Augustus Roebling of Trenton, who later gained fame for his part in building the Brooklyn Bridge, wrote many accounts of his experiences as a private under Gen. George McClellan in the Army of the Potomac. John B. Jones of Burlington won fame as an author of Civil War tales.

A pretty young Quaker nurse, Cornelia Hancock, played out her role as America's "Florence Nightingale," ministering to the wounded at the Battle of Gettysburg. Dr. Solomon Andrews of Perth Amboy, started as a volunteer in what is now the Medical Corps, but later tried to get the War Department to adopt his "Flying Machine." The list of those along the trails of New Jersey who participated in this tragic war goes on. We owe it to their memories not to forget them.

Heroes and Volunteers

I started last week to tell you something about the role that New Jersey played in the war that was fought to prove our nation's commitment to the equality of man. This was the statement that we so nobly trumpeted for the entire world to hear in our Declaration of Independence some 90 years before. The Civil War had to be fought to settle the slavery question, once and for all. It was a blemish on our purpose for existence that apparently could not be removed in any other way. The cost of this extreme procedure was almost beyond belief in both human and material sacrifice. New Jersey was deeply involved.

I had mentioned before that we were once a slave-holding state, and that our large numbers of Quakers were at the same time among the nation's earliest abolitionists. It is also noteworthy that the state had a large pro-southern segment. Not only did we do a lot of

413

business with the South, but it was, after all, to our Princeton that many sons of southern planters came to receive their higher education. Half of the student body was lost to the Confederate cause with the opening of the war. Furthermore, New Jersey's Cape May, which lies below the Mason-Dixon Line, was a prewar playground for the southern aristocracy and their families. They competed with one another at the Cape to see who could build the most luxurious villas.

But in spite of our background, New Jersey's role in the Civil War was one in which we could be justifiably proud. We had our heroes, and our long lines of volunteers. We had our military hospitals at Beverly and at Jersey City, at Newark and at Trenton. Two National Cemeteries for those who gave their lives during the Civil War were established at Beverly and at Newark. More than 6,000 young Jersey men made the supreme sacrifice that all men might be equal. Southern dead, too, have their final resting place on Jersey soil. At Finn's Point along the Delaware Bay are buried almost 2,500 Confederate soldiers. They were victims of a cruel internment at the prisoner's of war camp at nearby Fort Delaware. In a sense, they too paid the price for equality.

We hear a great deal about where Washington stayed while in New Jersey. Though President Lincoln did not spend anywhere near the amount of time in our state, he was here. And his funeral train passed through our state as well after the terrible tragedy of his assassination. As president-elect, he spoke at Jersey City in late February 1861, before an enthusiastic crowd. He was there again as president in June of 1862. He spoke also at Newark where he paraded down Broad Street. He made stops in Elizabeth, Rahway, and New Brunswick, too. In Trenton, he addressed our state Legislature and lunched at the Trenton House.

Once the war started, there was no question on whose side Jersey stood. There was much concern, though, that as Gov. Olden noted, New Jersey was a "natural highway form the South to the North." Remembering how the armies of the Revolution roared back and forth across our state, some feared the same role would befall us during the Civil War. From this, however, we were spared, though only the Delaware Bay separated us from the slave-holding states of the South.

Camp Olden and Perrine were established outside of Trenton for the four regiments that had assembled within a week after the call to arms had been issued by Lincoln. They became embarkation camps for New Jersey volunteers heading for duty in the South. Gen. Philip Kearney, already a national hero as a result of his action in the war with Mexico, became New Jersey's adopted hero when he was made the commander of the first Brigade that Jersey organized. The Town of Kearny, New Jersey was later named after this colorful figure. Originally a part of Harrison, it broke off in 1871.

Many other people and incidents involved in the Civil War are related to New Jersey. A pretty, young Quaker, Cornelia Hancock of Lower Alloway's Creek, was the first woman nurse on the field of battle at Gettysburg. Mullica Hill in Gloucester County sent an all-Quaker company of abolitionists into service almost immediately. Cumberland County sent more men in proportion to its population than any other county in the nation - its Cumberland Greys.

Cape May's Capt. Henry W. Sawyer gained notoriety when as a prisoner of war at the infamous Libby Prison he was chosen as one of two Union Captains destined to be executed in retaliation for two Confederates. The secretary of war threatened to execute Lee's son, if the plan was carried out. Jersey's Sawyer was immediately exchanged for Lee. The stories go on and on, but space prevents any further tales along the trails of New Jersey.

The "Jersey Brigade"

It was April of 1861 when the thunder of the cannon was heard in Charleston Harbor, a mere seven weeks after the newly elected Republican president, Abraham Lincoln, had visited New Jersey on his way to Washington, DC. He had made stops at Jersey City, Newark, Rahway, and New Brunswick, passed through Princeton and then spoke separately to the State Senate and General Assembly at Trenton. The war that was to engulf the nation for the next four long years had begun almost as a protest against the election of this "sectional" president, as the South called him.

The Republican Party had come into existence, due to the need for a spokesman for the growing antislavery concerns in the North. It

415

had won most of the nation's northern and western states in the election of 1860 - but not New Jersey. It attracted the support of some of the nation's ablest young leaders in both northern and western states. Its motto, "Free speech, free press, free soil, and free men..." was more than the pro-slavery South could stomach. Secession loomed its ugly head! Lincoln had just finished telling New Jersey's legislators what would happen if the secessionists got their way. They did, and it did.

The nation was now at war! The patriotic fervor that swept New Jersey in the cause of preserving the Union could hardly have been predicted even a week earlier. Neither could the grief that would come over the next four years to thousands of the state's young men and their families. Many a wounded Union soldier would return to New Jersey as a patient in one of the four hospitals set up there by the military at Beverly, Jersey City, Newark, and Trenton. Others would return to their final resting-places at national cemeteries established at Beverly and Newark.

Southern soldiers who died by the thousands as prisoners of war at New Jersey's Fort Delaware on Pea Patch Island occupy over 2,400 graves in New Jersey's Finn's Point National Cemetery. Officially dedicated by the United States Government in 1912, this place also contained the bodies of 135 Union soldiers, 127 soldiers from other wars and an "unknown soldier." The latter were all segregated in the "federal section" - an ironic monument in a sense to those divisions that had almost destroyed the nation.

Though New Jersey had been dubbed "a second-rate free state" before the war broke out, there was no doubt where it stood after the attack on Fort Sumter on April 12, 1861. Gov. Olden on April 17, called upon four regiments of the state militia to send volunteers for three months to federal duty. In a message to the state legislature on April 30, he said in part, "New Jersey is the national highway from the South to the North." This "fact is impressed upon us by the memories of the war of the Revolution..." Furthermore, he advised, "we should be prepared to resist invasion..." by "the selection of several positions in the southern part of the state...where troops may be posted, drilled in the duties of military service..." and be in that "general readiness...essential to our protection." Old Commodore Robert Stockton, a hero of the War of 1812, volunteered from his home in Princeton, "Morven," to assist in that home defense chore.

Within a week, New Jersey's four regiments were formed into the "Jersey Brigade" and on May 8, were the first fully organized state troops to arrive in Washington, DC, for which they received much acclaim, even from Lincoln himself. Camp Olden and Perrine had been hastily set up in fields outside of Trenton to accommodate raw recruits. After seemingly endless days of drilling and busy work, North and South's first real clash came in July of 1861 at Manassas Junction (Bull Run), Virginia. Though the Army of the Potomac fell back to Washington DC, it was considered an indecisive battle that shook both sides. The 9th Regiment of New Jersey Volunteers soon took part, however, in the North's first victories - the seizure of Roanoke Island in February and the capture of New Bern, NC, in March of 1862. It was beginning to become apparent to most that this was not to be the short war as first expected.

General Philip Kearny was placed in command of the first New Jersey Brigade to be organized at the outbreak of the Civil War. The men loved his dash and courage. He was the hero of the day at the Battles of Williamsburg and Seven Pines in the spring of 1862, and the Second Battle of Bull Run that summer. He became a true national hero and one of those New Jersey officers who would never return when he encountered the enemy at a battle that was a follow-up to Bull Run. He died in action at the Battle of Chantilly on Sep. 2, 1862. New Jersey's grateful citizens later named the area surrounding his home, "Bellegrove," Kearny, NJ, in his honor. His was only one of that parade of participants whose deeds were told along the trails of New Jersey by a citizenry who cherished their New Jersey connection.

NJ's Union Generals

Although, unlike the Revolution, no battles were fought in New Jersey during the Civil War, its people played a prominent role. Abolitionists had even established key stations in the state for the Underground Railroad.

It was April 12, 1861 when that fateful shot that opened the bloody War Between the States was fired on Fort Sumter. Women were wearing bustles and men stovepipe hats. New Jersey manufacturers were doing a bristling business with the south. There was a strong southern sentiment in this state where the southernmost counties laid below the Mason-Dixon Line.

The majority of the students at Princeton were sons of southern plantation owners. Cape May was the playground of the southern aristocracy. President Lincoln did not win New Jersey when he won the presidency in November of 1860. Families became divided over the issues that rent the nation, and some of its men became soldiers and officers in the Confederate Army.

But for the most part once the sides were drawn, New Jersey was whipped into a state of frenzied patriotism. Though Lincoln lost New Jersey in the November election, he was greeted with great cheers and a grand parade when he and Mrs. Lincoln passed through Newark on their way to his inaugural in Washington in late February of 1861.

The first recruits of the "Jersey Brigade" came from Warren County almost immediately after Lincoln's call for volunteers. The first fully uniformed Brigade in the nation's capital was from New Jersey - and that unit marched in parade across the White House grounds with Lincoln in review. Brig. Gen. Theodore Runyon of Newark became the state's first general officer.

A number of outstanding Union generals had New Jersey connections. Gen. Philip Kearny, who had a home called "Belgrove" in Harrison, was appointed a Brig. Gen. on May 17, 1861, and then given command of the New Jersey Brigade in the Army of the Potomac. Kearny, after a brilliant performance as a cavalry officer, was commissioned a Maj. Gen. of volunteers in 1862. Participating in a series of gallant campaigns thereafter, he was unfortunately killed at Chantilly, Virginia. After the war, in 1871, that part of Harrison containing his home was separated and incorporated as the Town of Kearny in his honor.

Another Union general, George B. McClellan, lived out his life in New Jersey. McClellan played an important role in a number of campaigns, before coming to Lincoln's attention. After receiving command of the Army of the Potomac, however, differences between him and the president over the conduct of the war eventually lost him his command. Fighting in a number of campaigns thereafter, he was returned to command, and then removed again. In the end, he was transferred to non-combat duty in Trenton. He ran unsuccessfully against Lincoln as the Democratic candidate for president in 1864. Elected New Jersey's Governor in 1877, he died at his home in Orange, in 1885.

But perhaps the most flamboyant of New Jersey's generals was a true native son, who was born at Deckertown in Sussex County. He was nicknamed the "Fighting Fool" by Gen. Sherman because of his daring and bravado. Gen. Hugh Judson Kilpatrick was given the task by Gen. William T. Sherman of carrying out his "Scorched Earth" campaign, in his famous march through Georgia. His troops called him "Kill Cavalry."

Raised on his father's farm in Sussex County, Kilpatrick left home for West Point in 1856. He was 18. He was graduated from the Academy in 1861 just in time to enter the Civil War. Shot in his first action at a battle in Virginia, he was sent home to recuperate. Back in Sussex County he recruited for the "Harris Light Cavalry," and returned to the war with that unit as a wild-riding Lt. Colonel. For outstanding performance in action, he was rewarded with a promotion to Brigadier General.

Much to the ire of his superiors, Kilpatrick went over their heads and got approval from Lincoln himself for a daring attack on Richmond. Bad weather foiled his hazardous plan, but before he could reap the scorn of his commanders, he was tapped by Sherman for his historic march to the sea. Sherman was looking for an enterprising aggressive leader for his bold plan, and Kilpatrick was a natural. Though the general from Sussex was wounded in a cavalry attack, he led another attack bouncing over the fields in a rented carriage! After that successful campaign, he was promoted to Major General. Returning to the trails of New Jersey after the war, he became active in Republican politics, was later named Minister to Chile, and died there in 1881.

Lincoln's War

The Civil War began on April 12, 1861, with the bombardment of Fort Sumter, off the coast of Charleston, SC. It ended four tragic years later on April 9, 1865, with the surrender at Appomattox Court House, Virginia, of Confederate commander Gen. Robert E. Lee, to the Union commander, Gen. Ulysses S. Grant. As we look back on those dramatic events now concluded for 125 years, on the surface it appeared to have been one saga of American history, which managed to elude New Jersey and its people. Not so!

Its people were very much involved in many aspects. In combatants alone, more than 88,000 of New Jersey's young men participated, more than 6,000 never came home. New Jersey was the first state to answer the call, and the state's first recruits, who were formed into the "Jersey Brigade," came from Warren County under the command of Capt. Edward Campbell of Belvidere. Let us not forget them.

Though the closest we actually came to what seemed a sure chance of invasion by enemy troops, was when Lee brought his army north, and was engaged in battle at Gettysburg in July of 1863, there seemed a constant threat hanging over us. With the Mason-Dixon Line crossing our southern counties, with the South considering us a "Border State," with the North considering us a "Second-rate Free State," our position seemed tenuous.

Gov. Olden spoke of us as being "the natural highway from South to North." He further reminded us of what happened to New Jersey during the Revolution, "when a ravaging army marching through our borders, preyed upon the substance, burned the houses, devastated the fields, and pillaged the granaries of the people." Old retired Commodore Robert Stockton of Princeton noted that only the Delaware River separated us from the slave states. He warned that we "consider the best means to preserve our own state from aggression," and that "we are in the presence of an awful danger."

Gov. Olden, in a message to the state legislature, called into special session on April 30, 1861, said "We should be prepared to resist invasion...the selection of several positions in the southern part of our state, or perhaps the establishment of a single central camp...may become essential to our protection...the states of New York and Pennsylvania, having a common interest with us in this defense, would doubtless, if necessary, cooperate with New Jersey."

Camp Olden and Perrine and an arsenal were soon erected in the fields outside of Trenton. That this concern about New Jersey's imminent invasion persisted is illustrated by Gov. Joel Parker's plea to President Lincoln on June 29, 1863. "The people of New Jersey," he said, "are apprehensive that the invasion of the enemy may extend to her soil." He went on to add that they want Gen. George McClellan "at the head of the New Jersey, New York, and Pennsylvania troops now in Pennsylvania, defending these middle states from invasion." The president had to assure him that, "I think you will not see the foe in New Jersey."

Following the Battle of Gettysburg, Lincoln spoke to Gen. Daniel Sickles, who had lost his right leg there, in the presence of another New Jersey officer, Col. James Fowler Rusling, born in Washington, Warren County. It was at that meeting, Col. Rusling later related, that Lincoln told of his great admiration for Gen. Grant, and he suggested at that time that Grant would receive a greater role in the war. Col. Rusling went on to become chief assistant quartermaster in the Department of the Cumberland and a brigadier General.

Lincoln finally did bring Grant east in the spring of 1864. Gen. Sherman was to take over his western command. Sherman soon encountered another New Jersey born officer, the formidable Confederate Gen. Samuel French, at the Battle of Kennesaw Mountain. French was a native of Gloucester County, New Jersey, who joined the Confederacy after inheriting a southern plantation through his wife's relatives.

On September 8, 1864, Gen. George B. McClellan accepted from his home in Orange, NJ, the nomination of the Democratic National Convention in Chicago in late August. He was to be their candidate for president to oppose Lincoln in the election of November 1864. New Jersey's McClellan was the general that Lincoln had twice dismissed from command for having "the slows," which was Lincoln's description of him for being overly cautious.

Having pinned their hopes upon the slogan that "Lincoln's War" was a failure, the Democrats were dismayed that Sherman soon began smashing his way east into Atlanta, making the war appear to be becoming successful. The election was another chapter in New Jersey's mixed role in support of "Lincoln's War."

The true feeling of the people along the trails of New Jersey concerning their martyred president was revealed following his assassination on April 14, 1865. "All New Jersey seemed to have come to the tracks," wrote a writer describing the passage of Lincoln's train across New Jersey 125 years ago.

Prisons and Cemeteries

In the recent oil spill along the lower Delaware River, reference was made to the damage expected to be suffered by the migratory bird stop on "Pea Patch Island." I was immediately reminded of another era in time - the 1860's. The name Pea Patch Island stirs images of the savage treatment there to some 12,000 Confederate prisoners of war held at Fort Delaware on Pea Patch Island by Union forces during the Civil War.

Of course, Union prisoners received equally inhumane treatment at the hands of the Confederates at such horrible prisons as Andersonville, GA or Libby, VA. So neither side was any more just or civilized in the way they treated the "enemy" of that day. It should remind us all of the depths to which humans seem capable of descending, particularly in times of war.

When the Civil War first started, both sides agreed to an exchange of prisoners on a regular basis, since neither had the facilities to keep them. But as the war extended far beyond anyone's wildest expectations, things changed. One of the events which apparently brought about the reversal in the previously agreed-to-rules was the execution by Union forces of two young Confederate officers who had been accused of being spies. This started a series of reprisals. Two Union officers being held at the Libby Camp, for example, were picked at random to be executed in return. On July 6, 1863, Capt. Henry W. Sawyer of the 1st New Jersey Cavalry was one of those unfortunate enough to have his name drawn. Though that particular incident was later resolved in Sawyer's favor, the changed attitude on both sides continued for the remainder of the Civil War.

Finn's Point, a land appendage on the Jersey side of the Delaware opposite Fort Delaware on Pea Patch Island, became the burying ground for more than 2,400 unfortunate southern victims of the fort. Today, the 104-acre site is the "Finn's Point National Cemetery." It was originally where the early Swedes and Finns built Fort Elfsborg, hoping to control the coming and going of ships on the Delaware. With the outbreak of the Civil War, the US Government bought the site with the same intention.

They then built Fort Delaware on nearby Pea Patch Island. Instead of it being used as a deterrent to possible attacks by the Confederate Navy, early in 1862 it was turned into a prisoner of war camp for captured rebels. The first Confederate prisoners to arrive at the infamous Fort Delaware came in the early spring of 1862. They had just been captured in Virginia in March 23, 1862.

For soldiers on both sides, being captured became a fate worse than death. In fact, they died by the thousands after suffering from the appalling conditions, including neglect, disease, starvation, and exposure to the elements. Death in northern prison camps came to 26,000 of the 220,000 southern prisoners taken. Perhaps they were the lucky ones. More than 2,700 of them were known to have died at Fort Delaware alone. Some 22,500 out of the 127,000 northern prisoners taken died in southern prison camps.

Pictures of the mass burials and of the skeletal-like bodies of some survivors look horribly familiar. Neither Union nor Confederate leaders seem to have shown any remorse for the inhumane conditions of their respective prison camps. They had no qualms, in fact, about allowing photographers free range in capturing the horrible sights. The only officer tried and hung for war atrocities following the Civil War was the commandant of the Andersonville, GA prison camp. Public wrath in the north following the war demanded it.

At first, dead prisoners were buried on Pea Patch Island itself. But as deaths grew into great numbers, the dead bodies from Fort Delaware were rowed ashore in open boats, loaded onto wagons and moved to Finn's Point. There is no accurate record of the mode of their burial. Some have said that long trenches received the bodies without identification or ceremony. Others said that each body was placed in a simple wooden box also unidentified.

You can accept either story. Perhaps both were true. At any rate, more than 2,400 soldiers were buried there unceremoniously in a period of about one and a half years. The miserable conditions at this prison were made worse by the fact that four times as many prisoners were being harbored there as the facility was built to handle.

Official government records list 2,436 Confederate men and boys lying at rest in what is now a National Cemetery along the trails of New Jersey. After much research, the US Government in 1912 erected an 85-foot obelisk monument at Finn's Point. Some 30 unknown soldiers are also buried there within sight of the infamous Pea Patch Island.

Memorial Day

Something that is designed to preserve the memory of a person or event is called a memorial. On May 5, 1868, Gen. John A. Logan, who was the Grand Army of the Republic's commander-in-chief, declared May 30, 1868, to be a day for the "decorating of graves of comrades who died in defense of their country in the late rebellion." Some states called it "Decoration Day," others "Memorial Day." It was first observed throughout the nation as a state holiday for decorating the graves of soldiers killed in the Civil War.

Today, it is a national holiday observed on the last Monday of May for remembering veterans of any of our wars. On this, the 125th anniversary of the end of the Civil War, however, this day takes on a special significance considering its origin. There were, as I mentioned earlier, over 88,000 men who served in the Civil War from New Jersey, over 6,000 of whom lost their lives. Many of those who did return also had tales to tell worth remembering.

One of these was a young New Jersey officer, who, for example, stood in the shadow of death in a case that became a cause to be celebrated. On May 25, 1863, Lt. Col. William Ludlow of the Union Army relayed to his counterpart in the Confederate Army, Col. Robert Ould, that two Confederate captains had been executed for spying. This was an accepted practice during wartime. It set off a chain of events, however, which captured the hearts of people on both sides.

On July 6, 1863, the commandant of Libby Prison in Richmond, VA was ordered by Confederate authorities to select two Union captains who were to be executed in retaliation. This was totally in violation of the rules of war. Slips of paper containing the names of all Union captains being held in that place as prisoners of war were placed in a box. A United States chaplain was given the awesome task of drawing the two names.

The first name to be drawn was that of Capt. Henry Washington Sawyer, 1st New Jersey Cavalry. He was a native of Cape May. New Jersey was thus once again to be a participant in another of the dramatic events that permeated this tragic war between brothers. The New Jersey press took up the cause with unrelenting headlines. Capt. Sawyer sought and was given permission to write home to his wife and family. His wife, in turn, immediately gained an audience with President Lincoln.

Lincoln personally interceded on behalf of this New Jersey officer and his comrade. He ordered a well-known Confederate prisoner, Gen. W.H.F. Lee, and another Confederate officer not below the rank of captain, to be held under special guard. If Captain Sawyer and Flynn (the other Union officer chosen for death) were executed or any other officer or enlisted man of the Union Army who had committed no crime, these two were to be hung immediately. Furthermore, any other such violations would be treated similarly.

Confederate reaction was swift. People on both sides recognized the injustices that were being perpetrated. Captain Sawyer and Flynn were returned to the main prison compound. Neither was made aware of what had happened. Both awaited their imminent execution. After living in the "shadow of death" in this fashion for some eight months, finally, in March of 1864, the two were suddenly released in an exchange for Lee and the other Confederate officer.

Another New Jersey officer to participate in one of the war's dramas was John James Toffey. On April 17, 1865, Toffey wrote home concerning an event that he had witnessed. He and several friends had heard that President Lincoln and General Grant were to attend a performance at Ford's Theater. They went, not in any particular interest in the play, but just to say they had personally seen these two national heroes. Much to his grief and dismay, he became a witness to the president's assassination. He also was the one who captured the assassin's spent horse and returned it to the authorities.

Some 20,000 of New Jersey's citizens later gathered in Trenton to pay homage to the body of the martyred president as it passed along the trails of New Jersey for the last time on his way home to Springfield, Illinois. Let us remember all of New Jersey's participants in that tragic war on this special Memorial Day.

UNIT 4: POTPOURRI

This unit offers a look at various aspects of the state of New Jersey including seasons, celebrations, and the diversity of the state.

Chapter 17: Seasons and Celebrations
Chapter 18: A State of Diversity

Henry F. Skirbst

CHAPTER 17: SEASONS AND CELEBRATIONS

Arbor Day

Grover Cleveland, the only president of the United States born in New Jersey, was inaugurated as the 22nd president in the spring of 1885, when "Arbor Day" first became a state holiday in Nebraska.

A tide of states, including New Jersey, began adopting this yearly tree-planting observance during this period. It had all gotten started back in 1872 when Julius Morton, then commissioner of agriculture from Nebraska, got the idea underway.

Soon the systematic planting of trees on a given day each year was being promoted all over the US by alarmed citizens concerned by the haphazard deforestation of many sections of the nation by zealous lumber industry.

April 22 eventually was chosen as "Arbor Day" by many northern states because it was Morton's birthday. In southern states, the date varied with the climate. It was the beginning of today's mass-conservation promotion movements in a nation previously governed solely by the frontier philosophy of, "if it's there, use it; when it's gone, move on."

In order to influence the minds of the nation's young people, this early conservation movement stressed "Arbor Day" as a regular springtime observance in just about every school in New Jersey in the early 1900's.

The population of the entire state when the first census was taken in 1790 was a mere 185,000 people! The predicted 1990 census will reveal it to be some 8 million people! In recent years, various groups dedicated to the conservation and preservation of our scenic, natural, and historic resources, have been trying desperately to arouse public awareness to the alarming disappearance of these precious open spaces in New Jersey and the dire consequences to our health.

Although the first county park system in the nation began in New Jersey's Essex County back in 1895 amidst a scoffing public who saw no need in what was then a growing, but still sparsely settled area, state preserves still had to await the 20th century!

With populations rapidly spreading out over the New Jersey countryside in what has come to be called "suburban sprawl," the state first introduced its "Green Acres" program as part of the environmental movement of the 1970's. It was a desperate attempt to preserve as much of its remaining open space as possible. Various state, county, and local parks have come into existence as a result.

From its smallest, six-acre Logan Pond at Repaupo Creek in Gloucester County, to its largest 14,000-acre pine and oak forest with about 20 waterways winding through it, known as the "Peaslee Fish and Wildlife Management Area" in Cumberland County, New Jersey now maintains some 50 wildlife sanctuaries and game preserves. They were all established to help maintain that balance of nature so essential to both human and wildlife inhabitants. Before they were consumed by the voracious appetites of the huge developers, about 150,000 acres of these wildlife management areas have been set aside.

These lands are located within as diverse a collection of habitats as is the state's terrain itself. They are, contrary to some misstatements widely scattered throughout every section of the state where open lands were still available. They are, today, places within an ever-engulfing megalopolis where both man and nature can find much-needed respite.

There are still, however, not nearly enough to ensure our present and future needs.

From the salt marshes along the coastal regions to forested mountains and meadowed valleys in its uplands, New Jersey has some of everything worth preserving. The 12,500-acre MacNamarra Wildlife Preserve in Atlantic and Cape May counties is a good example of the thousands of acres that have been set aside in South Jersey where probably our greatest effort has been undertaken because of national recognition and concern for preserving our unique Pine Barrens. Greater efforts need to be focused on the beautiful forested mountains of north Jersey as well.

The 1,500-acre Whittingham Fish and Wildlife Management Preserve in Sussex County and the 1,400-acre Wanaque Preserve next to Greenwood Lake in Passaic County are good examples of the smaller preserves set aside in New Jersey's northern counties.

Whittingham is one of the few places left in which beaver and otter can still be found in their natural habitats.

Lest you think that once they become state preserves they are forever safe, remember what has happened to Hamburg Mountain in Sussex County, what is happening in Allamuchy State Park, and, but for the vigilance of men like Hackettstown's Casey Kayes, what had been about to happen to the pristine Sunfish Pond in Worthington State Forest. Eternal vigilance is the cost of keeping our priceless natural heritage along the trails of New Jersey for today and for posterity.

Earth Day

When the first Europeans came to the Lenape's "Scheyichbi" in the 17th century, they found New Jersey to be a natural paradise endowed with a strikingly varied environment.

This April 22 will be observed as the 20th anniversary of the first "Earth Day," which began back in 1970 as a result of a movement emphasizing the need to stop and consider what we are doing to our environment.

It will be recognized this year all around the world.

New Jersey's US Senator, Bill Bradley, has been in the forefront, encouraging everyone to get involved. Sen. Bradley has been stomping the countryside both in and out of our state, urging people to do their share locally in protecting this Earth's natural resources.

In New Jersey, that means saving our wetlands and our wildlife habitat, as well as the quality of our air and water from human-generated pollution.

In promoting this great effort, all of the 1990's have been designated as the "Decade of the Environment." In New Jersey, already the most densely populated state in the nation, with more pollution-generating motor vehicles per square mile than any other state, we will be reaching a "crossroads," perhaps before many others, on how well mankind can manage this challenge.

Bradley has been expressing his concerns at many New Jersey schools about the loss of our wildlife habitat due to ever-spreading development. In his talks about an "environmental ethics" he is trying to influence our upcoming citizens to think in terms of "Every Day is Earth Day." He has been speaking out for wetlands-preservation, the need for recycling and a sensible approach to land use in New Jersey.

Like it or not, our tiny New Jersey is on center stage. From its mountains to its seashore, from rock-strewn hilly woodlands to the coastal plains and pinelands, from rural enclaves to bustling urban centers, New Jersey has it all.

From the unique Pine Barrens to the Delaware Water Gap, from the Palisades to the Great Falls of the Passaic, from the pristine loneliness of Sunfish Pond high in the Kittatinnies to busy Lake Hopatcong, New Jersey has it all.

From the New Jersey Turnpike to the Old Mine Road, from Interstate Routes 78 and 80 to Shades of Death road, New Jersey has it all. All, too, are haunted with a myriad of environmental problems that make it a microcosm on this year's "Earth Day" of what the whole nation will eventually confront.

Helen Fenski, a former housewife who almost 30 years ago took up the battle of stopping the powerful New York Port Authority from destroying the pristine Great Swamp region and turning it into a fourth jetport, has since been employed by New Jersey's Department of Environmental Protection.

Her task is to promote within our state an environmentally educated citizenry. If she does as well as a state employee as she did as a citizen-activist in the 1960's, helping to create the 7,000-acre "Great Swamp National wildlife Refuge," there is yet hope for New Jersey.

Fenske has undertaken the task of designing imaginative "nature centers" throughout the state that will excite the public about New Jersey's varied environment, and the dire need to preserve it. Her responsibility is to create centers that will illustrate the interdependence of the state's people with its natural resources - its land, water, and air. She must find ways of educating our citizens to an "environmental ethics," learning how its wildlife and its people, its woodlands and its parking lots, its farmers and its manufacturers, its environmentalists and its developers must live and work together as we enter the 21st century.

These "nature centers" are popping up in various sections of the state as resources make it possible. How well they are financed, and therefore can function, will depend upon how much support the people of New Jersey are willing to give them. It would be more prudent to educate our people now than to pay to restore later what they inadvertently destroy.

From Liberty State Park on the outskirts of Jersey City to the Pequest State Fish Hatchery in rural Warren County, they have begun to take root along the trails of New Jersey. From Allaire State Park near the Atlantic Seashore, to Washington Crossing State Park along the Delaware, they will tell their story.

From Cape May Point State Park in the south to High Point State Park in the north it is hoped that many will come to gain new insights into the importance to us all to preserve our states' land, water, and air as the "Decade of the Environment" opens the door of the 21st century upon the land the Lenape, our original people, once called "Scheyichbi."

Week of the Environment

As we near the end of the "Week of the Environment" in New Jersey (Apr. 22-28), I cannot help but think of the ghosts of the Lenape Indians as they surely must watch with despair the degradation of their beloved "Scheyichbi."

In April, 20 years ago, millions of Americans demonstrated their concern then by participating in an event known as "Earth Day."

Lester R. Brown, a Rutgers agronomist, commenting on what has taken place since, noted that "no comparable two-decade period in human history has witnessed such a wholesale destruction of the natural systems and resources on which civilization depends."

What a heritage we are passing along to the next generation! For Shame!

When the first Dutch explorers landed in New Jersey in the 17th century, both the place and its people were described in glowing terms. The land, they said, was a "Garden of Eden," and its inhabitants "a handsome, friendly people." An abundance of fish, fowl, and game was to be found for the taking in its clear waters, air, and forests.

The Lenape, its original people, were both farmers and hunters, taking from nature only what they needed. They clearly recognized their partnership with other species in the balance of nature; something we sorely lack. The English began calling them the "Delaware," since many seemed to cling to the valley of that mighty waterway as their more-or-less permanent home site.

Twenty years ago, an aroused public forced Congress to pass the first Clean Air and Water Acts. The Federal Environmental Protection Agency soon followed. In New Jersey the Department of Environmental Protection saw the light of day, and the state legislature set in motion our first "Green Acres" open-space acquisition program with overwhelming public approval.

In spite of all those bright beginnings 20 years ago, Brown says that "air and water pollution, hazardous wastes, and species loss have reached unprecedented levels." In some areas, "air pollution has even reached health-threatening levels." The gap between what we are doing and what needs doing has significantly widened. Our environmental problems grow worse; too much indifference.

Stephen Kaplan, in his book "The Experience of Nature: A Psychological Perspective," points to the healthful effects of nature. Prisoners who can see greenery out of their windows, he notes, use health services less. Patients with a view of nearby woods get out of the hospital sooner. Office workers who can take lunchtime breaks in a nearby park report fewer health problems. Even brief encounters with nature have a powerful healing effect. A natural environment is more than a nice amenity, he declared, people actually need it to sustain themselves from the stresses of daily life.

In a speech at Drew University in Madison, the naturalist, Bill McKibben, warned those New Jersey students that unless they make a strong commitment to change their attitudes and ways of life, the harm they are doing to their natural environment will be irrevocable. "Each time you burn one gallon of gasoline," he said, "you release five-and-a-half pounds of carbon dioxide into the atmosphere." In a state with already more autos in operation per square mile than any other, one can easily see what is happening to our air. To help, one of our major aims, McKibben noted, ought to be to convince our people and their political leaders of the dire need today to permanently set aside far more wilderness areas from the threat of development, before it is too late. More development brings more people and autos.

Lester Brown, the Rutgers agricultural specialist, noted that at a time of growing world food scarcity, we are ironically using up our prime farm acreage in unprecedented numbers. At a time of growing concern about excessive carbon emissions into our air, we are cutting down ever more of our carbon-consuming woodlands and planting less oxygen-producing trees. It is almost as though we were defying the laws of nature in a game of "Russian roulette."

"Reversing the deterioration," Brown notes, "depends on the wholesale reordering of priorities." Farmland preservation is not a choice, it is a must.

A New Jersey State Assembly Task Force was recently warned that development is imperiling the water supply of the seven-county (including Warren) North Jersey Highlands region. Unless something drastic is done to preserve its watershed lands from development, North Jersey by the year 2005 will not have enough safe water to sustain its burgeoning population. What is needed along the trails of New Jersey is a recommitment by every man, woman, and child to act responsibly toward their environment during the decade of the 1990's, and hope that it becomes a permanent way of life for them. We owe that much to the next generation.

The Fall Foliage in Northwestern New Jersey

In writing about New Jersey, you could hardly let October go by without calling attention to that brilliant natural spectacular - the fall foliage show.

Those who have moved from the state to Florida or the various states in the southwestern part of the country tell me it is the changing seasons that they miss the most. And of all the changes, the one that arouses the greatest emotional response is the splendor of autumn's annual leaf-turning exhibition.

New Jersey's color pageant panorama begins during the first few weeks of October. That is when the dogwoods, the sumacs, and the red maples first tease us with their brilliant scarlet tints. Our state's beautiful, rugged northern hill-country, interspersed as it is with lakes, and as heavily-wooded in many areas today as it was when the early Dutch migrants first laid eyes upon it some three centuries ago, is an appropriate starting place. To perpetuate this annual array the state has fortunately set aside thousands of naturally beautiful acres in the form of state parks and forests. Often these lands were donated by private individuals who wanted to preserve for future generations that they had enjoyed.

A journey westward along Route 23 will bring you to the far northwestern corner of the state where the 13,000-acre wilderness retreat know as High Point State Park first opens our fall presentation. From there at New Jersey's highest elevation, about 1803 feet above sea level, you will be able to view not only the Jersey fall landscape, but that of nearby Pennsylvania and New York State as well. A little further north at Tri-State Rock nearby Port Jervis you can almost stand in three states at the same time!

With the first curtain up, the show unfurls a continuing emblazonment of fall colors as more reds appear on our many scarlet oaks, sour gums, and sassafras trees. Along the ground, the leaves of the Virginia creepers and the blueberries add to this magnificent hue. The bright yellows of the various maples, birches, tulips, sweet gums, and locust will put a further contrast on our autumnal array.

Other maples and ashes will add mixtures of yellows and oranges and purples. Hickories, elms, and a variety of oaks as well will then complete the fall spectacle by turning to various shades of brown.

You can leave High Point and head south along 521 through Millville and Montague. Then take Route 206 into the 13,500 wooded acres of Stokes State Forest. There you can see some commanding vistas of fall foliage in its forested landscapes and picturesque gorges.

Continuing further south on 521 will bring you along the beautiful 700-acre Swartswood Lake State Park. Further to the south, you will meet Route 94. Along this road, you will pass through Blairstown, Walnut Valley, and Hainesburg on your way to Route 80 at Columbia. Follow Route 80 west to 70,000-acre Delaware Water Gap National Park. There the Delaware River, separating New Jersey from Pennsylvania cuts a 1200-foot deep gorge through the Kittatinny

Mountains. This natural formation, known as the Delaware Water Gap, is considered one of the scenic wonders of the east.

The Lenni-Lenape Indians called this "the place where the water is gone." The entire region was once the home of the Minsi Indians, the Wolf Clan of the Lenape Tribe. They were known to the early English settlers as the Delaware Indians. The Upper Delaware was once the ancient center of a flourishing Indian culture. Archaeologists have been excavating in the area between Flatbrookville and the Gap to uncover increasing evidence of the eastern woodland Indian settlements that were so prominent in this region.

Thousands of years of Indian habitation of the Upper Delaware ended with the coming of the Europeans. Though they lived at peace with the early Dutch and later English settlers from the mid 1600's to the mid 1700's, the coming of the French and Indian War in 1753 was the beginning of the end for them in New Jersey. By the close of the American Revolution (1783), most were gone from the Jersey side of the Delaware.

How appropriate that this part of New Jersey where Indians were once so prominent, has been preserved by the state and national governments. These thousands of wooded-acres and natural vistas now serve as a living memorial to its "original people," and especially so throughout the annual fall foliage spectacle in the season know as "Indian Summer." Just another of the sights you will see along the trails of New Jersey.

Fall Tour of Northern and Central New Jersey

We are in the midst of that beautiful season when Jersey's autumn colors are at their zenith. In as much as this state puts on as fine a show as can be found anywhere, it is appropriate to devote more time to New Jersey's fall foliage spectacular. While we view this annual splendor, we might also take in some of the historic sites that place New Jersey in the forefront of the Revolutionary War period. Though there are ample places right here in our state where we can successfully compete with New England, both in colorful foliage and historic events, New England seems to have captured the public fancy. I hope that someday our state will receive its just due.

We should point out that New England gets the jump on New Jersey because the annual autumn show always starts there before it does here. This is the result of the advent of earlier cool nights in the north. By the same token, the leaves in our northern counties begin turning colors before those of our southern sector. Coincidentally, the first shots of the American Revolution were also fired in New England. After which New Jersey played a far more significant role.

Exactly when the best time for viewing this color change is, will vary from year to year. The amount of rainfall during the growing season, as well as the arrival of long, cool nights help to determine when the colors will peak. The only certainty here is that shorter days will come with the fall. The scientific explanation for this natural occurrence involves a chemical process within the tree itself. Some of the colors we will see in any plant in the fall are actually always present.

It is in late summer, however, that the green chlorophyll, which up to that time is dominant, begins a breakdown process, which finally makes it possible to see those yellow and orange pigments. With the proper mixture of moisture and sunshine, other chemical action stimulates the manufacture of red and blue pigments while producing sugar for storage in the roots and stems. This blend of colors, not the same in every plant, gives us our fall foliage spectacular. A combination, then, of warm, sunshiny days and long, cool nights along with the variety of plants and the proper amount of moisture is the key to the perfect autumn festival.

Last week, we were in the northwest around High Point, Stokes, the Delaware Water Gap, and Swartswood Lake. Now moving eastward we will traverse the areas surrounding Wawayanda State Park in mountainous northeast Sussex, the Greenwood Lake region, and Ringwood State Park in the Ramapo Mountains of Passaic County. At Ringwood we will stop and visit the Ironmaster's Mansion constructed in those days when "iron was king" in north Jersey's mountains. This park is dedicated to preserving New Jersey's role as an arsenal of the American Revolution.

Heading west on Route 80, we then turn southward from the old Moravian village of Hope onto Route 519. A pleasant and colorful trip awaits us as we travel among this route, crossing Route 22 at Phillipsburg. Continuing south through Milford, we pick up Route 29 along the Delaware River at Frenchtown. Following Route 29 through Lambertville we will come upon Washington Crossing State Park. There we will stop at the Visitor's Center and view those stirring incidents through which New Jersey was involved in the crucial Battles of Trenton and Princeton. Washington Crossing is another Jersey landmark site reminding us of the vital role this state played during the American Revolution.

From there, we drive eastward along Routes 546 and 27 to that historic University town of Princeton. It was 200 years ago this fall, while the treaty ending the American Revolution was being negotiated in Paris, that Princeton served as the capital of the new United States. Congress was in session at Nassau Hall by invitation of Elias Boudinot, a Jersey resident, who, as president of the Congress at this time, was actually the first president of the new Republic.

There are a number of historic sites to visit in Princeton. On the outskirts in nearby Rocky Hill is the Berrien Mansion, called "Rockingham," where Washington stayed with his wife, Martha, while Congress was in session at Nassau Hall. It was here in this little New Jersey village that our revered national hero received the news of the war's end, and issued his "Farewell Orders" to his armies. This landmark location has been preserved as one of our state historic sites and is well worth a visit. Next week, we will continue our fall tour along the trails of New Jersey.

Fall Tour of Central and South Jersey

The first weekend in November is probably the last chance you will get to take to the trails of New Jersey in search of its remaining autumnal splendor. At the same time, it can be another occasion for visiting a few of its many historical sites.

If the weather holds out, there should still be places left where the brilliant hues of Jersey's fall foliage will delight your senses. At any rate, there is no doubt about the availability of those historic places. By now, the northernmost counties are no doubt on the decline. So we will aim for the central and southern stretch of the state.

I suggest we take Route 206, stopping first at Somerville. It was there, with his troops encamped at nearby Middlebrook, that General Washington and his wife, Martha spent the longest stay in any one place during the entire American Revolution. It was called Raritan at that time. In Raritan (Somerville), the Washington's stayed at the newly built "Wallace House" from the fall of 1778 through that unusually mild winter, until June of 1779.

It was a somewhat quiet time for the war, and so the Washington's were able to entertain many prominent Americans of that day at the Jersey residence. An elaborate "ball" was held there also, honoring the French ambassador to the fledging Republic and celebrating the second anniversary of the French alliance. Raritan became the county seat in 1782, and was known as Somerville by 1809.

Now a state historic site, a visit to the more than 200 year-old "Wallace House" on Washington Place can be coupled with a stop at another house laden with history, the "Old Dutch Parsonage" just across the street. General Washington was a good friend of the ardent patriot, the Rev. Jacob Hardenbergh, who lived there at that time. Hardenbergh was the first president of Queen's College, and now Rutgers University.

This house was built by John Frelinghuysen, and his young wife, Dinah, with bricks they brought over with them from Holland in 1751 as ballast for the ship on which they sailed. John Frelinghuysen established the first Dutch Reformed Church Seminary in America there in the "Old Dutch Parsonage." This was the forerunner of Queen's College - now Rutgers - and the present New Brunswick Theological Seminary. The Frelinghuysen family went on to gain state and national recognition in the field of politics.

Heading south on Route 206 to Route 514, we turn left toward Millstone. Along the way we'll pass the 65-acre Mettler's Woods, known as Hutchinson Memorial Forest. It's made up of ancient 90-foot high oaks and hickories towering over a forest of dogwoods. Managed since 1955 by the Rutgers University Botany Department, this uniquely virgin forest has been left untouched for at least the past 300 years while under the ownership of one family. Continuing south along Route 533, we arrive at the village of Griggstown. There the 19th century stood still. You can visit a mule-driver's barracks, a bridge-tender's house, and the old swing-bridge. All are reminiscent of the days in the 1800s when the busy Delaware and Raritan Canal passed through this once bustling canal-port town.

Also at Griggstown is the home of America's most famous Revolutionary War counter-spy, John Honeyman. Under the cover of a "notorious Tory," Honeyman spied for Washington while acting as a cattle-dealer for the British army. His detailed data about the British, and misinformation to them about the Americans, helped insure Washington's victories at Trenton and Princeton. The victorious outcomes of these Jersey battles were vital to both the morale of the nation, and the continuance of the Revolution. After the war, Washington had to assure Honeyman's neighbors, personally, that he was indeed a brave patriot. His exciting counter-spy activities deserve a more detailed accounting in a separate article. The Honeyman House is owned privately and is not open to visitors.

For a view of south Jersey's fall foliage, continue on Route 206 past Trenton, and head towards the 100,000-acre Wharton State Forest. Bypassing the vast Fort Dix Military Reservation, you will know you are on the outskirts of the Wharton Tract when you reach Indian Mills. There, in the twilight of Jersey's "Indian Summer," you will see the area where America set aside its first Indian Reservation by the Treaty of Easton during the French and Indian War. It was to this spot that north Jersey's proud Lenni Lenape nation was to be permanently encamped.

Continue through Wharton to Route 542. Turn left back into the state forest at Pleasant Mills. Visit the historic restored Iron Village of Batsto. Turn south on Route 563 to Egg Harbor, and continue on to May's Landing. There, time overcomes us again, on another of our journeys along the trails of New Jersey.

Outdoor Recreation in the Fall

"O suns and skies and clouds of June, and flowers of June together, Ye cannot rival for a single hour October's bright blue weather." They must have been experiencing a slice of the same kind of days that have graced New Jersey during these past several weeks to have inspired Helen Hunt Jackson to write those famous lines in her mid-19th century poem. In my generation, we had to commit it to memory as part of our schooling. I have never forgotten it and I am thankful for that. It is interesting, too, in this season known a Indian Summer, that Mrs. Jackson also wrote a great deal about our American Indians. Her most famous was perhaps "Century of Dishonor," published in 1881.

I cannot let October slip by though, without some comment about this fascinating season in New Jersey. Perhaps those of us who live here cannot fully grasp with the keenest sense of appreciation what beauty it beholds. It hit me most clearly when my wife, Ruth, commented that she thought she would collect a sampling of the colorful leaves surrounding our home, and send them to our daughter, Karen, now living in southern California. Karen, she said, misses the changing colors of the Jersey trees.

I've said it before, and its worth repeating now, you don't have to go to New England to enjoy this annual autumn leaf-changing spectacle. A drive through New Jersey's countryside will offer as awesome a display of fall colors as you will find anywhere. But it does not have to be limited to a drive in the family auto. For those with a little more zest I could suggest that you partake in the kind of activities my son, Peter, has enjoyed indulging in on these past several weekends. Both bicycling along Jersey's special trail-ways, and canoeing along its select waterways, will offer still other perspectives of the state's natural beauty in this season of changing colors.

One route that offers you both opportunities for viewing the Jersey countryside with its autumnal beauty, and at the same time helps you gain a sense of the state's interesting heritage, is that which takes you along the old paths of the Delaware and Raritan Canal and its feeder. Of course, it could not be accomplished in one weekend. This canal was completed in 1834, just 150 years ago, by thousands of Irish immigrants. These men labored on these canals for several years with pick and shovel, wheel barrows and horse-drawn scrapers. Hundreds died along its banks of cholera in the process.

For 100 years thereafter, it was part of one of the busiest transportation networks in the nation, as both mule-driven barges and magnificent yachts plied its waterways. Today, with portions of it as part of a State Park, it provides trail-ways for hikers and bikers as well as waterways for canoeists. Its former mule towpaths, now often overgrown with foliage, offer leisurely pathways through the natural serenity of the Jersey landscape. A part of the state, with which many are totally unfamiliar, is in fact these back area by-ways where its true beauty lies.

A dam was built across the Delaware at Raven Rock above Stockton. This dam insured both a steady supply of water for the canal by a feeder route to Trenton, where the actual canal started on its cross-state journey to New Brunswick, and, a water route for hauling coal from Pennsylvania's coal mines to the manufacturing centers. A link was also built from Trenton to Bordentown, but that is now filled in. The feeder route along the Delaware, however, is part of one of the finest 60 miles of waterways for recreational canoeing, as you will find anywhere.

Coming down the feeder route, you will pass the point where Washington and his heroic army crossed the Delaware for their historic Battle of Trenton. And along the bank of this feeder is a monument to John Honeyman, Washington's personal spy, who did much to make possible that historic event. Eastward beyond Trenton you will pass near historic Princeton and thence along Lake Carnegie to Kingston. Nearby is Rocky Hill, where Washington bid farewell to his troops at war's end. Further upstream are Griggstown and the house where John Honeyman lived with his family during the American Revolution.

The Millstone Valley Historic Trail, along the towpath from Kingston to the canal-bridge at Weston, was part of Washington's route to Morristown after the victorious Battles of Trenton and Princeton. Visits to such little Jersey villages as are along this canal route will help give you a better perception of what life was and is like along the many charming trails that cut across the unbeaten pathways of New Jersey.

Halloween in New Jersey

As the Halloween season rolls around, our minds begin to turn to thoughts of ghosts, goblins, witches, and such. New Jersey has plenty of authentic ghost stories to satisfy even the most ghoulish of appetites. Each area has its own local specters - depending upon its heritage. But let us look first to the origins of Halloween.

Many pagan tribes in the first centuries had recently been converted to Christianity. They had already been observing various festivals at this season of the year. Worshipping the spirits of their ancestors was often a part of these celebrations. Leaders of the early Church decided it would be a good thing to incorporate a Holy Day into this season, which could accommodate their ancient feast days.

It was finally resolved that Nov. 1 of each year should be set aside as "All saints Day." On this day, the "Feast of All Saints" would honor the memories of all those departed Christian souls who once lived on earth. In time, it became the custom to light bonfires the night before, called Holy Evening, or Hallow E'en. The purpose was to guide these good spirits back to the places where their memories were to be lauded. Halloween feasts, amidst gigantic bonfires, made for a happy night of reunion and dining, followed the next day by fasting and worship.

The superstitious early Europeans, however, soon imagined that the "evil spirits," jealous of all the attention being given to the departed "saints," were intermingling with the guests and creating havoc. Witches and goblins and the mysterious black cats became a part of this annual scene. An old custom returned of disguising oneself in various costumes to throw the evil spirits off. Treats were also left for them to appease their jealous lusts for revenge.

Many centuries later, new customs had evolved out of theses early traditions. Among early New Jersey residents was one called "Treat or be Tricked!" In later years, it was shortened to "Trick or Treat." Watered-down versions of many of these old practices eventually became our present Halloween customs.

But over the years, the idea that this was a special evening for ghosts to revisit the countryside persisted. The ghost of Johann Printz for instance. This once-gigantic, 400-pound Swedish Governor of New Sweden, who loved to eat, and whom the Indians called "The Big Tub," haunted the south Delaware region for centuries after the Dutch drove him out. The "Indian Slayer," Tom Quick, known also as the "Avenger of the Delaware," was often seen patrolling the woods of northwestern New Jersey with a particular vengeance on this night.

Always, he searched for the eluding 100th Indian to slay in revenge for the murder of his father.

The ever-persistent "Jersey Devil" frequented the Pine Barrens in South Jersey with a special vigor this night - eager to be returned to the heart and hearth of the mother who rejected him so many years before. Old canal-boat captains were often seen in the vicinities of the routes of the Morris or Delaware and Raritan canals on Halloween - long after the canal era had passed into Jersey history - as were ghosts of the riverboat men who plied the waters of the Delaware.

The "Murdering Parson of Pleasant Grove," Jacob Harden, for years revisited his old circuit on that night. He always ended the evening back in the vicinity of the Belvidere Courthouse - with the hangman's nooses still tight around his neck. Many people bore witness to the fact that "Old Blackbeard," the notorious Jersey pirate revisited his old haunts along the Jersey shore on this night. He was forever wailing about his lost buried treasures.

Then there was the "Ghost of Jerry Mack." Every year, he came back to the place where he lost his life to a mining mishap so long ago. Some say he still haunts the hills surrounding the Oxford Furnace - ever angry that his young life was snuffed out too soon. What about the "Ghost of Bonnel Moody?" That Tory activist lived in the vicinity of Newton back in the days of the American Revolution. His restless soul is still purported to be pleading his case in the Sussex countryside in the vicinity of Mood's Rock.

We still hear, too, of the apparition of Joseph Thomas, "The White Pilgrim" - often seen galloping his white stallion over the fields and through the woods around Johnsonburg, or Shiloh, or Allamuchy. Or the "Ghost of Joe Milliner, "the Robin Hood bandit of Pleasant Mills. Or that of the "Charlatan of Schooley's Mountain."

These are, of course, just some of the tales still heard along the trails of New Jersey, especially on Halloween Night!

Thanksgiving in New Jersey

The first national Thanksgiving holiday has a New Jersey connection. It was proclaimed by President George Washington in 1789, less than a year after he became the nation's first president under the new Constitution. It came, however, at the urging of a new Jersey congressman from Elizabethtown. But the history of that holiday is not nearly so clear-cut. The only thing about it that is clear is that mankind throughout the ages has set aside time, after harvesting his crops, to give thanks to God. Its origins are definitely rural in nature.

We know that the ancient Egyptians and the people of the Fertile Crescent in the Mid-East paid homage to the "Earth Mother" at an annual harvest festival. The Hebrews observed the festivals of Shuvuoth and Succoth, which were connected to both the beginning and ending of harvests. The ancient Greeks paid homage to Demeter and the Romans to Ceres. Medieval Europeans celebrated the Feast of St. Martin in November, at which time they gave thanks for bountiful crops.

Our American Indians were accustomed to observing a similar occasion, as well. So it was not at all unusual that the Pilgrims, and the friendly Indians, who had helped them through that first bitter year, celebrated together a great three-day feast of Thanksgiving in 1621. Those first Indian guests brought their own food to add to that which the Pilgrims provided. From what we know, venison, duck, geese, seafood, leek, watercress, and other greens, both wheat and cornbread, plums and dried berries for dessert were included among the meals that were served.

Various customs have been associated with our traditional American Thanksgiving Holiday throughout the years. Primarily it has become a day of family get-togethers and feasting. One tradition traced back to colonial days, continued among our early pioneers, and for years popular in rural America, was the annual, Thanksgiving morning turkey shoot. Pilgrims were the first to include sports among the activities enjoyed during their three-day festival. They teamed up for a game called "Stool ball." Today, football has become a Thanksgiving Day tradition.

Since 1924, when Macy's introduced the Annual Macy's Thanksgiving Day Parade extravaganza, parades have become popular in the United States on that day. In New Jersey, Bamberger's of Newark followed with its traditional Thanksgiving Day parade that soon became the official ushering in of the Christmas shopping season. Church services became traditional in the years following

446

Sara Hale's campaign to make it a permanent national holiday back in 1827. She emphasized the Biblical origins of the need for all people to bring "Thanksgiving offerings at the ingathering of the harvest." This was to "recognize (that) the goodness of God never faileth."

The holiday had sporadic observance throughout our history. During the Revolution, the Continental Congress each year recommended a national observance of Thanksgiving. A New Jersey congressman, Elias Boudinot of Elizabethtown, introduced the resolution in Congress, which led to Washington's proclamation establishing the new nation's first National Day of Thanksgiving in 1789. New Jersey had already had a long tradition of observing such a day. As early as 1673, Anthony Clove, then the Dutch governor, proclaimed our first official observance as a colony. In 1776, when our independence as a state was proclaimed, the second Wednesday of November was established as the first official state holiday of Thanksgiving.

That New Jersey congressman Elias Boudinot, was one of our state's prominent men who went on to achieve national recognition and is, therefore, worth pausing here to mention. He was a member of the revolutionary "Committee of Correspondence" in 1774.

In 1783, he was president of the Continental Congress at the signing of the Treaty of Paris, which gave us official worldwide recognition as an independent nation. As such, he was the president of the new United States. George Washington was our first president under the constitution.

Boudinot's home, "Boxwood Hall," is now a state historic site. Located at 1073 East Jersey Street in Elizabeth, it was one of George Washington's stops in New Jersey in 1789 on his way to be inaugurated president at Federal Hall in New York City. That city was then the nation's capital. It is well worth a visit. Down the street is the "Belcher-Ogden Mansion." Original home of John Ogden, it later became the residence of British royal governor Jonathan Belcher.

Members of the Ogden family, you recall, became involved in North Jersey's iron industry. Aaron Ogden, governor of New Jersey during the War of 1812, entertained Lafayette there on that celebrity's last visit to America in 1822. These are just a few of the many tales to be told along the historic trails of New Jersey.

Christmas in New Jersey

"Christmas in New Jersey" can mean many different things - in a state whose population is as diverse as its terrain. Time, too, varied the kinds of celebrations we witnessed for this holiday. There are some common threads, however, which, having woven their way into the fabric of our traditions over the years, have come to be associated with the season we call "Christmas" here in New Jersey. Of course, basic to all is that it celebrates a birthday - that of Christ, the Son of God, who came to earth to give man a rebirth and a promise of everlasting life.

Going back to the late 1600's, we had two separate cultures planting their ideas. The Dutch, who were here first, brought with them their concept of a joyful holiday. Birthdays were happy times and were associated with gift giving. So the Dutch evolved the idea of a Saint Nicholas (Santa Claus) coming in the night and leaving little gifts behind for all the good boys and girls who believed. The period between Christmas and the New Year was a time of festivities. The modern, overly commercial concept of elaborate gift-giving gradually evolved from a few pieces of fruit set in a child's wooden shoes which had been placed by the hearth at night to dry.

The early English Puritans of New Jersey, on the other hand, were far more serious in their outlook. The frivolity and gift giving were frowned upon. Their strong work ethic forbade taking off days for celebration. Laws were even passed to punish those who kept the day with such frivolous activities. But people being what they are, they eventually chose to follow the Dutch custom which has become almost universally accepted as a part of "Christmas in New Jersey."

North Europeans saw the evergreens as symbolic of the promise of Christmas - everlasting life. Decorating homes and churches with holly and mistletoe branches followed them to our shores. With the coming of large numbers of Germans to New Jersey, their custom of placing the decorated evergreen tree - the Tannenbaum - in every home soon caught on among the populace. By the 1870's, Santa Claus and Christmas trees, boughs of holly, and gift giving were here to stay. This was especially true when Thomas Nast, then living in Morristown, popularized them in his famous cartoons which began appearing in the daily newspapers.

With large Irish and then Italian migrations into New Jersey, their customs of placing lighted candles and manger scenes in homes, churches, and public places slowly became accepted practice among most Christians. Today, we see traces of all these various customs evolving in our celebration of the Christmas season. As each immigrant group takes its place in our heterogeneous society, the best tradition of each slowly works its way into our celebration of this most joyous of all holiday seasons.

A new custom has been catching on here in New Jersey over the past several years. It is the practice of visiting our state's many historic sites, which local citizen-groups are decorating, as they would have appeared at some Christmas of a bygone era. It started slowly. As others heard about it, the idea spread. Today, almost every historic site throughout the state can be visited during the month of December with the anticipation of seeing how it would have looked in perhaps the colonial, federal, or Victorian periods of our history during the Christmas season.

The custom is citizen-oriented. From Ringwood Manor in upper Passaic County to the Dey Mansion in Preakness Valley, you will see how New Jerseyans celebrated Christmas. From the elaborate Ballantine Townhouse in Newark's Washington Park to the country setting of Stanhope's Waterloo Village in Sussex County, you will get a taste of someone in New Jersey's Christmas past. From the Wallace House in Somerville to Rockingham in Rocky Hill outside of Princeton – you will experience a Christmas in a New Jersey of long ago.

You can travel to the Allaire Village outside of Asbury Park in Monmouth County or to the VonSteuben House at River Edge in Bergen County, and a Christmas experience from the past will await you. The custom is becoming a tradition at New Jersey's historic sites, from pageants and house tours to strolling minstrels and Christmas carolers. Some even include craft demonstrations within their Christmas settings. Some of those places you also might want to visit along the trails of New Jersey this year are the Clinton Historical Village in Hunterdon County and Warren County Historical Society

Museum's "Victorian Christmas" in Belvidere. Have a Merry Christmas!

Christmas, Through the Years

Caught up in the festivities that encompass the Christmas season in New Jersey today, it's hard to visualize that very little of what we now think of as "Christmas" was seen by New Jersey's first English-speaking settlers. Robert Treat and his little band of New England Puritans, who first settled along the banks of the Passaic River in 1666, would have no part in Christmas celebrations.

Throughout the colonial period to the majority of English settlers, most of whom were of the Puritan and later also the Quaker persuasions; it was a somber time.

Though the Dutch and Swedes, who were the first Christians to settle what is now New Jersey, had an entirely different attitude about the season. It must be remembered that they were few in number before the English takeover of the colony in 1664. As a result, their influence was minimal at that time.

After the English took over New Jersey, however, they invited large numbers of Dutch and German immigrants in an attempt to build up the colony's population. They came in great numbers during the 1700's. Only with people, after all, could they make it as a paying investment.

Making money on trade, you recall, was the major purpose of establishing the New Jersey colony. Though the individual settlers who came had their own goals, it was the trading companies, not the nations they represented, who paid for the establishment of the colonies, and they were in it for the profit they could make.

Anyway, the larger numbers of Dutch and even larger German immigration into New Jersey in the 18th century did eventually have a strong influence on their English neighbors. To them, Christmas was a season to be jolly.

The Dutch were first to introduce Saint Nicholas, or "Santa Claus" as he came to be called, and the Germans their festive evergreen trees (Tannenbaum), which became the universal "Christmas Tree."

These first evergreen trees were decorated with cookies and fruit symbolizing an everlasting life of plenty. Gift giving was limited to children, who represented the new generation. Among the later English settlers of the Anglican faith, plum-pudding, hot-toddy before a "Yule-log" at the fireplace, and homes decorated with holly greens became an accepted custom.

It was the marriage of the German Prince Albert to Queen Victoria in 1841, however, that revolutionized the celebration of Christmas throughout the English-speaking world. That included New Jersey even though the United State was no longer a part of the British Empire.

Albert introduced the German custom of decking out homes, churches, and public places with the evergreen, symbol of life eternal, the decorated "Christmas Tree" in every parlor, symbolizing paradise in eternity, and the gathering of family and friends and choral groups to sing or listen to Christmas carols.

English-speaking people throughout the world began following suit; after all, it was the "in thing" to do.

The large Irish immigration into the state, which came to build the Morris and Delaware and Raritan Canals among other projects, brought with them the custom of brightly lit candles in their window and the display of manger scenes, as well as the singing of lively Irish ditties.

The Dutch, German, and Irish gaiety brought a new holiday spirit to New Jersey's Christmas season, which lasted until New Year's Day. With the great wave of German and Irish immigrants in the 1840's and 50's, there was no longer any question about the recognition of the celebration of the Christmas and New Year's holidays in New Jersey.

By 1854, the custom had become so well established that New Jersey's state legislature was pressed by its citizens into recognizing "Christmas Day" as a legal state holiday.

During the 1880's, the famous German immigrant, Thomas Nast, then living in Morristown, immortalized the caricature we now recognize as Santa Claus. His depiction of the "right jolly old elf" as he appeared in the famous poem of that era, "Twas the Night Before Christmas," clinched it. His arrival on Christmas Eve with his reindeer and the placing of presents under the family Christmas tree, which were already accepted as part of the season, now were permanently etched in every New Jersey family's mind. The stage had been set for what the 20th century would permanently recognize as symbols of Christmastime.

As large numbers of newer immigrants, such as the Italians and Poles, emphasized the lighting of candles in their windows and the display of the nativity scene, these also became accepted traditions in New Jerseyans' concept of how this holiday season should be celebrated. Though today's commercialism and perhaps over-emphasis on expensive gift-giving crept up during the 20th century, much of what we celebrate along the trails of New Jersey today had its roots in those early Christians who came to the state during the 17th and 18th centuries.

The Christmas Tree

"Oh Evergreen tree, Oh Evergreen tree, / Your faithful needles will teach me / That hope and love and constancy / Give peace and joy eternally."

Thus does a verse from an old German Christmas carol explain why the custom of displaying Christmas trees in homes and churches and public places at this joyous season of the year has caught on in the hearts of New Jersey's people and throughout America, after a somewhat stormy beginning.

It is hard to realize today, with perhaps our overzealous observance of Christmas, that at one time the staid Puritan fathers of this nation actually went so far as to pass laws against such festivities in its celebration. In New England, where the Puritan influence was most dominant from its founding in the 1620's and throughout the 1700's, such displays were slowest in gaining acceptance. But in New Jersey, which was founded by the fun-loving Dutch during that same period, the acceptance of Christmas trees and visits by good ole Santa Claus were impossible to subdue. The New England Puritans, who began moving into New Jersey in great numbers after the first English takeover of the colony in 1664 tried unsuccessfully to impose their restrictive laws upon the Jersey Dutch.

By the 1680's, the early Dutch and Swedish settlers in New Jersey were being reinforced by large numbers of Germans who, at first, moved into the state from Pennsylvania. Among these groups were a religious sect known as Moravians who founded, among other places, the Warren County community of Hope. They brought with them from Germany their custom of displaying the lighted Christmas trees in their homes and churches. Decorated with apples, cookies, and other colorful objects, these trees were generally part of nativity scenes depicting the arrival of the Christchild.

During the American Revolution in the 1770's and early 80's, the Hessian soldiers stationed throughout New Jersey were purported to have introduced the sight of these beautifully lighted and decorated trees to areas of the state whose English residents had never seen them before. They are even supposed to have influenced George Washington to display them later in his celebration of the holiday. At any rate, many of these soldiers remained in the state after the war and added their influence to its final acceptance of this custom of celebrating the Christmas season.

With the great wave of German and Irish immigrants into New Jersey in the 1840's and 1850's, there was no longer any question of the recognition of the joyous celebration of the Christmas and New Year holidays. By 1854, the state of state of New Jersey finally was pressed by its citizens into recognizing Christmas as a legal holiday. During the early 1880's, the famous German immigrant, Thomas Nast, then living in Morristown, immortalized the caricature we now recognize as Santa Claus. His depiction of the jolly old fellow appeared in conjunction with the famous poem of that era, "Twas the Night Before Christmas." His appearance with his reindeers, placing presents under the family's Christmas tree indicated that those symbols of the season were already deeply engraved in the accepted customs of the people.

This month, we may enjoy displays of earlier Christmas celebrations in the various historic sites throughout the state. Such places as Waterloo Village in Stanhope, the Deserted Village of Allaire in Farmingdale, the VonSteuben House in the area of Hackensack, the Dey Mansion in Preakness Valley, the Botto House in Haledon, the Wallace House in Somerville, Ringwood Manor at Ringwood, and Rockingham in Rocky Hill near Princeton all will have exhibits of varying sorts during the Christmas holidays. Each will be depicting something of the observance in bygone days of New Jersey.

Today's acceptance of the Christmas tree, as one of the prominent symbols of the holiday's observance in New Jersey, can be attributed to the persistence of those early settlers. Its universal acceptance may be recognized by the ever-growing demand for evergreens. This demand, in fact, has made it a profitable crop for New Jersey farmers. Christmas tree farming in the state has been increasing in recent years, with some 400- tree growers now supplying between 100 and 200 thousand annually of a wide variety of evergreens. The tale of this once-outlawed Christmas custom now seems unbelievable, since it is today so permanently engraved in the hearts of the people along the trails of New Jersey.

CHAPTER 18: A STATE OF DIVERSITY

New Jersey: "The Garden State"

There has been some discussion recently in the papers about whether New Jersey should continue to use the nickname "the Garden State." It makes one wonder about what it was that started its use in the first place. We know, for example, that because of its reputation during the period of the American Revolution for its abundant grain production, New Jersey once was called, "the breadbasket" of the American colonies. Then, too, it had also been referred to by early European visitors as a "Garden of Eden." Since that latter term refers to a land of plenty, it seems to be still appropriate, although it may not be for long at the present rate of the depletion of its farmlands and woodlands by developers.

Though the state has always been home to a myriad of different occupations, farming, for centuries, was by far the most prominent in New Jersey, and thus the term, "Garden State," has always been closely connected with farming. The fact was that in earlier times the local blacksmith was most likely to be at least a part-time farmer. So also the area's best part-time carpenters or shoemakers were more than likely farmers most of the time. A farmer, more often than not, filled in too, as the local cabinetmaker, brewer, tanner, butcher, or cooper when time permitted. And generally one of the farmers would run a cider mill in season, pressing his own apples as well as those of his neighbors - who would come from miles around to use his press. Farmers farming and "the Garden State" have always been closely associated.

Even those who were not primarily farmers in our past, such as the storekeeper, the banker, schoolmaster, lawyer, or doctor, always had some connection nevertheless to farming. Usually they had a small farm of their own. Or they lived with a farm family. Or they rented out a farm they owned to a farm family. Everyone, at any rate, was well acquainted with life on the farm - its problems and its amenities. New Jersey, the "Garden State," was always thoroughly committed to its farming.

For many years, everyone in New Jersey also lived with a garden nearby, whether they resided in one of the few "big towns," or out in the countryside. In the earliest days, of course, they adopted the type of agriculture taught by neighboring Indians. Typically they grew Indian corn and beans and hunted wild game, which was in great abundance in this "Garden of Eden." Domesticated animals were added in time. Corn held sway as the most important crop grown in much of New Jersey for many years. Wheat, rye, oats, and barley followed. Nearby gardens grown for home use typically contained beans, cucumbers, cabbage and carrots, parsnips and peas, radishes, squash, onions, and turnips. Such fruits as apples, cherries, currants, grapes, gooseberries, mulberries, peaches, pears, plums, quinces, and strawberries also were common. In later years, "garden farming," became big business in the "Garden State" - and it still is. So, too, did the growing of fruit for sale. "Jersey peaches" gained a national reputation.

The abundance of wildlife for game food, and streams teeming with fish certainly had much to do with New Jersey's early reputation as a "Garden of Eden." Though predators such as wolves, panthers, and wild cats once were a source of considerable concern to early settlers, they soon were brought under control. Animals, such as beaver, deer, foxes, minks, muskrats, otter, raccoons, and skunks were found bountifully, and hunted for pelts or for food. Immense flocks of pheasants, plover, passenger pigeons, quail, snipe, and wild turkeys added to that feeling of plenty, which gave immediate recognition to the term, "the Garden State."

Dense forests were once in such profusion that, at first, trees were considered, by early settlers, as much of a foe as a friend. Though it was true that they provided the wood necessary for such uses as shelters, fences, furniture, farm equipment, fuel, and kitchen utensils, they also meant years of backbreaking labor in the cleaning of fields for the growing of crops. Early iron furnaces could never have existed without them, and for the most part their abundance gave meaning to, "The Garden State."

Time and science have since, of course, revealed our trees to be of even greater importance than realized by previous generations.

456

They not only serve as shelters for wildlife, which plays such an important role in maintaining that "balance of nature" so necessary to sustaining life, but they provide us with life-giving oxygen, and absorb such impurities as carbon dioxide. They also play an important role as aquifers, serving to control floods and provide adequate water supplies, vital to both life and industry.

As long as the trails of New Jersey are not allowed by greed to be depleted of these vital natural resources, we shall continue to be appropriately called, "the Garden State," just as we were by our fore-bearers.

Gardens in the Garden State

Some wonder why New Jersey was ever nicknamed the "Garden State." Others concede it may once have been true, but is no longer apropos. Occasionally, there are indignant demands that it be changed to a more appropriate tag. But to those who know New Jersey best, there are no doubts as to why it was, and still is, appropriate to so call this little patch of greenery among the nation's 50. How much longer this moniker will remain true depends upon what its people allow to happen in the near future. For now, though, statistics will back up the label.

In spite of the fact that heavily industrialized strips are concentrated along routes carrying the vast majority of out-of-state visitors passing through, there are about 3 million acres of New Jersey off the beaten track in garden-like settings. Considering the state's total acreage is only 4,813,000, that is not bad. That means that only about 1,813,000 acres are devoted to industry, commerce, and heavy residential use. The remaining three-fifths are still open country.

So what, then, is to be found in the remaining three millions acres? What is it, which still permits the "Garden" tag to remain? Well, for one thing, I have mentioned a number of times that it does have an enormous number of water bodies within its tiny peninsula. Enough so, in fact, to make it the greatest single source of fresh water in the East. That is what keeps its some 1 million acres of farmland and 2 million acres of woodlands so "garden fresh" most of the time - along with its usually very adequate rainfall.

It is true the state is the most urbanized and densely populated in the nation - the only one, in fact, to have reached 1,000 people per square mile. It also, fortunately, has had leaders of vision who established a "Green Acres" program within its boundaries. It is presently working, sometimes against great odds, to continue to preserve as much of its remaining greenery as is feasible. A recently enacted farm preservation program is part of that attempt.

From the mountainous northern counties to the southern coastal plains, some 50 wildlife preserves consume about 150,000 of those 3 million acres. About 600 local, county, state, and national parks occupy another 400,000 acres. As you can see, most of that open space is on private property, and so its future as a "garden spot" is very much in private hands. To meet current demands for public access to open-space and outdoor recreation, it has been estimated that an additional 200,000 acres of parklands should be acquired.

Obviously, it will only be through programs of private farmland and forest lands preservation that the state will retain its present image as a garden spot. Grazing horses and cattle in picturesque farmland settings - along with acres of waving grains and pasture, orchards and vineyards, rows upon rows of garden vegetables, acres of nursery stock and "Christmas" trees and controlled timber lands - are what, in the long run, will keep New Jersey "green."

But what about actual "gardens" in the "Garden State?" You may be surprised to know that there are an enormous number and variety of gardens within the bounds of this state. All are worth seeing, of course, but some have attained considerable prominence nationally and even worldwide. Others have achieved statewide recognition and are worth noting.

The Duke Gardens in Somerville, opened to the public in 1964, contain perhaps one of the greatest varieties of geographically and culturally different gardens in the world. From American colonial to American desert, from Indo-Persian to Edwardian English, from French parterre to Japanese, Duke Gardens has them all. At Fishing Creek in Cape May, you will find something entirely different. This is the home of the world-famous Sculpted Hedge Gardens.

A nationally renowned fern garden exists in Sparta. There, about 50 native species of fern intermingle with foreign varieties in a setting of wildflowers, shrubs, and various larger evergreens. Mountainside Park in Montclair is the site of still another kind of garden, Presby Memorial Iris Garden. There is to be found the world's largest collection of irises. This national historic landmark contains more than 200 species and 5,000 varieties among its 75,000 iris plants!

At the Tempe Wick Garden in Jockey Hollow national Park is a restored colonial garden. At the Macculoch Hall Garden in Morristown is a wide variety of old-fashioned plants. The 250-acre Skylands Gardens in Ringwood is the state's first attempt at a public botanical garden. These and many others scattered along the trails of New Jersey indeed do make this the "Garden State."

Geologic History

The familiar and splendid natural features of what we today call Warren County are, of course, the results of its geologic history. Though the thousands of acres of fertile muck-land that makes up the rich farming region called the "Great Meadows," for example, first came into existence after the completion of a successful, man-made reclamation program in 1876, its real creation goes back thousands of years to the advance of the last ice sheet - known as the Wisconsin Glacier.

Without belaboring the topic, or attempting to pretend to give you any detailed scholarly accounts, it is perhaps interesting to relate, just briefly, some general statements concerning these early beginnings. Geologists tell us that this entire area was once at the bottom of an ancient sea. This was millions of years ago. The lime deposits, the silty clays, which eventually became shale and slate - all familiar today, accumulated at that time on this sea bottom. Eventually, a great pressure from within the bowels of the earth uplifted thousands of feet of earth onto this sea. Sandstone, shale, and limestone layers covered it. In the course of additional millions of years, further eruptions pushed up folds extending the height of the land for miles above sea level. Mountains were thus born in the area.

Over more extensive periods of time, other forces of nature were busily at work re-carving these gigantic mountains of earth and rock. A "wearing-down" process had begun. Various aspects of weather played their dramatic roles over long periods of time in "wearing-down" the mountains to rolling hills. One of today's more notable natural features, that had worked its way through this landscape for some 300 miles from its source in the Catskill Mountains of NY State to its mouth at the Delaware Bay, was a mighty river the Indians called the Lenape Wihittuck.

When the Dutch came, they called it the South River. The English renamed it the Delaware, after their Lord De La Ware. It is said to have traveled its winding course virtually unchanged for millions of years. There is no doubt that this river has played an important role on this region's geography and history. Nor that it has had a profound influence on the lives of the people that lived in the Delaware Valley. Its very existence has carved out in Warren County one of the most scenic areas in the Eastern United States.

Over the ages, the Delaware river cut its way through the sandstone and conglomerate rock of what the Lenape came to call the Kittatinny - the Great Mountain, resulting in that most significant of Warren County's natural features - Delaware Water Gap. Highly regarded as one of New Jersey's "Natural wonders" for many years national recognition finally came on September 1, 1965, with the formation of the almost 70,000-acre "Delaware Water Gap National Recreation Area."

This National Park spans both sides of the Delaware for some 35 miles. From halfway up the western border of Warren County and throughout that of Sussex on the New Jersey side, and from the tip of Northampton County along Monroe and Pike Counties on the Pennsylvania side, it encompasses about 109 square miles today. About 56 of those are in New Jersey, 48 in Pennsylvania and the remaining 5 are the Delaware River itself.

In 1978, President Carter signed the legislation that designated that part of the river that lies within the park as part of the National Wild and Scenic Rivers System. Many other rivers and streams, brooks and creeks during the course of its long history began cutting their way through the countryside to empty into the mighty Delaware. Among the larger ones in Warren County were the Paulins Kill, the Pequest, the Pohatcong, and the Musconetcong. All played their roles in the lives of those with whom they came in contact.

Over the past million years, some three or four "ice sheets," or glaciers, are said to have moved southward from the Polar regions. The last, and comparatively recent, of these great natural events, which descended halfway through Warren County from the northlands, was known as the Wisconsin Glacier. This most modern "ice sheet" came into Warren about 11,000 years ago while stretching down over the northern tip of what is now New Jersey. Its presence here in areas still undeveloped remains noticeable to the educated eye.

The arrival and departure of the Wisconsin Glacier had a great impact on this region. This "ice sheet" was responsible for the present-day topsoil of Warren County, for much of it was moved there by its southward thrust. Another familiar characteristic for which it was responsible are the numerous swamplands and lakes. The stuff, which this sheet pushed before it, and left behind in its retreat, is called the "Terminal Moraine." Let us look at the effects of its presence along the trails of Warren County.

Water, Water, Everywhere

One of New Jersey's most valuable resources - which is also steeped deeply in it's past, vital to its present, and will play an increasingly significant role in its future - is its abundant supply of water.

Today, as in the past, New Jersey sits on top of the largest freshwater aquifier on the East Coast. It occupies the undersurface of one-quarter of the state's area. Everyone of its 567 municipalities has at least one waterway passing through, or along, its borders. It is surrounded on three sides by almost 450 miles of water. Some 700 square miles within its tiny land area are devoted to water. The state has more than 100 substantial rivers, streams, creeks, brooks, and runs, and numerous others too small to mention. More than 800 lakes, ponds, and reservoirs of varying sizes can be counted within New Jersey.

It thus seems unbelievable that in the midst of all of this water, the state has suffered from increasing numbers of ever-lengthening droughts in the past decade - even when rainfall has not been that lacking. The reason is obvious. The deepest and largest water barrel has its limits. Prudence would dictate that uncontrolled over-consumption of any resource can only lead to disaster. We have allowed ourselves to become the most densely populated of all the nation's states. What makes us flirt with calamity is the mistaken belief that somehow we are immune.

Our varied agricultural industry is totally dependent upon an adequate water supply. Our manufacturing industries located here to satisfy their needs for an ample source of water. The state's gigantic tourist industry counts on New Jersey's abundant clean water bodies - whether rivers, lakes, the ocean, bays, or inlets - to satisfy its recreational appetite. Every resident requires the support of an estimated 1,000 gallons of water per day to meet their needs. And yet we sup at the table as though there were no tomorrow. We deceive ourselves into believing that more is better.

From time immemorial, our waters quenched the needs of transportation, cleansing, and refreshment. The Lenni Lenape Indians, the state's "Original People," basked in its abundance for centuries - providing for both their sustenance and their recreation. With the coming of the Europeans, our ample waters served not only for these needs, but for still another dimension as well: power. The numerous communities that arose around their water mills are a memorial to what water can mean.

Swift-moving waters of nearby rivers and streams gave power to innumerable water wheels that turned out products at gristmills and sawmills, linseed oil mills and plaster mills, paper mills and limestone mills. Many places in New Jersey have retained names that tell the story of their origins. Such names as Milford, Millboro, Millbrook, Mill Creek, Millburn, Milldale, Millhurst, Millstone, Milltown, and Millville have their origins in Jersey water. Many others such as Helm's Mills (Hackettstown) and Hunt's Mills (Clinton) have buried their original purpose in new names.

The state's two largest rivers - the Hudson (306 miles in its entirety) and the Delaware (410 miles from source to mouth) - are shared with other states. The Delaware, possessing one of the natural wonders of the east, the Delaware Water Gap, also has been designated part of the nation's Wild and Scenic Rivers and is partially engulfed by a national park. Both have their beginnings in New York State. Both serve as partial borders, and both never become totally enveloped inside of our boundaries. Both have also played vital roles in our heritage, and both were "discovered" (as far as Europeans were concerned) by Henry Hudson. The Delaware was at first called "The South River" by the Dutch before our geography was fully understood.

The longest river totally within the state is the Raritan. The Indians called it "Laletan," meaning forded river. It consists of both a North and a South Branch winding through a diverse countryside before finally emptying into the Raritan Bay below New Brunswick. Another of the state's largest is the Passaic, meaning crooked river. It rises in Morris County's Great Swamp, which once was a part of the gigantic "Lake Passaic," and then meanders all over the place before finally emptying into Newark Bay.

The Passaic also contains two of the state's natural wonders, called Little Falls (with a drop of 40 feet) and Great Falls (with a drop of 77 feet). Then, there is the Hackensack, around which the Dutch first settled, and the Rockaway, which served the "Iron Kingdom." There are, of course, many others, which I will allude to among our journeys along the trails of New Jersey.

Wildlife Management Areas

From its smallest 6-acre Logan Pond at Repaupo Creek in Gloucester County, to its largest 14,000-acres of pine and oak forests and varied meadowlands - with about 20 waterways winding through it - known as the Peaslee Fish and Wildlife Management Area in Cumberland County, New Jersey maintains more than 50 wildlife sanctuaries and game preserves. They were established for the benefit not only of its natural wildlife, but for a wide variety of human inhabitants as well.

Within the most densely populated state of the nation, a conglomerate of sportsmen, naturalists, out-of-doors men, environmentalists, and just plain recreation lovers have been combining forces over the past half-century to pressure for the preservation of at least some of the state's remaining precious natural habitats.

Before they were consumed by the voracious appetite of the developers, these lovers of the great out-of-doors have so far managed to get about 150,000 acres of lands set aside. The lands where the state's wildlife preserves are located are contained within as diverse a collection of habitats as is the state's terrain itself. And they are so widely scattered throughout every section of the state that all of its citizens can find some type of natural preserve somewhere within a short distance of their home.

Unfortunately, in those areas of New Jersey where rapid development took root before men of vision saw the need for setting aside natural areas, there are few if any such preserves. Once land costs become prohibitive, the opportunity is lost forever. In fact, even once set aside, as we have seen at Hamburg Mountain in Sussex County and Sunfish Pond in Warren, the pressure to return it to private hands is not over.

Eternal vigilance, you see, is the price of land preservation as well as of liberty. I hope that these wildlife preserves will remain forever as enclaves of nature within an ever-deepening density of development, as open land decreases pressure for their development increases. They are today, however, places within an engulfing megalopolis where both man and nature can still find a much-needed respite - and should be preserved at all costs.

As I noted many times before, our small state has been blessed with an unbelievable variety of natural terrain. Within a day's ride, you can see quite an assortment of wildlife habitat. From the salt marshes along its coastal regions, to forested mountains and meadowed valleys in its uplands, New Jersey has them all. The MacNamara Wildlife Preserve in Atlantic and Cape May Counties is a good example of the thousands of acres that have been set aside in many areas of south Jersey.

Here, in a 12,500-acre setting, both canoeists and hikers can examine a primitive environment to their hearts' content. Within its bounds are found saltwater marshes, sandy pine-barrens, open fields, and forests of oak and pine. Parts of Cedar Swamp Creek and the Great Egg Harbor and Tuckahoe rivers, as well as six lakes and a number of ponds, make it a water-lover's delight.

Birdwatchers can feast their eyes upon bittern, coots, curlews, dowitches, assorted ducks, egrets, geese, grebes, gulls, heron, mallards, plovers, rails, sandpipers, teal, turnstones, willets, and even occasionally a bald eagle. Muskrats and mink, rabbits, and squirrels, woodcocks and deer are found scurrying everywhere. Both freshwater and saltwater fish abound.

In another environment, the 1,500-acre Whittingham Fish and Wildlife Management Area in Sussex County, and the 1,400-acre Wanaque Preserve, next to Greenwood Lake in Passaic County, are good examples of the smaller preserves set aside in the northern counties.

Whittingham is one of the few places left where beaver and otter can still be found in their natural habitats. The Wanaque River and Jennings Creek in the Wanaque Management Area, and the Pequest River in the Whittingham Preserve provide excellent trout fishing. Deer, duck, grouse, mallard, pheasant, rabbit, squirrel, and woodcock are also abundant enough there for the appetites of the state's out-of-doors men.

Moving to still another environment in the heavily urbanized northeast; we come up on the 727-acre Sawmill Creek Fish and Wildlife Management Area. This preserve in Bergen and Hudson Counties is a stark example of man's latest attempt to rescue what he had previously desecrated. It sits upon what had become the world's largest garbage dump. There in the Meadowlands, a yeoman's effort is paying off in the return of a variety of waterfowl and marshland fish, reptiles, and amphibians. I have here tried to select just a smattering of the natural habitat preserves that will reward you if you but travel along the trails of New Jersey.

Nature Centers

Because New Jersey is the most densely populated of all the states, and is already haunted by waste disposal, sewage elimination, water contamination, water shortages, air pollution, and a myriad of other environments problems - it is today, perhaps, a microcosm of what the whole country will one day confront. Therefore, how well, or how poorly, New Jersey handles these issues is of prime concern to the entire nation. Like it or not, our tiny New Jersey is on center stage.

Perhaps, it was no accident that our small state was endowed with such a varied environment. From mountains to seashore, from hilly woodlands to flat coastal plains, from quiet rural enclaves to bustling urban centers, New Jersey has it all. From the underlying granite rock belt where naturally decaying uranium emits deadly radon gas, to manmade methane gases spewing forth out of former dumpsites, New Jersey has it all. From the unique Pine Barrens in the south to the novel Delaware Water Gap in the north; from the unusual Palisades along the Hudson and the roaring Great Falls along the Passaic, to the ravaging, pounding waves of the Atlantic on our seashores, New Jersey has it all.

Within this splendid setting, Helen Fenske, the woman who 20 years ago took on the task of confronting the all-powerful New York Port Authority, has been given another huge task. She then helped create, in place of a proposed sprawling, bustling metropolitan jetport, today's 6,000-acre Great Swamp National Wildlife Refuge. Mrs. Fenske, a former housewife who had such a burning desire to preserve her beloved natural surroundings that she became an environmental activist, has been given a new responsibility. To her has fallen the task of promoting within our state, environmentally educated citizens - a must for our future survival.

To do this job, New Jersey has begun setting up a network of "nature centers" throughout the state. Mrs. Fenske must design the kind of imaginative centers that will excite the public about New Jersey's varied environment. She is responsible for creating centers that will illustrate the interdependence of the state's people with its natural resources - land, water, and air. To her has been given the responsibility of educating our citizens to the need for learning how its wildlife and its people, its woodlands and its parking lots, its farmers and its manufacturers, must learn to live together as we enter the 21st century.

About 12 of these "nature centers" are popping up in different environments in various sections of the state. Some will be in combination with other places of natural or historic interest in order to further draw citizen attention. How well they are financed, will depend upon how much support the people give them. In full view of the Manhattan skyline, for example, at the 800-acre Liberty State Park in Jersey City, you can already visit one of the first such

Environmental Education Centers. There, with the Statue of Liberty and the old Immigration Center at Ellis Island as a backdrop, films, speakers, and exhibits tell its millions of visitors the story of the interdependence of nature and man, within the most densely populated region of American.

At the brand new Pequest State Fish Hatchery in rural Warren County, another Natural Resource Education Center has already begun in a woodland setting. There, half a million visitors are expected to come and see its "living trout stream." Through displays and visual aids, lectures, and on-the-trail hikes, it is hoped that many will come and gain new understandings of the importance of preserving the state's natural resources.

Another such center has been created at Allaire State Park in Farmingdale. Here, at the site of a former bog-iron furnace and forge, history, sociology, economics, and nature reveal their interdependence. The historic Washington Crossing State Park along the Delaware is still another location for a "nature center."

There are other varied locales where modest beginnings have been made in what is hoped, with public support, will become "the best resource interpretive centers in America." They are at Cape May Point State Park, Bass River State Forest in Burlington, High Point State Park in Sussex, Island Beach State Park, Lebanon State Forest in the Pine Barrens, Swartswood Lake State Park, and the gigantic Wharton State forest in Burlington and Atlantic. At Wharton is also the Historic Batsto Iron Village.

These "nature centers," given the support they deserve, provide another of those unique public services to be found along the trails of New Jersey.

New Jersey at the Crossroads

From its beginnings as a European colony, New Jersey's basic occupation was farming. Soil, climate, and location made it a natural. Its reputation, as "the Breadbasket of the Revolution," was soon followed by its being dubbed as the "Garden State," because it supplied the tables of the New York and Philadelphia metropolitan areas with their fruit and vegetables.

For its first two centuries, however, New Jersey was merely a "corridor state" to the many travelers who passed through it on their way to somewhere else. Precious few of those travelers chose to remain as permanent residents. Farmers reigned supreme.

There was plenty of land, and because of the lack of demand, it remained comparatively cheap. In time, its beautiful diversity was recognized. Both its seashores and mountains turned it into the "playground state" for nearby city folk. Tourism became a major industry.

Sometime following World War II, seasonal vacationlands gradually were transformed into permanent home sites. The crush had begun.

What has happened, and is happening to New Jersey's once abundant open spaces over the past 20 years, should be a matter of grave concern to everyone. How the remaining "green acres" that are left within the "Garden State" are utilized is vital.

It will set the stage for the "quality of life" those estimated nine million who are expected to be living here in the next 10 years will have to endure.

Each year, another 50,000 acres of our precious coastal lands, farmlands, and woodlands are lost to development. That is a tremendous toll for a small state like New Jersey to have to endure.

Only a few decades ago, 950,000 acres in New Jersey were active farmlands. Today, we struggle to hang on to a minimum of 500,000 acres. That is what is needed for farming to remain a viable industry in the state. If not checked, our best farmlands and wildlife habitats will have disappeared by the end of the 1990's. We will be totally dependent on others for our food.

New Jersey already ranks first among all of the 50 states in terms of the number of people, cars, and roads per square mile. It is now the only state in the Union where none of its nearly eight million residents live "outside of a metropolitan area." With this "crush" of humanity upon its environment, every effort needs to be extended now to save what is left.

Healthful air to breathe, fresh water safe enough to drink (and swim in), marine life fit to eat, space to dispose of our wastes, the ability to move about without being forever caught up in unending traffic grids, and availability of an open countryside to retreat away from urban and suburban sprawl; all of these are vital to humanity's psychological as well as physical needs. Constantly crowded conditions breed all sorts of social, as well as physical, problems. All living beings need "space."

How New Jersey's remaining open lands are managed will determine whether or not its people are subjected to further pollution and congestion. Because of what is happening, "business as usual" has become impossible to tolerate. It has come down to the necessity for making decisions involving what is the best rational management of our remaining private lands. Property rights have now got to be balanced against a concern for the public's health and safety. The most densely populated state in the Union cannot continue to operate under the same rules as when it was merely a place to get through.

New Jersey is only about 166 miles, as the crow flies, from the tip of High Point to that of Cape May. It is only about 32 miles wide at its neck. Within its approximately 8,000 square miles, we are now attempting to squeeze some eight million people. With development going at its present pace, it will reach a saturation point of 10 million very shortly. We are creating an urban monster in which no one will want to live or work.

Early visitors found almost every kind of scenery imaginable: its famous seashore and the many lakes of its wooded mountains have been a source of recreational pleasure for untold generations. Its ideal location between two of the nation's large-metropolitan areas, New York City and Philadelphia, have provided both jobs and cultural and educational facilities for untold millions. It is, unfortunately, about to choke on its over abundance.

The very qualities that have made the trails of New Jersey such an attractive place to live, work and play are now being threatened by an over-development that has obviously gotten out of hand. New Jersey is at the crossroads. What kind of a heritage will we leave to our children? What are you doing about it?

New Jersey's Diverse Origins

From its earliest history, New Jersey attracted a wide assortment of people. Its contrasting surface features, despite its small area, seem to have partially served as the lodestone that pulled into its borders a great many people of varying interests and backgrounds. New Jersey's population became as mixed as its landscape.

Before Europeans came to the state, its first immigrants were members of the Algonquin nation, known as the "Original People," of Lenni Lenape. They too were attracted to New Jersey from elsewhere - drawn by the state's climate, the abundance of clear waters, good soil, deep forests, and easily accessible long, pleasant seashore. All of these translated into an abundant food supply, ample materials for their clothing, and their homes, which were called wigwams. In other words, the basics for a good life. In addition, such things as dyes from certain plants and shells gathered at the seashore were used for adorning themselves with those extra little luxuries that made life worth living.

In time, a variety of Europeans were lured to the lands the Indians called "Scheyichbi," and, in turn, gave it new names - New Netherlands, New Sweden, and finally New Jersey. Though the Italian explorer, Giovanni da Verrazano, first sighted New Jersey in 1524 while sailing for France (he called New York Bay the Sea of Verrazano), it was Henry Hudson, an Englishman employed by the Dutch, who first landed on the state's shores.

Hudson entered Jersey territory by way of the Delaware Bay in August of 1609, and sailed a short distance up the river. In September, he landed at Sandy Hook and explored the land around Raritan Bay. That same year, he also searched Newark Bay and the Passaic and Hackensack Rivers. Another Dutchman, Cornelius Mey, explored the region now called Cape May a few years later. The Dutch initially were interested in Jersey because its deep forests were rich in pelts for the fur trade. Later, they explored its mountains in search of minerals and eventually became engaged in the copper trade. In time, they also began to farm. Soon, Dutch and Flemish settlers, along with some French Huguenots, appeared inland from its trading posts.

Shortly after 1630, the Swedes came to the flatlands and deep forests of the southern reaches of the Delaware, also seeking a fur trade with the Indians. Later, they began to work south Jersey forests for lumber and farm its rich soil. They brought Finns and Danes to their lands, too. The first Englishmen were New England whalers who were attracted to its long seacoast. They started fishing villages on the

South Shore. Connecticut migrants came seeking a religious sanctuary at Newark, Elizabethtown, and Woodbridge. Soon, many others from the British Isles - Irish, Scotch, and Welsh - came to fish, farm, work its mines, and to engage in trade and shipbuilding.

The first Germans came to Jersey from Pennsylvania invited by William Penn as early as the late 1600's. They sought religious freedom and rich farmlands, settling along the Delaware and Raritan Valleys. Another group of German Moravians came from Pennsylvania to the region around Hope in the mid 1700's. They, too, sought to practice their religion in peace while engaging in farming. Large numbers of Germans were brought to the mountains around Ringwood by Peter Hasenclever around the same time to work its iron mines. Some moved to iron forges in the hills of Morris, Sussex, and Warren. Still other early Germans and Swiss came to work as glassblowers and potters in southwest Jersey and to the area of Egg Harbor as winemakers.

The first large wave of Irish immigrants came to work on the two great canals that crossed the state in the 1820's and 30's. The Morris Canal in the north was built to haul coal and farm products from Phillipsburg to Newark via Lake Hopatcong. The Delaware and Raritan had the same job in Central Jersey. The Irish canal diggers tended, eventually, to settle in Jersey's growing cities. A perpetual labor shortage in the early 1900's encouraged a large influx of Italian, Polish, Hungarian, and Russian immigrants. They also drifted to the cities where industrial centers provided jobs. Some also turned to farming. The Vineland area was especially attractive to large numbers of Italian farmers.

Today, about 15 percent of Jersey's population is foreign born. Italy, Germany, the United Kingdom, and Poland sent the greatest numbers. Sizable groups from Greece, Hungary, and Russia, as well as people from Asia, Africa, South America, Cuba, and Puerto Rico make the trails of New Jersey today a truly great "melting pot," and add to the enrichment of the tales that we have to tell.

"New Spain"

Most people have heard that for a good part of the 1600's New Jersey was included in what was called "New Netherlands." Some are aware, I am sure, that between 1638 and 1655 southwestern New Jersey was also known as "New Sweden." But I wonder how many know that for a time, during the early 1800's, New Jersey had also been dubbed "New Spain?" It all had to do with an event that occurred along the Jersey side of the Delaware River in 1816. The site of this historic event, as with so many others, was the little community of Bordentown in Burlington County.

Originally known as Farnsworth's Landing when it was founded as a haven for Quakers in 1682 by Thomas Farnsworth, Bordentown got its name from Col. Joseph Borden. The family gained notoriety for their patriotic zeal during the American Revolution. In 1777, "The Battle of the Kegs," which took place in the river there, led to the burning of Col. Borden's home by the British. It seems that the Borden Bushnell Plan to blow up British ships along the Delaware created a lot of nervous excitement on the part of His Majesty's Navy.

David Bushnell, a submarine experimenter from Bordentown, along with Joseph Borden, a local cooper, worked together in mining the Delaware with powder kegs made at Borden's cooperage. Though not much damage was done, the British were angry enough at the effort to see to it that Borden's home was burned. Borden was also the father-in-law of another famous resident, Francis Hopkinson, who was a signer of the Declaration of Independence and the designer of the Great Seal of the United States.

Still another onetime resident of Bordentown who achieved international fame was Thomas Paine. And he was probably the "New Spain" connection. A noted revolutionary thinker and writer, it was Paine, you recall, who wrote the pamphlet, "Common Sense." This did much in 1776 to incite the American public to the cause of Revolution against the King. He also coined the noteworthy phrase; "These are the times that try men's souls," which appeared in another of his pamphlets, "The Crisis." These stirring words were written while Paine was fleeing with Washington's army in their retreat across New Jersey.

At varying times during the 1790's, and into the early 1800's, Paine lived and wrote in Revolution-racked France. While there, he often extolled the virtues of his bucolic life in Bordentown, New Jersey. This may be why the dethroned King of Spain, Joseph Bonaparte, brother of the famed Napoleon, went there to live sometime after his flight from the Spanish throne.

Joseph had become acquainted with Paine when both served on the French Council of 500. He had been made King of Spain by Napoleon in 1808. He was deposed after having reigned for only five years. Following the Battle of Waterloo in 1815, Joseph Bonaparte sailed for the United States. Shortly after his arrival, he bought 1,500 acres in Bordentown and there created his magnificent Royal Estate on the banks of the Delaware, which he named, "Point Breeze."

The name, "New Spain," for New Jersey, came about after the Jersey Legislature had to enact special legislation in 1816 in order to allow the exiled King of Spain to purchase this royal estate on Jersey soil. The former Spanish King thought so well of his Jersey estate that in 1824, when he was offered the throne of Mexico, he declined, preferring his life in Bordentown. He finally did end his exile on the banks of the Delaware in 1832 when he then returned to Europe. After living for a time in England, he finally settled in Italy and died there in the City of Florence.

While he lived in exile in New Jersey's Bordentown, the former Spanish King entertained both European royalty and famous American Statesmen. Among the noted Americans who visited him at his "Point Breeze" Estate were President John Quincy Adams, Sen. Daniel Webster of Massachusetts, and Sen. Henry Clay of Kentucky. His former Royal Estate, now named Bonaparte Park, is a Catholic seminary, but is still open to the public.

Other historic sites in Bordentown are the Hopkinson and Borden houses and the Clara Barton School. It was in this one-room schoolhouse in 1853 that Clara Barton, founder of the American Red Cross, opened one of New Jersey's early free, public schools, so that children of the poor might also receive an education. Just a few more of those many tales about interesting and historic events that occurred so often along the trails of New Jersey.

The Nation's First "Melting Pot"

New Jersey was the first colony of the original 13 to become a sample of the multi-ethnic nation the United States would eventually become.

Though Henry Hudson visited sections of northeastern New Jersey in 1609 in his probing of the area for the Dutch in search of a northwest passage to Asia, and Adrian Block did much the same in 1611. It appears that the first actual European colonization of the state began when the Dutch established a trading post at Bergen in 1618. Pavonia, which included much of present-day Jersey City and Hoboken, soon followed. The Dutch officially designated their New World colonies as "New Netherland" in 1623.

Dutch maps of the period in the 1650's indicate that they were by then aware of the Passaic, Saddle, and Hackensack rivers as well as the region surrounding Newark Bay. From that, we may deduce that Dutch explorations in northeastern New Jersey had gone as far west as the Watchung Mountains. With the English takeover of the Dutch colony in 1664, we find that explorations went on into the lands further west during the next several decades. New Jersey's mutli-national settlement had begun.

Newark, in 1666, became the first English colony established along the banks of the Passaic River. It was a theocracy founded by a group of Connecticut Puritans who sought a place where they could worship, as they pleased, unmolested by neighbors of different religious persuasions. They first attempted such a move in 1661 while the Dutch were still in control. An agreement between the Dutch governor, Peter Stuyvesant, and the Puritan leader, Robert Treat, was reached, but not consummated, while the Dutch were in possession of the land.

When Berkeley and Carteret acquired all the Dutch claims between the Hudson and Delaware rivers in 1664, they guaranteed liberal religious toleration to all who would come and settle there. They even advertised this fact throughout northern Europe.

When Philip Carteret arrived in Elizabethtown in 1665 to become the first proprietary governor of the new province, he received a visit from Treat inquiring about the possibilities of establishing the colony they had negotiated with Stuyvesant. Eager to get settlers into their new lands, Carteret welcomed Treat and his band of Connecticut Puritans. The site on the Passaic was chosen and they finally arrived in the spring of 1666.

All was not to be that simple, however. A band of Hackensack Indians headed by their chief, Oraton, demanded payment for these lands before they would be allowed to settle. Fifty double hands of powder, 100 bars of lead, 20 axes, 20 coats, 10 guns, 20 pistols, 10 swords, 10 kettles, four blankets, four barrels of beer, two pair of breeches, 50 knives, 20 hoes, 850 fathoms of wampum, about 32 gallons of liquor, and three trooper's coats closed the deal. For this, the Puritans obtained (ownership of?) all lands from the Passaic west to the foot of the Waweack Creek on the Bayside north to the Yantacack River, where it emptied into the Passaic.

Originally called Milford, the settlement was officially named Newark, apparently in honor of Newark-on-Trent in England. This had been the home of the group's first pastor, the Rev. Abraham Pierson. By 1670, they had completed the construction of their first church, established a "Training Place," now called Military Park, a "Market Place," now known as Washington Park, and a cemetery. Six years later they hired their first schoolmaster. As the colony grew, settlements expanded west into Camptown (now Irvington), the Oranges, Livingston, and the Caldwells, and north into what are now Belleville and Nutley.

In 1668, Capt. Wm. Sandford had purchased the lands north of the Newark grants from the Indians. It included the area where the present communities of Arlington, Harrison, Kearny, Lyndhurst, and North Arlington are located. With permission of Gov. Carter, he began settling a small number of families into the region. Before the turn of the 17th century, all the lands of northeaster New Jersey were in the possession of English landowners, the various tribes of the Lenapes having moved further west. Shipping from around the world had encouraged a multi-ethnic settlement in the coastal villages.

In the meantime, Dutch settlers had continued pushing west from their settlements along the Hudson into the Delaware Valley, and across from Staten Island up into the Raritan Valley. Varying German religious groups as well as Scotch, Irish, and English Quakers followed. These, plus Swedes and Finns in the lower

Delaware, had made the trails of New Jersey into the nation's first "melting pot" where various peoples were learning to live together in Harmony.

"The Gateway" to America

When the first census was taken back in 1790, New Jersey was one of the smallest of the original 13 states. There were, at that time, less than 185,000 people to be found anywhere within its borders - all the way from the Atlantic in the east to the Delaware in the west; from High Point in the north to Cape May in the south.

Just 195 years later, we have become the most densely populated of all the 50 states. We have the ninth largest total population of any state in the nation. Though we remain 45th in area, today our population is midway between seven and eight million people.

One reason behind this tremendous increase is our geographic location. We are at the nation's front door. That is why the Statue of Liberty was placed on Jersey's doorstep back in 1886. It stands just a short distance off the coast of Jersey City. This French gift was to be placed at the entranceway to America, for all to see. That was one of the stipulations of the gift. The national government calls this region "The Gateway."

New Jersey was far different at its beginning and for many years after. The entire state used to be rural. Its population was made up primarily of farmers back in 1790. Its fertile fields produced ample yields of grain, such as corn and wheat, as well as a variety of garden vegetables. In fact, during the American Revolution, it was known as the nation's "breadbasket." Cattle, hogs, sheep, and poultry, as well as some of the nation's finest horses were raised on Jersey farms. Foraging parties from both British and American armies were a constant threat to our citizenry during the War for Independence. Jersey's substantial orchards produced large quantities of apples and peaches. In fact, hard cider from its apple orchards had achieved a national reputation. They called it "Jersey Lightning."

Our early settlers led a simple life. These independent farmers not only grew their own food, but also built their own homes and made their own clothing as well. There were plenty of fish to be taken from its many pristine lakes and steams, and an abundance of wildlife to be hunted in its fields and forests as well. The people of New Jersey were a self-sufficient breed. Mostly farmers, there were a few artisans and merchants in the scattered small villages, and deep-sea fishermen and shipbuilders along her broken coastline.

An urban population does not even appear on the graphs of New Jersey until the 1840 census, and then it was so small as to be practically unnoticeable. Not until the 1880 census, just 100 years ago, did town dwellers pull even with farm inhabitants in this state. By the 1890's, however, there were more people living in our towns and cities than on our farms for the first time in our history. The proportion of urban to rural dwellers finally doubled in the 1900 census - many of them European immigrants. By the 1920's and 30's, there was no doubt that New Jersey was becoming an urban state. Today, it is the most urbanized state in the Union. We still cling to almost 1 million acres of farmland, but that acreage is now under the most vigorous pressure to be developed than at any other period in our history. Once it is lost, of course, it will be gone forever.

Though we had become an overcrowded state for most of this century, the population centers of New Jersey were not evenly spread out across the entire state. Some areas, much to our benefit, clung tenaciously to their rural heritage, keeping the state somewhat in balance. Always providing that escape valve for those that had to find release from the pressures of overcrowding.

Most of the state's people were massed along two general regions. By far the largest population center developed in the northeast in the counties of Bergen, Essex, Hudson, Passaic, and Union, which bordered on the busy harbors along New York Bay and the Hudson River. About three-fifths of the state's people lived there. The smaller of the two urban areas was along the Delaware River in the regions centering near Trenton and Camden. One was part of the New York metropolitan area, the second that of Philadelphia. Benjamin Franklin always described New Jersey as "The cider barrel, tapped at both ends."

The two bastions of rural life that managed to keep the trails of New Jersey in balance throughout all of these years were its northwestern and southwestern counties. That is until the mid-1970's, when the pressure for development began to reveal itself in those far areas.

How much of rural New Jersey will remain, if any, following the current, seemingly unrelenting demands for new construction on our ever diminishing countryside, will determine what future tales are to be told along the trails of New Jersey.

The North American Phalanx

Some four miles west of Red Bank and about one mile north of Colts Neck, off of Route 34 in Monmouth County is the site of what was once considered by many prominent American writers, editors and social thinkers of the mid 1800's to be the answer to the world's social and economic ills. It was called the North American Phalanx.

Though based somewhat on ideas promoted earlier by Robert Owens of England and Charles Fourier of France, this American experiment in social living got its start in America at a time following the economic depression of 1837. As often happens when times are bad, people are willing to try out new ideas on how to live together in peace and harmony for the common good of all. An earlier experiment by Owens himself at New Harmony, Ind. had failed. But in 1842, such distinguished literary men of the day as Nathaniel Hawthorne, Ralph Waldo Emerson, Chares Dana, and Theodore Parker founded what appeared to be a very successful colony outside of Boston called Brook Farm. In time, about 69 such colonies arose throughout America.

With the seemingly flourishing Boston experiment in social living already in operation, a group of families from upstate New York purchased the old 700-acre Van Mater farm in Monmouth County in 1843. There they set up what was to be one of the longest operating and most successful social colonies in the nation - the North American Phalanx. One of its most distinguished backers was the famous editor of the New York Tribune, Horace Greeley.

The basic idea of the plan was that people should live together, away from the big cities, in self-supporting groups of about one to four thousand. They would be housed in large, hotel-like structures called phalanxes - from the Greek term for a military formation. Three or four of these phalanxes would form a union, three or four unions a district, and several districts a province. Within these colonies, there would be no extremes of poverty and wealth. All would find labor adapted to their tastes and talents. All would share in the fruits of their industry. Rich and poor would be unheard of. Everyone would work together for the common good. In time, a world unity would evolve with universal harmony. Want would be banished from the earth. There would be no need for fighting amongst one another, and so no need for armies or police department.

The New Jersey colonists were a cross-section of people. They included scientists, writers, farmers, lawyers, doctors, and artisans of all sorts. Each bore their share of the community's work. All had their appointed tasks. They practiced religious toleration, profit sharing, the 30-hour workweek, and equal pay regardless of age or sex. And all of this was in the mid 1800's, right here in New Jersey! The least desirable and most exhausting work paid the highest hourly rates. A reserve fund was set up for old age, accidents, emergencies, and equal education for all the children. There was no need for insurance or savings. People ate together in a main dining room where they could choose their meals from a menu. Evenings were devoted to dances, lectures, amateur plays and charades, or, political and social discussions.

In addition to a large farm, mills and machine shops were soon constructed. By 1852, New Jersey's North American Phalanx outside Red Bank was a productive and profitable colony. But because it was different, it was subject to constant outside criticism. One incident involved the introduction of the loose, Turkish trousers, known as bloomers, named after their designer, Amelia Bloomer of New York. Their use was begun by the women of the colony in 1848 because they found them much better suited to working in the fields. But they shocked the women of nearby Red Bank, and thus caused many bad reports to circulate about the type of women in the Phalanx.

In spite of its prosperity, an undercurrent of disagreement began to emerge within the community. Times had improved in the country. Reports of high wages on the outside began to bring on unrest. Soon after, a fire in one of the mills led to serious disputes as to where or how it should be rebuilt. One group split away and formed the Raritan Bay Union near Perth Amboy. By 1855, the majority voted to abandon the experiment. The property was broken up and sold at auction. The monies received were divided. New Jersey's famous social experiment - the North American Phalanx was dissolved. Just another one of those interesting tales that make the trails of New Jersey so unique.

A Microcosm of the Nation

As we approach the 1990 census, let us pause and take stock. According to the demographers, New Jersey, at its present rate of development, will reach a saturated population of 20,000,000 people by the year 2030.

Considering it took us some 260 years after the first Dutch settlement to reach our fist million that should indicate how fast the state is gobbling up its land resources in the current development cycle.

Demography also has some pretty sour dates concerning what this population explosion, assuming it remains as environmentally abusive, will do to our surroundings. The coming "Earth Day" should give us cause to pause.

Given our current preference for material comforts and financial gain over environmental sensitivity, we can expect such pleasantries as ever-increasing traffic gridlock and current garbage-disposal headaches becoming nightmares.

Water and air pollution will reach phenomenal proportions.

Land costs will force us to mortgage our housing upon our grandchildren, just as young Japanese couples do today, in order to meet monthly payments. And, as any psychologist will tell you, people will become increasingly cranky as their "space" becomes scarce. Thus, we will get cumulatively on each other's nerves, with all the ensuing dire social disruptions. Health problems thus created could easily bankrupt many.

New Jersey today is a microcosm of what the whole nation could confront in the future. How well New Jersey handles these problems is, therefore, of considerable concern to the nation.

If personal financial gain remains our only criteria for what we do with our remaining land resources, then we will pass on to our next generation the chilling results of our monetary greed.

Only the application today of common environmental sense for the common good will save our descendants from an environmental disaster. The Lenape should see their beloved Sheyichbe now.

When the first census was taken in 1790, New Jersey's population had reached some 185,000. Ten years later, in 1800, it was barely 200,000. Always a "crossroads" state between two large cities, Philadelphia and New York, New Jersey's population for 300 years remained concentrated in that corridor.

To the south lay the great Pine Barrens and the remote and seasonally desolate Jersey shore. To the north lay the frontier-like, heavily forested, rocky hill country. Both were primarily sparsely settled and somewhat agricultural in economy.

Not until the 1880 census, a period of some 260 years, did New Jersey's population finally reach its first million. In the ensuing 100 years, it would climb by eight times that amount! For example, by the time of the 20th century, what with a considerable increase in immigration, the 1900 census gave New Jersey about 1,800,000 people.

Twenty years later, with another surge of immigration, and an increase of development following both WWI and the coming of the automobile, the 1920 census took our population to three million! In the next 10 years in the midst of the Great Depression, the 1930 census registered a population of four million inhabitants in the Garden State. By that time, people began to become concerned.

Following the development boom brought on by the return of WWII veterans and an increasingly common possession of the automobile by just about every family, the 1960 census showed New Jersey with a six million population. As we approach the 1990 census, what has since become the most densely populated state, is expected to reach an unbelievable eight million people. That is more than many European countries.

Yet we still have not changed our 18th century attitude that more is better. With residential development becoming the largest consumer of land, we have obviously long since spilled over the originally stipulated population corridor. The once-pristine countryside to its north and south, which had for centuries been the "breadbasket" of the metropolitan area surrounding it, and the reason why New Jersey had been dubbed the "Garden State," was apparently to be gobbled up as well, regardless of the economic and environmental consequences.

In spite of all the warning on the horizon concerning what is surely coming lest we change our habits and monetary priorities, open space in New Jersey casually disappears at an alarming rate. What remains of prime farmlands and much needed "breathing spaces" is direly threatened.

Virtually no lands along the trails of New Jersey seem exempt. "Earth Day" and Census Day - 1990 should give us pause to consider the heritage we will leave to the next generation.

The Loss of Open Spaces

New Jersey today is in the throes of an unprecedented, unplanned, and inevitably costly and destructive sprawl, similar in motivation to what sent the pioneers on their westward trek across the nation in the post-Civil War period some 125 years ago. Just as that westward movement left valuable natural resources destroyed in its wake, so the present trek within our state, left virtually unchecked, has the same potential. Only the application of common sense, for the common good, will save us from a drastically significant change in the physical, social, and economic character of the state we now know and love.

When the census was taken for the first time, New Jersey's population was about 185,000. That was in 1790. By 1800, it was barely 200,000. Just over 100 years ago, in 1880, it had reached 1 million. By the turn of the 20th century, in 1900, there were about 1,800,000 people in the state. By 1920, following a surge of immigration, it had reached 3 million. In 1930, at the onset of the Great Depression, the state had 4 million inhabitants. The 1960 census showed 6 million. As we approach the year 1990, just 200 years from that first census, the number of people crowding into what has since become the nation's most densely populated state presses 8 million. Yet we still have not changed our 19th century attitude that more is better. Estimates based upon our continued, haphazard development predict an ultimate population of 20 million! By that point, drastic changes in our accustomed lifestyles will be forced upon us.

Residential development has become the state's largest consumer of land. It has increased more than three times the rate of population growth, and threatens to deplete all the available land for homes in northern New Jersey within 20 years. All usable residential land in the entire state, at our present rate of development, will be gone by the year 2050. At that point, we will finally have had to come to grips with the fact that land is a limited resource.

New Jersey's agricultural pursuits have been an important part of the life of the state, as well as the nation, since colonial times. When our villages and towns were first arising, the state's rural lands provided the major source of its daily food requirements. An abundance of fertile soil, a moderate climate, and an ample rainfall were the ingredients that made New Jersey the natural "breadbasket" of the growing young nation. Those ingredients still exist, and make this state a leading agricultural producer per acre in the nation in 1986! Such a valuable, irreplaceable resource should not be allowed to be destroyed at any cost.

Since the 1940's, farm acreage in New Jersey has been cut in half and the number of farms reduced from 25,835 to 9,100 due to its permitted intensive development. In spite of the fact that a growing urban population is more dependent than ever upon the products of a state with prime farmlands, its destruction by urban encroachment is treated casually and permitted without alarm for future consequences. In addition to food, agriculture has been "keeping New Jersey green" at no cost to the taxpayer. When that open-space is gone, our people will suddenly awaken to the knowledge that our land is a limited resource.

In recent years, various groups dedicated to the conservation and preservation of our nation's scenic, historic, and recreational areas have been trying desperately to arouse the public's awareness concerning the alarming disappearance of our open space in New Jersey. A return to the philosophy of the nation's first inhabitants, the Lenapes, is badly needed. The American Indians believed the land was to be used for the benefit of all men. Its use was on loan to individuals. Our zoning laws are an extension of that belief. If New Jersey is allowed to become even more overcrowded, in the name of "progress," individual rights to do whatever with the land will become increasingly restricted. Wherever crowds gather - more laws are imposed. We are writing our own tickets.

In spite of all the warnings on the horizon concerning what is coming, open spaces in New Jersey casually continue to disappear at a frightening rate. The outward expansion of the New York and Philadelphia metropolitan areas into New Jersey's open spaces has finally reached far out into its countryside, and now threatens to take even more of its prime farmlands. Deficiencies in providing needed recreational areas, "breathing spaces," and natural settings for the expanding population will hit with a sudden impact. Unique natural and historic areas will be lost forever. Development of natural aquifers and flood plains threatens our water resources. Yet virtually no lands along the trails of New Jersey seem exempt from the onslaught of development. The future, as was the past, is in the hands of the people.

Community Recreation

No matter how bad the times might have been, folks always seemed to fine some way to have a good time. Though the means of recreation may have varied throughout its history, New Jersey's people were able to find some way to entertain themselves. To the families living on the isolated New Jersey farms, and there were many, it often meant combining difficult everyday chores with social functions. Those who lived in the few larger "cities" could count on something more formalized, but for most of its people, fun was where they made it.

Since the most practical means of having a good time for these many farm families, who had little time and lots of work, was to lump the two together in various ways, all sorts of "parties" were arranged. Though done in the spirit of neighborliness, they also provided outlets for pent-up emotions, a break in the daily monotony, an excuse to get together socially, a chance to pit skills, and a way to get lots of jobs done that were often too much for one person or family to handle alone.

When a young couple got married, for instance, it was customary for their neighbors, along with their entire families, to come together for a "house raising" party. While the men busied themselves notching the logs and lifting them into place, the women worked on the noonday meal. The young people, depending upon their ages, either joined in, or played games together. Before lunch, the sides and floors were done. After the noon meal, the roof was put in place and clay was pressed into the cracks between the logs. All that the newlyweds had left to complete by day's end were the doors and windows. After supper, folks socialized for a while and then went home. The teenagers usually danced and "partied" into the night.

Once these young married couples were settled in their new home, they, in turn, were expected to provide still another break in the daily routine of their neighbors. This next occasion for socializing would be their "housewarming" party. Everybody who had helped at the house-raising would expect to be invited. A big evening meal was prepared, after which there would be games and dancing into the night.

Some entertainment was gained as well by community projects. These might be in the form of building a new or larger schoolhouse, or getting together to put up a new church or parson's home. Or sometimes it meant helping a neighbor with his barn raising. If disaster or illness struck a neighbor or his family, it might involve pitching in to do the farm work or house chores until the problem was solved. Whatever the occasion, it usually ended up by providing a combination of work and recreation for the families of his neighbors.

Throughout the 19th, and even into the early 20th century, spinning and weaving bees and quilting parties were popular neighborhood social events. The women had the opportunity to socialize all day, but in the evening the men-folk would arrive from the fields, and, after a hearty meal, dancing on the cleared barn floor would continue into the night. The young people might even stay until daylight.

In the earlier days, before fulling mills were erected, "fulling frolics" were also engaged in by the young folk of an area. The bundle of newly woven cloth was soaked with warm, soapy water and then "kicked about" by the young men who sat in a circle of chairs barefooted with their trousers rolled up above the knees. Amid much laughing and kidding the girls continually wrung out the wool cloth, hung it out to dry and replaced it with new bundles. By the end of the 18th century, 41 fulling mills were in operation in New Jersey and these "frolics" faded into history.

Apple-butter making bees, wood-cutting bees, corn husking bees - all were popular excuses for practical community get-togethers that both accomplished some necessary chore and provided a chance for lonely farm families to socialize. Much merriment and cider drinking took place during these affairs, and often contests between teams were introduced to add to the fun and excitement of the occasion. Loads of pies were consumed and dancing into the night usually rounded out the day's festivities.

Of course, there were also other community functions that brought neighbors together. Church suppers, strawberry festivals, spelling bees, picnics, turkey-shoots, trap-shooting contests, barn dances, all were among them. Hunting and fishing were both sport and functional. Horseracing and fistfights were also arranged. The many taverns and inns that dotted the trails of New Jersey often provided such a center of community life that their role made them an 18th century institution. Only the church and school exceeded their importance.

Entertainment Before TV

Before television or movie houses, the people of New Jersey had to find other sources of entertainment to break the monotony of daily life. The current popularity of the TV show, "People's Court," reminds me that at one time in our past, a trip to the County Seat while court was in session used to be a popular source of amusement. It served as a sort-of live soap opera. People sat for hours listening to the unraveling drama of someone else's tragedies, much as they sit glued to the TV today watching their favorite soaps.

Notices of scheduled court sessions were as much looked forward to then as people today check TV guides or movie listings.

Lawyers and judges, with varying personalities, were listened to and rated with as much enthusiasm as modern movie or TV stars. And, in between trials, or during breaks, the more inventive New Jerseyans organized group or individual competitions, and often collected side bets to make them more interesting. Some used the occasion for family shopping. Having a County Seat is one's town in those early days was good for business.

If a public punishment could be anticipated, as a result of a given trial, that trial could expect to arouse even more excitement. The whipping posts, the stocks or public dunkings were some of the more entertaining punishments meted out. Lockups were no fun for the spectators and more costly to the taxpayers. But the real crowd-pleasers were the public hangings. Specially constructed gallows were put up outside of the courthouse. It is hard to imagine today the great hoopla this event stirred up among the entertainment-starved people of the past. Crowds would come to the county seat from miles of the surrounding countryside for such a stimulating experience.

One such exciting trial was held in Belvidere in the mid-19th century. It had all of the drama of a modern "soap," involving as it did a popular young minister, the Rev. Jacob S. Harden.

Harden was indicted in April of 1859 for the murder of his wife. He had been a Methodist circuit-rider preacher serving many little churches of the area. At the time the murder was committed, he was officiating at the Anderson Church in Mansfield Township. Not long after his marriage, he fell madly in love with one of the young ladies he met on his travels. In order to marry her, he plotted to murder his wife by poisoning. A systematic placing of arsenic in the apples she was eating seemed the perfect crime. The plot was uncovered upon her death.

Though the evidence presented during his 14-day trial in April of 1860 was strictly circumstantial, the jury, composed of Edwin Albertson, James Blair, Aaron Crammer, John Deshong, Philip Hartung, Horace Norton, David Smith, George Stillwell, John Tell, Charles Walker, and George and Philip Weller, found him to be guilty.

His execution on the gallows constructed at Belvidere in the early summer of 1860, was one of the most dramatic occurrences in the history of Warren County. It was celebrated as though it were a county fair. Refreshment tents were set up along the roadsides. Special trains ran into town by the Bel-Del RR. People poured in by the thousands.

Though this carnival-like atmosphere hardly seems appropriate by today's standards, it was a common practice in those days. Tickets were even sold for special close seats. Printed copies of his confession were also for sale as souvenirs. The trial and hanging became the chief topic of conversation, much as a World Series game might be today. Local folklore has it that his anguished ghost returned to that scene each Halloween for many years thereafter.

The county fair was another "happening" that served as one of New Jersey's chief sources of entertainment. Three-day fairs twice yearly, each May and October, were authorized by the General Assembly as early as 1686. Burlington, Newark, Perth Amboy, Princeton, Salem, Trenton, and Woodbridge were among the earlier places set aside. Decorated booths with varieties of merchandise to see, exhibits, carriage and horse races, and many other contests and activities were arranged to attract the outlying farm families as well as city-folk. And they did. They came by the thousands.

Between 1781 and 1826, some 10 County Agricultural Societies were holding one or two fairs a year each. By 1860, another 33 clubs came into existence. The NJ Agricultural Society held its first State Farmer's Fair at Camden in 1855. Each year, it was held in another city until a permanent fairground was established in Newark in 1867. That lasted until 1899. In addition to providing educational and business opportunities, these fairs once served as vitally important recreational outlets for the hundreds of thousands of lonely farm families who lived along the trails of New Jersey in that by-gone era.

Recording Industry

Edison's genius was in the application of science to technology.

When the US Congress awarded this prolific New Jersey inventor its gold medal in 1928, it noted that his inventiveness, up to

that date, had contributed a monetary value to society of .
$15,599,000,000.

In fact, no monetary value can be placed on the pleasure,
convenience and improvement to life this man's inventions have
provided mankind. He is regarded by many as one of the greatest
technical geniuses that ever lived.

Most of his early inventions, such as the phonograph,
developed first in 1877, have come a long way since their inception.
His crude phonograph was the grandfather of today's highly technical
recording industry - with all of its ramifications for science, business,
and entertainment.

The National Academy of Recording Arts and Sciences
established a "Hall of Fame" in the early 1970's just to "bring to the
American public a greater awareness of the cultural riches that have
been amassed since the invention of sound recording."

In 1975, its first entrants were five all-time hit records:
Coleman Hawkins' "Body and Soul," put out by Bluebird Records in
1939; Nat King Cole's "The Christmas Song," by Capitol Records in
1946; Paul Whiteman and George Gershwin's "Rhapsody in Blue,"
by Victor Records in 1927; Louis Armstong's "West End Blues," by
Okeh Records in 1928; and Bing Crosby's "White Christmas," by
Decca Records in 1942.

I had mentioned before that a retired audio-engineer in the
recording industry, Clair Krepps of Warren County's Franklin
Township, had won his place in the "Hall of Fame" - acknowledging
his contribution as chief engineer in the production of "The Christmas
Song." Krepps is also credited with a number of audio improvements
he introduced during his four decades in the recording business. These
innovations have helped Edison's original phonograph rise to the
musical perfection that its heirs have achieved today.

Krepps obviously believes that Edison's invention was one of
the greatest of all times. Constant improvements have led to such
refinements as "hi-fi" and stereophonic sound. This incessant flow of
new techniques is what keeps the industry alive. During his early
years in the recording business, Krepps worked with two of Edison's
machinists, Fred Van Epps Sr., and Larry Scully Sr. Van Epps was
the father of one of the great, jazz guitar players of all times. He lived
and worked in New Jersey, building recording lathes, and turntables.

Scully furnished master recording lathes to the industry for many years.

After five years with Capitol Records, Krepps was approached in 1951 by the president of MGM Studios, Frank Walker, to build a recording studio for them. Walker had just completed the world's largest record-pressing plant in Bloomfield, New Jersey and wanted his own recording studio in New York City.

Krepps accepted, and for the next seven years operated MGM's New York studio as its chief engineer. Primarily a movie producer, MGM at first gave Krepps the task of taping the sound tracks for such big hit movies of theirs as "The Wizard of Oz," "Showboat," and "Some Like It Hot."

During his years with MGM, he worked with such recording stars as George Shearing, Joni James, Hank Williams, and numerous other country artists such as Brenda Lee. Also recorded by him at that time were Blue Barron's Orchestra, Rudy Vallee, Kate Smith, Connie Francis, and many of the jazz artists of the day.

While at MGM, a former British Army major, John O'Sullivan, offered Krepps the vice presidency of a record-manufacturing plant he was planning in Puerto Rico under the United States Government's "Operation Boot Strap" program.

Krepps accepted. Unfortunately, the business went bankrupt. After a series of other positions, he finally opened his own studios in New York City in 1963, "Knickerbocker Sound Studios" and "Mayfair Recording Studios." During that time, he and his brother, Edgar, worked on a new idea for a recording studio console that would record with eight tracks instead of the conventional four.

It was fantastically successful and led to United Artists Studios buying him out in 1970.

After an extended tour of Europe with his wife, Lee, Krepps returned to America to take over as chief engineer for the recording studios of Warner Communications- Atlantic Records.

During the ensuing years, he worked with such artists as Aretha Franklin, Roberta Flack, the Rolling Stones, the YES group, Emerson Lake and Palmer, the Bee Gees and numerous other Rock acts.

He still maintains a consulting attachment with a division of Warner Communications in Scranton, PA, but mainly he is enjoying his retirement along the trails of New Jerseys' Montana Mountain. How do I know? I have lunch with him every Wednesday.

A *"Sporting State"*

As New Jersey enters the last years of the 20th, and approaches the threshold of the 21st century, it seems to be intent upon carving out a reputation for itself as a "sporting state." Or perhaps an entertainment center would be a better term.

To those who know nothing of its history, of course, this appears to be a wholly new lifestyle that it's launching. The truth of the matter is that New Jersey's prominence as the locale for "play" has its roots buried deep in the very beginnings of its existence.

As a well-traveled crossroads colony lying between the cities of Philadelphia and New York, as well as of New England and the south. New Jersey from earliest times was heavily dotted with numerous inns and taverns. They were there to accommodate the needs of the weary travelers constantly passing through.

All along both its main and crossroads, and at its various ferry landings, inns were to be found. Each had a variety of activities to lighten the burdens (and often the pocketbooks) of those who were enduring the painful hardships of travel. These activities ranged through every conceivable sort of gambling and showmanship to more serious music and theater.

We hear much of the state's current obsession with all forms of gambling. It might come as a surprise to know that by the mid-1700's, New Jersey's lotteries, which had been in existence since earliest colonial times, outnumbered those of any of the other colonies.

Almost every church, college, road, jailhouse, school, or other public building or project in New Jersey's early history was financed by the sale of lottery tickets. All were with the approval of the General Assembly. Both rich and poor, hopefully according to their means, were thus permitted to contribute to praiseworthy projects, while enjoying a chance to win sizeable prizes. And they enabled the avoidance of having to take money from the public till to finance them.

491

Among the various amusements which both travelers and local folk might find these inns was the traveling artist. For a fee, he would outline the profile of your head and bust - quite popular in the days before photography. Of course, such sporting activities as billiards, card playing, and shuffleboard were also most likely to be found at these many stopovers.

Some of the inns, as well as other public meeting places, also hosted such entertaining events as traveling wax works, ventriloquists, magicians, magic lantern shows, and even wild animal shows or exhibits.

Although cockfights were declared illegal in New Jersey as early as 1748, they, too, continued to draw large crowds - to secluded spots. They became especially popular in the little towns along both sides of the Delaware following the Civil War. Two larger towns, Trenton and Easton, were particularly notorious centers for these contests.

Both foot races and horse races were popular sporting events in New Jersey from earliest times. They were held at various towns throughout the state with each providing for an admission charge to spectators and varying-size purses for the participants.

Col. Lewis Morris complained as early as 1700 that New Jerseyans were "perhaps the most...wicked people in the world," preferring to spend their Sundays going "to fighting and running of races."

Some 10 New Jersey communities were sites of fairly regularly scheduled horse races. Monmouth County was an early leader in the very profitable pursuit of horse breeding. Some of the best race horses in the United States in the decades of the 1820's and 30's were New Jersey bred and owned.

Balloon ascensions also became popular events in New Jersey, ever since the first flight in the United States took off from Philadelphia in 1793 - and landed in Woodbury.

P.T. Barnum was putting on his Wild West shows at the amusement fields in Hoboken as early as the 1840's.

In fact, Hoboken in east Jersey, as well as Camden along its western border, provided their respective out-of-state city neighbors from across their rivers, with considerable rural entertainment fields throughout the first half of the 1800's.

Each had a ferry service crowded with visitors on weekends. They came to enjoy picnics, garden walks, food, and drink concessions, merry-go-rounds, etc.

The first recorded baseball game in America took place at Hoboken's "Elysian Fields" on June 19, 1846 - between two New York teams, I might add.

Of course, the "Jersey Shore" had been an amusement center since the days of the Lenape Indian's annual summer trek and throughout its history. Long Branch was probably the earliest shore resort for New Yorkers, while Little Egg Harbor and Tuckerton were drawing Pennsylvanians as early as 1765. Cape May was the playground for the southern plantation owners from about 1801 to the Civil War.

Throughout its history, then, the trails of New Jersey have served as a haven for man's inborn craving for entertainment. Some things seem never to change.

The First American Football Game

This is the season, according to my son, John Skirbst, who is a graduate of Rutgers, to write about the first intercollegiate football game in America - or even the world as far as we know. Of course, it took place here in New Jersey, and Rutgers was one of the teams.

Oh, the game had been played in one version or another between various classes on college campuses as early as the 1820's. There had even been interscholastic secondary school competition in the Boston area by 1860. But it was not until after the Civil War when the students of Rutgers challenged those at the College of New Jersey (now Princeton) to play a series of three football games, that intercollegiate football began. In those days, neither the faculty nor the administration played any official part in those arrangements.

It is interesting to note that this first, American football game was more like what we now call soccer. A round, inflated rubber ball was used, which one player moved toward the opposing goal posts with short kicks. While advancing the ball he would be protected by his teammates. The ball could be moved forward in the air by battling it with the hands or head, but there was no carrying or catching allowed. A point was made by getting the ball between the two single standing goal posts. There were apparently no crossbars yet at that time. There were 25 men on each side. No uniform or protective padding was worn.

Those first games were agreed upon by the students before game time. That first game began at 3 p.m. Stories vary, as to how soon after the arrival of the Princeton team the game began. The agreement for that match was that the first team to score six goals would win. Rutgers scored first. The score was tied at 4-4 when Rutgers, in quick succession, kicked the remaining two, making them the winner of that historic first intercollegiate football match in the world - by a score of 6 goals to 4.

The second of the series was held a week later at Princeton in a field that was located across from the Sidell Mansion. This house was later to become the retirement home of the only president of the United States to be born in New Jersey, Grover Cleveland. Princeton won that game, 8-0. The third game was not played.

Though there were no uniforms, many Rutgers players wore either scarlet bandanas or Jerseys, to distinguish them from the Princeton players. That this was necessary was indicated by the fact that during the first game, one of the Rutgers players had mistakenly helped the opposition advance the ball to score a goal. William Gummere, who was captain of the Princeton team, later went on to become Chief Justice of the NJ Supreme Court for some 25 years. William Leggett, captain of the Rutgers squad, became a prominent Dutch Reformed clergyman.

A great deal of competition existed between the two colleges, so this football game was a natural. There already had been an annual battle between the two student bodies to capture and keep several historic cannons. One is said to have been struggled for between Gen. Washington and the British Gen. Howe. The second is said to have been loaned to New Brunswick by the Town of Princeton during the War of 1812. Rutgers students were accused of stealing it. The one was finally sunk by Princeton into a bed of concrete on their campus. Rutgers students retaliated with the other. That ended the struggle. Another rub was the defeat of Rutgers at the first intercollegiate baseball game in 1886. A football rivalry would continue their competition.

The playing field for that first game was located off College Avenue where the present gymnasium is. The Rev. Chester D. Hartranft was one who helped coach the Rutgers' team. When a little train steamed out of Princeton at 9 a.m. that morning, it was loaded with eager students. Rutgers students met them en masse at the New Brunswick station. They were immediately taken to be entertained at varying spots about town. In the meantime, the two captains met to discuss the rules for that day's game. Once those preliminaries were settled and announced, the time of the game was called for 3 p.m.

After the match was over, and the Rutgers team had won, the men of Rutgers provided the men of Princeton with a hardy supper and an evening of entertainment. All in good spirits, they then accompanied their rivals to the railroad station for the train rides back to Princeton. And so began along the trails of New Jersey on that Nov. 6, 1869, the first intercollegiate football competition, which was to become so much a part of both the college and the American tradition. Another New Jersey beginning for another bit of our American heritage, and you can thank my son, John, for doing the research on this morsel of Americana.

Ski Resorts

As we have mentioned before, New Jersey has a great variety of surface features, in spite of is small size. Because of this asset, it offers some natural settings to please the palate of almost everyone. It is long, wide beaches stretch for some 125 miles along its southeastern coast, and offers a diversity of nautical features to satisfy the desires of a wide range of tastes. Its beautiful streams, lakes, and forested mountains make up that part of the state lying chiefly in the northern sector. One fourth of the state is in the unique Pine Barrens of southern New Jersey.

For the time being, I am going to concentrate, however, on New Jersey's share of that beautiful eastern range known as the Appalachian Mountains. This range cuts across northern New Jersey in a northeast to southwesterly direction. It is made up primarily of three regions called the Valley, the Highlands, and the Piedmont. Throughout the first two regions we find many forested ridges and

495

hills separated by deep valleys. They are mainly in Warren, Sussex, and Morris, and western Passaic and Hunterdon Counties. Rising to elevations from 800 to 1800 feet, they are not high by western standards, but once were much higher. Because these mountains are old, millions of years of winds, rains, running water, and glaciers have worn them down. In Northwestern Jersey in Sussex and Warren Counties, the best known range is the Kittatinny Mountains. Also in Sussex there are the Pochuck, Hamburg, Wawayanda, and Sparta Mountains. In Warren, we also find the Jenny Jump, Marble, Scotts, and Pohatcong Mountains. In Morris County, the Schooley's, Bowling Green, Green Pond, and Copperas Mountains are found. Western Passaic County has its Bearfort and Kanouse Mountains.

The Piedmont or foothills of these mountains extend into sections of eastern Passaic, Bergen and Hudson Counties, and southeastward into Essex, Union, and Somerset Counties. They are chiefly gently rounded hills with steep-sided ridges rising sharply above the surrounding surface - and are generally forested. Elevations range from 40 to 900 feet. The best known ridges in the northeast are the Palisades, along the west bank of the Hudson, the Ramapos bordering Passaic and Bergen counties, the rolling hills called the Sourlands in Somerset, and Watchung Mountains stretching from north of Paterson in Passaic through Essex and Union to bound Brook in Somerset County.

I emphasize New Jersey's mountains and hills because they are the scenes of many interesting sites and folklore, and I want to pint out a growing recreational activity found in them. Though it has been slow in coming, skiing in New Jersey has flourished to the point where it has become a major winter sport in the state.

I am sure people must have been skiing in New Jersey for many years before the Craigmeur Ski Area opened, nevertheless its opening in 1937 marked a real beginning for this sport. Located south of New Foundland in a region containing the Green Pond, Bearfort, and Kanouse Mountains near the Morris and Passaic borders, Craigmeur appeals mainly to family groups and beginner skiers. It is an excellent place to learn to ski. Its slope is not frightening for the novice. It also provides cross-country skiing on marked trails.

Peapack is another old-timer among ski areas. In operation at least since the 1940's, it is on Mine Mountain between Peapack and

Bedminster in Somerset County. An old-fashioned ski area, Peapack, with slopes 200 feet high and 1000 feet long, is strictly a natural snow area. In the Ramapo Mountains, there are two ski areas of note. The Campgaw Mountain Ski Area outside of Mahwah in Bergen County is still very popular in the region. Across the border in Passaic, the Eagle Mountain Ski Area in Ringwood also had toboggan slides and ice-skating. On the other side of the state near Lambertville in Mercer County, above the Delaware River, is the Belle Mountain Ski Area. In the Pohatcong Mountains near West Portal in Hunterdon County, just south of the Musconetcong River, was the Jugtown Mountain Ski Area. In the Bearfort Mountain area in Passaic, was the Apple Acres Ski Area near West Milford.

After Craigmeur, the next area in North Jersey to gain prominence was the Snow Bowl. Lying within the Green Pond and Bowling Green Mountains the Snow Bowl was in Milton. It was gaining in popularity until half a dozen years of poor snow conditions made it impossible to keep going.

The event that really made skiing a major New Jersey sport was the opening of Great Gorge in 1966. Located in the Wawayanda Mountains in McAfee, Great Gorge started the ski boom. Because of its success, another ski area opened some two miles away called Vernon Valley. The two soon became the giants of New Jersey's skiing fraternity. In 1975, still another area opened nearby called Hidden Valley. It lies between the Pochuch and Wawayanda Mountains in Vernon.

Though snow machines now make a lack of snow no problem, the onset of cycles of extended warm weather when the machines are useless is a problem. This happened in New Jersey for a period of years in the early 1970's and ruined some of the ski areas. Great Gorge and Vernon Valley merged to stay afloat and also had to promote its facilities for year-round use to keep in business. They have thus made it the number one ski area of the state. It has been host to world championship pro races and US Ski Team events. More than 50 slopes and trails spread over three 1,000 foot mountains, a new triple chair lift, 14 double chair lifts and three tow ropes make it among the great ski areas of the Northeast. Hidden Valley got over the slump periods by including the Club Plan in its program.

So you do not have to make the long trip to New England or New York to enjoy the thrills of skiing. New Jersey has managed to produce world championship ski racers on its slopes. Yet its real value is for the beginners and the intermediates. Although there are the more challenging slopes, New Jersey also provides good skiing without scaring the novice half to death. Ski enthusiasts now flock to New Jersey's annual winter events making our mountains a real economic asset to the state. We will have more about other aspects of New Jersey's mountains next time.

Doctors and Medicine

In the latter part of the 17th century, after the British takeover from the Dutch of what came to be called New Jersey, there was an increased effort made to entice settlers into this new English territory. Empty land, of course, brings no profits, and making money, after all, was the whole purpose of taking over these new territories. One of the enticements offered was its "very healthful air."

People, then as now, were ever in search of good health, and places to live that were thought to provide it, were sought out. New England's cold, cruel, winters were not particularly inviting, nor was the oppressive summer heat and "malaria" of the southern colonies.

But ah, New Jersey! It's "serene" climate was plugged as being most agreeable and offered by late 17th and 18th century promoters as a good reason why people should come there to settle.

But diseases were as rampant in colonial New Jersey as they were everywhere. Epidemics of these curses of the human race made regular invasions of the Jersey countryside.

Early plagues included the measles and smallpox epidemics that were known to ravage the colonies throughout the 1700's. Diphtheria, malaria, scarlet fever, typhoid fever, and even yellow fever all took their terrible tolls among New Jersey settlers throughout the 17th, 18th, and 19th centuries.

Quarantines of the sick were one of the most used tools of the medical profession of those days to try and keep those diseases under control. Large-scale gatherings, such as the popular farmers' fairs of the day, were often cancelled due to one epidemic or another.

By the 1760's, inoculation with a bit of the smallpox virus was beginning to become another means among some New Jersey doctors of curtailing at least that dread disease. George Washington was the first to use it on a large scale when he ordered his army inoculated at Morristown during the smallpox epidemic of 1777.

But most health problems in the early days were handled in the home by mothers. In a day when doctors were scarce and money even scarcer, it was the New Jersey housewife's lot to become familiar with all sorts of medical folklore among her many other chores. Some kept notes of the various "cures" available. To them we owe much of our knowledge today of how these problems were handled. Herb gardens provided many plants in common use for a variety of illnesses. Farmer's almanacs were often the source of what to use for what.

By the mid-1770's, "patent medicines" were appearing in the general stores and in the increasing number of "drug" stores or apothecaries popping up. Various "elixirs" and "pills" were offered. Many were advertised to be used to "cure" a wide-variety of ailments.

Doctors, barber-surgeons, chemists, physicians, apothecaries, and surgeons all began making their appearances throughout the late 17th and 18th century New Jersey settlements.

For the most part, they were not MD's, as we know them today. They were usually educated men with some special interest. Often, they were clergymen as much interested in mending the soul as the body. Only a few had some medical training. The first president of the New Jersey Medical Society in 1766, for example, was the Rev. Robert McKean, a clergyman from Perth Amboy.

As the 19th century dawned, fewer and fewer members of the New Jersey Medical Society were clergymen and an apprenticeship with a practicing physician had become the chief means of learning the trade. More and more "doctors" were receiving some kind of formal training.

In 1800, at least 10 New Jersey doctors had bona fide "doctor of medicine" degrees from either New York or Philadelphia medical schools. The tide only turned as the people themselves began demanding more of their "doctors" in the way of formal training. Even so, a serious lack of knowledge still plagued those who plied this trade in New Jersey. As late as 1881, the New Jersey Medical

499

Society still admitted that "malaria" was a term often attributed to a disease if they didn't know what else to call it.

For many years, a much-held belief among New Jersey doctors was that various ailments were the result of disturbances brought into the circulatory system. Bloodletting, including leeches on the neck and throat, was a popular 19th century treatment. The invasion of the digestive system, likewise, called for the use of strong purgatives to induce vomiting or cleanse the bowels. As early as the 1830's, two rural doctors, Dr. Jabez Gwinnup, speaking to the Warren County Medial Society, and Dr. William Johnson of Hunterdon County, warned of its danger. The confusion over the treatment of ailments must have been a terrible torment to those fine people who practiced medicine along the trails of New Jersey in those "good old days" gone by.

History of Education

One of the areas of our lives today, which most adults share in common with their neighbors, is the "school days, school days, dear old golden rule day's" experience.

My wife, Ruth, and I recently attended my high school graduation class's 40th anniversary reunion. So I was forcefully reminded of those days as I chatted with old friends who had been so much a part of my life from kindergarten through high school. I was also reminded of how mobile our society is. I had not seen most of those people in 40 years. Many had come from all over the country to be there. Only a handful still lived in the same community where we grew up!

Though the free education of all its citizens from kindergarten through post-high school is an ideal that many of the people of New Jersey today cherish as an ultimate goal, a bit of historical perspective will reveal that it was not always so. We have grown so accustomed to our public schools that many have come to assume that their establishment was written into our nation's constitution by the founding fathers. Others even believe the institution to be a part of our bill of rights: Not so.

It will come as a shock to some to find out that some 100 years after the first shot was fired in the American Revolution and 10 years after the last shot was fired in the Civil War, there was in New Jersey little of any recognized state obligation to support a free public-school system. It was not until 1875 that the people of New Jersey, through their state legislature, first adopted an amendment to the State Constitution of 1844 declaring this responsibility.

This 1875 amendment stated for the first time that "the legislature shall provide for the maintenance and support of a thorough and efficient system of free public schools for the instruction of all children in the state between the ages of five and eighteen years."

In 1912, the legislature, by law, extended the age of free public education to all those under 20. Publicly funded schools were "permitted" in New Jersey as early as 1820. But raising money by taxation for schools was only "for the education of such poor children as are paupers." Until 1820, education of the poor was left to charity. Private and church schools were the rule of the day for everyone else!

The first actual school of record in New Jersey (not free) was built in the Village of Bergen (now Jersey City) in 1662. Its teacher collected his annual salary of 250 guilders from his students. In addition to being expected to instruct his pupils, he was required to conduct church services in the absence of the minister, be a choirmaster and also act as sexton and gravedigger!

Rebuilt in 1708 and in use until 1790, the school was re-established as the Columbia Academy that year.

Students were assigned to grades according to their abilities. The curriculum in the lower grades was reading, writing, and the catechism of the Dutch Reformed Church. Upper grades studied arithmetic, higher mathematics, the Psalter, and both the English and Dutch languages.

Discipline in those early schools was not a matter of debate. It was extremely strict. Punishments were freely permitted to be meted out by the schoolmaster without restriction. A whip or ruler was commonly in use for that purpose. "Sparing the rod" was not expected.

Though many schools were established by early New Jersey communities, they were not comparable to today's, nor were they for everyone. A public school system as we know it did not come about until the latter part of the 19th and the early 20th centuries.

As early as 1851 the City of Newark was unique in establishing a board of education. By 1855, it had 16 schools and a Normal School for training teachers. The latter was the forerunner of Kean College. By 1857, it had organized an evening school for both immigrants, then flooding into the city, and apprentices training for the various grades. Average class size was reported to be between 60 and 70 pupils until 1897. In 1886, it introduced the state's first summer school. The first Kindergarten came in 1897, and by 1900, all of its grammar schools had them.

The state of New Jersey did not enact its first compulsory education laws, requiring all youngsters to attend school, until 1913 and 1914. These same laws first provided for the establishment of county vocational school.

Physical Education became mandatory in the schools of New Jersey as a result of the sad physical fitness that tests revealed to exist among our young men being drafted for World War I.

As you can now begin to see, the majority of those innovations that make our common school experience along the trails of New Jersey recognizable did not come about until well after the dawn of the 20th century.

Printed in the United States
1468200002B/1-27